AN

ANALYSIS AND SUMMARY

OF

OLD TESTAMENT HISTORY

AND THE

LAWS OF MOSES.

WITH A

CONNECTION BETWEEN THE OLD AND NEW TESTAMENTS.

BY

J. T. WHEELER, F.R.G.S.,

AUTHOR OF

"AN ANALYSIS AND SUMMARY OF HERODOTUS," "AN ANALYSIS AND SUMMARY OF THUCYDIDES," ETC.

WIPF & STOCK · Eugene, Oregon

Wipf and Stock Publishers
199 W 8th Ave, Suite 3
Eugene, OR 97401

An Analysis and Summary of Old Testament History
and the Laws of Moses With a Connection Between
the Old and New Testaments
By Wheeler, J. T.
Softcover ISBN-13: 978-1-7252-9142-3
Hardcover ISBN-13: 978-1-7252-9141-6
eBook ISBN-13: 978-1-7252-9143-0
Publication date 11/3/2020
Previously published by W. R. Work & Co., 1879

This edition is a scanned facsimile of
the original edition published in 1879.

CONTENTS.

As complete Analytical Contents and tables will be found at the beginning of each book, and a Comprehensive Index at the end of the volume, it is presumed that the present condensed contents will be found sufficient for reference.

	PAGE
PREFACE	7
INTRODUCTORY OUTLINE OF THE HISTORY AND GEOGRAPHY OF THE COUNTRIES NOTICED IN THE OLD TESTAMENT	11
OUTLINE OF THE CRITICAL HISTORY OF THE OLD TESTAMENT	28
JEWISH MONTHS	31
CHRONOLOGICAL TABLE	33

THE PENTATEUCH, OR FIVE BOOKS OF MOSES	35
GENESIS: Patriarchal history from the birth of Adam till the death of Joseph. B. C. 4004 to 1635: about two thousand three hundred and sixty-nine years	35
I. History of the world prior to Abraham	36
II. Lives of Abraham, Isaac, Jacob, and Joseph	44
EXODUS: History of the Jews as a nomad family from the death of Joseph until the building of the tabernacle and consecration of the priesthood. B. C. 1635 to 1490: about one hundred and forty-five years	68
I. History of the Exode from Egypt, the journey to Sinai, and the delivery of the Law	69
II. The Moral and Civil Law	80
Jewish Constitution	86
III. The Ceremonial Law—viz. 1. The Tabernacle	89
LEVITICUS: History of the Levitical priesthood, sacrifices, etc. B. C. 1490: about one month—viz. from the building of the tabernacle to the numbering of the people	98

CONTENTS.

PAGE

The Ceremonial Law continued from Exodus—viz.:

    2. Priests, Levites, and Nethinim.................................... 96
    3. Sacrifices, oblations, and meat- and drink-offerings...... 100
    4. Annual feasts and festivals; sabbatical year and jubilee. 107
    5. Vows... 113
    6. Purifications.. 116

NUMBERS: History of the Israelites from the delivering of the Law at Sinai to the conquest of the country east of the Jordan. B. C. 1490 to 1451: about thirty-eight years and nine or ten months.. 120

    I. Wanderings in the wilderness................................... 120
    II. Conquest of the country east of the Jordan................ 124

DEUTERONOMY: Repetition and confirmation of the Law. B. C. 1451: about two months.. 130

    The last acts of Moses.. 130
    Canaan prior to its conquest by the Israelites.................. 133

THE TWELVE HISTORICAL BOOKS... 136

JOSHUA: History of the conquest of Canaan and settlement in the country under Joshua. B. C. 1451 to 1426: about twenty-five years.. 136

    I. Conquest of Canaan.. 136
    II. Settlement in Canaan.. 141

JUDGES: History of the Jews as a federative republic. B. C. 1425 to 1095: about three hundred and thirty years.............. 145

    I. Period prior to the Judges.. 145
    II. The seven servitudes or tyrannies, and the fifteen judgeships.. 149

    (This period includes the first ten chapters in 1 Samuel.)

RUTH: An episode in the history of the Judges. About B. C. 1320 162

1 AND 2 SAMUEL AND 1 AND 2 KINGS: History of the Jews under a monarchy. B. C. 1095 to 588: about five hundred and eight years 163

    I. History of the single monarchy.................................. 169
        Saul.. 169
        David.. 178
        Solomon 191
    Prefatory review of the history of the divided monarchies.. 199

    II. History of the divided monarchies of Judah and Israel. 201
        First Period: from the revolt of the ten tribes until Jehu destroyed the dynasty of Ahab in Israel, and slew Ahaziah in Judah..................................... 201

CONTENTS.

                                                                       PAGE

    Second Period: from the simultaneous accession of Jehu in Israel and usurpation of Athaliah in Judah until Israel was carried away captive by the Assyrian power.......... 215

    Third Period: from the Assyrian captivity of Israel until the Babylonian captivity of Judah.............. 225

    History of Assyria.......... 238

1 AND 2 CHRONICLES. B. C. 4004 to 536: about three thousand four hundred and sixty-eight years.......... 238

History of the Chaldee-Babylonian empire during the seventy years' captivity, forming a connection between the 2 Kings and 2 Chronicles and the book of Ezra. B. C. 606 to 536....... 241

EZRA: History of the edict of Cyrus and first return from captivity under Zerubbabel, and the governorship of Ezra. B. C. 536 to 445: about ninety years.......... 244

NEHEMIAH: History of the government of Nehemiah. B. C. 445 to 420: about twenty-five years.......... 253

ESTHER: An episode. About B. C. 461 to 451.......... 255

Chronology of the kings of Media and Persia, with their names as given in Scripture and in profane history.......... 257

THE FIVE POETICAL BOOKS:.......... 258

    JOB.......... 258
    PSALMS.......... 262
    PROVERBS.......... 263
    ECCLESIASTES.......... 264
    SOLOMON'S SONG.......... 265

THE SIXTEEN PROPHETICAL BOOKS.......... 266

    THE FOUR GREATER PROPHETS.......... 267

    1. Isaiah.......... 267
    2. Jeremiah (Prophecies and Lamentations).......... 271
    3. Ezekiel.......... 272
    4. Daniel.......... 272

    THE TWELVE MINOR PROPHETS—viz. 1. Hosea; 2. Joel; 3. Amos; 4. Obadiah; 5. Jonah; 6. Micah; 7. Nahum; 8. Habakkuk; 9. Zephaniah; 10. Haggai; 11. Zechariah; 12. Malachi....... 278

PRINCIPAL PROPHECIES, INTIMATIONS, AND TYPES OF THE MESSIAH IN THE OLD TESTAMENT.............. 283

CONNECTION BETWEEN THE OLD AND NEW TESTAMENTS, including the history of the Jews from the administration of Nehemiah to the birth of Jesus Christ.............. 288

CONTENTS.

PAGE

 I. Jewish history from Nehemiah to the revolt under
   the Maccabees... 290
 II. History of the Maccabees, or Asamonean princes..... 299
 III. History of the Jews under the Herodians to the com-
   mencement of the New Testament history............ 321
 Jewish sects... 330

THE FOURTEEN APOCRYPHAL BOOKS:

 1 Esdras; 2 Esdras; Tobit; Judith; Rest of the chapters of
 the Book of Esther; Wisdom of Solomon; Ecclesiasticus,
 or Wisdom of Jesus the Son of Sirach; Book of Baruch;
 Song of the Three Children; History of Susanna; Bel and
 the Dragon; Prayer of Manasses; 1 and 2 Maccabees......... 332

EXAMINATION QUESTIONS, including the Cambridge Examination Papers for various years, in chronological order.......... 335

INDEX OF NAMES, PLACES, ETC..................................... 351

PREFACE.

THE success which attended the publication of an *Analysis and Summary of Herodotus* has induced the author to compile an *Analysis and Summary of Old Testament History* on a similar plan. Accordingly, the present work contains an Analytical Summary of all the most important events recorded in the Old Testament Scriptures, arranged in chronological order, but retaining the canonical division into books. Each book of this Summary is separated into divisions, excepting where one book contains merely a repetition of the history of a preceding one; and each of these divisions is again subdivided into paragraphs, all of which have the Contents appended in a peculiar type. These Contents are also thrown together and reprinted at the beginning of each book; full references are also given at the end of each paragraph to the chapters or verses in the Bible in which the original facts are recorded.

By means of these Analytical Contents the biblical student can at once see the exact scope and subject-matter of each book, and by reading the Summary he will easily call back a multitude of facts and events the relation of which frequently spreads through several chapters in the original; whilst the references will at once enable him to obtain from his Bible a more extended account of any particular period of the history which he may require.

In carrying out this general design every opportunity has been seized for explaining or illustrating any obscure part of Jewish history, and particularly those portions which are more frequently the subjects of college examinations. The authorized chronology of our marginal-reference Bibles, which is based upon that of Archbishop Usher, is added to every page; the history of the divided monarchies of Judah and Israel is printed in parallel columns; the scriptural and profane names of the kings of Media and Persia are given at page 257; a chronological table of the prophets, at page 266; a table of the principal prophecies, intimations, and types of the Messiah, at page 283; examination-questions, including the Cambridge examination-papers in Old Testament history for various years, in chronological order, at page 335; and a complete index of names, places, etc., at the end of the volume. To these are added an introductory outline of the geography, political history, etc., of every country mentioned in the Old Testament, and an outline of the critical history of the Scriptures; together with chronological tables. Moreover, in order to complete the book as an analysis of Jewish history, two connecting chapters have been inserted: I. A history of the Chaldee-Babylonian empire during the seventy years' captivity, which forms a connection between 2 Kings and 2 Chronicles and the book of Ezra; II. Jewish history from the governorship of Nehemiah to the taking of Jerusalem by Titus, which forms a connection between the Old and the New Testaments. A comprehensive analysis of the Mosaic laws and ordinances has also been included. The moral and civil law is classified under each commandment, both for the convenience of reference, and because by such arrangement they are made to form a very useful and practical commentary upon the Decalogue. This classification is based upon a harmony of the Mosaic law, taken from a manuscript presented to St. John's College by Archbishop Laud, and reprinted in *Horne's Introduction*, and other similar works. The ceremonial law has been chiefly arranged according to the classification of Michaelis.

In conclusion, the author must acknowledge his many obligations to the following works: to the valuable *Introduction to the Study of the Holy Scriptures*, by the Rev. T. H. Horne; *The Historical Researches and Manual of Ancient History*, by Professor Heeren, of the University of Göttingen; the *Commentaries* of Patrick, Lowth, Whitby, etc.; the *Oxford Chronological Tables*, published by the lamented Mr. D. A. Talboys; and the *Works* of Dean Prideaux, Jahn, Calmet, Michaelis, Tomline, Bishop Horne, etc., etc.

J. T. W.

CAMBRIDGE, Jan. 20, 1850.

NOTICE.

In giving to the Christian public this very remarkable book, it is believed a great kindness will be done to every lover of the Bible. The analysis and arrangement seem to be almost perfect, and withal so simple that a child may understand them. To the student of the Bible *The Analysis and Summary* will supply a place which, it is believed, no other book can fill. The full merit of this book is to be found not only in the almost incredible amount of information it contains, but in the wonderful arrangement of the author, by which the reader can find just what he wants and when he wants it. To all members of Bible classes, teachers in Sabbath and secular schools, and in all family instruction, this book, it is fully believed, will prove one of the best of human helps in the study of the word of God.

INTRODUCTORY OUTLINE

OF

I. THE HISTORY AND GEOGRAPHY OF THE COUNTRIES NOTICED IN THE OLD TESTAMENT;

II. THE CRITICAL HISTORY OF THE OLD TESTAMENT.

I. THE HISTORY AND GEOGRAPHY.

ANALYSIS.

The "World" of the Old Testament—in four divisions; viz.

I. *Egypt.*

Boundaries and divisions.—Political history.—Religion.—Commerce and manufactures.

II. *Countries between the Mediterranean and the Euphrates.*

1st. ASIA MINOR—in twelve provinces.
2d. SYRIA PROPER.—Geography.—Political history.
3d. PHŒNICIA. — Geography. — Political history. — Colonies. — Sea trade.—Land trade.—Home manufactures.
4th. ARABIA.—Geography.—Political history.—Divisions: Moabites, Ammonites, and Edomites.
5th. **Palestine.**—Geography: divisions—viz. 1st. Into twelve tribes; 2d. Into a single monarchy; 3d. Into the two monarchies of Judah and Israel; 4th. Into five districts.—The Philistines.—Political history: 1. The nomad state, 1921-1426; 2. The federative republic, 1426-1095; 3. The single monarchy, 1095-975; 4. The divided monarchy of Judah and Israel, 975-588; 5. The province and principality, B. C. 588 to A. D. 70.—Productions.—Commerce.

III. *Countries between the Euphrates and the Tigris.*

1st. MESOPOTAMIA, or Aram, or Padan-aram.
2d. ARMENIA, containing the garden of Eden.
3d. BABYLONIA, or the land of Shinar.—Geography.—Political history.—Commerce.

IV. *Countries between the Tigris and Indus.*

Eleven provinces, sometimes forming one empire.—Character of the great Asiatic empires.—Ruling empires of South-western Asia: viz.
1st. ASSYRIA.—Geography of Assyria Proper.—Political history.
2d. MEDIA.—Geography.—Political history.
3d. PERSIA.—Geography.—Political history.—Religion.

SUMMARY.

1. The "World" of the Old Testament.—The nations whose history is noticed in the Old Testament lay between the 40th degree north lat. and the equator, and were included in the tracts of South-western Asia and the territory of Egypt.* The "world" of Old Testament history was therefore bounded on the east by the rivers Oxus and Indus; on the south by the Indian Ocean; on the west by the Libyan desert (Sahara); and on the north by the Caspian and Euxine Seas, with the intervening range of Caucasus, whose lofty summits were never crossed by any Asiatic conqueror before Genghis Khan.

This region may be divided into four tracts—viz. 1. Egypt; 2. Countries between the Euphrates and the Mediterranean and Red Seas; 3. Those between the Euphrates and the Tigris; 4. Those between the Tigris and the Indus.

2. I. Egypt: Boundaries.—Egypt is redeemed from the surrounding desert by the waters of the Nile, and is bounded on the north by the Mediterranean; on the east by the Red Sea; on the south by the Nubian desert and Ethiopia; and on the west by the Libyan desert.

3. Divisions.—1st. *Upper or Southern Egypt, or Thebais*, extending from Syene to Chemmis; crowded with temples, palaces, tombs, huge obelisks, colossi, sphinxes, etc. Capital, Thebes.

2d. *Central Egypt*, from Chemmis to Cercasorus; divided into seven nomoi or governments; contained the pyramids of Gizeh and Lake Mœris. Capital, Memphis.

3d. *Lower or Northern Egypt*, comprising the Delta and land on both sides. Full of cities, of which Sais was the most remarkable; but subsequently Alexandria became the capital, and the first trading city in the world.

---

* Some allusions are made to the "isles of the sea," which included the islands and coasts of the Mediterranean (Isa. xi. 11; Ezek. xvii. 3, etc.); also to "Javan," or "Greece" (Isa. lxvi. 19, etc.), and to "Tarshish" or "Tartessus," a Tyrian colony on the southern coast of Spain. Isa. xxiii., etc. India is twice mentioned in the book of Esther, but must have been unknown to the Jews.

INTRODUCTORY OUTLINE.

4. Political History.—Egypt was governed by a monarchy and sacerdotal aristocracy.

1. *The Pharaohs.*—1st dynasty—Menes and his successors. 2d dynasty—Shepherd-kings, who were Bedouin Arabs, and termed Hyksos. 3d dynasty—Sesostris the Great to the overthrow of the oligarchy of twelve princes, about B. C. 650; Shishak (probably Cephrines) invaded Judah in the reign of Rehoboam, B. C. 972 (sect. 375). 4th dynasty—Psammetichus, sole king to the conquest of Egypt by Cambyses, B. C. 650–525. Pharaoh-Necho, who defeated Josiah (sect. 528), and Pharaoh-Hophra, or Apries, who tried to assist Zedekiah (sect. 548), belonged to this time.

2. *The Persians, 525–323.*—Egypt was conquered by Cambyses, and was a Persian province, though frequently revolting, until the overthrow of the empire by Alexander the Great, who died B. C. 323.

3. *The Ptolemies, 323–30.*—Ptolemy Lagus, first governor, and afterward king, of Egypt, which remained an independent monarchy until the death of Cleopatra, B. C. 30, when it became a Roman province.

5. Religion.—Animal idolatry; but different animals were sacred in different districts, except Apis, who was the national god of all Egypt.

6. Commerce, Manufactures, etc.—*Imports.*—Gold, ivory, and slaves from Ethiopia; incense from Arabia; wine from Greece and Phœnicia; salt from the African desert.

Exports.—Corn, linen, and cotton. The Egyptians did not themselves export these wares; the African caravans were chiefly composed of nomad hordes.

Manufactures.—Weaving, dyeing, working in metal, and pottery.

Productions.—The byblus, from which the papyrus was prepared; the lotus; flax; various kinds of grain, pulse, etc.; no lofty trees but the date and sycamore.

7. II. Countries between the Mediterranean and the Euphrates.—These comprise—1st. Asia Minor; 2d. Syria Proper; 3d. Phœnicia; 4th. Arabia; and 5th. Palestine.

8. Ist. Asia Minor.—Anciently consisted of twelve provinces, which are mentioned only in the New Testament—viz. Bithynia, Paphlagonia, Pontus, Mysia, Lydia, Caria, Lycia, Pisidia and Pamphylia, Cilicia, Phrygia and Lycaonia, Galatia, and Cappadocia.

9. 2d. Syria Proper: Geography.—SYRIA, or ARAM, in its widest signification, included not only all the countries between the Mediterranean and the Euphrates, but also those between the Euphrates and the Tigris, and even Assyria Proper, and was thus the first habitation of mankind after the deluge, and included the birthplace of Abraham, and probably the garden of Eden. SYRIA PROPER was, however, bounded on the east by the Euphrates, west by the Mediterranean, north by Cilicia, and south by Phœnicia, Palestine, and Arabia Deserta. Cities, Damascus, Antioch, Riblah, Helbon, Hamath, Seleucia, Tadmor or Palmyra, Baal-Gad or Heliopolis, now Baalbec, and Tiphsah or Thapsacus. Rivers, Abana, Pharpar, and Orontes.

10. Political History.—1. *Independent States, ante 1040.*—Syria Proper was divided into cantons, such as Zobah, Damascus, Hamath, Geshur, Rehob, Ishtob, Maachah, etc., and these were governed by petty kings.

2. *A Jewish Province, cir. 1040–975.*—David reduced Syria to a Jewish province, but in Solomon's reign Rezon seized Damascus and erected a kingdom.

3. *Kingdom of Damascus, 975–740.*—The kingdom of Damascus now comprised the greater portion of Syria; the kings of the other cities became tributary, and it soon became a flourishing monarchy, and extended its boundaries chiefly at the expense of the divided monarchies of Judah and Israel (see sect. 491); but it was at length overthrown by the Assyrian conqueror Tiglath-pileser.

4. *A Dependent State, 740–64.*—Syria was successively in subjection to Assyria, Babylonia, and Persia, and was at length reduced by Alexander the Great; but after his death, B. C. 323, it formed part of the kingdom of Syria, which extended from the Mediterranean to the Indus, and was governed by the Seleucidæ until B. C. 64, when it became a Roman province.

11. 3d. Phœnicia: Geography.—Phœnicia was a mountainous tract extending along the shore between Syria Proper and the Mediterranean. Cities, Tyre, built first on the mainland, afterward on an island, Sidon, Byblus, Berytus, Tripolis, and Aradus. Mountains, Lebanon, consisting of two parallel ridges, Libanus and Anti-Libanus, which extended from Sidon to Damascus, and enclosed the fertile vale of Cœle-Syria, now Baalbec.

12. Political History.—Consisted of several cities and their territories under separate governments, of which Tyre was the head.

1. *Tyrian kings, cir. 1050–586.*—This line of kings, extracted by Josephus from Menander, commenced with Abical, the contemporary of David, and concluded with the sacking of Tyre by Nebuchadnezzar. Hiram, successor of Abical, allied with David and Solomon. Three remarkable females belonged to this line: JEZEBEL, daughter of Ethbaal I., and wife of Ahab—paganized Israel; ATHALIAH, daughter of Jezebel and Ahab—usurped Judah; DIDO, sister of Pygmalion—founded Carthage.

2. *Tributary to Persia, 586–332.*—New Tyre was afterward founded, with tributary kings under the Persian rule, but was taken by Alexander the Great, B. C. 332.

3. *Decline.*—Phœnicia was now ruined and its trade transferred to Alexandria. It often changed its Syro-Grecian and Egypto-Grecian masters, and at length fell into the hands of the Romans.

13. **Colonies.**—The Phœnicians were originally pirates and anciently possessed many islands in the Archipelago, but were expelled by the Greeks. They subsequently formed settlements on the south of Spain—Tartessus, Gades, Carteia; on the north coast of Africa—Utica, Carthage, Adrumentum; on the north-western coast of Sicily—Panormus and Lilybæum; and also probably settled in the Persian Gulf, on the islands of Tylos and Aradus—Bahrein.

14. **Sea Trade.**—The Phœnicians sailed—1st. To North Africa and Spain for silver; 2d. Beyond the Pillars of Hercules to Britain and the Scilly Isles for tin, and probably amber; 3d. They joined the Jews under Solomon in voyages from Elath and Eziongeber on the Red Sea to Ophir—*i. e.* the rich lands in the south, particularly Arabia Felix and Ethiopia (sect. 357); 4th. From the Persian Gulf to India and Ceylon; 5th. On voyages of discovery, and, particularly, they circumnavigated Africa.

15. **Land Trade.**—This was mostly carried on by caravans—viz. 1st. With Arabia for spices and incense, imported from Arabia Felix, Gerrha, and the Persian Gulf; 2d. Through Palmyra to Babylon, which opened an indirect communication, by way of Persia, with Lesser Bukharia and Little Thibet, and probably with China; 3d. With Armenia and neighboring countries for slaves, horses, copper utensils, etc.*

16. **Home Manufactures.**—1st. Stuffs and dyes, particularly the purple dye made from the juice of a marine shell-fish, and of every possible shade; 2d. Manufactures of glass and toys, much used in their commercial barterings with uncivilized nations. The invention of letters is attributed to the Phœnicians.

17. **4th. Arabia: Geography.**—A peninsula abounding in vast sandy deserts, and chiefly occupied by the nomad descendants of Ishmael; but its northern and eastern coasts rendered it a most important seat of trade.

18. **Divisions.**—*1st. North,* Arabia Petrœa, extending from Palestine to the Red Sea, and inhabited by the southern Edomites, Amalekites, Midianites, Hivites, Amorites, Kenites,

---

* The twenty-seventh chapter of Ezekiel contains an exact and interesting account of Phœnician commerce.

Horim, Maonim, and Cushites, called Ethiopians in Scripture. Capital, Petra. Mountain, Sinai.

2d. Inland, Arabia Deserta, with Euphrates on the east and Mount Gilead on the west, and comprehended the Itureans, Nabatheans, people of Kedar, etc. The Rephaim, Emim, Zuzim, and Zanzummim (Gen. xiv. 5; Deut. ii. 10, 11) anciently possessed the territories afterward occupied by the Moabites, Ammonites, and Edomites.

3d. South, Arabia Felix, bounded on the east by the Persian Gulf, south by the Indian Ocean, and west by the Red Sea. Rich in spices and perfumes, particularly frankincense, and rich also as being the ancient staple for Indian merchandise. Probably included the territory of the queen of Sheba.

19. **Political History.**—Arabians are divided into two classes: 1st. Dwellers in cities; 2d. Nomads. Abimelech, king of Gerar, was visited by Abraham and Isaac. Moses, after slaying the Egyptian, fled to the Midianites, descendants of the fourth son of Abraham and Keturah, who subsequently joined the Amalekites and other nomad Arabs in ravaging Palestine (sect. 279). The Amorites, Amalekites, and others were conquered by Moses. The Moabites, Ammonites, and Edomites were petty kingdoms frequently at war with the Israelites, and lay on the east of the Jordan.

20. **Moabites.**—Incestuously descended from Lot; defeated the giants Emim, and occupied a territory on the banks of the Arnon. Capital, Ar or Ariel, called also Rabbah-Moab and Kirharesh. Idols, Chemosh and Baal-peor. Lost territory to the Amorites, but not attacked by Moses, though Balak tried to persuade Balaam to curse the Israelites. Eglon subsequently oppressed Israel (sect. 276), but was assassinated by Ehud. Saul subdued them (sect. 308), and David (sect. 329), but after the death of Ahab its king, Mesha, refused to pay tribute (sect. 423), and was closely besieged by Jehoshaphat and Jehoram in his capital, and sacrificed his eldest son on the wall (sect. 429). Moab was afterward carried captive by Assyria, and probably followed the fortunes of Israel.

21. **Ammonites.**—Incestuously descended from Lot; subdued the Zanzummim, and occupied their country northeast of the Moabites. Capital, Rabbath. Lost territory to the Amorites, which was afterward occupied by the tribes east of the Jordan. Assisted Moab in conquering Canaan (sect. 276), but were defeated by Jephthah (sect. 291), by Saul (sect. 306), and by David (sect. 331), and Rabbath was taken by Joab (sect. 333). They subsequently united with the Edomites and Moabites in attacking Judah, but were defeated by Jehoshaphat (sect. 422). Their country afterward followed the fortunes of Israel.

INTRODUCTORY OUTLINE.

22. **Edomites.**—Descendants of Esau; settled in Mount Seir, in the land of the Horites, and spread through Arabia Petræa from the Dead Sea to the Mediterranean. Capitals, Bozra and Petra. First governed by dukes or princes, afterward by kings, but subdued by Saul (sect. 308), by David (sect. 329). Hadad became an independent king toward the close of Solomon's reign (sect. 362). In Jehoram's reign Edom rebelled, and Amaziah subsequently took Petra and obliged ten thousand people to leap from the rock (sect. 464). It was subsequently ravaged by Nebuchadnezzar (sect. 559), and conquered by John Hyrcanus (*Con.*, sect. 45).

23. **5th. Palestine: Geography.**—Palestine Proper was bounded on the north by Syria and Phœnicia, on the east by Arabia Deserta, on the south by Arabia Petræa, and on the west by the Mediterranean. The limits of the territory were, however, perpetually changing. Under the judges the country east of the Jordan was often oppressed by the Ammonites and Moabites, whilst the Philistines held a considerable district in South-western Judah. Under David and Solomon the limits of the kingdom were much enlarged, extending from the Euphrates to the Red Sea, and from the Mediterranean to Arabia Deserta, thus comprising Syria Proper and Philistia, Moab and Ammon in Arabia Deserta, and nearly all Arabia Petræa, including Edom, etc. Mountains, Gilead, Carmel, Tabor, Hermon, Gilboa, and Lebanon. Rivers, Jordan, Arnon, Jabbok, and Kishon. Lakes, Merom, Gennesareth, and the Dead Sea.

24. **Divisions: 1st. Into Twelve Tribes** by Joshua (sect. 263), during which the tabernacle was set up in Shiloh. The territory of each tribe was subdivided according to the families (sect. 128).

25. **2d. Into a Single Monarchy,** during the reigns of Saul, David, and Solomon. Capital, Jebus or Jerusalem.

26. **3d. Into the two Monarchies of Judah and Israel.**—Judah comprised two tribes. Capital, Jerusalem. Israel comprised ten tribes. Capital, first Shechem, then Tirzah, and finally Samaria.

27. **4th. Into five Districts,** under, successively, the Persians, Ptolemies, Seleucidæ, Asamoneans, Herodians, and Romans. WEST OF THE JORDAN.—1st. Judæa, on the south. Capital, Jerusalem. 2d. Samaria, in the centre. Cities, Samaria, or Sebaste, and Sichem. 3d. Galilee, on the north. Towns, Nazareth, Cana, Bethsaida, etc. EAST OF THE JORDAN.—4th. Peræa.* Cities, Pella, Machærus, etc. ON THE SOUTH.—5th. Idumæa, the ancient Edom.

---

* **Division of Peræa.**—Peræa, which signifies "the country on the opposite side," was a general name for any district belonging to or closely con-

28. **Political History.**—A spirit of theocracy prevailed more or less throughout every form of Jewish government.

29. **I. The Nomad State, 1921–1426,** from Abraham until the death of Joshua.—1st period—Patriarchal government under Abraham, Isaac, and Jacob, 1921–1706. Canaan occupied by ten races: Kenites, Kenizzites, and Kadmonites east of the Jordan; west, by the Hittites, Perizzites, Rephaims, Amorites, Canaanites, Girgashites, and Jebusites. Divided into states governed by petty kings, many of whom were subdued by Chedorlaomer, king of Elam or ancient Persia (sect. 24). 2d period—Israelites divided into ten tribes, resided in Egypt, 1706–1491. Dynasty of Menes expelled by the Hyksos or Shepherd-kings, and the Israelites reduced to slavery and their male infants slain. Moses born, 1571. 3d period—A strict theocracy during the wanderings in the wilderness under Moses, and conquest of Canaan under Joshua, 1491–1426. Exode from Egypt; law delivered on Mount Sinai, 1490; Moses died, 1451; Joshua died, 1426.

30. **2. The Federative Republic, 1426–1095.**—Each tribe was governed by its own patriarch, but all were united in one federate state and one common bond by the worship of Jehovah; introduction of idolatry punished by the oppression of neighboring powers; heroes or judges raised up at various times to deliver the people, and govern them in the spirit of theocracy; ill-government of Samuel's sons induced the people to demand a king.

31. **3. The Single Monarchy, 1065–975.**—Saul made king, but acted in opposition to the divine commands. David succeeded him, and extended his dominions to the Euphrates and Red Sea, and made Palestine the ruling monarchy in Western Asia. His son Solomon succeeded and allied with the Phœnicians, and carried on an extensive commerce by land and sea. Built the temple, but afterward tempted to idolatry, and the nations conquered by David rebelled.

32. **4. The Divided Monarchy of Judah and Israel, 975–588.**—Rehoboam, son of Solomon, refused to lighten the people from the heavy taxation imposed by Solomon, and the ten tribes revolted under Jeroboam. The kings of Israel introduced

---

nected with a country from the main part of which it was separated by a sea or river. The name *Peræa* was therefore applied in its more extended sense to the whole territory stretching from the river Arnon to Mount Hermon, between the Jordan and the desert, and was subdivided into eight districts or cantons—viz. 1. Peræa, in the more limited sense, which only extended from the Arnon to the Jabbok; 2. Gilead, or Galaaditis; 3. Decapolis, or Ten Cities, of which little is known for certain; 4. Gaulonitis; 5. Batanea, the ancient Bashan: 6. Ituræa or Auranitis; 7. Trachonitis; 8. Abilene, in the extreme north, among the mountains of Anti-Libanus, between Baalbec and Damascus.

idolatry to prevent their subjects from worshipping at Jerusalem; and, defying the warnings of Elisha, Elijah, and other prophets, the nation was carried into Assyrian captivity by Shalmaneser, B. C. 721. The early kings of Judah reigned righteously, but subsequently allied and intermarried with the kings of Israel and followed in their idolatrous steps; and though Isaiah, Jeremiah, and others warned the people, and Hezekiah, Josiah, and other good kings deferred the punishment of the kingdom, yet the nation was at length carried into Babylonian captivity, B. C. 588.

33. **6. The Province and Principality, B. C. 588 to A. D. 70.**
—*1st. The Babylonian Captivity, 606–536*, reckoning from the first taking of Jerusalem by Nebuchadnezzar to the edict of Cyrus, lasted seventy years, during which time the land lay desolate.

2d. The Persians, 536–323.—Cyrus, having overthrown the Babylonian empire and established the Medo-Persian, permitted the Jews to return to Judæa under Zerubbabel (sect. 572). They were subsequently governed by their high priests, under the satrap of Syria, and paid tribute to Persia. Alexander the Great overthrew the empire B. C. 330, and died B. C. 323.

3d. The Successors of Alexander, 323–300.—Violent disputes broke out amongst Alexander's generals after his death, and Palestine frequently changed masters, until a permanent treaty was established between the four kings.

4th. The Ptolemies, 300–202.—The high priests governed the Jews and farmed the revenues under the Ptolemies. Flourishing period of Jewish literature, and completion of the Septuagint.

5th. The Seleucidæ, 202–166.—Antiochus III., or the Great, wrested Palestine from Ptolemy V., or Epiphanes, and the Jews now paid tribute to Syria, but were governed by their own high priests and Sanhedrim. Antiochus IV., or Epiphanes, persecuted the Jews for not following the Greek idolatry, and the latter revolted under Mattathias, who died B. C. 166.

6th. The Maccabees, 166–37.—War under Judas Maccabæus and his successors for religious freedom, not for political independence, and the Jews still paid tribute to Syria; but in B. C. 143, Demetrius Nicator acknowledged the independence of the Jews, and relinquished all claims for taxes. The quarrels between Hyrcanus II. and Antigonus and their appeal to Pompey made the Jewish state dependent on Rome, and Herod, having obtained the favor of Antony by gifts and assiduous attention, was made king of Judæa.

7th. The Herodians and Romans, B. C. 37 to A. D. 70.—Our Saviour was born B. C. 4, and Herod died B. C. 3. His kingdom was divided by his three sons into three tetrarchies, which were subsequently appended to Syria and became a Roman province.* Our Lord was crucified under Pontius Pilate, a Roman procurator, A. D. 29, in the thirty-third year of his age. The Jews rebelled under Gessius Florus. Titus destroyed Jerusalem, A. D. 70.

34. **Productions.**—Wheat, honey, grapes, oil, olives, pomegranates, apples, figs, almonds, citrons, balm, etc. The principal shrubs, herbs, and trees are aloe, hyssop, the rose, spikenard, mandrake (a species of melon), myrtle, mustard tree, cedar, oak, palm, etc. The mountains contained iron and copper. The valleys afforded capital pasture for sheep, oxen, goats, camels, and asses. The rivers and lakes abounded in fish, which were cured by salt from the Dead Sea.

35. **Commerce.**—Palestine was an agricultural country, but allied with Phœnicia during the reigns of David and Solomon, and carried on an extensive commerce by land and sea. (See sect. 357.)

36. **Philistia: Geography.**—Philistia was a small territory bordering on the south-west of Judæa. Cities, Ekron, Gath, Askelon, Ashdod, and Gaza.

37. **Political History.**—The Philistines were not Canaanites, but originally Egyptians from the Pelusiac branch of the Nile, and they had migrated from Caphtor (Cyprus) not long before the arrival of the Hebrews, and expelled the Avim from the low country in Southern Palestine, and there established five governments or lordships in five cities. They were defeated by Shamgar and Samson (sect. 277 and 297), and by Saul (sect. 307), and rendered tributary by David (sect. 329). They revolted under Jehoram (sect. 436), but were defeated by Uzziah (sect. 472), and again rebelled from Ahaz (sect. 493), but were reduced by Hezekiah (sect. 506). They subsequently suffered from the same enemies as the Jews, but were at length wholly subdued by Alexander Jannæus.

38. **III. Countries between the Euphrates and the Tigris.**—These comprised—1st. Mesopotamia; 2d. Armenia; and 3d. Babylonia.

39. **1st. Mesopotamia, or Aram, or Padan-aram,** anciently included both Armenia and Babylonia, and even part of Syria, and is considered to be the first habitation of mankind after the deluge, and gave birth to Terah, Abraham, Nahor, Sarah, Rebekah, Leah, and the sons of Jacob. Mesopotamia Proper consisted of a table-land occupied by nomad hordes, with Armenia on the north and Babylonia on the south, and

---

* See the *Analysis and Summary of New Testament History*, by the author of the present volume.

INTRODUCTORY OUTLINE. 21

it successively became a part of the Assyrian, Persian, Macedonian, and Syrian empires.

40. 2d. Armenia was a mountainous territory north of Mesopotamia, watered by the rivers Cyrus, Araxes, and Phasis. It is supposed to have included the garden of Eden, and its history is similar to that of Mesopotamia.

41. 3d. Babylonia, or the Land of Shinar: Geography.—Babylonia was a level plain south of Mesopotamia Proper, remarkable for the richness of its soil. Anciently, by its high cultivation, its canals and lakes, and the erection of dams, it was the most fruitful, and from its situation the most opulent, state of Inner Asia. Capital, Babylon, on the Euphrates.

42. Political History.—*1st Period, prior to the Chaldean Conquest, cir. B. C. 2234–626.*—Nimrod founded Babel or Babylon, from whence Asshur migrated and founded Assyria, which was afterward conquered by Nimrod. See "Assyria" and sect. 16, *note.*

2d. From the Chaldean Conquest to the taking of Babylon by Cyrus, B. C. 626–539.—The Chaldeans, a nomad race, descended from Caucasus and Taurus, overwhelmed Southern Asia, and mastered Babylonia.* (See sect. 535.) Ptolemy enumerates thirteen Chaldean kings as reigning prior to this conquest of Babylonia, which seems to have been completed by Nabopolassar, whose son and successor, Nebuchadnezzar, subdued Asia from the Mediterranean to the Tigris, and founded the Chaldee-Babylonian empire. For a history of Nebuchadnezzar and his successors down to the taking of Babylon by Cyrus, see sect. 558–570. Babylon subsequently followed the fortunes of the Persian empire.

43. Commerce.—Babylon owed its extensive commerce to its superior geographical position, which, while it afforded admirable facilities for traffic by land, was equally convenient for maritime and river navigation on the Euphrates and Tigris and the Persian Gulf. By land the Babylonians imported from the countries east of Persia—1st. Onyxes, sardines, emeralds, jaspers, etc., which they obtained from the Ghaut Mountains and Bactrian desert; 2d. Indian dogs, dyes, wool, gold, and gold-dust; 3d. Silk from China, etc. By sea they imported—1st. Incense from Arabia; 2d. Cotton, spices, ivory, ebony, etc., from India; 3d. Bamboos,

---

* Mr. Grote (*Greece*, iii. p. 392, third edit.), resting on Herodotus and Strabo, can see nothing in the Chaldeans but *Babylonian priests*. This was certainly their later position (or the later use of their name), but the Chaldeans are familiarly spoken of by the prophets as coming from the *north*, and Ur of the Chaldees was in *Northern* Mesopotamia. Magians and Chaldeans seem both to have fallen from dominant tribes into priesthoods.

teak-wood, etc., from Tylos; 4th. Cinnamon from Ceylon; 5th. Pearls from the Persian Gulf, etc. Their chief manufactures were woven stuffs, carpets, brilliantly-colored and finely-textured cottons, of which the principal factories were at Borsippa on the Euphrates, about fifteen miles from Babylon. They were also famous for their sweet waters, engraving on precious stones, seal-rings, chased walking-sticks, costly perfumes, etc.

44. IV. Countries between the Tigris and Indus.—These comprised, 1. Assyria, or the province of Adiabene; 2. Susiana; 3. Persis; 4. Carmania; 5. Gedrosia; 6. Media; 7. Aria; 8. Arachosia; 9. Parthia and Hyrcanus; 10. Bactria; 11. Sogdiana. The empires successively founded by Assyria, Babylonia, Media, and Persia included, however, the principal portions of this territory.

45. Character of the great Asiatic Empires.—The mighty empires of the East were, with the exception of the one founded by Alexander, erected by warlike nomad hordes, who, pressed by necessity or circumstances, forsook their northern and sterile climes to carry war and conquest into the fruitful and cultivated lands of Southern Asia. Here they established a brilliant but evanescent empire, for they quickly adopted the luxurious habits of the vanquished nations, and consequently were soon overthrown by fresh swarms of uncorrupted warriors, who also in their turn degenerated and gave way to new invaders. The general features in the gradual internal development of all empires formed by nomad conquerors are—1st. The mere occupation of rich territories and levying of tribute, when the constitutions already established among the conquered or tributary nations are generally suffered to remain; 2d. The gradual progress toward the adoption of a fixed abode and the building of cities, together with the assumption of the customs and civilization of the conquered; 3d. The division into provinces, and, as a necessary consequence, the establishment of satrap government; 4th. Insurrections of the satraps and pernicious influence of the seraglio, which quickly produce the dissolution of the empire or its total annihilation by some violent attack from without.

46. Ruling Empires of South-western Asia: 1st. Assyria.—Assyria Proper, or the province of Adiabene, consisted of a table-land east of the Tigris, having Armenia on the north, Mesopotamia on the west, Babylonia on the south, and Media and Susiana on the east. Cities, Nineveh (Ninus) and Arbela. "Assyria" was, however, a name given to an ancient and vast empire erected among the nations bordering on the Euphrates and Tigris, and included, according to Strabo and other geographers, all the Asiatic countries south of the Taurus, excepting Persia, Arabia Proper, and Palestine.

47. Political History.—*1. Primeval Period.*—Asshur, or Assur, third son of Shem, migrated from the land of Shinar to the country called, after him, Assyria, which was afterward subdued by Nimrod, son of Cush, who built Nineveh on the Tigris, and named it after his son Ninus. (See sect. 486, *note.*) Nineveh became a great city in the time of Jonah, cir. B. C. 862. Mythical accounts of Ninus, Semiramis, Ninyas, etc.

2. Jewish Period.—Line of kings recorded in Scripture B. C. 771–604: Pul, Tiglath-pileser, Shalmaneser, Sennacherib, and Esarhaddon. Seat of the nation in Assyria Proper. Israel carried into captivity by Shalmaneser, B. C. 721. Sennacherib invaded Egypt and his army destroyed by an angel of the Lord, B. C. 710. Medes revolted from Assyria and formed a separate empire under Deioces, B. C. 709. Babylon separated from the Assyrian empire, B. C. 626. Babylonians and Medes take Nineveh, B. C. 612. (See sect. 535.)

48. 2d. Media.—Media Proper lay north of Persis, and was an extensive and very fruitful country, mountainous toward the north. Rivers, Araxes, Cyrus, and Mardus. Cities, Ecbatana and Rages. The name of Medes, however, is frequently used as a common appellation of the ruling nations in Western Asia, from Tigris to the Indus, or Persia (in the more extensive sense of that word) before Cyrus. It is generally noticed in Scripture as a conquering nation.

49. Political History.—Medes revolted from Assyria, B. C. 709, and formed a separate empire under Deioces [Arphaxad], who founded Ecbatana, allied with the Babylonians, and took Nineveh, B. C. 612. (See sect. 535.) The empire of the Medes now became a ruling monarchy in Asia, and extended its conquests from the Tigris to the Indus, whilst the Chaldee-Babylonian empire subdued the countries from the Tigris to the Mediterranean. Darius the Mede (Cyaxares II.) died B. C. 537, and was succeeded by Cyrus the Persian, when Media Proper became a province of the Persian empire.

50. 3d. Persia.—Persis, or Persia Proper, lay north of Media. It was rugged and mountainous toward the north, level and fruitful in the centre, and sandy toward the south. Rivers, the Cyrus and Araxes. City, Persepolis, or Pasargada, the national palace and cemetery of the kings of Persia. "Persia" subsequently became the designation of the vast empire established by Cyrus.

51. Political History.—*Primitive Condition.*—The Persians were a highland people, subject to the Medes, dwelling in the mountainous parts of the province of Persis, and leading a nomad life. They were divided into ten clans, of which that of the Pasargadæ was the noblest and the ruling horde.

Cyrus, or Kai Khosru, cir. B. C. 560-530.—His early life is obscured by romance, but it is evident that he was elected chief of all the Persian tribes, then subject to Media, in the same way as Genghis Khan in a later age was placed at the head of all the Mogul hordes. Three ruling monarchies now existed in Asia: 1. The Medes, from the Tigris to the Indus; 2. The Babylonians, or Chaldeans, from the Tigris to the Mediterranean; 3. The Lydians, who, under their king Crœsus, had conquered the greater part of Asia Minor, to the river Halys. Cyrus overthrew the Medes, or Medo-Bactrian empire, by the defeat of Astyages, subdued all the Lydian territory, seized the Greek colonies in Asia, captured Babylonia, and subjugated the Phœnicians. In B. C. 536 he granted an edict permitting the Jews to return from captivity. Cyrus, having extended the frontiers of the Persian empire in Southern Asia to the Mediterranean, the Oxus, and the Indus, made an unsuccessful campaign against the Massagetæ (the nomad races inhabiting the steppes of Central Asia), and fell in the contest (sect. 576).

Cambyses, 530-522.—The Ahasuerus of Ezra iv. 6; conquered Egypt, but was unsuccessful against the Ammonians and Ethiopians. Magians revolt. (See sect. 576.)

Smerdis Magus, 522.—The Artaxerxes of Ezra iv. 7-23. An usurper. (See sect. 577.)

Darius Hystaspis, 521-485.—Called Darius the Mede. Ezra iv. 4; vi. Invaded Scythia. Babylon revolted and was retaken. Ionian colonies in Asia revolted, which was followed by a war with Greece. Battle of Marathon, B. C. 490. (See sect. 578.)

Xerxes, 485-464.—Subdued the Egyptian revolt and made an expedition against Greece. Battles of Thermopylæ and Salamis, B. C. 480. Battles of Platæa and Mycale, B. C. 479. (See sect. 582.)

Artaxerxes Longimanus and his Successors, 464-330.—For a summary of this period, down to the overthrow of the empire by Alexander the Great, see sect. 583.

52. **Religion.**—The ancient religion of the Persians was the Magian, or worship of fire, and included, according to the Zendavesta, two conflicting principles—Ormuzd, god of light, and Ahriman, god of darkness. Zoroaster, who flourished, according to Prideaux and Hyde, during the reign of Darius Hystaspis, was the great reformer of the Persian religion. The Magian doctrine still exists among the Ghebres in Persia and the Parsees in India.

II. THE CRITICAL HISTORY OF THE OLD TESTAMENT.

ANALYSIS.

The Bible.—Divisions of the Old Testament: I. The Pentateuch, or five Books of the Law; II. The twelve Historical Books; III. The five Poetical Books, or Holy Writings; IV. The seventeen Prophetical Books; The Apocrypha.—Original language of the Old Testament.—The Septuagint.—The Vulgate.—English translations.

SUMMARY.

53. **The Bible**—$\beta\iota\beta\lambda o\varsigma$, i. e. *the Book*—is comprised in the OLD TESTAMENT, which contains thirty-nine books, and the NEW TESTAMENT, which contains twenty-seven books; in addition to these are the APOCRYPHAL WRITINGS, which are contained in fourteen books.

54. **Division of the Old Testament.**—The thirty-nine books of the Old Testament are divided into four classes—viz. I. THE PENTATEUCH, or five Books of the Law. II. The twelve HISTORICAL BOOKS. III. The five POETICAL BOOKS, or HOLY WRITINGS. IV. The seventeen PROPHETICAL BOOKS—viz. 1. The five Books, including *Lamentations*, by the four *Greater Prophets* and 2. The twelve Books of the twelve *Minor Prophets*.

55. **I. The Pentateuch,** or Five Books of the Law, from Πεντε, *five*, and τευχος, *a volume*. It comprises GENESIS, EXODUS, LEVITICUS, NUMBERS, and DEUTERONOMY, and was all written by Moses, excepting perhaps the last chapter of Deuteronomy, which contains an account of the death of Moses, and was therefore probably written by Joshua or Samuel, or some other later prophet.

The history of the Pentateuch extends from the creation to the death of Moses, B. C. 4004–1451, and includes a period of 2453 years. It is divided into three sections—viz.

1. History of the creation and deluge and the generations prior to Abraham. Gen. i.-xi.

2. History of the Jews as a nomad family—their patriarchal state, Egyptian slavery, and wanderings in the wilderness under Moses. Gen. xii.-l.; Ex. i.-xix.; Numbers.

3. The Mosaic code of laws and ordinances. Ex. xx.-xl.; Leviticus and Deuteronomy.

56. II. The Twelve Historical Books—viz. JOSHUA, JUDGES, RUTH, 1 and 2 SAMUEL, 1 and 2 KINGS, 1 and 2 CHRONICLES, EZRA, NEHEMIAH, and ESTHER. The authors of these books are unknown. It seems certain that from the commencement of the theocracy scribes were employed to write the records of their times; which records were subsequently deposited in the tabernacle or temple. It is therefore conjectured that the historical books, to the end of KINGS, were compiled from these original records by *Jeremiah*, shortly before the Captivity, and that the remaining five books, from 1 Chronicles to Esther, were compiled by Ezra. The history of these twelve books extends from the death of Moses to the end of Nehemiah's history, B. C. 1451 to about B. C. 434—a period of 1017 years. It is divided into five sections:

I. History of the conquest of Canaan under Joshua. Joshua.

II. History of the Jews under a federative republic. Judges; 1 Sam. i.-viii.; including the episode of Ruth.

III. History of the Jews under a single monarchy—viz. of Saul, David, and Solomon. 1 Sam. ix. to end; 2 Sam.; 1 Kings i.-xii.; 1 Chron.; 2 Chron. i.-ix.

IV. History of the Jews under the divided monarchy of *Judah* and *Israel*. 1 Kings xii. to end; 2 Kings; 2 Chron. x. to end.

V. History of the Jews from the Babylonian captivity to the end of Nehemiah's history. Ezra; Nehemiah; with portions of Jeremiah, Daniel, etc., and including the episode of Esther.

During the period of the Pentateuch and historical books, the whole of the five poetical books must have been composed, and all the prophecies in the seventeen prophetical books delivered.

57. III. The Five Poetical Books, or *Holy Writings—Hagiographa*, from αγιως, *holy*, and γραφη, a *writing*. They comprise JOB, PSALMS, PROVERBS, ECCLESIASTES, and SOLOMON'S SONG. They are called poetical books because they are almost wholly written in Hebrew metre. JOB is supposed to have been written by *Moses;* the PSALMS by ten persons—viz. *Moses, David, Solomon, Asaph, Heman, Ethan, Jeduthun,* and the three sons of *Korah;* the PROVERBS chiefly by *Solomon*, though in the thirtieth and thirty-first chapters the proverbs of *Agur* and *Lemuel* are inserted. ECCLESIASTES and SOLOMON'S SONG are undoubtedly by *Solomon*.

58. IV. The Seventeen Prophetical Books. These writings are divided into two kinds—viz.

INTRODUCTORY OUTLINE. 27

I. *The Five Prophetical Books* (including *Lamentations*) of the four GREATER PROPHETS—viz. ISAIAH, JEREMIAH, (Prophecies and Lamentations), EZEKIEL, and DANIEL.

II. *The Twelve Prophetical Books of the Twelve Minor Prophets*—viz. HOSEA, JOEL, AMOS, OBADIAH, JONAH, MICAH, NAHUM, HABAKKUK, ZEPHANIAH, HAGGAI, ZECHARIAH, MALACHI.

59. **The Fourteen Apocryphal Books**—$\alpha\pi o\kappa\rho\upsilon\pi\tau\omega$, i. e. *to hide*—which comprise 1 and 2 ESDRAS, TOBIT, JUDITH, REST OF ESTHER, WISDOM OF SOLOMON, ECCLESIASTICUS, BARUCH, SONG OF THE THREE CHILDREN, BEL AND THE DRAGON, PRAYER OF MANASSES, and 1 and 2 MACCABEES. The history of these books will be found in the *Connection*, sect. 103, *et seq.* They are of doubtful origin, and consequently not included in our canon of Scripture, though the Roman Catholic Church, by the authority of the Council of Trent, admits them as canonical. (See "Apocryphal Books," *Con.*, sects. 103–117.)

60. **Original Language of the Old Testament.**—The Old Testament is written in Hebrew, excepting some chapters of Ezra and Daniel, which are in Chaldee, the Jews having become more familiar with the Chaldee than the Hebrew during the Babylonian captivity. There are, however, two editions of the *Pentateuch*—viz. the SAMARITAN and the HEBREW. The SAMARITAN is written in the ancient Hebrew character, and has been preserved by the Samaritans distinct from the other ever since the Babylonian captivity, "for the Jews had no dealings with the Samaritans." The comparison of the two has been found useful in correcting the errors of transcribers.

61. **The Septuagint.**—This ancient Greek version was originally made for the use of the Egyptian Jews, and called *Septuagint—septuaginta*, i. e. *seventy*—because, according to the tradition of one Aristeas, which is now generally rejected, it was supposed to have been made in seventy-two days, by seventy elders, or learned Jews, who had been sent by the Jewish high priest Eleazar to Alexandria at the request of Ptolemy Philadelphus, king of Egypt. It is also called the *Alexandrian* version, from having been executed at Alexandria. Some say that the seventy elders were shut up in the isle of Pharos, and completed their task in seventy-two days, while Demetrius Phalerus, the king's chief librarian, transcribed it from their dictation. Others say that the seventy, being shut up in separate cells, wrote each a separate translation, and all were afterward found to exactly coincide in words and sentiment.

This version was most probably made during the joint reigns of Ptolemy Lagus and his son Ptolemy Philadelphus, about B. C. 285 or 286 (see *Con.*, sect. 12), and the introduction of Coptic or pure Egyptian words and the rendering of Hebrew words in the Egyptian manner clearly prove that the translators were natives of Egypt; whilst the difference of style and ability shows that this version was the work not of one, but of several individuals.

The *Septuagint* gradually acquired the highest authority amongst the Jews of Palestine, and subsequently amongst the Christians, and all the quotations in the New Testament from the Old are taken from it. It was, however, abandoned by the Jewish synagogue about the first century after Christ. It is still employed by the Greek and other Christian churches.

62. **The Vulgate.**—This was an ancient Latin version of the Septuagint and Greek New Testament, made in the early part of the second century, and called the VETUS ITALA, or *Old Italic*, but its author is unknown. In the fourth century, Jerome commenced revising this old Italic translation, but before it was completed he undertook and finished a new Latin version of the Bible, which gradually acquired so great an authority in Western Europe that it has been exclusively adopted by the Romish Church ever since the seventh century. Some parts only of Jerome's revision of the *Old Italic* version have been preserved, but his Latin translation, under the name of *Latin Vulgate*, was at length pronounced to be authentic by the Council of Trent in the sixteenth century, and ordered to be exclusively used in the service of the Romish Church. Several revisions of the Latin Vulgate have been since undertaken by learned men, which were rendered necessary from the errors of copyists and the occasional intermixture of the *Old Italic* version with Jerome's *Latin Vulgate*. Of these revisions, the most celebrated is that by Pope Sixtus V., which was published at Rome in 1590, but suppressed by Clement VIII., whose authentic edition appeared in 1592.

63. **English Translations.**—No complete version of all the Scriptures appears to have been made in Saxon, though Bede translated certain parts, and other Saxon versions still exist of the most important portions.

The First English translation known to be extant was made by an unknown indivividual about 1290; of this there are but two manuscript copies preserved—one in the Bodleian Library, and the other in Christ Church College Library, Oxford.

John de Trevisa, about a century after, is said by Caxton to have translated the whole Bible into English; but this is uncertain.

John Wickliffe, about the same time—viz. 1380—either translated the whole Bible from the Latin Vulgate, or collected

INTRODUCTORY OUTLINE. 29

previous translations which completed an *English Bible*. His version of the New Testament has been often published.

William Tyndale, in 1526, printed his English version of the New Testament. Two years after, he also printed a translation of the Pentateuch. He was martyred at Antwerp in 1536.

Miles Coverdale, in 1535, printed at Zurich the *first complete English translation of the Bible*, composed of Tyndale's versions, as far as they went, and his own.

John Rogers, in 1537, having previously assisted Tyndale, now edited a Bible (probably at Hamburg) under the assumed name of Thomas Matthews; his Bible is therefore generally called *Matthews' Bible*. This translation was revised by *Cranmer* and *Coverdale*, and printed in London, 1539, in large folio, and from this was called the *Great Bible*.

The Geneva Bible was published between 1557 and 1560, at Geneva, being a new version by Coverdale, Knox, Goodman, and others, with short annotations. The New Testament in this Bible was the first one divided into verses.

The Bishops' Bible was published in 1568, with two prefaces by Archbishop Parker, who employed several critics to make the translation, amongst whom were eight bishops; hence it was called the *Bishops' Bible*. This Bible was read in churches, but the *Geneva* was preferred in families.

THE PRESENT AUTHORIZED ENGLISH VERSION was published in 1611. At the Hampton Court Conference, in 1603, several objections were made to the *Bishops' Bible*, and, in 1604, James I. issued a commission to fifty-four of the most eminent divines of both universities to undertake a new version. This was not commenced until 1607, when seven of the divines had died and only forty-seven were living. The forty-seven survivors were now divided into six committees— two at Oxford, two at Cambridge, and two at Westminster— and each had a certain portion assigned it. In 1610 the great work was completed, and then revised by a committee of six of the translators, and finally reviewed by Bishop Bilson and Dr. Smith; the latter prefixed the Arguments and wrote the Preface. The whole was printed and published in 1611.

64. Division into Chapters and Verses.—The invention of *chapters* has been ascribed to both Archbishop Lanfranc and Stephen Langton, but the real author was Cardinal Hugo de Sancto Caro, who, having projected a concordance to the Latin Vulgate about the middle of the thirteenth century, divided both the Old and New Testaments into chapters, the same as we now have. These chapters he subdivided into smaller portions, which he distinguished by the letters A, B,

C, D, etc. In the fifteenth century Rabbi Mordecai Nathan made a Hebrew concordance on the same plan, and adopted the cardinal's divisions. The introduction of verses into the *printed* editions of the Hebrew Bible was made by Athias, an Amsterdam Jew, in 1661, and into the Greek by Robert Stephens in 1551. The first English New Testament with verses appeared at Geneva in 1557, and the first English Bible so printed was also executed at Geneva, in 1560. The *Bishops' Bible*, and subsequently the *Authorized Version*, were also divided into chapters and verses.

JEWISH MONTHS.

The Jews had two principal kinds of years, the *Ecclesiastical* and the *Civil.*

I. *The Ecclesiastical or Sacred Year* began on the first day of the month *Nisan,* corresponding to about the middle of March, this being the time when the Jews departed out of Egypt. (See sect. 97.) From this month *Nisan,* or *Abib,* the Jews computed their feasts, and the prophets also occasionally dated their oracles and visions.

II. *The Civil Year* began on the first day of the month *Tisri,* from a traditionary supposition that this was the date of the creation of the world. By this year the Jews computed their jubilees and dated their contracts, the births of their children, and the reigns of their kings.

Months of the Ecclesiastical *and* Civil *years compared with our months.*

Ecclesiastical Year.	Civil Year.	
1. Nisan or Abib,	7.	part of March and April.
2. Jyar or Zif,	8.	" April and May.
3. Sivan,	9.	" May and June.
9. Kisleu or Chisleu,	10.	" June and July.
10. Thebet,	11.	" July and August.
11. Sebat,	12.	" August and September.
12. Adar,	1.	" September and October.
4. Thammuz,	2.	" October and November.
5. Ab,	3.	" November and December.
6. Elul,	4.	" December and January.
7. Tizri,	5.	" January and February.
8. Marchesvan,	6.	" February and March.

As the Jewish years were lunar years, and therefore consisted of only 354 days and 8 hours, they were accommodated to solar years by the addition of a month at the end of the Ecclesiastical year, and this intercalary month, which came after the month Adar, was called Ke-Adar, or the Second Adar.

CHRONOLOGY OF THE PRINCIPAL EVENTS RECORDED IN THE OLD TESTAMENT.

1st Period.

Patriarchal State.—From the Creation to the Death of Joseph.

B.C. 4004–1635—about 2369 years.

	B. C.
The creation	4004
Enoch's translation	3017
Noah born	2948
Building of the ark commenced	2469
The deluge	2349–2348
Confusion of tongues about	2234
Noah's death (aged 950)	1998
Abram born	1996
Call of Abram	1921
Ishmael born	1910
Sodom and Gomorrah destroyed	1898
Isaac born	1897
—— offered by Abraham	1872
—— marries Rebekah	1857
Esau and Jacob born	1837
Abraham died (aged 175)	1822
Ishmael died	1773
Jacob goes to Padan-aram	1760
—— marries Leah and Rachel	1753
Joseph born	1745
Jacob leaves Laban	1739
Joseph sold to Potiphar	1729
Isaac died (aged 180)	1716
Joseph interprets Pharaoh's two dreams	1715
Seven years' plenty	1715–1708
Seven years' famine	1708–1701
First visit of Joseph's brethren	1707
Second visit " " "	1706
Israelites migrate to Egypt	1706
Jacob died (age 147)	1689
Joseph died (aged 110)	1635

2d Period.

Nomad State.—From the Death of Joseph to the Death of Moses.

B. C. 1635–1451—about 184 years.

Birth of Moses	1571
Flies to Midian	1531
The exodus	1491
Tabernacle completed	1490
Rebellion of Korah	1471
Moses and Aaron sin	1453
Aaron died	1452
Moses died (aged 120)	1451

3d Period.

A Federative Republic—From the Death of Moses to the Anointing of Saul.

B. C. 1451–1095.

Passage of the Jordan	1451
Canaan divided among the twelve tribes	1444
Joshua died	1426
Judges	1402–1095

For the chronology of this very obscure period, see p. 148.

Ruth	about 1322–1312

4th Period.

The Single Monarchy.

B. C. 1095–975.

1. SAUL king	1095
David anointed	1063
Slays Goliath	1063
Saul committed suicide (reigned forty years)	1056
2. DAVID king	1056
Reigned at Hebron	1056–1048
—— over all Israel	1048–1015
3. SOLOMON king	1015
Building of the temple	1012–1005
Dedication	1005
Rehoboam king	975

5th Period.

The Divided Monarchies of Judah and Israel, and seventy years' Captivity.

B. C. 975–536.

Revolt of the ten tribes	975
Kingdom of Israel	975–721
Kingdom of Judah	975–588
Jonah prophesied	about 840
Amos and Hosea	800

CHRONOLOGICAL TABLE.

	B.C.
Isaiah	758–698
Joel	about 800
Micah	758–699
Israel carried into captivity by Shalmaneser	*721*
Nahum	720
Zephaniah	640
Jeremiah	628–586
Habakkuk	612

Nebuchadnezzar took Jerusalem in the reign of Jehoiakim, from which date—viz. B.C. 606, *to the edict of Cyrus*, B.C. 536—*is calculated the seventy years' captivity.*

	B.C.
The seventy years' captivity	606–536
JERUSALEM AND THE TEMPLE TAKEN AND BURNT, AND JUDAH CARRIED AWAY CAPTIVE	588
Daniel prophesied	606–534
Ezekiel prophesied	595–536
Obadiah prophesied	588–583

See also tables at p. 166, and p. 266.

6th Period.

From the Edict of Cyrus, B.C. 536, *to the Taking of Jerusalem by Titus,* A.D. 70.

	B.C.
Edict of Cyrus and return of the Jews	536
Second temple begun	535
Second temple finished	515
Governorship of Ezra	458–445
Nehemiah's first administration	445–433
Nehemiah's second administration	428–420
Close of Old Testament history	420
Alexander the Great at Jerusalem	332
His death	323
Palestine under the Ptolemies	300–202
Septuagint made	about 280
Palestine under the Seleucidæ	202–166
Antiochus Epiphanes profaned the temple	170
Revolt of Mattathias	167
Palestine under the Maccabees	166–37
Judas Maccabæus	166–161
Feast of dedication instituted	165
Apocryphal history ends	135
Samaritan temple on Mount Gerizim destroyed by John Hyrcanus	129
Judæa subjected to Pompey	63
Crassus plundered the temple	54
Cæsar assassinated	44
Herod king	37–3
Rebuilds the temple	19
Jesus Christ born	4

THE PENTATEUCH.

[ΠΕΝΤΕ, "FIVE," AND ΤΕΥΧΟΣ, "A VOLUME," THE FIVE BOOKS OF THE LAW—VIZ. GENESIS, EXODUS, LEVITICUS, NUMBERS, AND DEUTERONOMY; ALL WRITTEN BY MOSES.—SEE INTRODUCTION.]

GENESIS.

(Γένεσις, "generation"—the generation of all things.)

PATRIARCHAL HISTORY FROM THE BIRTH OF ADAM TILL THE DEATH OF JOSEPH, B. C. 4004 TO 1635.—ABOUT 2369 YEARS.

ANALYSIS.

I. *History of the World prior to Abraham.*

Antediluvian Period, 4004-2348.—THE CREATION, B. C. 4004. Plurality of Persons in the Godhead.—God blesses man.—The garden of Eden.—The fall.—Promise of a Redeemer.—Murder of Abel.—Posterity of Adam through Cain.—Posterity of Adam through Seth.—Building of the ark, 2469-2349.—THE DELUGE, 2349-2348.

Settlement after the Flood, 2348-1996.—Noah's prophecies concerning his sons; dies, 1998.—Posterity of Noah, fulfilment of his prophecies, etc.—Building of Babel, 2234.—Generations from Noah to Abram.—Haran, Nahor, and Abram.

page 36

II. *Lives of Abraham, Isaac, Jacob, and Joseph.*

Abram, 1996-1822, lived 175 years.—Early life and call of Abram, B. C. 1996-1921.—Journeys through Canaan to Egypt, 1921.—Returns to Canaan and encamps at Mamre, whilst Lot dwells at Sodom, 1918.—Inhabitants of Canaan.—Abram rescues Lot from captivity, 1913.—Character of Melchizedek.—God promises Abram a son; Ishmael born, 1910.—God renews his covenant with Abram, 1898.—Institutes circumcision and changes Abram and Sarai's names, 1898.—Abraham visited by three angels; intercedes for Sodom.—Destruction of Sodom and origin of Moab and Ammon.—Abraham removes to Gerar.

Isaac, 1897-1716, lived 180 years.—ISAAC BORN.—1897.—Hagar and Ishmael exiled, 1892.—Digging of Beersheba, 1891.—Abraham tempted to offer Isaac, 1872.—Isaac a type of Christ.—DEATH OF SARAH, 1860.—Isaac marries Rebekah, 1857.—Abraham marries Keturah, 1853.

Jacob, 1837-1689, lived 147 years.—Jacob and Esau born to Isaac, 1837.—ABRAHAM DIES, 1822.—Esau sells his birthright, 1805.—Famine in Canaan; Isaac leaves Mamre for Gerar and deceives Abimelech, 1804.—Esau marries two Hittite women, 1796.—Ishmael dies, 1773.—Isaac blesses Jacob instead of Esau, 1760.—Jacob goes to Laban at Haran; his dream.—Esau marries Mahalath.—Jacob marries Leah and Rachel, 1753.—His family.—Makes a new covenant with Laban, 1745.—Leaves Laban, 1739.—His vision at Mahanaim and message to Esau.—Wrestles with a MAN at Peniel.—Meeting with Esau.—Resides at Succoth and Shechem; slaughter of the Shechemites, 1739-1732.—Buries the idols of his household and goes to Bethel.—Death of Rachel; birth of Benjamin, 1732.—Reuben's incest with Bilhah.—JACOB RESIDES WITH ISAAC AT MAMRE, 1729.

Joseph, 1745-1635, lived 110 years.—Joseph excites his brethren's envy, and sold to the Ishmaelites, 1729.—Judah marries a Canaanite; his incest with his daughter-in-law.—Joseph sold to Potiphar and imprisoned, 1729-1715.—[ISAAC DIED, 1716.]—Joseph interprets the dreams of Pharaoh's butler and baker, 1720-1718.—Interprets Pharaoh's two dreams, 1715.—Made chief ruler of Egypt, and marries Asenath.—Seven years' plenty, 1715-1708; birth of Manasseh, 1712; of Ephraim, 1711.—Seven years' famine, 1708-1701; first visit of Joseph's brethren, 1707; second visit of Joseph's brethren, 1706.—Israelites migrate to Egypt, 1706.—Policy of Joseph during the famine, 1702, 1701.—Dying acts and prophecies of Jacob, 1689.—Fulfilment of Jacob's prophecies.—JACOB'S DEATH AND BURIAL, 1689.—Joseph again forgives his brethren.—DEATH OF JOSEPH, 1635.—Joseph a type of Christ.—Scriptural meaning of a *type*.—Typical intimations of the Messiah in Genesis.—Prophetical intimations and their fulfilment.—Names, and meanings of the names, of the principal persons mentioned in Genesis. . . . . page 44.

SUMMARY.

I. *History of the World prior to Abraham.*

Antediluvian history, B. C. 4004-2348.
1. ***The Creation, B. C. 4004.***—In the beginning* God created the heavens and the earth.

---

* At present there are some apparent discrepancies between geology and astronomy and the sacred writings; but the Bible was not intended to instruct mankind in the sciences, and therefore only alludes to things

1st day—LIGHT, and the separation of day from night.

2d day—FIRMAMENT or AIR, and separation of the ocean from the clouds.

3d day—DRY LAND, HERBS, and TREES, and separation of the earth from the sea.

4th day—SUN, MOON, and STARS.

5th day—FISHES and BIRDS.

6th day—ANIMALS and MAN.

7th day—God rested, and sanctified his work. Gen. i.; ii. 1–3.

2. *Plurality of Persons in the Godhead.*—Before God created man he said, " Let *us* make man in *our* image, after *our* likeness; and let them have dominion over the fish of the sea, and over the fowl of the air, and over the cattle, and over all the earth, and over every creeping thing that creepeth upon the earth." These expressions *us* and *our* distinctly imply a plurality of Persons in the Godhead.

3. *God blesses Man.*—After God had created man, male and female, he blessed them, saying, " Be fruitful, and multiply, and replenish the earth, and subdue it: and have dominion over the fish of the sea, and over the fowl of the air, and over every living thing that moveth upon the earth." Gen. i. 26–28.

4. *The Garden of Eden.*—God, having created Adam, placed him in the garden of Eden to cultivate the trees and subsist upon the fruit, but under an express command to refrain from the tree of knowledge of good and evil. The Almighty then brought him all the beasts and birds to be named, and made a woman from one of his ribs, and gave her to him for a wife.* Adam called his

---

as they *appear* to the uninstructed mind, and not as they are in reality, leaving the physical creation for the delightful exercise of our faculties. Geology, however, substantially agrees with the biblical accounts. It proves the successive creation of plants and animals, ending with man; it shows that every part of the earth is marked by the effects of a deluge occurring at one time or at many times; and it points to a beginning, when neither plants nor animals nor man existed. But both the Scriptures and geology are silent as to the period when the fiat of our Creator first called our earth and the planetary systems into being. Conf. Silliman's *Introduction to Geology;* Pye Smith's *Reconciliation of Geology and Scripture,* etc.

* Thus were instituted the two ordinances of the *Sabbath* and of *marriage;* the first is a type of that rest which remaineth to the peo-

wife Eve, "the mother of all living." Eden was watered by four rivers—viz. the Hiddekel, Euphrates, Pison,* and Araxes. Gen. ii.

5. ***The Fall.***—After this the serpent tempted Eve to eat of the forbidden fruit, and she prevailed on her husband to share her sin. The sentence of God was then pronounced upon the criminals. To Adam he said, "Cursed is the ground for thy sake, in sorrow shalt thou eat of it all the days of thy life. Thorns also and thistles shall it bring forth to thee, and thou shalt eat of the herb of the field. In the sweat of thy face shalt thou eat bread till thou return unto the ground: for out of it wast thou taken; for dust thou art, and unto dust shalt thou return." To Eve he said, "In sorrow shalt thou bring forth children: and thy desire shall be to thy husband, and he shall rule over thee." The tree of life was then guarded by flaming cherubim, lest the man should eat of it and live for ever, and Adam and Eve were clothed by the Almighty with coats of skins and expelled from Paradise. Gen. iii.

6. ***Promise of a Redeemer.***—When the Almighty denounced our first parents, he intimated the future redemption of mankind. To the serpent he said, "Thou art cursed above all cattle: upon thy belly shalt thou go, and dust shalt thou eat all the days of thy life. *And I will put enmity between thee and the woman, and between thy seed and her seed; it shall bruise thy head, and thou shalt bruise his heel.*" By the "seed of the woman" is meant Jesus Christ, and by "bruising the serpent's head" is meant that Christ would destroy the works of the

---

ple of God, and the latter of the mystic union between Christ and his Church.

* The attempts to discover the site of the garden of Eden have been hitherto numerous and contradictory, and in many cases so ridiculous as to make all modern researches appear vain and useless. The Tigris and Euphrates have now been turned from their course, and their ancient channels are unknown, as is proved from local traditions and Arabian geographers. Of the two most probable conjectures, one fixes the terrestrial Paradise in Armenia, between the sources of the Euphrates, Tigris, Phasis, and Araxes, and the other identifies the *land* of Eden with the country between Baghdad and Bassorah, which comprehended ancient Babylonia; and they only contend that the *garden* stood in some part of this territory, where an ancient junction, and subsequent separation, of the Euphrates and Tigris took place. For a further inquiry, see Kitto's *Chapter on the Site of Paradise.*

devil. "When the fulness of time was come, God sent forth his Son, made of a woman." Gal. iv. 4. "The God of peace shall bruise Satan under your feet shortly." Rom. xvi. 20.

7. *Murder of Abel.*—Two sons were now born to Adam and Eve; Cain, the elder, became a tiller of the ground, whilst Abel, the younger, was a keeper of sheep. After a time the two brothers offered sacrifices to God, Cain bringing a portion of the fruit of the earth, and Abel the firstlings of his flocks. The offering of Abel was alone accepted by Jehovah, but he fell a victim to the envy of Cain; and the agonized parents, who had brought sin into the world, now saw its terrible consequences in the fratricide by their first-born. Gen. iv. 1–15. "As by one man sin entered into the world, and death by sin." Rom. v. 12.

8. *Posterity of Adam through Cain.*—There is no Mosaic account of the births or deaths of the posterity of Cain, and only the heads of families appear to be mentioned.

1. CAIN begat Enoch, and built a city after his name.
2. ENOCH begat Irad.
3. IRAD begat Mehujael.
4. MEHUJAEL begat Methusael.
5. METHUSAEL begat Lamech.
6. LAMECH married two wives:

1st. ADAH, mother of—1. *Jabal,* the father of dwellers in tents and cattle-grazers; 2. *Jubal,* the father of instrumental musicians.

2d. ZILLAH, mother of—1. *Tubal-Cain,* who instructed artificers in brass and iron; 2. *Naamah,* a daughter. Gen. iv. 16–23.

9. *Posterity of Adam through Seth.*—There were ten generations from Adam to Noah inclusive—viz.

1. ADAM, 4004–3074. Lived 930 years; begat Seth in his 130th year, from whom Christ was descended.
2. SETH, 3874–2962. Lived 912 years; begat Enos in his 105th year.
3. ENOS, 3769–2864. Lived 905 years; begat Cainan in his 90th year.
4. CAINAN, 3679–2769. Lived 910 years; begat Mahalaleel in his 70th year.

5. MAHALALEEL, 3609–2714. Lived 895 years; begat Jared in his 65th year.

6. JARED, 3544–2582. Lived 962 years; begat Enoch in his 162d year.

7. ENOCH, 3382–3017. Lived 365 years; begat Methuselah in his 65th year. "Walked with God, and he was not, for God took him." Gen. v. 24. "By faith Enoch was translated that he should not see death; . . . for before his translation he had this testimony, that he pleased God." Heb. xi. 5. Enoch also prophesied God's judgments on sinners, saying, "Behold, the Lord cometh with ten thousand of his saints, to execute judgment upon all." Jude 14, 15.

8. METHUSELAH, 3317–2348. Lived 969 years; begat Lamech in his 187th year. The oldest of all men; he was contemporary with Adam for 243 years, and with Noah for 600 years.

9. LAMECH, 3130–2353. Lived 777 years; begat Noah in his 182d year. He predicted the blessing. Gen. v. 29.

10. NOAH, 2948–1998. Lived 950 years. In his 500th year he had begotten three sons—Shem, Ham, and Japheth. Gen. v. 3–32; ix. 28, 29.

10. *Building of the Ark, 2469–2349.*—The earth was now corrupt and filled with violence; the sons of God married the daughters of men,* and the Almighty threatened to destroy mankind by a deluge. But Noah was a just man and "a preacher of righteousness" (2 Pet. ii. 5), and, having thus found grace in the eyes of Jehovah, he was desired to build an ark for the deliverance of himself and his family. "By faith Noah, being warned of God of things not seen as yet, moved with fear, prepared an ark to the saving of his house." Heb. xi. 7. "The long-suffering of God waited while the ark was preparing." 1 Pet. iii. 20. Ample directions were given by the Almighty for this undertaking. The ark was to be made of gopher-wood, and to be 300 cubits [547 feet] long, 50 cubits [91 feet] wide, and 30 cubits [54½ feet] high, and to have three stories. Noah was engaged upon

---

* By the sons of God were probably meant the descendants of Seth, who practised the worship of Jehovah. These seem to have intermarried with the rest of mankind, or the descendants of Cain.

it for one hundred and twenty years, during which he continued to preach repentance, but in vain. In his six hundredth year [B. C. 2349] the ark was completed, and he entered it, with his wife and his three sons and their wives, together with one pair of every species of unclean animals and seven of each clean species. This ark was a type of our salvation by Jesus Christ. Gen. vi.

11. *The Deluge, 2349, 2348.*—On the seventh day after entering the ark the flood began, and the rain fell for forty days and forty nights. The waters prevailed for one hundred and fifty days, and covered the highest hills; every land-animal was destroyed; but at length the mountain-tops were seen, and the ark rested on Ararat in Armenia, between the Black Sea and the Caspian. After successively sending forth a raven and a dove, Noah at length left the ark, having remained in it for one year and seventeen days. The lonely family then sacrificed to Jehovah, and God blessed Noah and his sons, and promised that for the future neither the order of the seasons nor of day and night should cease; but he forbade them to eat flesh with the blood in it, or to shed the blood of their fellow-man: "Whoso sheddeth man's blood, by man shall his blood be shed; for in the image of God made he man." Finally, the Almighty set his rainbow in the clouds in token of this everlasting covenant. Gen. vii.; viii.; ix. 1–17. Before the deluge the earth was probably watered by mist, and not by rain. Gen. ii. 5, 6.

12. *Noah prophesies concerning his Sons; dies, 1998.*—Noah now became a husbandman and planted a vineyard, but, [Settlement after the Flood, B. C. 2348-1996.] having drank too freely of the wine, his son Ham, the father of Canaan, discovered him naked, but Shem and Japheth covered him with a mantle. Noah, on awaking, discovered what had been done, and said of Canaan, the son of HAM, "Cursed be Canaan; a servant of servants shall he be to his brethren;" of SHEM, "Blessed be the Lord God of Shem; and Canaan shall be his servant;" and of JAPHETH, "God shall enlarge Japheth, and he shall dwell in the tents of Shem; and Canaan shall be his servant." Noah lived three hundred and fifty years after the deluge, and died B. C. 1998. Gen. ix. 18–29.

13. *Posterity of Noah, and fulfilment of his Prophecies.*—The three sons of Noah are supposed to have been the progenitors of the following races, in whom the patriarch's prophecies appear to have been fulfilled.

14. *1st. Japheth,* whose posterity appear to have extended to Northern Asia and Asia Minor, and from thence to have been ultimately impelled into Europe. He had seven sons—viz.

1. GOMER, father of the Cimbri or Cimmerians.
2. MAGOG, " " Scythians or Tartars.
3. MADAI, " " Medes.
4. JAVAN, " " Greeks.
5. TUBAL, " " Tibarenians, on the coast of Pontus.
6. MESHECH, " Muscovites.
7. TIRAS, " " Thracians.

The prophecy concerning Japheth was thus fulfilled in his posterity occupying vast territories, and in their subjugation of Asia and Africa, by which they dwelt in the tents of Shem, with the descendants of Canaan for their servants.

15. *2d. Ham,* whose children remained in chief possession of Mesopotamia; formed settlements at the head of the Persian Gulf, in Arabia, and in Canaan; established the old empires in Assyria and Egypt; and, as their numbers multiplied, advanced into Ethiopia and other remote parts of the African peninsula. He had four sons, viz.

1. CUSH, father of the Cushites or Ethiopians, in Arabia and Africa.

His son Nimrod built four very ancient cities, including Babel, and founded the ancient empire of Assyria. Asshur, son of Shem, migrated from this country, and built Nineveh and three other cities.

2. MIZRAIM, father of the Egyptians—literally, the two Egypts.
3. PHUT, " " Libyans.
4. CANAAN, " " Canaanites, including Phœnicians.

The prophecy concerning Ham has been fulfilled in the conquest of Palestine by the Hebrews, and the past and present degraded state of Africa.

16. *3d. Shem,* whose descendants gradually spread over the east and north-east of the Tigris. He had five sons—viz.

1. ELAM, father of the Elamites or Elymæans.
2. ASSHUR, " " Assyrians.
3. ARPHAXAD, " Hebrews, Ishmaelites, and other Abrahamic nations.

>For the descent of Abraham from Arphaxad see sect. 18.

4. LUD, " " Lydians.
5. ARAM, " " Aramites in Syria and Mesopotamia.

The prophecy concerning Shem was fulfilled in the Messiah being born of his posterity, and the worship of God being preserved amongst them. Gen. x.*

17. *Building of Babel.*—After the death of Noah the whole earth was of one language, and all the families journeyed from Armenia in the east to a plain in the land of Shinar, near Chaldea or the Euphrates. Here they commenced building a city and tower, afterward called "BABEL" ($\beta\alpha\beta\upsilon\lambda\grave{\omega}\nu$) †—*i. e.* "confusion"— which they presumptuously intended should reach the heavens; but God confounded their language, and the generation became scattered. Nimrod, the son of Cush, "a mighty hunter before the Lord," founded the kingdom of Babel in the fourth generation, or about one hundred and twenty years, after the deluge. Gen. xi. 1–9.

18. *Generations from Noah to Abram, 2446–2056.*—There were ten generations from Noah to Abram inclusive—viz.

1. SHEM, 2446–1846. Lived 600 years; begat Arphaxad in his 100th year.

---

* There are many different opinions about the exact territories occupied and nations founded by the several branches of Noah's descendants. The account in the text appears the most probable. A careful and valuable critical review of the table of nations is to be found in Hävernick's *Introduction to the Pentateuch.*

† The building of this city is one of the earliest recorded facts subsequent to the deluge. According to secular history it was founded by Belus, and afterward enlarged by Ninus and Semiramis, and was seated on both banks of the Euphrates.

2. ARPHAXAD, 2346–1908. Lived 438 years; begat Salah in his 35th year.
3. SALAH, 2311–1878. Lived 433 years; begat Eber in his 30th year.
4. EBER, 2281–1817. Lived 464 years; begat Peleg in his 34th year.
5. PELEG, 2247–2008. Lived 239 years; begat Reu in his 30th year.
6. REU, 2217–1978. Lived 239 years; begat Serug in his 32d year.
7. SERUG, 2185–1955. Lived 230 years; begat Nahor in his 30th year.
8. NAHOR, 2155–2007. Lived 148 years; begat Terah in his 29th year.
9. TERAH, 2126–1921. Lived 205 years. Lived 70 years (B. C. 2056), and begat

19. 10. HARAN, NAHOR, AND ABRAM.—Though Haran was born when Terah was seventy years old—viz. B. C. 2056—Abram could not have been born before B. C. 1996, or sixty years afterward. Haran died before Terah, leaving one son and two daughters—viz. 1. LOT; 2. MILCAH, who married her uncle Nahor; and 3. SARAI or ISCAH, who married her uncle Abram. Gen. xi. 10–27.

II. *Lives of Abram, Isaac, Jacob, and Joseph.*

Abram, B. C. 1996–1822; aged 175 years.
Isaac, B. C. 1897–1716; aged 180 years.
Jacob, B. C. 1837–1689; aged 148 years.
Joseph, B. C. 1745–1635; aged 110 years.

Patriarchal history.
Abram, B. C. 1996–1822.

20. ***Early Life and Call of Abram, 1996–1921.***—Abram, Nahor, and Haran were born to Terah, in Ur of Chaldea,* and here Haran died. At Ur, God said to Abram, "Get thee out of thy country, and from thy kindred, and from thy father's house, into a land that I will show thee."

---

* The original seat of the Chaldeans was probably in the mountains of Armenia and Kurdistan, whence they descended into the plains of Mesopotamia and Babylonia. *Ur* was a district in Northern Mesopotamia occupied by the Chaldees. It was also the name of a very ancient city, subsequently called Edessa, which formed the capital of Osroene. *Haran* lay farther south, on the road toward Palestine.

Accordingly, Abram and his wife Sarai, his father Terah, and his nephew Lot, left Ur for Canaan, but stopped at Haran in Mesopotamia, where Terah died, B. C. 1921. Joshua appears to say that whilst at Ur both Abram and his father were idolaters: "Your fathers dwelt on the other side of the flood in old time, even Terah, the father of Abraham, and the father of Nahor; and they served other gods." Josh. xxiv. 2; Gen. xi. 28–32; xii. 1; Acts vii. 2, 3.

21. *Journeys through Canaan to Egypt, 1921.*— After Terah's death, Abram, who was now 75 years old, departed, under divine direction, to Canaan, with Sarai and Lot, God having said, "In thee shall all families of the earth be blessed." Abram passed through Sichem* to the plain of Moreh,† where the Almighty said to him, "Unto thy seed will I give this land." Abram then encamped upon a mountain between Bethel and Hai, and afterward journeyed southward, but was at length driven by a famine to Egypt, where he deceived Pharaoh by passing off his wife Sarai as his sister; but she was preserved from the Egyptian king by divine interference. Gen. xii. 2–20.

22. *Returns to Canaan and Encamps at Mamre, while Lot Dwells at Sodom, 1918.*—At Pharaoh's command, Abram and Lot left Egypt and returned to the mountain between Bethel and Hai with increased possessions and herds; but, a dispute having arisen between their several herdsmen, they agreed upon an amicable separation, Lot pitching his tent in the vale of Siddim, toward Sodom, while Abraham proceeded to the vale of Mamre in Hebron,‡ where he fixed his residence and built an altar to the Lord. Gen. xiii.

23. *Inhabitants of Canaan.*—Some time prior to this period a division of the posterity of Canaan, youngest son of Ham, settled in this country, and named it after their father. They appear to have been divided

---

* This was afterward included in *Samaria*.

† The plain or valley of *Moreh* lies between the mountains of Ebal and Gerizim, also in Samaria, and must not be confounded with Mount *Moriah*, on which the temple was built.

‡ *Mamre* was about a mile from the town of *Arba*, afterward called *Hebron*, and lay in a central part of what was subsequently the tribe of Judah.

into ten families, or tribes; the Kenites, Kenizzites, and Kadmonites inhabited the region east of the Jordan; whilst the Hittites, Perizzites, Rephaims, Amorites, Canaanites,* Gergashites, and Jebusites occupied the territory from the Jordan to the Mediterranean. They were separated into a number of small independent communities, governed by petty kings, who, however, appear to have been regarded more as military commanders than as civil rulers. Gen. v. 19–21. (See also sect. 247–249.)

24. *Abram rescues Lot from Captivity, 1913.*— About fourteen years prior to the present date, an Assyrian force crossed the Euphrates and subjected five petty kings, including those of Sodom and Gomorrah, who occupied the vale of Siddim. This invading force was composed of four nations, who probably formed a part of the Assyrian power, which seems at this period to have predominated in Western Asia; and each of these nations was commanded by its own king—viz. Chedorlaomer, king of Elam, or Elymais; Amraphel, king of Shinar, or Babylonia; Arioch, king of Ellasar; and Tidal, king of nations—*i. e.* of a mixed people or union of small tribes. Chedorlaomer was probably left viceroy of these conquests, for we are told that the five conquered kings in the vale of Siddim served him faithfully for twelve years, but rebelled in the thirteenth. In the fourteenth year Chedorlaomer and his confederates again invaded the country to punish the rebellion, and after reducing the races in the neighborhood, who had probably participated in the revolt, they reached the vale of Siddim. The five kings came out to meet them, but were soon defeated, and their forces either driven into the slime-pits or compelled to flee to the mountains. Chedorlaomer then ravaged the towns, seized all the movable property and provisions and the women and children, and carried away Lot and his family among the captives. Abram was still sojourning in the vale of Mamre when the tidings were brought to him. Three Amorite brothers, Mamre, Eshcol, and Aner, joined him with their clans,

---

* The whole of these tribes were of Canaanite origin, and the Canaanites here specially mentioned were probably only put for all their clans not intended to be particularly enumerated, such as the Phœnician tribes. See Kitto.

and he then armed his own three hundred and eighteen servants, and, dividing his small army into several bands, he fell upon the conquerors by night near Dan, and routed and pursued them to Hobah, north of Damascus, and recovered the plunder and prisoners. On his return he was met by Melchizedek, the king of Salem, and priest of the most high God, who brought bread and wine and blessed the conquering patriarch, who seems to have acknowledged him as priest of Jehovah, for "he gave him the *tithe* of all." The king of Sodom then offered to Abram the goods which he had recovered, in return for the captives whom he had delivered, but the present was generously declined. Gen. xiv.

25. *Character of Melchizedek.*—The character and office of Melchizedek are involved in mystery. His birth, death, and parentage are alike unknown. (See Heb. vii. 1–3.) St. Paul and David both allude to him as a type of Jesus Christ, who they say "is a priest for ever after the order of Melchizedek." Ps. cx. 4; Heb. v. 6; vi. 20; vii. 17, 21.

26. *God promises Abram a Son, and prophesies Four Hundred Years' Affliction to his Seed.*—After Abram's return to Mamre, he was encouraged by God in a vision, and promised a son whose descendants should be numerous as the stars and inherit Canaan. Abram then, by the divine command, offered a prescribed sacrifice, and, falling into a deep sleep, the Lord appeared to him in a vision and prophesied the four hundred years' Egyptian captivity of his descendants and their final possession of the Promised Land: "Know of a surety that thy seed shall be a stranger in a land that is not theirs, and shall serve them, and they shall afflict them four hundred years." Gen. xv. 13. These four hundred years cannot be reconciled with chronology, which makes the Egyptian bondage extend to only two hundred and fifteen years; but, calculating the affliction to have commenced in Canaan at the birth of Isaac, it will make a period of four hundred and thirty years.

27. *Ishmael born, 1910.*—Sarai still continued childless, and in B. C. 1911, being ten years after Abram's first sojourn in Canaan, she persuaded her husband to take her Egyptian handmaid Hagar as his concubine.

Hagar became pregnant and despised her mistress; but, being hardly dealt with by Sarai, she fled to the wilderness of Shur, in Arabia Petræa, where an angel encouraged her by a well, and promised her a son who should be named Ishmael: "And he will be a wild man; his hand will be against every man, and every man's hand will be against him." Hagar then returned, and gave birth to Ishmael in B. C. 1910, being the 86th year of Abram's age. Gen. xv.; xvi. Ishmael and Hagar were again expelled after the birth of Isaac. (For a further account of him see sect. 34.)

28. *God renews his Covenant with Abram, 1898.*—When Abram was ninety-nine years old and Ishmael thirteen, the Lord renewed his promises to the father—viz.

1st. That he should have a son by Sarai, notwithstanding their old age.

2d. That in his seed all the nations of the earth should be blessed.

3d. That his descendants should possess Canaan and be as numerous as the stars.

The first promise was fulfilled in the birth of Isaac, the second in the birth of the Messiah, and the third *literally* in the rapid increase of the Israelites, Ishmaelites, and Edomites, and *spiritually* in the multitude of believers in all nations. Acts iii. 25; Rom. iv. 12–17. St. Paul says, "They which are of faith, the same are the children of Abraham." Gal. iii. 7. Hence Abraham has been called the "father of the faithful." (See sect. 42.)

29. *Institutes Circumcision, and changes Abram's and Sarai's Names.*—Circumcision was then instituted by Jehovah, and Abraham circumcised all the males of his household, himself included, on the same day, he being ninety-nine years old and Ishmael thirteen years. God also changed Abram's name to ABRAHAM, which signifies "the father of a great multitude;" and Sarai's name to SARAH, which signifies "princess." Gen. xvii.

30. *Abraham visited by three Angels; intercedes for Sodom, 1898.*—The same year three strangers visited Abraham, and were hospitably entertained, when one of them, who was the angel Jehovah, again promised him a son by Sarah, and reproved his wife for laughing

at the prediction. The angel also intimated to Abraham the forthcoming destruction of Sodom and Gomorrah, but when the patriarch pleaded for the doomed city, he was assured that if fifty or even ten righteous men could be found there, it should be spared. Gen. xviii.

31. *Destruction of Sodom, and Origin of Moab and Ammon, 1898.*—Two angels were now sent to warn Lot and his family of the impending doom. They were suitably entertained by the nephew of Abraham, but only escaped from the inhabitants of Sodom by smiting them with blindness. The household were now aroused at the miracle. Lot and his wife and two unmarried daughters left the city, but the husbands of his married daughters refused to move, and his wife, looking back, was turned to a pillar of salt. Sodom and Gomorrah were then destroyed by fire and brimstone, and the plain in which they stood was overflowed by the Jordan, and now forms the Dead Sea. Lot and his two daughters escaped to Zoar, which was saved at his request. He and his daughters afterward dwelt in a neighboring cave, where Moab and Benammi, the progenitors of the Moabites and Ammonites, sprang from an incestuous connection. Gen. xix.

32. *Abraham removes to Gerar, 1898.*—Abraham now left Mamre and journeyed southward to Gerar, in the territory afterward occupied by the Philistines, where he deceived Abimelech by saying that Sarah was his sister; but she was preserved by divine interference, and Abimelech rebuked her husband, but made him large presents of cattle and servants, and one thousand pieces of silver,—*i. e.* shekel's weight, or £129 3*s.* 4*d.**—and permitted him to settle in the land. Gen. xx.

33. *Isaac born, 1897.*—Isaac was born Isaac, B. C. in the one hundredth year of his father's age, 1897–1716. and circumcised on the eighth day. He was called Isaac —*i. e.* "laughter"—because his mother had laughed when the three angels had promised his birth. (See sect. 30.)

34. *Hagar and Ishmael exiled, 1892.*—Sarah now returned the mocking of Hagar, and Abraham, though

---

* Silver is reckoned here and throughout the book at 5*s.* per oz., and gold at £4 per oz.

sanctioned by God, was reluctantly compelled to send away his concubine and child, who were afterward reduced to the greatest distress in the wilderness of Beersheba; but an angel appeared, and, God having opened her eyes, she saw a well. Ishmael then became a great archer in the wilderness of Paran, and afterward married an Egyptian wife and had twelve sons, who became the fathers of twelve Arabian tribes, which still exist. He also had a daughter, Mahalath, who subsequently married her cousin Esau. (See sect. 48.) He died, aged one hundred and thirty-seven, in the presence of all his brethren. Gen. xxi. 1–21; xxv. 18.

35. *Digging of Beersheba, 1891.*—Abraham, who still resided at Gerar, now entered into a covenant with Abimelech and Phichol, his captain of the host, and dug the well of Beersheba. Gen. xxi. 22–34.

36. *Abraham tempted to offer Isaac, 1872.*— When Isaac was twenty-five years old, Abraham was desired by God to offer him up as a burnt-offering on Mount Moriah. The faithful patriarch took his son and two servants, and arrived at the appointed place after a three days' journey. Abraham and Isaac ascended Moriah alone. The fire and wood were prepared, when Isaac said, "My father, behold the fire and the wood, but where is the lamb for a burnt-offering?" Abraham replied, "My son, God will provide himself a lamb for a burnt-offering;" and the father was about to offer the fearful sacrifice, when his hand was stayed by an angel, and a ram caught in the thicket was offered and accepted as a substitute for the son. Abraham then called the place "Jehovah-jireh"—"the Lord will provide"—and after receiving another special testimony of the approbation of God, he returned and dwelt at Beersheba.* Gen. xxii.

---

* **Isaac a Type of Christ.**—Isaac was a type of Christ in the following ways: 1. In his miraculous birth from an aged mother, whilst Christ was born of a virgin. 2. In his being, like Jesus, obedient unto death. 3. In his carrying the wood on which he was to be sacrificed to Mount Moriah, whilst Christ carried his cross to the same place. 4. In his meek obedience to his father's will. 5. In his father's willingness to sacrifice his only son, who was heir to a *temporal* Canaan, like to our Saviour, through whom we are heirs to a *heavenly* Canaan. Moreover, the lamb which Abraham had told his son that "God would provide" seems to point to the "*Lamb of God;*" whilst the substituted ram re-

37. *Death of Sarah, 1860.*—Sarah, having attained the age of one hundred and twenty-seven years, died at Mamre, when Abraham purchased the cave of Machpelah for four hundred shekels' weight of silver [about 182 oz., or £45 10s. 8d.] from the sons of Heth as a burial-place for his wife, and it subsequently became the sepulchre of himself and of Isaac, Rebekah, Jacob, Leah, and Joseph. Gen. xxiii.

38. *Isaac marries Rebekah, 1857.*—Isaac was now forty years old, and Abraham sent Eliezer, who was the steward or eldest servant of his house, to Haran in Mesopotamia to seek a wife for Isaac in the family of Nahor. At a well in the outskirts of the city of Nahor, Eliezer prayed to Jehovah, in the name of the God of his master Abraham, that the damsel of whom he should ask a drink, and who should accede to his request, might be the woman appointed for Isaac's wife. Before he had done speaking he saw Rebekah, the daughter of Bethuel and granddaughter of Nahor and Milcah, with whom events occurred as he had prayed. Accordingly, he gave Rebekah a golden earring and two bracelets; and after delivering his errand to her brother Laban and her father Bethuel, he was permitted to escort her to the residence of Abraham, where she was married to Isaac. Gen. xxiv.

39. *Abraham marries Keturah, 1853.*—After this Abraham married Keturah, who bore him six sons,* amongst whom was Midian, the progenitor of the Midianites. Gen. xxv. 1-3.

40. *Jacob and Esau born to Isaac, 1837.*—Isaac had been married twenty years without offspring; but, having entreated the Lord, his wife, Rebekah, brought forth twins—ESAU, the elder, a hairy man, who became a hunter and was the favorite of his father, and JACOB, the younger, who became a shepherd and the darling of his mother. Gen. xxv. 19-28. Jacob obtained his name because at his birth he held his brother's heel, *Jacob* signifying "a heeler," or "one who

---

sembles those temple-sacrifices which were typical of Christ's atonement.

* These sons Abraham, before his death, sent away with gifts, and they subsequently became founders of Arabian tribes, and traces of their names may still be discovered in Arabia.

heels or strikes up his adversary." This explains Esau's subsequent remark: "Is not he rightly named Jacob? for he hath supplanted me these two times."

41. *Abraham dies, 1822.*—Abraham died at the age of one hundred and seventy-five, and was buried by Isaac and Ishmael in the cave of Machpelah. The sons of his concubines he had previously sent away from Isaac with gifts. Gen. xxv. 5–10.

42. *Abraham the Father of the Faithful.*—Abraham was remarkable for three particular acts of faith— viz. 1. Obeying the call of God and leaving his father's house to go he knew not whither, and in sojourning in the land of promise as in a strange country, dwelling in tabernacles; 2. Offering up his son Isaac; 3. Believing God's promise that he should be the father of many nations, though he was one hundred years old and Sarai past child-bearing, which faith was imputed to him for righteousness. Heb. xi.; Rom. iv.

43. *Esau sells his Birthright, 1805.*—One day, when Esau and Jacob were each thirty-two years old, Esau came in hungry and sold his birthright to Jacob for a mess of red pottage. Gen. xxv. 29–34. Esau was named EDOM, which signifies "red," either from this *red* pottage or from the *redness* of his hair and complexion. Gen. xxv. 25, 30.

44. *Famine in Canaan; Isaac leaves Mamre for Gerar, and deceives Abimelech, 1804.*—On account of a famine and by divine command, Isaac left Mamre for Gerar, where, like his father, he deceived Abimelech, the king of the Philistines, by saying that Rebekah was his sister. This deceit was discovered by Abimelech, and Isaac, after reopening the wells which Abraham had dug, but which had been filled up by the Philistines, removed to Beersheba, where God confirmed to him the promise which he had made to his father; and Abimelech and Phichol also renewed the covenant which they had made with Abraham. Gen. xxvi.

45. *Esau marries two Hittite women, 1796; Ishmael dies, 1773.*—When Esau was forty years old he married Judith (or Aholibamah) and Bashemath (or Adah), the daughters of Hittites—an alliance which grieved the minds of both Isaac and Rebekah. Ishmael

had now begat twelve princes, who dwelt between Havilah and Shur, and he died in B. C. 1773, at the age of one hundred and thirty-seven years. Gen. xxvi. 34, 35; xxv. 12–18; xxxvi.

46. *Isaac blesses Jacob instead of Esau, 1760.*— When Isaac was one hundred and thirty-seven years old he sent Esau to hunt venison, that he might eat the savory meat and bless him before he died. Rebekah heard the instructions, and hoped to transfer the blessing to her favorite son, Jacob. She accordingly desired Jacob to fetch two goat-kids from the flock, from which she made savory meat, and, after placing the skins upon Jacob's neck and hands and clothing him in Esau's raiment, she sent him to the bedside of her aged husband. The deception was successful, and Isaac took the meat from Jacob and pronounced over him the patriarchal and prophetical benediction of abundance, dominion, and superiority. Scarcely had Jacob left his presence when Esau returned, and Isaac discovered the imposition. The agitated father trembled exceedingly at hearing the bitter lamentations of Esau, but confirmed the blessing on Jacob, and only pronounced an inferior benediction on his first-born; and the enraged hunter resolved, when his father should die, to be revenged by the murder of his brother. Gen. xxvii.

47. *Jacob goes to Laban at Haran; his Dream, 1760.*—The threat of Esau was reported to Rebekah, and she prevailed on Isaac to send Jacob to Padan-aram [Mesopotamia] for the purpose of seeking a wife amongst the daughters of her brother Laban. Jacob, having received the directions of his father, left Beersheba for Haran in Mesopotamia, where Laban dwelt, and on the approach of night he arranged some stones for his pillows and lay down to sleep. The ancestor of the Israelites was here encouraged by a celestial vision. A ladder appeared to connect earth with heaven, upon which angels ascended and descended, whilst Jehovah stood on its summit and announced himself to Jacob as the God of his fathers, and confirmed in him the promises which he had made to Isaac and Abraham. Jacob awoke with trembling, and, actuated by pious awe, he built a monument with the stones he had used for pillows; and, pouring oil

upon it, he called the place Bethel—"the house of God"—and vowed that if God would fulfil his promise of protection, he would devote to him a tenth of his possessions. Gen. xxviii.

48. *Esau marries Mahalath, 1760.*—Meantime, Esau, seeing that his marriages had hitherto displeased his father, took his cousin Mahalath, daughter of Ishmael, for wife. Gen. xxviii. 9.

49. *Jacob marries Leah and Rachel, 1753.*—Jacob, on reaching a well in the outskirts of Haran, saw his cousin Rachel, the daughter of Laban, and immediately fell in love with her. He was then welcomed by Laban, who had two daughters—Leah, the eldest, who was tender-eyed, and Rachel, who was exceedingly beautiful. Jacob promised to serve his uncle Laban for seven years for Rachel; but when the time had expired and he claimed his wife, Laban artfully substituted Leah for Rachel. Jacob was incensed at the deceit, but Laban pleaded the customs of the country, but promised to give Rachel to his son-in-law at the expiration of the marriage-week, upon his engaging to serve him for another seven years. The two marriages were then consummated, Zilpah being the handmaid of Leah, and Bilhah the handmaid of Rachel. Gen. xxix. 1–30.

50. *Family of Jacob.*—Jacob loved Rachel best, but, as for some time she was barren and Leah fruitful, there was constant rivalry and jealousy between the two wives. His children were born in Haran in the following order:

By *Leah*, his first wife,
   1. REUBEN, born B. C. 1752.
   2. SIMEON, born B. C. 1751.
   3. LEVI, born B. C. 1750.
   4. JUDAH, born B. C. 1749.

By *Bilhah*, Rachel's handmaid,
   5. DAN, born B. C. 1748.
   6. NAPHTALI, born B. C. 1747.

By *Zilpah*, Leah's handmaid,
   7. GAD, born B. C. 1748.
   8. ASHER, born B. C. 1747.

By *Leah*, who gave mandrakes to Rachel,
   9. ISSACHAR, born B. C. 1747.

10. ZEBULUN, born B. C. 1746.
And afterward DINAH, a daughter.
By *Rachel*, his second and favorite wife,
11. JOSEPH, born B. C. 1745.
Several years afterward, at Ephrath in Bethlehem,
12. BENJAMIN, born B. C. 1729. Gen. xxx. 1-24.

51. *Jacob's new Covenant with Laban, 1745.*—
Jacob had now served Laban fourteen years for his two wives, and was desirous of returning to Beersheba; but Laban pressed him to stay, and promised to give him all the cattle which were born with particular marks. By singular expedients Jacob contrived that all the healthy cattle should be born with the marks required, which so excited the envy and discontent of Laban and his sons that Jacob determined on returning to Isaac, and his wives readily agreed with his resolve. Gen. xxx. 25-43; xxxi. 1-16.

52. *Jacob leaves Laban, 1739.*—Jacob, having now faithfully served Laban for twenty years, was indignant at his conduct; and, being a fearful man, he secretly and suddenly left Padan-aram—*i. e.* Mesopotamia—with his wives, sons, possessions, and herds. Laban was ignorant of his departure until three days afterward, when he immediately commenced pursuit, and overtook his son-in-law in Mount Gilead, but, being warned by God in a dream not to injure Jacob, he only expostulated with him on the secrecy of his departure, and accused him of having stolen his gods. Jacob was unaware that Rachel had taken these images, and vehemently denied the charge and begged Laban to look over the whole of his goods, threatening to execute whoever should be found to have carried off the idols. But Rachel contrived to conceal the gods, and Jacob rebuked Laban for the ungrateful return which he made after receiving from him twenty years' faithful service. A reconciliation then took place, a heap of stones was made, and it was agreed that Jacob should not afflict the daughters of Laban or take other wives besides them, and that Laban should never pass the heap with the design of injuring Jacob. After a friendly feast the two parties separated, Laban to Padan-aram and Jacob toward Beersheba. Gen. xxxi. 17-55.

53. *His Vision at Mahanaim and Message to Esau.*—At Mahanaim, Jacob was met by angels, and

from thence he sent messengers to Seir and Edom to endeavor to propitiate his brother Esau, but they returned with the tidings that Esau was advancing to meet him with four hundred men. Jacob was now terrified and distressed, and divided his people and cattle into two divisions, that if Esau attacked one the other might escape. He then prayed to the God of his fathers, and made up a present to his brother of two hundred she-goats, twenty he-goats, two hundred ewes, twenty rams, thirty milch-camels with their colts, forty kine, ten bulls, twenty she-asses, and ten foals. All these he arranged in droves with a space between each two, and desired his servants to proceed with them, and when asked by Esau as to whose they were to reply that the cattle belonged to his servant Jacob, who was behind them, and were a present for *his* lord, Esau. Gen. xxxii. 1-20.

54. *Wrestles with a Man at Peniel.*—Jacob now sent his wives and family over the Jabbok and was left alone, but he spent the night in a mysterious wrestle with a celestial Being, who touched and disjointed the hollow of his thigh, and, after blessing him, changed his name from Jacob to ISRAEL, or "prevailer with God." Jacob then named the place PENIEL, "the face of God;" and his descendants continue to refuse to eat of that sinew which shrank. Gen. xxxii. 20-32.

55. *Meeting with Esau.*—The next morning Jacob passed the ford and saw his brother approaching with four hundred men. He immediately placed Rachel and Joseph in the rear of his train, and, advancing before it, he bowed seven times in obeisance to Esau. The heart of the huntsman was touched; he fell upon the neck of Jacob and kissed him, and they both wept. Leah and Rachel were then introduced and the present forced upon Esau, who afterward returned to Seir, and Jacob journeyed on slowly to Succoth.* Gen. xxxiii.

56. *Resides at Succoth and Shechem; Slaughter of the Shechemites, 1739-1732.*—At Succoth, Jacob dwelt for about two years, and then removed to Shalem, a city of Shechem, where he bought a field of Hamor, the prince of the country, and pitched his tent and erected an

---

* See note to sect. 100.

altar. Here Dinah, his daughter by Leah, having mingled with the daughters of the land, was carried off by Shechem, son of Hamor. The young man wished to atone for his conduct by marriage, and both himself and his father endeavored to propitiate Jacob and his sons. The brethren of Dinah agreed to the alliance, but demanded the circumcision of the Shechemites; and the third day after the ceremony Simeon and Levi fell upon the city, slew all the males, including Hamor and Shechem, took Dinah from the house of the young prince, and carried off the women and cattle. Jacob bitterly rebuked his children for this cruel and treacherous act, and remembered it in his dying predictions regarding Simeon and Levi. Gen. xxxiii. 18-20; xxxiv.

57. *Buries the Idols of his Household and goes to Bethel, 1732.*—The Lord now commanded Jacob to go to Bethel, which he obeyed, after collecting all the idols from his household and burying them under the oak at Shechem. Here Deborah, the nurse of Rebekah, died, and Jehovah again appeared to Jacob and renewed his promise of a numerous posterity and possession of Canaan. Gen. xxxv. 1-15.

58. *Death of Rachel; Birth of Benjamin, 1732.* —Jacob now left Bethel, but when his family had nearly reached Ephrath, Rachel was seized with the pains of labor, and died after giving birth to Benjamin, and was buried at Ephrath in Bethlehem. Gen. xxxv. 16-20. Rachel with her dying lips called the child BENONI— *i. e.* "the son of my sorrow;" but Jacob, wishing to forget his sorrow, afterward called the child BENJAMIN— *i. e.* "the son of my right hand."

59. *Reuben's Incest with Bilhah.*—Jacob proceeded on his journey, but dwelt a while beyond the tower of Edar, where Reuben committed incest with Bilhah, Rachel's handmaid and Jacob's concubine. For this crime Reuben received the dying curse of Jacob, and his birthright was transferred to Judah. (See sect. 72.) Gen. xxxv. 22.

60. *Jacob resides with Isaac at Mamre, 1729.*— Jacob now joined his father Isaac at Mamre in Hebron in Canaan, and lived with him till he died, thirteen years afterward, B. C. 1716. Gen. xxxv. 27-29.

61. *Joseph excites his Brethren's Envy, and is sold to the Ishmaelites, 1729.*—

Joseph, B. C. 1745–1635.

Scarcely had Jacob settled in Canaan when Joseph, the elder son of Rachel, who was then seventeen years old, excited the hatred and envy of his brethren by three circumstances: 1st. He reported to his father the misconduct of the sons of Bilhah and Zilpah; 2d. Jacob loved him more than his other children, and gave him a coat of divers colors; 3d. Having dreamed two dreams prophetical of an elevated career—one that his brothers' sheaves bowed before his sheaf, and another that the sun, moon, and eleven stars did obeisance to him—he related the visions to his brethren. After this he was sent by Jacob to his brethren, who were supposed to be keeping their father's flocks at Shechem; but, on arriving at Shechem, Joseph learnt that they were gone to Dothan, where he accordingly followed them. The sons of Jacob saw their younger brother afar off and resolved on slaying him, but Reuben persuaded them to throw him alive into a pit, thinking to deliver him afterward and return him to his father. The brethren then stripped Joseph of his coat and threw him into a dry pit; but shortly afterward some Ishmaelite [Arabian] merchants passed by, and, upon Judah's proposition, the ten brethren, whilst Reuben was absent, sold Joseph for twenty pieces of silver, and he was carried to Egypt. When Reuben discovered the deed he rent his clothes, but the others dipped Joseph's coat in the blood of a kid and carried it to Jacob, who immediately supposed that his favorite son had been devoured by a wild beast, and refused to be comforted for his death. Gen. xxxvii.

62. *Judah marries a Canaanite; his Incest with his Daughter-in-law, cir. 1727.*—About this time Judah married the daughter of a certain Canaanite named Shuah, and begat three sons, Er, Onan, and Shelah. Er married Tamar, but was cut off for his sins; Onan, who was to have raised up an heir to his brother, met with a similar fate; and Judah desired Tamar to remain a widow in her father's house until Shelah should be grown up. Years passed, and Judah was afraid to marry Shelah to Tamar lest he should die like his brethren. At length Tamar heard that Judah's wife had died and that he had gone with Hirah to Timnath to shear his sheep. Tamar accordingly veiled herself as a harlot, and, after tempting Judah to visit her, she received from him his staff, signet, and bracelets as a pledge that he would send her a kid, and returned to her father's house before Judah could regain his pledges. Three months afterward it was reported to Judah that Tamar had played the harlot, and he ordered her to be brought out and burnt, when she showed him his pledges and he acknowledged his guilt. She afterward bore twin sons, Pharez and Zarah. Gen. xxxviii.

63. *Joseph sold to Potiphar and imprisoned, 1729-1720.*—Meantime, Joseph was carried to Egypt and bought by Potiphar, a captain of Pharaoh's guard. Here he rose to be overseer in Potiphar's household, and the house was blessed for his sake; but, having resisted Potiphar's wife, she falsely accused him, and he was thrown into prison, where he rose in the favor of the keeper and kept charge of the other prisoners. Gen. xxxix.

64. *Interprets the Dreams of Pharaoh's Butler and Baker, 1720-1718.*—About B. C. 1720 the king's butler and baker were cast into the same prison by Pharaoh, where they each had a remarkable vision, which they described to Joseph. The butler dreamed that he saw a vine with three branches bud, blossom, and bring forth grapes, which he pressed into Pharaoh's cup and gave into Pharaoh's hand. This Joseph interpreted to signify that in three days he should be released from his prison and restored to his place, and the captive Hebrew begged the butler then to remember his innocent fellow-prisoner and attempt his release. The baker dreamed that he had three white baskets on his head, the uppermost one containing baked meats for Pharaoh, but which were eaten by the birds while he was carrying it. This was explained by Joseph to mean that he too should be taken from prison in three days, but only to be hung upon a tree for birds to eat his flesh. The two dreams were fulfilled: the chief baker was hanged and the butler was restored to his place, where he soon forgot the condition of Joseph. Gen. xl.

65. *Interprets Pharaoh's two Dreams, 1715.*—

After two full years Pharaoh dreamed that he saw seven fat kine come out of the river and feed in a meadow, but were followed by seven lean kine, who ate up the seven fat ones. Again, he dreamed that seven full ears of corn sprang from one stalk, and seven thin ears, blasted with the east wind, sprang up after them and devoured them. These two visions troubled the king, and none of the Egyptian magicians could interpret them, when the chief butler remembered the interpretations of Joseph and reported them to Pharaoh. The Hebrew captive was hastily released from prison and brought to the royal presence, where he thus interpreted the visions. "The two dreams," said Joseph, "are one: the seven fat kine and seven full ears are seven years of plenty, and the thin kine and blasted ears are seven years of famine, which shall follow the years of plenty and consume all that they produced." Joseph now advised Pharaoh to choose a wise man who might appoint officers to take a fifth of the produce during the seven years of plenty, and store it up for the seven years' famine. Gen. xli. 1-36.

66. *Made chief Ruler of Egypt and marries Asenath, 1715.*—Joseph was now thirty years old, having been thirteen years in prison, but his counsel pleased Pharaoh and his princes, and he was immediately exalted to the highest honors next the king, and married to Asenath, daughter of Potipherah, priest of On.* Gen. xli. 37-45.

67. *Seven years' Plenty, 1715-1708; Birth of Manasseh, 1712; of Ephraim, 1711.*—For seven years the new ruler went through Egypt and collected corn as the sand of the sea and stored it up in vast granaries. Two sons were born to him by Asenath—Manasseh and Ephraim, who became the fathers of two of the twelve tribes. Gen. xli. 46-57.

68. *Seven years' Famine, 1708-1701; first Visit of Joseph's Brethren, 1707.*—A famine now commenced and spread over all nations, but the storehouses of Joseph became the granaries of the world. The family of Jacob felt the famine, and the patriarch was compelled to send

---

* On is the same as *Heliopolis*, a celebrated city in Lower Egypt, whose priests were particularly renowned for their learning. See *Herodotus*, ii. 3.

ten of his sons to Egypt to buy corn; for he kept back Benjamin, lest he should meet with the supposed fate of Joseph. The governor of Egypt recognized his brethren without their knowing him, but he charged them with being spies and threw them into prison, but released them after three days, with the exception of Simeon, whom he kept as a pledge that they should bring him their younger brother. The nine sons of Jacob now returned to their father, but on their way discovered that the money they had paid for the corn was enclosed in their sacks; this terrified Jacob, and he refused to send Benjamin, though Reuben offered his own sons as a surety for his life. Gen. xlii.

69. *Second Visit of Joseph's Brethren, 1706.—* Famine at last compelled Jacob to send Benjamin with his other brethren to Egypt to buy corn, but the old man strictly charged his sons to propitiate the Egyptian ruler by presents and to take double money, lest that which they had discovered in their sacks should have been placed there through inadvertence. On their arrival in Egypt, Joseph ordered his steward to take them to his house and make ready the noonday meal. The brethren were now frightened, and on reaching the house they explained to the steward the restoration of their money, but he replied that he had received it, and it must have been their God who had restored it; he further reassured them by bringing out Simeon. Joseph soon followed his brethren and the meal was served, but Joseph sat at one table, his brethren at another, and the Egyptians at a third, " as shepherds were an abomination to the Egyptians." The brethren were entertained liberally, but were surprised at finding themselves placed at table exactly in the order of their ages, and that Joseph sent a fivefold portion to Benjamin. The next morning they left the city, but Joseph had first commanded his steward to restore the money as before, but to place his silver cup in the sack of Benjamin. They had not, therefore, proceeded far before the steward overtook them and charged them with robbery. They immediately protested their innocence, challenged investigation, and invoked death on the man who should be proved guilty; but the cup was found with Benjamin, and the distressed brethren were compelled to re-

turn to Joseph. Judah now made to the supposed Egyptian ruler an affecting relation of the disappearance of Joseph, and of Jacob's peculiar affection for Benjamin; and then, after stating that the death of their aged father would certainly follow the detention of his beloved son, he offered to abide himself as a bondman if the lad were permitted to return. Joseph could now refrain no longer, but speedily told his brethren that the brother whom they had sold for a slave had become the governor of Egypt; he then assured them of his hearty forgiveness, and invited both themselves and Jacob to settle in Egypt during the remaining years of famine. The invitation was seconded by Pharaoh, and wagons, changes of raiment, and asses laden with provision were sent by Pharaoh and Joseph for the accommodation of the children of Israel. Gen. xliii.–xlv.

70. *Israelites migrate to Egypt, 1706.*—When Jacob's sons returned from Egypt, their venerable father could scarcely believe their report; but, on seeing the wagons, he cried, "It is enough; Joseph my son is yet alive; I will go and see him before I die." He accordingly commenced the journey; and, having sacrificed at Beersheba and been again encouraged by God, he arrived in Egypt with his sixty-four sons and grandsons, one daughter, Dinah, and one granddaughter, Sarah, amounting in all to sixty-six persons. Gen. xlvi. 26. These, with himself and Joseph and his two sons, made seventy persons (v. 27); whilst the sixty-six persons, with his nine sons' wives, make the seventy-five persons mentioned in Acts vii. 14. Jacob migrated to Egypt B. C. 1706, being exactly two hundred and fifteen years from the call of Abraham in B. C. 1921. Joseph then presented his father and five of his brethren to Pharaoh, and the old man, with one hundred and thirty years' experience, declared that his years were evil and few, and blessed the Egyptian king. The land of Goshen* was then assigned to the

---

* **Goshen** was the best pasture-land in Egypt, and probably included the district of Heliopolis. It certainly lay eastward of the Pelusiac branch of the Nile, and stretched to the desert, or even to the Gulf of Suez, as no mention is made of the Israelites crossing the Nile in their **exode** under Moses.—*Heeren's African Researches.*

Hebrews for a residence, as shepherds were an abomination to the Egyptians. Gen. xlvi.; xlvii. 1-12.

71. *Policy of Joseph during the Famine, 1702, 1701.*—The famine soon pressed heavily upon the Egyptians; all their money had been spent in buying corn, and they were at length compelled to give, first their cattle, and afterward their lands, in exchange for corn. Joseph thus destroyed the free proprietors and made the king the lord-paramount of the soil; whilst the people became the hereditary tenants of their sovereign, and paid a fifth of their annual produce as rent for the soil they occupied. The priests only retained their estates through this trying period.* Gen. xlvii. 13-26.

72. *Dying Acts and Prophecies of Jacob, 1689.*—After the Hebrews had resided for seventeen years in Egypt and multiplied exceedingly, the time came that Jacob should die. The aged patriarch raised himself on his dying bed, and having blessed his two grandsons through Joseph, and blessed Ephraim, the younger, above Manasseh, the first-born, and made them both equal to his own sons, he thus prophesied concerning the future destinies of the twelve:

1. Reuben, the first-born, who had committed incest with Bilhah: "Unstable as water, thou shalt not excel."
2. Simeon, 3. Levi, who had treacherously slain the

---

* Heeren states that this policy of Joseph weakened the nation, and ultimately led to the irruption of the Hyksos, or Shepherd-kings, who are generally supposed to have been Bedouin Arabs. The administration of Joseph has, however, been fully defended by Kitto; and, indeed, there is every reason to believe that the invasion of the Shepherd-kings was prior to the time of Joseph. We read that when Abram visited Egypt, some centuries before, he was treated with great consideration by the reigning Pharaoh (sect. 21), though he was in the character of a pastoral chief, which was regarded with abomination by the native government in the time of Joseph. It is most probable, therefore, that the pastoral dynasty existed at the time of Abram's visit, but was extinguished prior to the government of Joseph; which accounts for the fact that under the latter every nomad shepherd was detested at the Egyptian court (sect. 69), in consequence of the oppressive and humiliating dominion which the pastors had exercised in the country. This is also confirmed by the testimony of Mr. Wilkinson. Kitto thinks it not improbable that the Shepherd-kings were Assyrian viceroys; and if this can be proved by the future researches of Mr. Layard or Major Rawlinson, it will throw great light on many circumstances in the lives of the patriarchs.

Shechemites for their insult to Dinah: "Cursed be their anger, for it was fierce; and their wrath, for it was cruel: I will divide them in Jacob, and scatter them in Israel."

4. *Judah:* "Thou art he whom thy brethren shall praise: thy hand shall be in the neck of thine enemies; thy father's children shall bow down before thee. Judah is a lion's whelp: from the prey, my son, thou art gone up: he stooped down, he couched as a lion, and as an old lion; who shall rouse him up? *The sceptre shall not depart from Judah, nor a lawgiver from between his feet, until Shiloh come; and unto him shall the gathering of the people be.* . . . His eyes shall be red with wine, and his teeth white with milk."

5. *Zebulun:* "Shall be an haven for ships."

6. *Issachar:* "Is a strong ass couching down between two burdens: . . . and bowed his shoulder to bear, and became a servant unto tribute."

7. *Dan:* "Shall judge his people, . . . shall be a serpent by the way, and an adder in the path."

8. *Gad:* "A troop shall overcome him: but he shall overcome at the last."

9. *Asher:* "His bread shall be fat."

10. *Naphtali:* "A hind let loose; he giveth goodly words."

11. *Joseph:* "A fruitful bough by a well. . . . The God of thy father, who shall help thee; and the Almighty, who shall bless thee with blessings of heaven above, blessings of the deep that lieth under, blessings of the breasts, and blessings of the womb: . . . the blessings of thy father have prevailed above the blessings of my progenitors unto the utmost bound of the everlasting hills: they shall be on the head of Joseph."

12. *Benjamin:* "Shall ravin as a wolf: in the morning he shall devour the prey, and at night he shall divide the spoil." Gen. xlviii.; xlix.

73. ***Fulfilment of Jacob's Prophecies.***—The history of all the tribes would furnish striking instances of the fulfilment of these prophecies, and more particularly the history of the descendants of Judah and Joseph. From Judah the country was called "Judæa," and the people "Jews." This tribe was famous—1. For its conquests; 2. For the kingdoms of David and Solomon; 3. For the birth of the Messiah; 4. For being a distinct people, and having governors of their own down to the time of the Messiah or Shiloh. Moreover, whilst the ten tribes of Israel were carried captive into Assyria and entirely lost, those of Judah and Benjamin were held in Babylonian captivity for seventy years only, after which they returned to the land of their fathers.

In Joseph the blessing of Jacob was fulfilled, in his

being the progenitor of the two large tribes of Ephraim and Manasseh, from whom sprang the celebrated Joshua, etc.

The curse of Levi was afterward taken off on account of the pious zeal of the Levites in destroying the worshippers of the golden calf and consecrating themselves to God.

74. *Death and Burial, 1689.*—Having closed his prophetical benedictions, Jacob charged his sons to bury him in the cave of Machpelah, and yielded up the ghost at the age of one hundred and forty-seven years. His body was embalmed by the physicians of Joseph, which process occupied forty days,* and the mourning lasted seventy days; after which, Joseph obtained the permission of Pharaoh to attend the funeral of his father. Accordingly, all the house of Jacob and Joseph, together with all the servants of Pharaoh and elders of Egypt, left Goshen and buried Jacob in the cave of Machpelah, having mourned at the threshing-floor of Atad beyond Jordan for seven days; which place was afterward called Abel-mizraim, or "the mourning of the Egyptians." Gen. l. 1–13.

75. *Joseph again forgives his Brethren.*—After Joseph's return to Egypt, his brethren feared that he would now seek revenge for their former cruelty, but, having sent a message praying for his forgiveness, he reassured them by kind words and good offices. Gen. l. 14–21.

76. *Death of Joseph, 1635.*—At length, fifty-four years after the death of his father, Joseph, having seen the grandsons of his two sons, felt that his dying hour was approaching. He assured his brethren that God would certainly lead them to the land of promise, and enjoined them to carry his bones with them. He died, aged one hundred and ten years, and his body was embalmed and placed in a coffin, in which it was preserved till the exode of the Hebrews. Gen. l. 22–26; Josh. xxiv. 32.

77. *Joseph a Type of Christ.*—Joseph was a type of

---

* Herodotus says that the Egyptian embalmers steeped the body in natrum or in nitre for seventy days (lib. ii. c. 86–90).

Christ in being—1. A dearly-beloved son; 2. A firm resister of temptation; 3. An inspired interpreter and prophet; 4. A patient sufferer of trials and inflictions; 5. The preserver or saviour of a nation.

78. *Scriptural meaning of a " Type."*—*Typical* or *type* means literally "a resemblance," but scripturally it signifies a symbol of something future, or an example designed by God to prefigure that future thing; the thing so prefigured is called an *antitype*.

79. *Typical Intimations of the Messiah in Genesis.*—The Messiah was typified in—1. ADAM, who was the natural father of mankind, as Christ, the second Adam, was the spiritual father; 2. NOAH, who like Christ was a preacher of righteousness, whilst the ark was a figure of our salvation; 3. MELCHISEDEK, who was "without father, without mother, without descent, having neither beginning of days, nor end of life; but made like unto the Son of God" (Heb. vii. 1–3); 4. ISAAC (see sect. 36, *note*); 5. JOSEPH (see sect. 77). Abel's sacrifice and the offering of Isaac are also typical of our Saviour.

80. *Prophetical Intimations and their Fulfilment.*—Genesis records three intimations of the Messiah—viz.

1st. By God to the serpent: "It (the seed of the woman) shall bruise thy head, and thou shalt bruise his heel." Gen. iii. 15. FULFILMENT: "When the fulness of time was come, God sent forth his Son, made of a woman." Gal. iv. 4. "The God of peace shall bruise Satan under your feet shortly." Rom. xvi. 20. "The Son of God was manifested that he might destroy the works of the devil." 1 John iii. 8. "That old serpent." Rev. xii. 9. (See also Heb. ii. 14.)

2d. By God to Abraham: "In thee shall all the families of the earth be blessed" (Gen. xii. 3; xviii. 18; xxii. 18); also to Isaac (Gen. xxvi. 4), and to Jacob. Gen. xxviii. 14. FULFILMENT: "I bring you good tidings of great joy which shall be to *all* people." Luke ii. 10. "It is evident that our Lord sprang out of Judah." Heb. vii. 14.

3d. By Jacob to Judah: "The sceptre shall not depart from Judah, nor a lawgiver from between his feet, until Shiloh come." Gen. xlix. 10. FULFILMENT: "The high priesthood did not cease to exercise their authority until A. D. 70.—*Horne.*

Names, and Meanings of the Names, of the principal Persons mentioned in Genesis.

ADAM (*earthy*).
EVE (*living*).
Cain (*possession*, or *acquisition*).
Abel (*vanity*).
Seth (*appointed*).
Enoch (*dedicated*) taken up into heaven without dying.
Methuselah (*he has sent his death*), the oldest man.
Lamech (*poor, debased*).
Noah (*rest*).
} Antediluvian patriarchs.

Shem (*renown*), the progenitor of the nations of Asia.
Ham (*heat*), of Africa.
Japheth (*enlarged, persuading*), of Europe.
} Sons of Noah.

Terah (*breathing*), father
Haran (*anger*), brother
Sarah (*lady, princess*), wife
Laban (*shining*), nephew
Lot (*wrapt up*), nephew
} of Abraham.

Isaac (*laughter*), the child promised to Sarah.
Ishmael (*God will hear*), the son of Hagar (*a stranger*), Sarah's bondwoman, and progenitor of the Arabians.
} Sons of Abraham.

Esau or Edom (*red*), founder of Idumæa and the Edomites.
Jacob (*heeler, supplanter*), bought Esau's birthright and inherited his blessing, afterward called Israel (*prevailer*).
} Sons of Isaac.

Reuben (*vision of a son*).
Simeon (*obedient*).
Levi (*associated*).
Judah (*praise*).
Issachar (*a hiring*).
Zebulun (*dwelling*).
Joseph (*increase*).
Benjamin (*son of my right hand*).
Dan (*judging*).
Naphtali (*my wrestling*).
Gad (*troop*).
Asher (*happiness*).
} The twelve sons of Jacob.

Dinah (*judgment*). . . . . Jacob's daughter.

Ephraim (*very fruitful*). } Sons of Joseph.
Manasseh (*forgetfulness*).

EXODUS.

Εξ, "*out*," and οδος, "*a way*"—*the way out or going out from Egypt.*

HISTORY OF THE JEWS AS A NOMAD FAMILY, FROM THE DEATH OF JOSEPH UNTIL THE BUILDING OF THE TABERNACLE AND CONSECRATION OF THE PRIESTHOOD. B. C. 1635 to 1490.

ANALYSIS.

I. *History of the Exode from Egypt, the Journey to Sinai, and Delivery of the Law.*

Moses, 1571—1451.—Condition of the Jews after the death of Joseph, 1635-1571.—Birth of Moses, 1571.—His flight to Midian, 1531.—Called by God at Horeb, 1491.—Returns to Egypt, circumcises his son, and meets Aaron, 1491.—Moses and Aaron stand before Pharaoh.—1st plague, Blood; 2d, Frogs; 3d, Lice; 4th, Flies; 5th, Murrain; 6th, Boils; 7th, Hail; 8th, Locusts; 9th, Darkness.—Passover instituted.—10th plague, Death of the first-born.—THE EXODUS, 1491.—Feast of unleavened bread and sanctification of the first-born.—Journey from Raamses to Pihahiroth.—Passage of the Red Sea.—Wanderings to Marah (bitter water), Elim, and Sin, or Sinai.—Water, quails, and manna.—Properties of manna.—Journeying to Rephidim; water obtained from Horeb.—Joshua defeats the Amalekites.—Visit of Jethro; magistrates appointed.—Encampment before Mount Sinai—Promulgation of the moral law (ten commandments) by Jehovah.—Promulgation of the civil and ceremonial law through Moses.—Idolatry of Israel with a golden calf.—Renewal of the tables of stone.—[Completion of the tabernacle, 1490, p. 94.], ... page 69.

II. *The Moral and Civil Law.**

First and second commandments, against idolatry, false prophets, divinations, etc.—*Third commandment,* against taking God's name

---

* As the civil law was based on the moral law, or ten commandments, it is in the present work analyzed and classified under each commandment for the convenience of reference.

in vain, blasphemy, etc.—*Fourth commandment*, against breaking the Sabbath.—*Fifth commandment*, against disobedience to parents. —*Sixth commandment*, against murder; law of manslaughter; minor corporal injuries.—*Seventh commandment*, against adultery, unlawful marriages, divorcements, fornication; other matrimonial laws. —*Eighth commandment*, against stealing; arson, trespass, and landmarks; men-stealing and fugitive servants; usury, pledges, and things committed in charge; law respecting heirships.—*Ninth commandment*, against false witnessing.—*Tenth commandment*, against covetousness. Miscellaneous precepts.—LAWS RESPECTING SLAVERY. . . . . page 80.

§ *Jewish Constitution.*

Composition of the Jewish state.—The comitia, or legislative assemblies.—Method and place of convening the comitia.—Powers of the comitia.—Connection of the tribes with each other.—Tribunal instituted by the advice of Jethro. . . . . . . page 86.

III. *The Ceremonial Law.**

1. *The Tabernacle.*—External description:—THE HOLY AND THE MOST HOLY PLACE.—*Furniture of the Holy Place*, viz. 1st. The altar of incense; 2d. The shew-bread table; 3d. The candlestick.—*Furniture of the Most Holy Place*, viz. 1st. The ark, and its subsequent history; 2d. The mercy-seat; 3d. The cherubim, the Shechinah.—COURT OF THE TABERNACLE—*its furniture*, viz. 1st. The altar of burnt-offering; 2d. The laver. . . page 89.
§ Typical intimations of the Messiah in Exodus. . page 95.

SUMMARY.

I. *History of the Exode from Egypt, the Journey to Sinai, and Delivery of the Law.*

81. *Condition of the Jews after the Death of Joseph, 1635-1571.*—During the sixty-four years which extended between the death of Joseph and birth of Moses,† the Israelites

Moses, B. C. 1571-1451.

---

* The ceremonial law is divided into six branches—viz. 1. The tabernacle; 2. The priests and Levites; 3. Offerings, including sacrifices, oblations, etc.; 4. Feasts and festivals; 5. Vows; and, 6. Purifications. Of these, the first only is to be found in Exodus; the remaining five are contained in Leviticus. (See "Analysis of Leviticus.")

† The only historical fact recorded of the Israelites between the death of Joseph and the period recorded in Exodus is to be found in 1 Chron. vii. 21. From this it appears that a body of Ephraimites, headed by the sons of Zabad, the sixth in descent from Ephraim, un-

had increased so rapidly as to alarm the Egyptians, and another Pharaoh* had ascended the throne, who knew not Joseph. The children of Jacob were oppressed by tyrannical demands of personal service; they built two treasure-cities, Pithom and Raamses, and labored in every variety of public work, but continued to multiply in spite of their bondage and afflictions. Pharaoh then ordered the two Hebrew midwives, Shiphrah and Puah, to destroy all the male infants of the Israelites; but the two women did not comply, and Pharaoh then commanded his people to throw the male infants of the Hebrews into the Nile. Ex. i.

82. *Birth of Moses, 1571.*—At this time a child was born to two Levites, Amram and Jochebed, and its mother was tempted by its extreme beauty to conceal it for three months; after which, she placed it in an ark of bulrushes [papyrus] and laid it on the flags beside the Nile. Here the child Moses—*i. e.* "saved from the water"—was discovered and adopted by the daughter of Pharaoh, who accidentally gave him to his own mother to be nursed, and had him educated in the several branches of Egyptian learning. Ex. ii. 1–10.

83. *His Flight to Midian, 1541.*—When Moses was forty years old he observed the burdens of his brethren, and on one occasion slew an Egyptian who was smiting a Hebrew. The next day he was mediating between two Hebrews who were striving together, when one of them referred to the murder, and soon afterward Pharaoh sought to slay Moses, and he was obliged to flee to Midian, in the deserts of Arabia Petræa. Here he sat down by a well and assisted the seven daughters of Reuel, Raguel, or Jethro, priest of Midian—*i. e.* sheikh or prince of a Midianite clan—to water their flocks, for the

---

dertook a kind of freebooting expedition into the land of the Philistines, with the view of driving off the cattle belonging to the men of Gath; but they were repulsed by the Philistines with much slaughter, and Zabad lost all his sons.

* It has been generally supposed that this Pharaoh belonged to the race of Shepherd-kings; but it has been proved (see note to sect. 71) that these Shepherd-kings were expelled prior to Joseph. Who the monarch was that knew not Joseph must be left for future historical researches to decide. Present opinions are conflicting and inconclusive.

shepherds had tried to drive them away. Jethro then invited Moses into his house, and afterward gave him his daughter Zipporah for a wife, who bore a son, named Gershom. Ex. ii. 11-22.

84. *Called by God at Horeb, 1491.*—Forty years after this Pharaoh died, and God heard the prayers of the Hebrews and appeared to Moses, who was then eighty years old, in a flaming bush, while he was keeping his flocks at Horeb [Sinai]. The Almighty first commanded Moses to pull off his shoes, and then announced himself as the God of Abraham, and desired Moses to demand of Pharaoh the deliverance of his brethren, and to lead them to Canaan. Moses was diffident of his success with Pharaoh, and afraid that the Israelites would desire to know the name of that God who had sent him; but the Lord replied, "I AM THAT I AM," and desired Moses to tell the Hebrews that the God of their fathers had sent him to lead them from Egypt to Canaan, and to request of Pharaoh permission for them to go three days' journey into the wilderness to worship their God. He then further encouraged Moses by the two miracles of the serpent-rod and the leprous hand, assuring him that if these should fail with Pharaoh, other miraculous signs and plagues should follow, and that, as he was wanting in eloquence, his brother Aaron should be spokesman to the people. Ex. ii. 23-25; iii.; iv. 1-17.

85. *Moses returns to Egypt, circumcises his Son, and meets Aaron, 1491.*—Moses now returned to Jethro, and obtained permission to visit his brethren. On his way from Midian to Egypt he was met by an angel of the Lord, who sought to kill him, upon which his wife Zipporah circumcised their son. Meantime, Aaron, the elder brother of Moses by the same parents, by a divine command went to meet Moses in the wilderness; and the two brothers arrived at Egypt, assembled the elders of Israel* and told their mission, and confirmed it by the two signs of the serpent-rod and leprous hand. Ex. iv. 18-31.

86. *Moses and Aaron stand before Pharaoh.*—

---

* For an account of the political and civil condition of the elders of Israel, see "Jewish Constitution," sect. 133.

Moses, who was eighty years old, and Aaron, eighty-three years, then entered Pharaoh's presence and requested permission for the Hebrews to go three days' journey into the wilderness to sacrifice to Jehovah; but Pharaoh not only contemptuously refused, but added to the burdens of the Israelites by obliging them to collect the straw with which to make the bricks. Moses shrank from appearing again before Pharaoh, but in answer to his reiterated objections fresh assurances were given of the divine presence and protection. The two brethren again entered Pharaoh's presence, when Aaron's rod was transformed into a serpent before him; and though the Egyptian enchanters were permitted to imitate the miracle with their rods, yet that of Aaron swallowed them all up. Ex. v.; vi.; vii. 1–13.

87. *The Ten Plagues.*—The heart of Pharaoh was still hardened, and the plagues threatened by Jehovah were now to be accomplished.

88. *First Plague, Blood.*—Rivers, pools, and all water in vessels were turned to blood for seven days, and the fishes died. The enchanters imitated the miracle. Ex. vii. 19–25.

89. *Second Plague, Frogs.*—The river [Nile] brought forth swarms of frogs, and the enchanters imitated the miracle, but could not *remove* the plague. Pharaoh begged for relief and promised compliance to Moses, but after the frogs were destroyed he recalled his word. Ex. viii. 1–15.

90. *Third Plague, Lice.*—The dust turned to lice, and the enchanters failed to imitate this miracle; but Pharaoh continued hardened. Ex. viii. 16–19.

91. *Fourth Plague, Flies.*—All Egypt except Goshen swarmed with flies. Pharaoh begged the Israelites to worship where they were, which Moses refused. He then promised to let them go into the wilderness; but when the flies had vanished, he again broke his word. Ex. viii. 20–32.

92. *Fifth Plague, Murrain.*—A deadly murrain attacked the Egyptian cattle only, and left the Israelite herds untouched; but Pharaoh was still hardened. Ex. ix. 1–7.

93. *Sixth Plague, Boils and Blains.*—Moses flung

ashes toward heaven, which turned to dust and produced boils and blains upon man and beast, including the magicians; but Pharaoh was still hardened. Ex. ix. 8–12.

94. *Seventh Plague, Hail.*—Hail was now threatened, but Pharaoh was still hardened, though some of the Egyptians placed their cattle in safety. Fire and hail then destroyed man, beast, herb, tree, barley, and flax. Pharaoh again entreated Moses; but when the storm was allayed, he refused to let the Israelites go. Ex. ix. 13–35.

95. *Eighth Plague, Locusts.*—Moses threatened locusts, when Pharaoh offered to let the Israelites go for the three days if they would leave their children and cattle as hostages. This was rejected, and locusts devoured all that the hail had left. Pharaoh again promised, was again relieved, but again broke his word. Ex. x. 1–20.

96. *Ninth Plague, Darkness.*—Darkness covered all Egypt save Goshen for three days. Pharaoh offered to let the Israelites go if they would leave their flocks and herds as security for their return. But this proposition was rejected, as the cattle would be required for the sacrifices. Moses then threatened the death of the first-born, but Pharaoh ordered both Moses and Aaron from his presence, and assured them of death if they again entered it. Ex. x. 21–29.

97. *Passover Instituted.*—Moses now at God's command ordered each of the elders of Israel to choose a male lamb of the first year, without blemish, from the sheep or goats, one for every family or for two small families uniting. The lamb was to be chosen on the tenth day of the month, and eaten on the evening of the fourteenth day; and the month [Abib, corresponding to part of March and April] was from that time to be called the first month of their year, though previously it had been counted as the seventh.* The Hebrews were to kill the lamb in the evening and sprinkle its blood over the doorposts with a bunch of hyssop, that the destroying angel might know their houses and pass them by. They were also to roast the lamb whole and eat it with unleavened

---

* From this time the Israelites reckoned Abib as the first month of their *sacred* year, but as the seventh of their *civil* year.

bread and bitter herbs, and to eat it in haste, with their loins girded, their shoes on their feet, and their staves in their hands. Foreigners, hired servants, and uncircumcised strangers were not to eat it, and what was left in the morning was to be burnt. Defiled and unclean persons could not eat it until purified; then they might keep it on the fourteenth day of the second month. This feast was to be kept as an ordinance for ever. (See sect. 188.) Ex. xii.; xiii. 1–16.

98. *Tenth Plague, Death of the First-born; Exode of the Hebrews, 1491.*—The awful hour at length arrived, and whilst the Hebrews were eating the paschal lamb the Lord smote all the first-born of the Egyptians, both man and beast. Amid the fearful mournings which ensued, Pharaoh hastily summoned Moses and Aaron and commanded both them and the Israelites to depart. The Egyptians cried, "We be all dead men," and readily lent jewels and raiment to the Hebrews to expedite their exode; whilst the latter were compelled to carry off their dough in its unleavened state, bound upon their shoulders in leathern kneading-troughs. Ex. xi.; xii. 29–36.*

---

* **Individual Design and Character of the Miracles in Egypt.**—The miracle of the *serpent-rod* of Aaron authenticated the mission of Moses and proved the fallacy of the serpent-worship of the Egyptians. The plagues of *blood* and *frogs* were directed against the worship of the Nile. The plague of *lice* was a general judgment on Egyptian idolatry, by the laws of which the priests wore only linen garments, and shaved their whole bodies once a day to guard against the slightest risk of contamination from so impure an insect. The plague of *flies* was designed to destroy the trust of the people in Beelzebub—*i. e.* "lord of flies"—who was supposed to protect them from such ravenous swarms. The *murrain* which destroyed the cattle also aimed at the destruction of the entire system of brute-worship amongst the Egyptians. The plague of *boils* and *blains* will be better understood by the mention of the following fact. Human victims were occasionally burnt alive on several altars to propitiate Typhon, or the evil principle, after which the officiating priest cast their ashes into the air in order that evil might be averted from every spot to which an atom was wafted. Moses cast a handful of the ashes into the air, which, instead of averting the evil, brought down boils and blains, and thus made the bloody rites of Typhon a curse to the idolaters. The plague of the *locusts* showed the impotence of Serapis, who was supposed to protect the country against these destructive insects, which now appeared and retired only at the command of Moses. The plagues of *hail* and *darkness* were directed against the worship of Isis and Osiris—the sun and moon—who were supposed to control the light and the elements. Thus Jehovah, the Lord of hosts, summoned nature to proclaim him the true God. The God of Israel asserted his supremacy, and exerted his power to degrade

99. *Feast of Unleavened Bread and Sanctification of the First-born.*—In remembrance of these events the Israelites were ordered to eat unleavened bread during the seven days after the passover for ever—viz. from the fourteenth day of Abib till the twenty-first. (See sect. 188.) They were also commanded to sanctify the first-born male of both man and beast to Jehovah, but they might redeem the firstling of an ass with a lamb, and their children with money. (See sect. 182.) Ex. xii. 15-20; xiii. 1-16.

100. *Journey from Raamses to Pihahiroth.*—The Israelites, to the number of 600,000, exclusive of children, left Raamses with their cattle and a mixed multitude of people exactly four hundred and thirty years from the calling of Abraham—viz. B. C. 1921-1491—having dwelt in Egypt two hundred and fifteen years—viz. B. C. 1706-1491. They left Egypt harnessed—*i. e.* five in a rank—and carried with them the bones of Joseph, according to his dying injunction; and, being led by a pillar of cloud by day and of fire by night, they encamped successively at Succoth* and Etham, and at length reached Pihahiroth, on the western arm of the Red Sea, after making a circuitous route through the wilderness. Ex. xiii. 17-22.

101. *Passage of the Red Sea.*—Meantime, Pharaoh repented the liberation of the Hebrews, and hastily pursued them with six hundred chariots and a host of cavalry. The trembling Israelites at Pihahiroth saw the army approaching, and cried to Moses, "Because there were no graves in Egypt, hast thou taken us away to die in the wilderness?" Moses replied, "Fear ye not, stand still and see the salvation of the Lord." The angel of God then removed the pillar of cloud to the rear, where it became a light to the Israelites and a darkness to the Egyptians. The outstretched hand of Moses then opened

---

the idols, destroy idolatry, and liberate the descendants of Abraham from the land of their bondage. And in the last miracle of all, when the "angel of pestilence breathed in the face" of all the first-born of the land, the true God showed himself to be a God not only of power, but of judgment, and as such to be feared by the wicked and reverenced by all.

* Succoth signifies "tents" or "booths," and the name therefore only appears to denote a place where caravans passing that way usually encamped. This *Succoth* must not therefore be mistaken for the *Succoth* near the banks of the river *Jabbok* where Jacob encamped (sect. 55).

a path for the fugitives through the obedient waves. The presumptuous monarch dared to follow in their track, but was checked by the loss of his chariot-wheels; and when the Hebrews had reached the opposite shore in safety, the chivalry of Egypt was buried beneath the returning waters. The triumph was celebrated by the song of Moses, the timbrel of his sister Miriam, and the dances of the Israelite women. Ex. xiv.; xv. 1–21.

102. *Wanderings to Marah, Elim, and Sin; Water, Quails, and Manna sent.*—Having thus crossed the Red Sea, the Israelites entered the wilderness of Shur, where they wandered three days without finding water; at length, journeying southward, they obtained a supply at Marah, but on account of its bitterness reproached Moses, who then healed it by casting in a tree. From Marah they proceeded still on a southward course to Elim, where there were twelve wells and seventy palm trees, and from thence they entered the wilderness of Sin, which lies between Elim and Sinai. At Sin their provisions were exhausted, and they again murmured and regretted the flesh-pots of Egypt, but the same evening quails were sent, and the following morning God rained bread from heaven and manna began to descend. Ex. xv. 22–27; xvi. 1–15.

103. *Properties of Manna.*—Manna, "the bread of heaven" (Heb. *manhu*, "what is it?"), was found upon the ground every morning like hoar-frost or coriander seed, and tasted like honey wafers. Every morning each man gathered about one omer, or five pints, for the day's eating, and on the sixth day two omers, or ten pints; and thus it fed the Hebrews during forty years, and Aaron was commanded to lay up an omer of it [five pints] in a pot as a lasting memorial. It had five miraculous qualities: 1. It only fell six days in the week, and not on the Sabbath; 2. A double quantity fell on the sixth day as a supply for the Sabbath; 3. That which was gathered on the first five days was putrid if kept more than one day, but that which was gathered on the sixth day remained sweet for two days; 4. It sustained nearly three million of souls; 5. It ceased to fall after the Israelites had entered Canaan. Ex. xvi.

104. *Journey to Rephidim; Water obtained from*

Horeb.—From Sin the Israelites journeyed to Rephidim, where they thirsted for water, and again reproached Moses and were almost ready to stone him; but he prayed to God, and obtained a miraculous supply by striking his rod against the rock in Horeb, which he afterward called Massah, or "temptation," and Meribah, or "strife." This rock lies to the south of Sinai. Ex. xvii. 1-7.

105. ***Joshua defeats the Amalekites.***—At Rephidim, Moses commanded Joshua to choose an army and attack Amalek, whilst he himself stood on the hill, attended by Aaron and Hur and with the rod of God in his hand. Joshua accordingly fought against the Amalekites and prevailed whilst Moses held up his hands, but was repulsed if his hands fell down. Aaron and Hur then placed a stone for Moses to sit on, and, standing on each side of him, they held up his hands till the sun had set and Amalek had been defeated. Moses, in obedience to God, recorded the victory in a book and built an altar— Jehovah-nissi, or "The Lord my banner." Ex. xvii. 8-16.

106. ***Visit of Jethro; Magistrates appointed.***— Jethro, or Reuel, the father-in-law of Moses, having heard of the wonders God had performed, visited his son-in-law, bringing with him Zipporah and her two sons by Moses— viz. Gershom and Eliezer. Moses went out to meet Jethro, and received him affectionately. Jethro then offered a sacrifice to Jehovah, and joined with Moses, Aaron, and the elders of Israel in a solemn feast. The next day Jethro observed that Moses judged the people from morning till evening, and that the duty was too heavy; he therefore advised him to appoint subordinate judges over thousands, hundreds, fifties, and tens to decide in small matters, whilst he himself only settled the more difficult causes. Moses followed this counsel, and Jethro then returned to his own land.* Ex. xviii.

107. ***Encampment before Mount Sinai.***—In the third month from the exodus the Israelites had left Rephidim and encamped in the wilderness of Sinai before the mount, which was situated toward the south of the peninsula of Arabia Petræa, which lies between the two

---

* For a further account of these magistrates, see "Jewish Constitution," sect. 133.

northern arms of the Red Sea. Here the Lord, having reminded them through Moses of the deliverance he had wrought, called upon them to obey his commands. He then spoke to Moses out of a thick cloud, and ordered him to direct the people to cleanse themselves and wash their clothes, and to be ready on the third day; and none were to touch the mount, either man or beast, on pain of death. Ex. xix.

108. *Promulgation of the Moral Law.*—The third day was ushered in with thunders and lightnings; fire and smoke enveloped the mount, and the trumpet of the Lord summoned the people to the appointed audience, when Jehovah came down from Sinai in a thick cloud and promulgated the ten commandments to the terrified assembly. Ex. xx. 1, 18.

109. *The Civil and Ceremonial Law.*—The people then retired from their fearful proximity to Deity, and begged Moses that they might receive the future laws from him instead of from Jehovah, swearing to perform all that God should command. Moses accordingly ascended the mount to receive from God a more detailed code of civil and ceremonial law. At first he went up alone, but he was subsequently partly attended by Aaron and his two sons, Nadab and Abihu, and by the seventy elders of Israel, who worshipped afar off whilst the laws were being written and delivered to Moses by Jehovah on two tables of stone, called the *Tables of the Law*, or *Tables of the Covenant*. They, however, all saw the God of Israel with the semblance of paved work of a sapphire stone under his feet. Moses also dwelt in the cloud that rested on the mount seven days with his servant Joshua, whilst the charge of the people was delegated to Aaron and Hur; but on the seventh day Moses alone was called into the midst of the cloud, where he stayed for forty days and forty nights. Moses also built an altar and twelve pillars, according to the twelve tribes; and, offering up a sacrifice of peace-offerings of oxen, he sprinkled the blood partly on the altar, partly on the book of the covenant, and partly on the people, who then pledged themselves to obey all the words of Jehovah. Jehovah, having given to Moses the two tables, revealed to him the idolatry of Israel and his intention to consume them;

but Moses interceded for the seed of Abraham, and the Lord repented of the evil which he thought to do. Ex. xx. 18, 21; xxiv.; xxxi. 18; xxxii. 7–14.

110. *Idolatry of Israel with a Golden Calf; three thousand slain.*—Meantime, the Hebrews, having grown impatient at the absence of their leader, forgetful of their recent terrors, and unmindful of their promises of obedience, had given their golden earrings to Aaron and prevailed upon him to make them a molten calf,* which they then worshipped as their deliverer from Egypt. Moses, having been informed of this idolatry by Jehovah and descended the mount with Joshua, heard the noise of their worship as he approached the camp, and saw the calf and the dancing. His righteous anger was now uncontrollable. He broke the two tables of stone beneath the mount, and burnt the calf, ground it to powder, and, mixing its ashes with water, he made the Israelites drink it. He reprimanded Aaron, who made the paltry excuse that he was forced by the people to make the calf. He then called upon the adherents of Jehovah to fall upon the idolaters, and the Levites arose and slew three thousand of their brethren. The following day he admonished the people of their sin and interceded with God, who had smitten the people with plague. The people then humbled themselves and stripped off their ornaments, and the tabernacle was removed without the camp, when the pillar of cloud once more returned, and the Lord, having talked familiarly with Moses, favored him with an unveiled view of his glory. Ex. xxxii.; xxxiii.

111. *Renewal of the Tables of Stone.*—Moses was now commanded to hew fresh tables of stone, upon which Jehovah would rewrite his laws. He again abode upon Sinai for forty days and forty nights without bread or water, and when he returned to the camp his face shone so brightly that he was compelled to wear a veil when conversing with the Israelites. He then rehearsed to the people the commandments he had received, and invited them to contribute toward the tabernacle and the priests; and when the sacred building was completed, he conse-

---

* This golden calf was no doubt in imitation of the Egyptian Apis. See Herodotus, ii. 38.

crated Aaron and his sons according to divine appointment. (See "Consecration of Priests," sect. 166.) Ex. xxxiv.; xxxv.; xl.

II. *Moral and Civil Law.*

112. *First and Second Commandments, against Idolaters, False Prophets, Divination, etc.*—Whoever sacrificed to any god save Jehovah was to be utterly destroyed. Ex. xxii. 20. Whoever gave his seed to Moloch was to be stoned. Lev. xxi. 1–5. All wizards and those who had familiar spirits were to be stoned. Lev. xix. 31; xx. 6, 27; Deut. xviii. 9–14. Prophets and dreamers who prophesied in the name of false gods were to be stoned, even though their prophecies came to pass, together with brothers, sisters, daughters, wives, or friends who enticed to idolatry. If a prophet presumptuously foretold a thing in the name of the Lord which never came to pass, he also was to be stoned. Cities infected with idolatry were to be burnt and destroyed. Deut. xiii.; xvii. 2–7. No alliance or covenant was to be made with idolaters. Ex. xxiii. 32, 33; Deut. vii. All monuments of idolatry were to be destroyed (Num. xxxiii. 50–56; Deut. xii. 1–4), and none were to inquire after other gods. Deut. xii. 29–32.

113. *Third Commandment, against taking God's Name in Vain, Blasphemy, etc.*—Whoever cursed God or blasphemed his name was to be stoned. The son of Shelomith blasphemed, and was stoned by the congregation. Lev. xxiv. 10–16, 23; Num. xv. 30, 31.

114. *Fourth Commandment, against breaking the Sabbath.*—Whoever defiled the Sabbath was to be put to death. Ex. xxxi. 12–17; xxxv. 1–3. A man gathering sticks on the Sabbath was stoned by the congregation. Num. xv. 32–36. The seventh day was to be kept because God rested on the seventh day when he created the world. This shows its universal application.

115. *Fifth Commandment, against Disobedience to Parents.*—Whoever smote or cursed his father or mother was to be put to death. Ex. xxi. 15, 17; Lev. xx. 9. A stubborn, drunken, or rebellious son was to be stoned. Deut. xxi. 18–21.

116. *Sixth Commandment, against Murder; Law of Manslaughter, etc.*—Murder, when it proceeded from hatred, revenge, or premeditation, and was proved by more than one witness, was to be punished by death without redemption. In cases of manslaughter where the death occurred by accident or mistake the murderer might flee to one of the cities of refuge, of which three were appointed in Canaan and three east of the Jordan. The congregation might also judge between the slayer and the revenger of blood; and if they found the accused guiltless of wilful murder, they might restore him to a city of refuge, where, however, he must remain until the death of the high priest, for if found without the outskirts the revenger might slay him. Ex. xxi. 12–14; Lev. xxiv. 17, 21; Num. xxxv. 9–34; Deut. xix. 1–13. If a man killed a thief breaking into his house at *night*, it was *justifiable homicide*; but if he killed the thief when the sun was up, it was *manslaughter*, because in the latter case the man robbed might have obtained reparation by selling even the person of the thief. Ex. xxii. 2, 3. If a man struck his slave not of Hebrew descent, and the slave died immediately, the master was to be punished; but if the slave survived one or two days, the master escaped. Ex. xxi. 20, 21. If a man was found murdered and the murderer was unknown, the elders of the nearest city were to sacrifice a heifer in a valley neither eared nor sown and wash their hands over it. Deut. xxi. 1–9.

117. *Minor Corporal Injuries.*—If a man injured another in a fray, he was to pay the expenses of his cure and recompense him for his loss of time. Ex. xxi. 18, 19. If a pregnant woman was hurt in a fray and miscarried, her husband could demand compensation, though the amount might be referred to arbitrators. Ex. xxi. 22. This law of retaliation did not extend to slaves; but if a master knocked out his slave's eye or tooth, the slave received his freedom as compensation. Ex. xxi. 26, 27. If an ox killed a man, it was to die; and if the owner knew of its propensity, he was to make compensation, but not otherwise. Ex. xxi. 28–32.

118. *Seventh Commandment, against Adultery.*—In cases of adultery both the man and woman were to be put to death. Lev. xx. 10; Deut. xxii. 22. If a man

suspected his wife's virtue, but could find no proof, he was to take her to the priest with a jealousy-offering of the tenth of an ephah [about five pints] of barley-meal without oil or frankincense. The priest was then to take the jealousy-offering from the woman's hand and burn it upon the altar, and afterward to take holy water, and dust from the floor of the tabernacle, and mix them together, and make the woman drink the mixture, saying that if she was guilty the water would make her belly swell and thigh rot, and the woman was to reply "Amen." The water would afterward prove her innocence or confirm the charge. Num. v. 11–31. If a man defiled a bondmaid betrothed to a husband, but unredeemed, they were not to be put to death, but she was to be scourged, and he was to take a ram for a trespass-offering to the priest, who would then make atonement for his crime. Lev. xix. 20–22.

119. *Unlawful Marriages.*—A man might not marry, under pain of death both to him and the woman—1. His father's wife; 2. His father or mother's daughter or granddaughter; 3. His son's wife; 4. A wife and her mother. If he married the following he would die childless: 1. His father or mother's sister; 2. His brother's wife;* 3. His uncle's wife. He was also forbidden to marry—1. A wife and her sister whilst the former was alive; 2. A heathen woman. Lev. xviii. 6–18; xx. 11, 12, 14, 17, 19–21; Deut. vii. 3.

120. *Divorcements.*—If, after marriage, a man was dissatisfied with his wife, he might write her a bill of divorcement, and each was at liberty to marry again; but if the woman did take a second husband, she could never return to her first husband, even after the death of the second. Deut. xxiv. 1–4.

121. *Fornication, etc.*—If a man debauched an unbetrothed maid, he was to marry her; but if her father refused to let them marry, he was to pay her dowry. Ex. xxii. 16, 17. In Deuteronomy it is ordered that the man marry the woman and pay her father fifty silver shekels [$22\frac{3}{4}$ oz. = £5 13s. 10d.], and be deprived of all power of obtaining a divorce. Deut. xxii. 28, 29. If he debauched

---

* If a man's brother died childless, however, he was to marry his widow. (See "Other Matrimonial Laws.")

a betrothed maid in the city, they were both to be stoned, because she might have cried out; if in the field, only the man was to be stoned. All unnatural defilement was to be punished by death. Ex. xxii. 19; Lev. xviii. 22–30; xx. 13, 15, 16.

122. *Other Matrimonial Laws.*—If a man approached an unclean woman, they were both to be put to death. Lev. xviii. 19; xx. 18. If a man took a female captive in battle and desired to marry her, he was first to shave her head, pare her nails, and suffer her to bewail her parents a full month. After this he might divorce her, but could not sell her. Deut. xxi. 10–14. If a man impugned his wife's virginity, her parents were to take the proofs of it to the elders; and if the elders were satisfied of her innocence, they were to chastise the man and fine him one hundred silver shekels [$45\frac{1}{2}$ oz. = £11 7s. 8d.]; but if they found her guilty, she was to be stoned. Deut. xxii. 13–21. A newly-married man was not to go out to war for one year after his marriage. Deut. xxiv. 5. If a man's brother died childless, he was to marry the widow, and the first-born of this union was to succeed to the deceased brother and take his name. If a man refused to marry the widow, she was to complain to the elders, and both she and the man were to be brought before them. If the man then refused to take her, she was to take off his shoe and spit in his face, and his name was to be called "The house of him that hath his shoe loosed." Deut. xxv. 5–10. If, when two men strove together, the wife of one immodestly assisted her husband, her hand was to be cut off. Deut. xxv. 11, 12.

123. *Eighth Commandment, against Stealing.*—If a man stole an ox and killed or sold it, he was to restore fivefold; if a sheep, fourfold; if either were found in his possession alive, he was only to restore double. If a thief was slain whilst breaking into a house at *night*, no blood was to be shed for him (sect. 116). If a thief had nothing with which to make restitution, he was to be sold into slavery. Ex. xxii. 1–4.

124. *Arson, Trespass, and Landmarks.*—If a fire broke out and consumed either standing corn or stacks, whoever kindled it was to make restitution. Ex. xxii. 6. If a man put his beast into another man's field or vine-

yard, he was to make double restitution. Ex. xxii. 5, 9. Old landmarks were never to be removed. Deut. xix. 14.

125. *Men-stealing and Fugitive Servants.*—If a man stole an Israelite and sold him, he was to be put to death. Deut. xxiv. 7. Fugitive servants were not to be delivered up or oppressed. Deut. xxiii. 15, 16. (See also sect. 132.)

126. *Law of Sale.*—In the sabbatical year all debts were to be remitted save those incurred by foreigners, and in the jubilee year all land-possessions were to be restored. Deut. xv. 1-3; Lev. xxv. 8-24. If a man had been compelled by poverty to sell his estate, the price of its redemption was to be regulated by the number of years before the jubilee year. Lev. xxv. 25-28. If a man sold a house in a walled city, he might redeem it within a year of the sale; but after that he could never redeem it, nor would it revert to him at the jubilee. The houses in unwalled villages and those in Levitical cities might be redeemed at any time, and would revert to the original possessor in the jubilee. Lev. xxv. 29-34.

127. *Usury, Pledges, and Things committed in Charge.*—If a man borrowed anything of his neighbor and it died or was hurt, he was to make it good, unless the owner were with it or hire was paid for it. Ex. xxii. 14, 15. Money might be lent to a stranger upon usury, but not to an Israelite. No usury was to be charged to a poor man, whether stranger or not. Ex. xxiii. 25; Lev. xxv. 35-47; Deut. xxiii. 19, 20. Any raiment taken as pledge was to be returned by sunset. Ex. xxiii. 26, 27. If a man received money or stuff to keep for another, and it was stolen whilst under his charge, the thief, when found, was to pay double. If the thief could not be found, the man himself was to be tried by the judges. Ex. xxii. 7, 8.

128. *Law respecting Heirships.*—The land of Canaan was to be divided by lot among the Israelite families according to their tribes, and each family was to keep their inheritance for ever; for if sold it was to revert to its original possessors in the jubilee year. Num. xxxiii. 50-56. The sons always equally inherited their father's possession, except the first-born, who received a double portion; and in no case was the first-born to be

disinherited—not even if a man had two wives and loved one and hated the other, and his first-born was the son of the hated wife. Deut. xxi. 15-17. If a man died without sons, the possession went to his daughters—a privilege first obtained by the daughters of Zelophehad; only, in such cases, the daughters were not to marry out of their father's tribe. If a man left neither sons nor daughters, his possession went to his brethren; if he left no brethren, it went to his father's brethren; and if his father had no brethren, it went to his nearest kinsman. Num. xxvi. 52-56; xxvii. 1-11; xxxvi.

129. *Ninth Commandment, against False Witnessing.*—Whoever concealed his knowledge of a sin was to bear the iniquity of the sinner. Lev. v. 1. Two or more witnesses were required to establish a criminal accusation. Deut. xvii. 6.

130. *Tenth Commandment, against Covetousness.*—No one was to desire anything belonging to his neighbor. Ex. xx. 17. No money was to be lent to the poor on usury. Ex. xxii. 25. No unjust weights or balances were to be used. Lev. xix. 35, 36.

131. *Miscellaneous Precepts.*—A kid was not to be seethed in its mother's milk. Ex. xxiii. 19. The stranger was not to be oppressed. Ex. xxiii. 9. Fat or blood, or unclean beasts, birds, or fish, or beasts that had died a natural death, might not be eaten. Lev. iii. 17; xii.; Deut. xiv. Gleanings were to be left to the poor and the stranger. Wages due were not to be kept till morning. Talebearers were denounced. Cattle of different species were to be kept distinct, and mingled seeds were not to be sown in a garden. Lev. xix.; Deut. xxii. 9. Israelites were not to cut themselves or shave their heads for the dead. Deut. xiv. 1, 2. Strayed or fallen cattle were always to be assisted. Neither men nor women were to wear each other's apparel. In taking nests, the dam was never to be taken with the young. Battlements were to be built to the roofs of houses. Deut. xxii. A neighbor's grapes or standing corn might be gathered and eaten, but not carried away. Deut. xxiii. 24, 25. Controversies were to be referred to arbitrators. Oxen were not to be muzzled when treading out corn. Deut. xxv.

132. *Law respecting Slavery.*—Men became slaves

by the following means—viz. 1. CAPTIVITY in war; 2. DEBTS, when the debtor was unable to pay them; 3. THEFT, when a thief could not make reparation; 4. MAN-STEALING, an act of violence which was to be punished by death; 5. BIRTH, when a slave had children; 6. PURCHASE, when a man sold himself or was purchased from another master. The medium price of a slave was about thirty silver shekels [about $13\frac{1}{2}$ oz. = £3 8s. 3d.]. Ex. xxi. 16, 32; xxii. 2; Lev. xxvii. 1-8; Deut. xx. 14; xxi. 10, 11; xxiv. 7; 2 Kings iv. 1. Moses instituted the following laws concerning slaves—viz. I. That all servants or slaves should be treated with humanity, especially Hebrews (Lev. xxv. 39-53); II. If a master slew a slave, he was to be judged accordingly and punished; but if the slave lived a day or two after being smitten, the master was unpunished (Ex. xxi. 20, 21); III. If a master injured the eye or tooth of his slave, the latter was to be freed (Ex. xxi. 26, 27); IV. Slaves were to rest on Sabbaths and festivals (Ex. xx. 10; Deut. v. 14); V. Slaves were to be invited to feasts made from the second tithes (Deut. xii. 17, 18; xvi. 11); VI. Slaves were to receive an adequate subsistence (Deut. xxv. 4); VII. A master was bound to provide for the marriage of maid-servants, unless he took them as concubines for himself or gave them to his son (Ex. xxi. 8); VIII. Hebrew slaves were not obliged to serve for more than six years; but if one wished to continue to serve, he had his ear bored at his master's doorpost in sign of perpetual servitude (Ex. xxi.); IX. In the year of jubilee all servants or slaves of Hebrew descent were to be emancipated (Lev. xxv. 39-41); X. A runaway slave from another nation was to be treated with kindness, and not forcibly returned. Deut. xxiii. 15, 16.

§ *Jewish Constitution.**

133. **Composition of the Jewish State.**—In the old patriarchal form of government which was maintained

---

* To this section but a few of the leading Scripture references have been given, as otherwise the page would be overloaded with references to isolated passages in various parts of the Old Testament, to which few readers would think it necessary to turn. Those biblical students who may be desirous of examining all the authorities are referred to the learned works of Jahn and Michaelis.

by the Hebrews during their sojourn in Egypt, every father exercised a father's authority over his own household, and every tribe obeyed its own prince, who was originally the first-born of the founder of the tribe, but subsequently appears to have been elected. As the people increased various heads of families united together and elected a leader, who was sometimes called the head of a thousand. The princes also, whose duty it had been originally to keep genealogical tables, subsequently employed scribes for that purpose, who in progress of time acquired so much authority as to be permitted to exercise a share in the government. We have thus,

1st. The heads of families, or elders.
2d. The princes of the tribes.
3d. The heads of associated families, or of thousands.
4th. The genealogists, translated "officers." All of them, however, were sometimes designated as "elders."

Under the Mosaic economy the authority of these heads and princes continued the same as before, with the addition of the judges of tens, of fifties, of hundreds, and of thousands.

These judges were elected by the suffrages of the people from those who, by their authority and rank, might be reckoned amongst the rulers or princes of Israel; and they did not forfeit their civil authority by accepting this judicial office. The judges of smaller numbers were subordinate to those who judged larger numbers, and accordingly difficult cases went up from the inferior to the superior judges; and the very difficult causes were submitted to Moses himself, or to the supreme ruler of the commonwealth, and in the time of the monarchy to the king himself; and sometimes a further appeal was made to the high priest. Ex. xviii. 13–26; Num. i.; v. 46; Deut. i. 13–18.

134. *The Comitia, or Legislative Assemblies.*—The various civil and judicial officers mentioned in the foregoing section were necessarily dispersed throughout the country. Those who dwelt in the same city or the same neighborhood formed the *comitia, senate,* or *legislative assembly of their immediate vicinity;* when all that dwelt in any particular tribe were convened, they formed the *legis-*

lative assembly of the tribe; and when they were convened in one body from all the tribes, they formed, in like manner, the *legislative assembly of the nation,* and were the representatives of the whole people. The *priests,* who were the learned class of the community and hereditary officers in the state, had, by the divine command, a right to a sitting in this assembly. The elders, princes, genealogists, and judges, in their collective capacity, were called the " elders of the assembly " or " of the people," the "princes of the assembly," or "congregation," the "whole assembly," etc. Sometimes an assembly included the whole mass of the people. Deut. ix. 12; xxv. 8, 9; Judg. i. 1-11; viii. 14; ix. 3-46; xi. 5; 1 Sam. viii. 4; xvi. 4.

135. *Method and Place of convening the Comitia.*—The comitia were convened by the judge or ruler for the time being, and, in case of his absence, by the high priest. The members appear to have met at the door of the tabernacle, though sometimes some other celebrated spot was selected. During the sojourn in the wilderness the comitia were summoned by the blowing of the holy trumpets, *one* trumpet being the signal for a more select convention, composed merely of the heads of associated families and of the princes of the tribes; whilst the blowing of *two* trumpets convened the great assembly, which, in addition to the heads of associated families and princes of the tribes, included the elders, judges, and genealogists. After the settlement in Palestine the comitia were assembled by messengers. Num. x. 2-4.

136. *Powers of the Comitia.*—The comitia, or assembly, exercised the rights of sovereignty. It declared war, concluded peace, and ratified treaties, and it chose the civil rulers, generals, and eventually kings. The oath of office was administered to its members by the judge or the king, and the latter in turn received their oath from the comitia, acting in the name of the people. The comitia acted on their own authority and according to their own views, without instructions from the body of the nation; but, though no single instance occurs in which the latter sought to interfere in the deliberations of the assembly, yet the assembly were in the habit of proposing their decisions and resolutions to the people for their ratification and consent. When Jehovah was chosen as

the special King of the Hebrews, it was not done by the comitia, but by the people themselves, all of whom, as well as their rulers, took the oath of obedience. Ex. xxiv. 3-8; Deut. xxix. 9-14.

137. *Connection of the Tribes with each other.*—Each tribe was governed by its own prince and heads of families, etc., and therefore, to a certain extent, constituted an independent community. Judg. xx. 11-46. If, however, any one tribe found itself unequal to the execution of any proposed plan, it might connect itself with another, or even a number of the other tribes; and if any affair concerned the whole or many of the tribes, it was determined by them in conjunction in the legislative assembly of the nation. But still, all the tribes were bound together so as to form one Church and one civil community—not only by the common promises vouchsafed by Jehovah to their common ancestors, not only by the need in which they stood of mutual counsel and assistance, but also by the circumstance that God was their common King, and that they had a common tabernacle for his palace, and a common sacerdotal and Levitical order for his ministers. Judg. xi. 1-11; i. 1-3, 22.

138. *The Tribunal of Seventy instituted by Moses.*—The tribunal of seventy elders instituted by Moses (sect. 219) seems to have been merely intended for a supreme senate, to take a share with Moses in the government, and was not probably of long continuance. Frequent mention is made in the New Testament of a Sanhedrim, which appears to have been instituted at Jerusalem after the return from the Babylonian captivity, for from the death of Moses until this latter period we do not find the least mention of this council or tribunal.

III. *The Ceremonial Law.**

1. THE TABERNACLE.

139. *External Description.*—The Israelites made voluntary offerings for the building of the tabernacle and its appurtenances so liberally that Moses was obliged to

---

* The Jewish ceremonial law was divided into six branches—viz. 1. THE TABERNACLE; 2. THE PRIESTS, LEVITES, and NETHINIM; 3. OFFER-

restrain them. The tabernacle was built by two inspired architects—Bezaleel the son of Uri, of the tribe of Judah, and Aholiab the son of Ahisamach, of the tribe of Dan. It was 30 cubits [18 yards 8 inches] long, 10 cubits [6 yards 2 inches] broad, and 10 cubits [6 yards 2 inches] high. The two sides and western end were made of shittim- [acacia] wood boards, overlaid with gold. Each of these boards was 10 cubits [6 yards 2 inches] long and 1½ cubits [2 feet 8 inches] broad; and they were fixed upright in silver sockets, and secured by shittim-wood bars overlaid with gold, which passed through golden rings on the boards. The eastern end was the entrance, and, instead of boards, was enclosed with a richly-embroidered hanging suspended by golden hooks from five pillars of shittim-wood, which stood in five brazen sockets. Four veils or coverings were cast over the whole building: 1. The innermost one, which formed a ceiling, and consisted of fine linen embroidered with cherubim and shaded with blue, purple, and scarlet; 2. A covering of goats' hair; 3. Rams' skins dyed red; 4. The outermost one of dyed badger skins. Ex. xxvi.; xxxi. 1–11; xxxv. 4–35; xxxvi.

140. *The Holy and the Most Holy Place.*—The tabernacle was divided into two apartments, the HOLY and the MOST HOLY PLACE, by means of a rich hanging like the one at the entrance, stretched upon four pillars of shittim-wood overlaid with gold, and standing in silver sockets. Ex. xxvi. 31–37.

141. *Furniture of the Holy Place.—1st. The Altar of Incense,* which was placed in the centre of the Holy Place. It was made with shittim-wood overlaid with gold, with horns of the same material, and was 1 cubit [1 foot 9 inches] square and 2 cubits [3 feet 7 inches] high. The crown or ornamental cornice was of gold, with four golden rings underneath it to receive the staves of shittim-wood overlaid with gold by which the altar was carried. Incense was burnt on this altar both morning and evening. It was also sprinkled with the blood of the

---

INGS, including sacrifices, oblations, and meat- and drink-offerings; 4. FEASTS and FESTIVALS; 5. VOWS; 6. PURIFICATIONS. Of these, the first only is to be found in Exodus; the remaining five are contained in Leviticus.

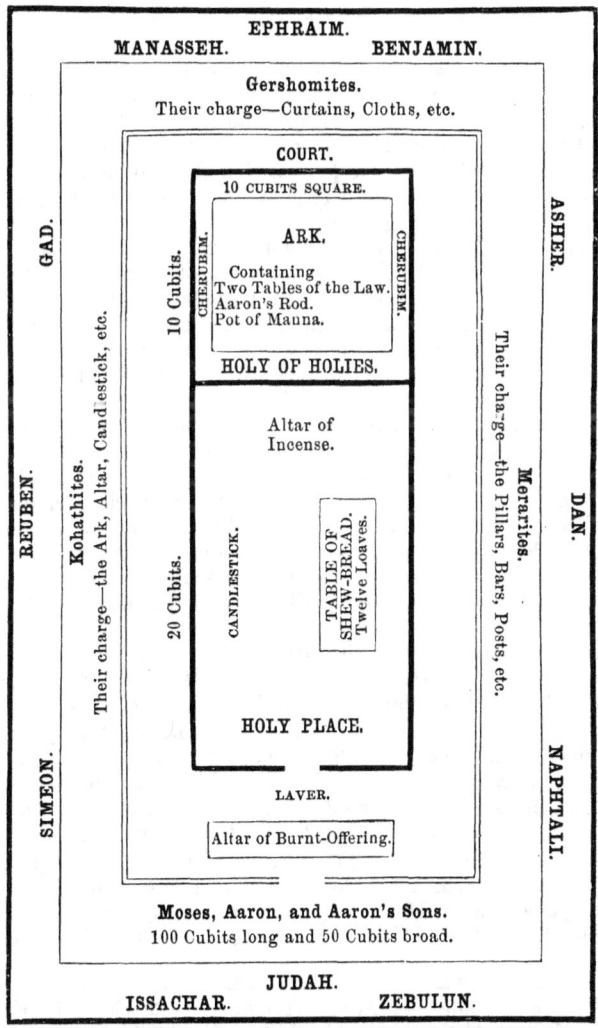

THE TABERNACLE, AND ORDER OF THE ENCAMPMENTS OF THE SEVERAL TRIBES.

sacrifices that were offered for the sins of ignorance. Ex. xxx. 1-10; xxxvii. 25-29.

142. *2d. The Shew-bread Table,* which stood north of the altar of incense—that is, on the right hand of the priest as he entered. It was made, like the altar, of shittim-wood overlaid with gold. It was 2 cubits [3 feet 7 inches] long, 1 cubit [1 foot 9 inches] broad, and 1½ cubits [2 feet 8 inches] high, and had a crown or ornamental cornice of gold, with a border or second crown above it. It also had four golden rings and staves of shittim-wood and gold, like the altar of incense. Shew-bread was always kept upon this table, twelve fresh loaves of which (one for each tribe) were offered every Sabbath, the priests alone eating the removed bread. Dishes, spoons, covers, and bowls were made for the table of pure gold. Ex. xxv. 23-30; xxxvii. 10-16.

143. *3d. The Candlestick,* which stood south, or on the left of the altar of incense. It was made of beaten gold, and weighed one talent, or about one hundredweight = £5464. It had six branches, three on each side, and three bowls like almonds, with a knop and a flower in each branch. It also had seven lamps, which were kept burning with pure olive oil both morning and evening, with tongs and snuff-dishes all of pure gold. Ex. xxv. 31-40; xxxvii. 17-24.

144. ***Furniture of the Most Holy Place, or "Holy of Holies."—1st. The Ark.***—The ark was made of shittim-wood overlaid with gold. It was 2½ cubits [4½ feet] long, 1½ cubits [2 feet 8 inches] broad, and 1½ cubits [2 feet 8 inches] high. It had an ornamental cornice of gold round the top, with four golden rings to receive the staves of shittim-wood and gold by which it was carried. The ark contained—1. The testimony or tables of the covenant; 2. A golden pot with an omer of manna; 3. Aaron's rod that budded. In the side of the ark was a place where Moses enjoined that a copy of the law should be kept.* Ex. xxv. 10-16; xxxvii. 1-5; Heb. ix. 4.

---

* **Subsequent History of the Ark.**—It led the Israelites, under Joshua, across the Jordan on dry land (Josh. iv.), and subsequently the walls of Jericho fell down after it had been carried round them once a day for six days, and seven times on the seventh. Josh. vi. On entering

145. *2d. The Mercy-seat,* which was a golden covering for the ark, was so called because God was propitiated by the blood of the goat sprinkled upon or before it on the day of atonement. Ex. xxv. 17; xxxvii. 6.

146. *3d. The Cherubim,* or two figures of beaten gold. Each of these figures had four faces—viz. that of a lion, man, calf, and eagle, attached to a human body with four wings, and four hands under the wings, and standing on feet like those of a calf or ox. Two of the wings of each cherub covered its body, whilst the other two were stretched above the mercy-seat. Jehovah promised to commune with his people from between the cherubim, and there dwelt the miraculous light of Shechinah. Ex. xxv. 18–22; xxxvii. 7–9.

147. *The Shechinah.*—This miraculous light rested like a cloud between the cherubim, and was a visible token of the presence of God in his holy temple. It had led the Israelites through the wilderness like a pillar of cloud by day and of fire by night. It appeared to the shepherds at our Saviour's birth, to Paul at his conversion, and to the disciples at Christ's transfiguration.

148. *Court of the Tabernacle.*—The tabernacle could be taken to pieces and put together again as occasion required. It was carried by the Levites and pitched in the

---

Canaan it was first set up in Shiloh, but many years afterward, when the Israelites were oppressed by the Philistines during the judgeships of Eli's sons, it was carried into the Hebrew camp, and fell into the hands of the enemy. The Philistines were so afflicted whilst it was in their possession that they passed it to Ashdod—where the god Dagon fell before it—to Gath, to Ekron, and from thence to Beth-shemesh, where the people were struck dead for looking into it. From this place the Israelites carried it to the house of Abinadab at Kirjath-jearim, after having been deprived of it for seven months. 1 Sam. iv. 11; vii. 1. In the reign of Saul it was at Nob, and afterward at Kirjath-jearim again, whence David carried it in a new cart, first to the house of Obed-edom, because Uzzah was struck dead for touching it on the journey, and afterward to his own house at Jerusalem. 2 Sam. vi. 10–15. When David fled from Absalom he took it with him, but sent it back again to Jerusalem, and at last it was deposited by Solomon in the temple. 2 Sam. xv. 24–29; 2 Chron. v. 2–5. Here it remained until the temple was profaned by the idolatry of Judah, when the priests carried it from place to place to preserve it from pollution. Josiah afterward ordered it to be replaced, but what became of it subsequently is unknown; it was lost during the destruction of the temple by Nebuchadnezzar, and was wanting in the second temple. 2 Chron. xxxv. 3.

midst of every encampment, the tribes being stationed round it in a quadrangular form under their respective standards. It was always stationed in an open oblong space 100 cubits [182 feet 4 inches] long and 50 cubits [91 feet 2 inches] broad, due east and west, and surrounded by brazen pillars filleted or fluted with silver, and 5 cubits [3 yards 1 inch] high and at 5 cubits' [3 yards 1 inch] distance from each other. These pillars were hung with fine twined linen yarn, except at the entrance on the eastern end, which was of blue, purple, scarlet, and fine white twined linen, with cords to draw it either up or aside when the priests entered the court. Ex. xxvii. 9–21; xxxviii. 9–20.

149. *Furniture of the Court.—1st. The Altar of Burnt-offerings.*—The altar was placed in a line between the entrance of the court and that of the tabernacle, and was 5 cubits [3 yards 1 inch] long, 5 cubits broad, and 3 cubits [5 feet 5 inches] high. It was hollow, and made of shittim-wood boards overlaid with brass, and had a horn at each corner. All the pans, basins, shovels, flesh-hooks, and vessels belonging to it were made of brass, and it was surmounted by a brazen grate or network, on which the victims were consumed. It also had four brazen rings to receive staves of shittim-wood overlaid with brass, by which it was carried. The first sacrifice upon this altar was consumed by fire from heaven, which was never afterward suffered to go out. Ex. xxvii. 1–8; xxxviii. 1–7; Lev. vi. 13; ix. 24.

150. *2d. The Laver.*—The laver was placed between the altar of burnt-offering and the entrance of the tabernacle. It was made of brass, and had a foot, also of brass, and held water, in which Aaron and his sons were to wash their hands and feet whenever they entered the tabernacle or approached the altar. Ex. xxxviii. 8.

---

151. *Completion of the Tabernacle, 1490.*—On the first day of the first month of the second year of the exode from Egypt—viz. B. C. 1490—the tabernacle was completed, and "a cloud covered the tent of the congre-

gation, and the glory of the Lord filled the tabernacle." Ex. xl.

152. *Typical Intimations of the Messiah in Exodus.*—In this book the Messiah was typified in—I. AARON: "Seeing then that we have a great High Priest, that is passed into the heavens, Jesus the Son of God" (Heb. iv. 14); II. THE PASCHAL LAMB: "For even Christ our Passover is sacrificed for us" (1 Cor. v. 7); III. MANNA: "And did all eat the same spiritual meat" (1 Cor. x. 3); IV. ROCK IN HOREB: "And did all drink the same spiritual drink: for they drank of that spiritual Rock that followed them: and that Rock was Christ" (1 Cor. x. 4); V. THE MERCY-SEAT: "Whom (Jesus Christ) God hath set forth to be a *propitiation* through faith in his blood." Rom. iii. 25.

LEVITICUS.

(Λευιτικον—*Levitical Priesthood and Sacrifices.*)

HISTORY OF THE LEVITICAL PRIESTHOOD, SACRIFICES, AND ORDINANCES, B. C. 1490.—ABOUT A MONTH—VIZ. FROM THE BUILDING OF THE TABERNACLE TO THE NUMBERING OF THE PEOPLE.*

ANALYSIS.

[*Ceremonial Law*, continued from Exodus.]

2. *Priests, Levites, and Nethinim.*—*Classification.*— I. PRIESTS—their duties and requirements; sacerdotal dress; sources of livelihood.—II. HIGH PRIEST—his office; his typical character; his robes—viz. 1st. The ephod; 2d. The coat or robe of the ephod; 3d. The breastplate of judgment (Urim and Thummim); and 4th. The mitre or crown.—III. THE LEVITES—their duties, livelihood, and consecration.—IV. THE NETHINIM—Consecration of Aaron and his sons. . . . . page 96.

3. *Sacrifices, Oblations, and Meat- and Drink-Offerings.*—*General Classification of Jewish Sacrifices and Offerings.*—1. SACRIFICES OR OFFERINGS OF BLOOD, *four classes of—*

---

* Ex. xl. 2; Num. i. 1.

viz. 1st. Burnt-offerings; 2d. Peace-offerings; 3d. Sin-offerings; 4th. Trespass-offerings; typical character of the sacrifices.—II. OBLATIONS, OR UNBLOODY OFFERINGS, *three classes of*—viz. 1st. Ordinary oblations (shew-bread and incense); 2d. Free oblations (fruits of promises or vows); 3d. Prescribed oblations (first-fruits, firstlings, and tithes).—Meat-offerings.—Drink-offerings.—National sacrifices. . . . . page 100.

4. Annual Feasts and Festivals; Sabbatical Year and Jubilee.—*Classification of Annual Festivals instituted by Moses*—viz. 1. The Feast of Passover, or Unleavened Bread; 2. Feast of Pentecost, or of Weeks, Harvest, or First-fruits; 3. Feast of Tabernacles; 4. Feast of Trumpets; and 5. Feast or Fast of Expiation, or Great Day of Atonement.—[Later Feasts—Purim, Dedication, etc.]—The Sabbatical year.—The Jubilee.—Typical character of the feasts and festivals, and the Jubilee. . . . . page 107.

5. Vows.—Nature of vows.—How far valid.—*Classification:* 1. Vows of dedication; 2. Vows of interdiction and Nazaritism.— The cherem or anathema. . . . . page 113.

6. Purifications.—*Nature and Classification of Purifications.* —Materials for purifying.—1. PURIFICATION AS A RELIGIOUS CEREMONIAL.—II. PURIFICATION FROM PERSONAL UNCLEANNESS.—III. PURIFICATION FROM LEPROSY.—*Classification*—viz. 1. LEPROSY IN MAN: character and symptoms; laws for distinguishing it; purification from it.—2. LEPROSY IN HOUSES.—3. LEPROSY IN CLOTHES. . . . . page 116.

§ Typical intimations in Leviticus. . . . . . page 119.

SUMMARY.

[*Ceremonial Law*, continued from Exodus.]

2. PRIESTS, LEVITES, AND NETHINIM.

153. *Classification.*—The tribe of Levi were exclusively devoted to the service of the temple, under the name of LEVITES, but of these only the males of the family of Aaron were permitted to sacrifice at the altar of burnt-offering, under the name of PRIESTS, and of them the HIGH PRIEST alone was permitted to enter the Holy of Holies or Most Holy Place. In addition to the priests, high priest, and Levites was a class of inferior assistants, including Gibeonites and captives; these were called NETHINIM.

154. *The Priests: their Duties and Requirements.* —The priests were chosen from the family of Aaron exclusively. They served immediately at the altar, prepared the victims, and offered the sacrifices. They also kept up a perpetual fire on the altar of burnt-offerings and in the golden candlestick; prepared, brought, and removed the shew-bread; offered up prayers for the people; judged of leprosy, the causes of divorce, the waters of jealousy, vows, uncleanness, etc.; carried the ark in war, sounded the trumpets, and animated the army; were consulted as interpreters of the law, and publicly blessed the people in the name of the Lord. Every priest was required to establish his descent, and none were permitted to marry a harlot or a profane woman, or one who had been divorced. Bodily defects, blemishes, leprosy, or uncleanness would exclude any priest from sacrificing at the altar or entering the tabernacle, and no one might make his head bald, nor shave off the corner of his beard, nor cut his flesh; nor might he defile himself by mourning for any of his relations, save for his father, mother, son, daughter, brother, or virgin sister. Lev. xxi.; xxii.; Num. iii.

155. *Sacerdotal Dress.* —The priests were not distinguished by sacerdotal habits excepting whilst they were officiating, when they wore linen drawers, tunic, and girdle; also a tiara shaped like the mitre or crown (sect. 163), worn by the high priest, but not so ornamented, and without the golden plate. Ex. xxviii.; Lev. viii.

156. *Sources of their Livelihood.* —Besides the thirteen cities and the tithe which they derived from the Levites (sect. 164), they received the following things, which were to be dedicated to God (sect. 181–183)—viz. 1. The first-fruits of the wheat, oil, and wine. 2. The first fleece of the sheep. 3. The price paid for the redemption of the first-born of men and impure animals. 4. The first-born of sheep, cows, and goats, whose blood and fat were sacrificed on the altar, and the remainder given to them. 5. The right shoulder and breast of peace-offerings. 6. All the sin-offerings, except the fat which covered certain parts of the victim, and which was burnt on the altar, and excepting in the cases of sin-offerings made for a priest himself or for the congregation. 7. The skin or fleece of burnt-offerings. 8. The shoulder, cheeks, and maw of the oxen and sheep killed by the Israelites for their own use. 9. The first-fruits of trees—that is, those of the fourth year. 10. A share in the spoils of war. Lev. vii.; xix.; Num. xviii.; xxxi.; Deut. xviii. 3.*

157. *The High Priest: his Office.*—The high priest was placed over the other priests, and alone could enter the Most Holy Place—once a year, on the day of atonement. He was also the final judge in all controversies, and the chief man in Israel, and in later times presided over the Sanhedrim. He held his office until incapacitated by age or polluted by crime. Lev. xvi.

158. *His Typical Character.*—The high priest was an eminent type of our spiritual High Priest, Jesus Christ: "Seeing then that we have a great High Priest, that is passed into the heavens, Jesus the Son of God," Heb. iv. 14.

159. *His Robes.*—Besides the dress which was common to himself and the inferior priests, he wore four peculiar garments.

160. *1st. The Ephod,* a kind of vest fastened to the shoulders, the hinder part reaching to the heels, whilst the fore part descended only a little below the waist. It was of fine twisted linen, splendidly wrought with gold and purple, and was fastened to the shoulders by two straps of similar material, to which were affixed the *breastplate of judgment.*

161. *2d. The Coat or Robe of the Ephod,* which was made of blue wool bound round with woven work to prevent its rending. Seventy-two golden bells were fastened upon the hem, with an artificial pomegranate of blue, purple, or scarlet between each. Whilst these pomegranates beautified the robe, the sound of the seventy-two bells informed the congregation of the high priest's entrance into the Most Holy Place to burn incense, so that the prayers of the people and the incense from the altar might ascend together as a fragrant odor before God.

---

* The priests afterward became so numerous that King David divided them into twenty-four classes, which were each to serve a week in rotation. 1 Chron. xxiv. After the captivity, only four of these classes returned, but they were again divided into twenty-four, each of which class or course had a chief or head, which are supposed to be the chief priests of the New Testament.

162. 3d. *The Breastplate of Judgment,* or oracle, was a piece of cloth doubled, one span [about 11 inches] square, and of similar workmanship and materials with the *ephod.* On it were set twelve precious stones, containing the engraved names of the twelve sons of Jacob and the words *Urim* and *Thummim.* [The real nature of the Urim and Thummim is unknown; but when the high priest went to ask counsel of Jehovah, he presented himself arrayed in this breastplate and received the divine commands.]

163. 4th. *The Mitre or Crown,* on the front of which was tied, by a blue ribbon, a plate of pure gold, on which was engraven " Holiness unto the Lord." The high priest alone entered the Most Holy Place on the day of atonement. Ex. xxviii.; Lev. xvi.

164. *The Levites, their Duties, Livelihood, and Consecration.*—The Levites were divided into three families, called after the three sons of Levi—viz. GERSHOMITES, KOHATHITES, and MERARITES. Their office was to wait upon the priests, to carry the tabernacle and its furniture from place to place, and to cleanse the sacred vessels, take charge of the sacred loaves, and sing psalms and perform on musical instruments. They were supported by a tenth of the corn, fruit, and cattle belonging to the other eleven tribes, and on their entering Canaan, instead of a portion of the territory, forty-eight cities were assigned them, with the suburbs, extending to three thousand cubits beyond the city wall. The Levites were, however, obliged to give a tenth of this tithe for the support of the priests of the family of Aaron, together with thirteen of their cities. Six of these cities were also made cities of refuge. They were to serve in the tabernacle from their thirtieth to their fiftieth year, though afterward they commenced serving at twenty. 1 Chron. xxiii. 24. They were consecrated by shaving their bodies, washing their clothes, and being sprinkled with water, and then by taking two young bullocks to Aaron, with the necessary appendages, one to be offered as a burnt-offering, and the other as a sin-offering. Num. iii.; iv.; viii.; xviii.

165. *The Nethinim.*—Besides the Levites, there were subsequently an inferior class of persons, who performed the more servile offices of the tabernacle, such as carrying wood and water, and these were called Nethinim. The Gibeonites (sect. 258) were the first of this class of assistants, but it was afterward increased by the addition of captives taken in war. Josh. ix. 21–27; 2 Chron. ii. 17; Ezra viii. 20.

166. *Consecration of Aaron and his Sons.*—Aaron and his family were originally invested with the priesthood. by Moses, who was appointed by Jehovah to officiate at their consecration, and directed to perform the following ceremonies: Moses first washed Aaron and his sons with water, arrayed them in their pontifical vestments, and anointed Aaron with the holy oil; he then offered three sacrifices:

1*st*. *A sin-offering*, as a kind of expiation by which they were to be purified. (See "Sacrifices," sect. 171.)

2*d*. *A burnt-offering*, as a gift or present to recommend them to the Lord.

3*d*. *A peace-offering*, as a sacred feast by which they were introduced into the family of God, for even the offerers were permitted to eat of their own peace-offerings.

After this original consecration of the sons of Aaron no subsequent consecration was required for their descendants and successors in the priesthood. But in the *high priesthood* the case was different, for every fresh high priest after Aaron was anointed and arrayed in the pontifical robes for the same number of days as Aaron himself had been. [After the consumption of the sacred oil made by Moses, which the Jews affirm was never made again, an investment with the pontifical robes was deemed a sufficient consecration.] Ex. xxix.; Lev. viii.

3. SACRIFICES, OBLATIONS, AND MEAT- AND DRINK-OFFERINGS.

167. *Jewish Offerings classified.*—Jewish offerings were of two kinds: I. SACRIFICES, or offerings of blood; II. OBLATIONS, or unbloody offerings. A sacrifice was an entire change or destruction of the thing offered; an oblation was a simple offering or gift.

I. Sacrifices, or *blood-offerings*, were of four classes—viz. 1. Burnt-offerings; 2. Peace-offerings; 3. Sin-offerings; 4. Trespass-offerings.

II. Oblations, or *unbloody offerings,* were of three classes—viz. 1. *Ordinary oblations,* including shew-bread and incense; 2. *Free oblations,* including the fruits of promises or *vows;* 3. *Prescribed oblations,* including first-fruits, firstlings, and tithes.

In addition to these sacrifices and oblations were *meat-offerings* and *drink-offerings,* which were the frequent accompaniment of both bloody and unbloody offerings.

1. *Sacrifices.*

168. ***Selection of Victims.***—Only five species of animals might be sacrificed—viz. bullocks, sheep, goats, turtle-doves, and young pigeons, the two latter to be offered when the circumstances of the offerer would not enable him to furnish either of the three former. The victim was to be *without spot or blemish,* not less than eight days old, and yet not too aged, and it was not to be procured by the price of a dog or by that of whoredom. In sacrificing birds no particular sex was required, but in cattle it depended on the nature of the sacrifice or circumstances of the offerer. The peace-offerings of individuals were both males and females; the sin-offering of an individual was to be a female lamb or kid; but all victims of every class of sacrifice offered for the whole congregation, and all burnt-offerings, sin-offerings, and trespass-offerings for a ruler or high priest, were to be males. Lev. xxii.; Deut. xxiii. 18.

169. ***1st. Burnt-offerings.***—These were freewill-offerings, wholly devoted to God, except the skin, which alone was taken by the priests. The offerer was himself to lead one of either of the above five species of animals to the court of the tabernacle (afterward to the court of the temple), and, laying his hands upon its head, he was to repeat a prayer. If several persons united in offering the victim, they were to lay their hands upon it in succession.* The priest then was to take the animal, cut its

---

* " By this imposition of hands the person presenting the victim acknowledged the sacrifice to be his own; that he loaded it with his iniquities; that he offered it as an atonement for his sins; that he was worthy of death because he had sinned, having forfeited his life by violating the law of God; and that he entreated God to accept the life of the innocent animal in the place of his own."—*Horne.*

throat and windpipe in one stroke, and, receiving the blood in a vessel, he was to sprinkle some of it around the altar and pour out the remainder at the altar's foot. The skin was then stripped from the neck of the victim, its breast opened, the bowels taken out, the backbone cleft, and the whole divided into quarters. The legs and inwards were then washed, and, the various parts having been salted, they were all utterly consumed upon the altar of burnt-offering. If a turtle-dove or pigeon was offered, the priest wrung off its head and sprinkled its blood as above, but plucked away the crop with the feathers, and cast them east of the altar amongst the ashes. He then cleft the bird without dividing it, and salted and burnt it. If the person was too poor to bring a dove or pigeon, he was to bring a mincha, or meat-offering, for which see "Meat-offerings" (sect. 184). The fire used on this altar first came down from heaven, and was never suffered to go out (see sect. 149). Nadab and Abihu, the two elder sons of Aaron by Elisheba, were destroyed by fire from heaven because they presumed to use strange fire. Lev. ix.; x.

170. *2d. Peace-offerings.*—These comprehended thank-offerings, freewill-offerings, and offerings made in consequence of vows, and were made in token of peace and reconciliation between God and man. The common offerings were a calf, lamb, or goat, accompanied by a proper meat-offering. In the case of vows and thank-offerings, the victim was to be without any blemish whatever; but in the case of freewill-offerings, it might be either lacking or superfluous in its parts. The victim being brought, the offerer laid his hand upon its head as an acknowledgment of his guilt, and it was killed before the tabernacle. Its blood was then sprinkled round about the altar: the fat, kidneys, caul, and, if it was a lamb, the rump also, were burnt on it; the breast was then *waved* and the shoulder *heaved*, and both became the property of the priests; and the remainder was eaten by the offerer under THREE RESTRICTIONS: 1st. If the peace-offering was for a thanksgiving, its flesh was to be eaten on the same day that the sacrifice was made, and all that remained on the morrow was to be burnt; but if the peace-offering was for a vow or a voluntary offering,

its flesh might be eaten on the morrow also, and all that remained on the third day was to be burnt. If this law was infringed, the sacrifice was of no effect. 2d. If the flesh touched any unclean thing, it was to be burnt. 3d. The persons who partook of it were not to be unclean from any circumstances, and it was declared that whoever infringed this law would be cut off. The appointed seasons and occasions of the peace-offering were—1. At the consecration of a priest; 2. At the expiration of the Nazarite vow; 3. At the solemn dedication of the tabernacle; 4. At the purification of a leper. Lev. iii.; vii. 11–38.

171. *3d. Sin-offerings.*—These were made for sins committed through ignorance, either by individuals or by the whole congregation, also as a purification from sin or uncleanness, as one was offered at the consecration of Aaron, and others were to be made at the cleansing of a leper and the purification of a woman after childbirth. Sin-offerings were made in four different ways—for a priest, a ruler, a common individual, or for the whole congregation.

172. *Sin-offering for a Priest.*—The priest was to kill a young bullock at the door of the tabernacle, and dip his fingers into the blood and sprinkle it seven times before the veil of the sanctuary. He was then to put some of the blood upon the horns of the altar of sweet incense within the tabernacle, and pour the remainder at the foot of the altar of burnt-offering at the door of the tabernacle. He was then to take all the fat, with the two kidneys and caul, and burn them upon the altar of burnt-offering, but all the remainder of the bullock, skin and all, was to be burnt without the camp.

173. *For the Congregation.*—A young bullock was to be brought as before to the door of the tabernacle, and after the elders of the congregation had placed their hands upon its head, it was to be killed with the same ceremonies, saving that only its fat was to be burnt on the altar. The remainder of the bullock was in this case also to be burnt without the camp.

174. *For a Ruler.*—The offerer was to bring a male kid of the goats and place his hand upon his head. The priest was then to kill it with the same ceremonies, burn

only the fat upon the altar, and receive the remainder for his portion.

175. *For a Common Individual.*—The offerer was to bring a female kid or lamb, which was to be slain with the same ceremonies. The fat only was to be offered, and the priest was to receive the remainder. In the case of purification of a leper or of a woman after childbirth, if the offerer could not bring a lamb, two turtles or young pigeons were to be offered, one for a sin-offering and the other for a burnt-offering. Lev. iv.; vi. 24–30.

176. *4th, Trespass-offerings.*—These were made when the party had committed any trespass unwittingly, and also in the purgation of certain corporeal impurities. It is difficult to define the difference between the two classes of *sins* or *trespasses* for which sin-offerings and trespass-offerings were made. In both sacrifices the offerer placed his hand upon the victim's head and confessed his sin or trespass over it, and neither of them was ever admitted as a voluntary oblation. The sex of the victims and the sacrificial rites were, however, different. The offerings for trespass were to consist of rams or he-lambs, which were never used for sin-offerings, though turtle-doves or pigeons might be brought in both cases. Again, the blood of the sin-offering was to be put upon the horns of the altar, whilst that of the trespass-offering was to be sprinkled on the altar's sides. Sin-offerings were also offered for the whole congregation, whilst the trespass-offering was only required from individuals; and the latter was also accompanied by a restitution for damage, and one-fifth added. Trespass-offerings were made in six cases—viz. 1. For things stolen, unjustly gotten, or detained; 2. For sacrilege; 3. For inadvertent uncleanness; 4. For violating a bondmaid; 5. For a Nazarite; 6. For a leper. Lev. v.; vi. 1–7; vii. 1–10.

177. *Typical Character of the Levitical Sacrifices.*—I. THE BURNT-OFFERING prefigured the full, perfect, and sufficient sacrifice of Christ "to put away sin," and who by his "one offering hath perfected for ever them that are sanctified." Heb. ix. 26; x. 14. II. The PEACE-OFFERING represented Christ's oblation of himself, whereby he became our peace and salvation: "For he is our

peace." Eph. ii. 14. III. THE SIN-OFFERING for *sins of ignorance*, being consumed without the camp, signified Christ's suffering "without the gate, that he might sanctify the people with his own blood." Heb. xiii. 11–13. IV. THE TRESPASS-OFFERING for sins knowingly committed represents Christ, who is said to have "made his soul an offering for sin." Isa. liii. 10.

2. *Oblations.*

178. *1st. Ordinary Oblations: Shew-bread and Incense.*—Ordinary oblations were of two kinds—viz. 1st. SHEW-BREAD, or twelve loaves, according to the twelve tribes, which the priests placed hot every Sabbath morning on the golden table in the sanctuary, at the same time that they removed the stale loaves which had been exposed during the preceding week; and they alone were permitted to eat this stale shew-bread; 2d. INCENSE, consisting of fragrant spices mixed with frankincense and beat small, which was offered every morning and evening on the golden altar of incense within the tabernacle, whilst the people silently prayed without. No similar incense was to be used by the people under pain of death. Ex. xxv. 30; xxx. 34–38.

179. *2d. Free Oblations.*—These were the fruits of promises and vows. Of *vows* there were two kinds—1st. THE VOW OF CONSECRATION, when anything was devoted either for the sacrifice or for the service of the temple, as wood, salt, wine, etc.; 2d. THE VOW OF ENGAGEMENT, when persons engaged to do something that was not in itself unlawful, as not to eat some particular meat or wear some particular habits, or not to cut their hair or drink wine, etc. (See "Vows," sect. 197.)

180. *3d. Prescribed Oblations.*—These were of three kinds: FIRST-FRUITS, FIRSTLINGS, and TITHES.

181. *1. First-fruits.*—All first-fruits were consecrated to God, being made both for the whole nation and for each particular family. The Jews were prohibited from gathering in the harvest before they had offered the omer or new sheaf, which was presented on the day after the great day of unleavened bread; neither were they allowed to bake any bread from the new corn before they

had offered two new loaves on the day of Pentecost. Without this all the corn was unclean. The person presenting the *first-fruits* was to give them to the priest, who was to place them by the side of the altar; and the offerer was then to repeat a prayer of thanksgiving to God for delivering him from Egypt and leading him to the land of milk and honey. The *first-fruits* of corn, wine, oil, and wool afterward belonged to the priests.

182. *2. Firstlings.*—The first-born of all males of both men and animals belonged to God. The firstling of a cow, sheep, or goat was unredeemable and sacrificed, its blood sprinkled and fat burnt upon the altar, and the remainder given to the priests. But the firstling of a man or an unclean animal was to be redeemed by the payment of 5 shekels [2 oz. 5½ dwts. = 11s. 4d.].

183. *3. Tithes.*—The Jews paid tenths or tithes of all they possessed to the Levites every year, except the sabbatical year, and the Levites, again, paid a tenth of the tithe they received to the priests. When the owners had paid this first tithe they gave a second tithe, which was eaten at offering feasts as a sign of rejoicing and gratitude to God. A third tithe was given to the poor, together with a corner of every field, which it was not lawful to reap with the rest, and such ears of corn, grapes, or sheaves as were dropped, scattered, or forgotten. Field-tithes might be redeemed by paying one-fifth more than the estimation of their value, but tithes of cattle could not be redeemed. The payment and valuation of the tithes were left to the people, though the Levites were not prohibited from seeing after them. The payment of the second tithe was merely secured by the declaration which they made every three years before God. If a person had not paid his tithes, and afterward repented, he could atone for his omission by paying an additional fifth with his tithe and making a trespass-offering. Lev. xxvii.; Num. xviii.

184. *Meat-offerings.*—The meat-offerings, or *mincha*, consisted of meal, bread, cakes, ears of corn, or parched grain, prepared with oil and frankincense in different proportions according to the victims or occasions. They were always to be salted, but to be free from leaven or

honey. They always accompanied *burnt-offerings* and *peace-offerings*, excepting when the victims were birds, which were not substituted for quadrupeds, but were never presented as a *sin-offering*, excepting when the offerer was too poor to afford two pigeons or turtle-doves, and as accompanying the sacrifice of a purified leper. Lev. ii.; vi. 14–23; Num. xv.

185. *Drink-offerings.*—These were never used separately, but were an accompaniment to both sacrifices and oblations. They consisted of wine, part of which was poured upon the victim and meat-offering whilst lying on the altar, and the remainder was allotted to the priests. Num. xv.

186. *National Sacrifices.*—These were of four kinds —viz. 1. The *perpetual* or *daily sacrifice*, consisting of one lamb offered as a burnt-offering every morning, and another every evening, at the third and ninth hours, by a small fire, and accompanied by a meat and drink-offering; 2. The *weekly* or *Sabbath-day sacrifice*, which was equal to the daily sacrifice, and offered in addition to it; 3. The *monthly* or *new-moon sacrifice*, at the beginning of each month, consisting of two young bullocks, one ram, and seven lambs of a year old for a burnt-offering, and one kid for a sin-offering, all of which were to be accompanied by suitable meat- and drink-offerings; 4. The yearly sacrifices on the great annual festivals—viz. 1st. *The Passover;* 2d. *Tabernacles;* 3d. *Pentecost;* 4th. The new moon or beginning of the civil year, called the feast of *trumpets;* 5th. The *day of expiation* or *atonement.* Num. xxviii.

4. ANNUAL FEASTS AND FESTIVALS, SABBATICAL YEARS, JUBILEE, ETC.

187. *Classification.*—Moses instituted five annual festivals—viz. those of *Passover, Pentecost, tabernacles, trumpets,* and *expiation.* At the three first all the males of the twelve tribes were bound to be present, and were promised that when residing in Canaan *no man should desire their land* whilst they were absent at Jerusalem; and on these occasions no Israelite was to appear before the Lord without some offering. The last two festivals

were celebrated with great solemnity, though the presence of every male Israelite was not absolutely required.

188. *First Feast, Passover, or Unleavened Bread.* This feast was first instituted on the night before the exode of the Israelites from Egypt, and was ordered to be kept as a perpetual memorial of their deliverance. (Sect. 97.) It lasted for seven days, commencing on the fourteenth day of the first month, Nisan or Abib, when the paschal lamb was slain, and continuing until the twenty-first day, during which unleavened bread only was eaten, in remembrance of the bread which the Israelites were obliged to carry from Egypt in the hurry of their departure. All Israelites were compelled to keep the feast under pain of death; but if any were unclean or on a journey, they might postpone its celebration until the fourteenth day of the second or ensuing month. The paschal lamb was to be a male without blemish, and to be taken from the sheep or goats four days before the feast; it was to be roasted whole, eaten with unleavened bread and bitter herbs, no bones to be broken, and all that remained in the morning was to be burnt. One lamb was to be killed for every family, but two or three families might join together; and they were to eat it standing, with their loins girded, their sandals on their feet, and their staves in their hands. Ex. xii.; Lev. xxiii. 4–8.

189. *Second Feast, Pentecost, or Weeks, Harvest, or First-fruits.*—This feast was called—1st. The feast of WEEKS, because it was celebrated seven weeks, or a week of weeks, after the first day of unleavened bread; 2d. The feast of HARVEST and the day of FIRST-FRUITS, because on this day the Jews presented the first-fruits of the wheat-harvest in two loaves baked of the new corn; and 3d. The feast of PENTECOST ($\Pi\varepsilon\nu\tau\eta\varkappa\omicron\sigma\tau\eta$), because it was kept on the fiftieth day after the first day of the feast of unleavened bread. Its object was also to commemorate the promulgation of the law on Mount Sinai, and it lasted seven days. Wheaten loaves and first-fruits were presented; seven lambs of the first year, one young bullock, and two rams were sacrificed as burnt-offerings, accompanied with meat- and drink-offerings; one kid of the goats was offered as a sin-offering, and two lambs of the first year were offered for a peace-offering. Lev. xxiii.

15-21. [It was at this feast that the Holy Ghost descended on the apostles in the shape of cloven tongues. Acts ii. Christians keep it on Whitsunday, fifty days after Easter.]

190. *Third Feast, Tabernacles.*—This feast, the last of the three great festivals, lasted also for a week, and was instituted to commemorate the dwelling of the Israelites in tents in the wilderness. During the whole festival the people dwelt in tents or tabernacles made of boughs and branches, and carried in their hands branches of palm trees, olives, citrons, myrtles, and willows. On the first day, which was accounted a Sabbath, thirteen bullocks, two rams, and fourteen lambs were sacrificed as a burnt-offering, with their accompanying meat- and drink-offerings, and one kid was offered as a sin-offering. For the six succeeding days these sacrifices were regularly decreased one bullock daily, and on the eighth day, which was accounted a Sabbath, there were only one bullock, one ram, seven lambs, and one kid offered as burnt- and peace-offerings, together with their meat- and drink-offerings. Lev. xxiii.; Num. xix. 33-44.

191. *Fourth Feast, Trumpets.*—This feast was held on the first and second days of the month Tizri, and formed the commencement of the CIVIL YEAR, in the same way that the Passover commenced the SACRED YEAR. During this festival no labors were performed, a religious convocation of all the people was held, and trumpets were continually blown. The extra burnt-offering consisted of one young bullock, one ram, and seven lambs, with their meat- and drink-offerings, and one kid of the goats was offered for a peace-offering. Lev. xxiii. 23-25; Num. xxix. 1-6.

192. *Fifth Feast, or Fast of Expiation, or Day of Atonement.*—This was celebrated on the tenth day of Tizri, and was observed as a strict fast, the people abstaining from all servile work, taking no food, and afflicting their souls. The sacrifices on this day were the most solemn and important of all that were ordained in the Mosaic ritual. On this day only was the high priest alone permitted to enter the sanctuary, and not even then without preparation, under pain of death. Having washed himself in water and put on his holy

linen garments and mitre, the high priest performed the following ceremonies:

1. *Offerings for Himself, Household, Priests, and Levites.*—He was to go into the outer sanctuary and present to the Lord a ram for a burnt-offering, and a young bullock as a sin-offering for himself, his household, and the priests and Levites.

2. *For the Congregation.*—He was to present two young goats at the door of the tabernacle, to be a sin-offering for the whole congregation, together with one ram for a burnt-offering.

3. *Casts Lots for the Scapegoat.*—He was to cast lots upon the two goats, to see which was to be sacrificed for a sin-offering to the Lord, and which was to be let go for a SCAPEGOAT into the wilderness.

4. *Sprinkles Blood on the Mercy-seat.*—He was to sacrifice the bullock as a sin-offering for himself and household, etc., and to take some of the blood into the inner sanctuary, bearing in his hand a censer of burning incense kindled at the sacred fire on the altar, and to sprinkle the blood seven times with his finger upon and before the mercy-seat, to purify it from the pollution it might be supposed to have contracted from his sins and transgressions during the preceding year.

5. *Sacrifices one Goat.*—He was to sacrifice the allotted goat for the sins of the whole nation, and to enter the inner sanctuary a second time and sprinkle it with the blood as before, to purify it from the pollution of the people's sins and transgressions of the preceding year; after which he was also to purify the tabernacle and altar in the same manner.

6. *Ceremonies with the Scapegoat.*—He was to bring the live goat, lay both his hands upon its head, and confess over it all the sins, iniquities, and transgressions of the children of Israel; and after thus transferring them to the animal, he was to send it away by the hand of a fit person into the wilderness, to bear away all their iniquities into an unpeopled land, where they should be remembered no more.

7. *Concluding Ceremonies.*—He was to put off his linen garments and leave them in the sanctuary, and wash himself again in water, and put on his usual raiment, and

then to offer burnt-offerings for himself and people at the evening sacrifice. After the fat of the bullock and goat sacrificed for sin-offerings had been burnt upon the altar, the remainder of their carcass, skin, etc. was to be burnt without the camp, and the burner was afterward to wash his clothes and bathe in water. The person who let the scapegoat go in the wilderness was likewise to wash his clothes and bathe. Lev. xvi.; xxiii. 26–32; Num. xxix. (See sect. 196.)

193. [*Later Feasts—Purim, Dedication, etc.*—Besides the above annual festivals, the Jews introduced in later times several fasts and feasts in addition to those instituted by Moses. The two principal festivals of this kind were—

I. THE FEAST OF PURIM, when all the people assembled to curse Haman. Esth.

II. THE FEAST OF DEDICATION, which was instituted by Judas Maccabæus, in imitation of those by Solomon and Ezra, as a grateful memorial of the cleansing of the second temple and altar, after they had been profaned by Antiochus Epiphanes. 1 Macc. iv. 52–59.

Besides these two festivals, several fasts were instituted on various occasions, particularly to commemorate the disastrous events which preceded or followed the Babylonian captivity.]

194. *The Sabbatical Year.*—Whilst every seventh day was consecrated as a day of rest for man and beast, every seventh year was set apart as a year of rest for the land. During that year the earth was to lie entirely fallow, and its spontaneous produce was to be enjoyed by the servants, strangers, and cattle. All Hebrew debtors and Hebrew servants were also to be released from their debts or service. If the latter chose to remain with his master, he must have his ears bored. Deut. xv. In order to prevent famine in this and the ensuing year, triple produce was promised on the sixth or preceding year. Lev. xxv.

195. *The Jubilee.*—This was a more solemn sabbatical year, held every fiftieth year or every seventh sabbatical year. On the tenth day of Tizri, being the great day of atonement, the trumpets were to be sounded throughout the land, all debts to be cancelled, and all slaves and cap-

tives, even those who had their ears bored, to be set at liberty. All estates which had been sold were now to revert to their original proprietors, or to the families to which they had originally belonged. The value and purchase-money of estates were thus diminished as the year of jubilee approached. Houses in walled towns were excepted from this rule; these were to be redeemed within a year, or otherwise belonged to the purchaser, notwithstanding the jubilee. During this year the land was uncultivated, as in the sabbatical year. Lev. xxv.

196. *Typical Intimations of the Messiah to be found in the Fasts and Festivals.*—The three great feasts may be considered to be typical of the principal events in the life of Christ. I. THE PASSOVER prefigured his death and passion, and is the analogue of the Christian institution of the Eucharist. II. THE PENTECOST commemorates the first-fruits of his Spirit, which subsequently descended at the commemoration of the festival. III. THE FEAST OF TABERNACLES prefigures his birth and incarnation, when "the Word was made flesh and dwelt [*tabernacled*] among us." John i. 14.

The solemn day of expiation was, however, the most strikingly typical of Christ's ministry and atonement, and in the following ways:

1. Our Lord, the High Priest of our profession, commenced his ministry by baptism "to fulfil all legal righteousness." Matt. iii. 13–15.

2. He was led by the Holy Spirit into the wilderness as the true scapegoat, who "bore away our infirmities, and carried off our diseases." Matt. viii. 17.

3. Before his crucifixion "he was *afflicted*," and "his soul *was* exceedingly *sorrowful unto death*" when he was to be made a sin-offering like the allotted goat. Matt. xxvi. 38; 2 Cor. v. 21; Heb. i. 3.

4. "His sweat, as great drops of blood falling to the ground," corresponded to the sprinkling of the mercy-seat. Luke xxii. 44.

5. To prepare for his own sacrifice, he consecrated himself in prayer to God, and then prayed for his household —apostles and disciples—and for all future believers. Matt. xxvi. 39–46; John xvii. 1–9, 20–26.

6. He put off his garments at his crucifixion, when he

became the sin-offering (John xix. 23, 24), and, as our spiritual High Priest, entered into the most holy place, heaven, to make intercession with God for all his faithful followers. Heb. vii. 24–28; ix. 7–15. "Who was delivered for our offences, and was raised again for our justification." Rom. iv. 25.

The jubilee year had also a typical design and use, which is thus pointed out by Isaiah: "The Spirit of the Lord God is upon me, because the Lord hath anointed me to preach good tidings unto the meek; he hath sent me to bind up the broken-hearted, to proclaim liberty to the captives, and the opening of the prison to them that are bound; to *proclaim the acceptable year* of THE LORD." Isa. lxi. 1, 2. The acceptable year of the Lord, when liberty was proclaimed to the captives and the opening of the prison to them that were bound, evidently refers to the jubilee, but in the prophetic sense means the gospel state and dispensation, which proclaim spiritual liberty from the bondage of sin and Satan and the liberty of returning to our own possession, even the heavenly inheritance, to which, having incurred a forfeiture by sin, we had lost all right and claim.

5. Vows.

197. *Nature of Vows.*—Vows were religious engagements or promises voluntarily undertaken by a person toward the Almighty. Though the Israelites were not counselled or encouraged to make them, yet Jehovah himself had declared his acceptance of them, and they were therefore binding not only in a moral view, but according to the national law, and the priest was authorized to enforce and estimate their fulfilment.

198. *How far Valid.*—To render a vow valid three things were required by Moses: 1st. That it should be actually uttered with the lips, and not merely made in the heart; 2d. That the party making it should be independent of the authority of others and competent to undertake the obligation: thus the vows of minors, unmarried daughters under the parental roof, wives, slaves, etc., were all invalid unless ratified by the express or tacit consent of their fathers, husbands, or masters; 3d. That the things

vowed should not be the hire of a prostitute or price of a dog. Lev. xxvii.; Num. xxx.; Deut. xxiii. 18.

199. *Classification*.—Common vows were of two kinds: I. VOWS OF DEDICATION; II. VOWS OF SELF-INTERDICTION AND NAZARITISM. Besides these was the CHEREM, a solemn kind of anathema, which was accompanied by a form of execration, and could not be redeemed.

200. *I. Vows of Dedication*.—These were undertaken when a person engaged to bring an offering to God or to dedicate anything to him. There were four kinds of things vowed in this way—viz.:

1st. UNCLEAN BEASTS. As these could not be offered to God, they were to be redeemed by the vowers, who paid one-fifth more than the value as estimated by the priest.

2d. CLEAN BEASTS FOR OFFERINGS. These could not be redeemed nor exchanged for others, under penalty of both being forfeited to the Lord. No firstlings could be vowed, because they were already devoted to God. (See "Firstlings," sect. 182.)

3d. HOUSES AND LANDS.—*Houses* might be redeemed by paying one-fifth more than the value, as estimated by the priest. *Land* might be redeemed in the same manner, but was to be estimated according to the seed it would require (fifty shekels [$22\frac{3}{4}$ oz. = £5 13*s*. 10*d*.] to each homer [7 bushels 3 pecks $1\frac{3}{4}$ pints] of barley-seed), and also according to the years that remained before the year of jubilee, when, of course, it would revert to its hereditary owner. If, however, the person who vowed or sanctified the land would not redeem it, and the priest, upon his refusal, should sell it to another man, then the land would not revert to its original possessor at the jubilee, but would remain holy unto the Lord, and its possession would revert to the priests.

4th. A VOWER DEDICATING HIMSELF.—In these cases the vower was always to redeem himself according to the following scale:

	Shekels.	£	s.	d.
MALES, from 1 month to 5 years old	5 =		11	4
FEMALES, " " "	3 =		6	9
MALES, from 5 years to 20 years old	20 =	2	5	6
FEMALES, " " "	10 =	1	2	9

	Shekels.	£	s.	d.
MALES, from 20 years to 60 years old	50 =	5	13	10
FEMALES, " " "	30 =	3	8	3
MALES, from sixty years old and upward	15 =	1	14	1
FEMALES, " " "	10 =	1	2	9

If the person who vowed himself was very poor, the priest might estimate him at a still lower value. Lev. xxvii.

201. *II. Vows of Self-interdiction and Nazaritism.*—These consisted in a person's engaging to abstain from wine, food, or any other thing. The most important of these vows were those appertaining to Nazaritism. Of Nazarites there were two classes: 1st. Those who were Nazarites by birth (as Samson and John the Baptist); 2d. Those who were Nazarites by engagement and for a limited time. All Nazarites were required—1. To drink no wine or strong drink of any kind; 2. To eat no grapes or anything belonging to the vine; 3. To let their hair grow; 4. Not to defile themselves by touching the dead or mourning for their relations. If any one died in the presence of a Nazarite of the second class, the latter was compelled to shave his head, make the usual offerings, and recommence his Nazariteship. At the expiration of the vow the Nazarite was to offer at the door of the tabernacle one male lamb of the first year for a burnt-offering, one ewe-lamb of the first year for a sin-offering, and one ram for a peace-offering, together with a basket of unleavened bread and meat- and drink-offerings. He was also to shave his head and place the hair on the fire underneath the peace-offering, and the priest was to take the sodden shoulder of the ram, one unleavened cake, and one unleavened wafer, and, placing them in the hands of the Nazarite, he was to wave them for a wave-offering. After this the Nazarite might drink wine.* Num. vi.

202. *The Cherem or Anathema.*—This was a solemn

---

* The *Rechabites* are not to be confounded with the Nazarites. The former were the descendants of Jehonadab, the son of Rechab, and became famous for implicitly following these directions of their father—viz. 1. To drink no wine; 2. To possess no houses, fields, or vineyards; 3. To dwell in tents. In consequence of their obedience, God promised that the posterity of Jehonadab should never cease. They appear to have gained their living by being scribes. Jer. xxxv.; 1 Chron. ii. 55.

kind of excommunication, which was accompanied by a form of execration and could not be redeemed. The species of CHEREM with which we are best acquainted was the imprecation pronounced upon hostile cities, when the inhabitants were to be put to death, the cattle slain, the houses and treasures utterly burnt and destroyed, and a curse pronounced upon any who should attempt to rebuild it. A CHEREM was thus pronounced against Jericho and the king of Arad, and against any Israelite city which should introduce or practise idolatry. (See "First Commandment," and Num. xxi. 1–3; Josh. xii. 14.)

6. PURIFICATIONS.

203. *Nature and Classification of Purifications.*— Jewish purifications were of three kinds: 1st. PURIFICATION AS A RELIGIOUS CEREMONIAL, which was necessary for all persons and things engaged in divine worship; 2d. PURIFICATION FROM PERSONAL UNCLEANNESS; 3d. PURIFICATION FROM LEPROSY.

204. *Materials for Purifying.*—Purifications were performed with three different materials: 1. By the sprinkling of blood; 2. By the anointing with oil; 3. By the water of purification, which was drawn from a spring or running stream, and was either pure, or mixed with blood or with the ashes of a red heifer. The last case alone requires description. The people were to bring a red heifer without blemish, and which had never borne a yoke, to the high priest, who was then to take it without the camp, kill it before the people, sprinkle its blood seven times before the gate of the tabernacle, and then to burn the whole (including the flesh, hide, blood, and excrements), casting into the fire a bundle of cedar-wood, some hyssop, and double-dyed scarlet. The ashes were then carefully collected and put in a clean place, and both the high priest and the men who burnt the heifer and gathered together its ashes were to wash their clothes, bathe their flesh, and be unclean until the evening. Num. xix.

205. *1st. Purification as a Religious Ceremonial.* —All persons and things dedicated to divine worship were to undergo purification. The Levites, priests, and high priest all underwent a purification previous to their consecration. The Israelites washed their flesh and clothes previous to receiving the law; and after its promulgation and the people had declared their assent to the book of the Covenant, Moses sprinkled them with blood. The tabernacle and all its sacred vessels were also anointed with oil. Those about to offer sacrifices or prayers were also lustrated, and especially the priests and high priest before executing their respective offices. Lastly, all who were adjudged by the Mosaic law to be impure or unclean required to be purified before they could be admitted into the congregation of the Lord. Num. xix.; Lev. viii.

206. *2d. Purification from Personal Uncleanness.*—If an unclean person did not purify himself, he was to be cut off from the congregation. There were six species of uncleanness—viz. I. Dead bodies; II. Gonorrhœa, or seed-flux; III. Emisso seminis; IV. Childbirth; V. Menses and issues of blood; VI. Leprosy. If a clean person touched an unclean one, he contracted a similar uncleanness, and both were excluded from the tabernacle until their purification was completed.* Lev. xi.; xii.; xv.; Num. xix.

207. *3d. Purification from Leprosy.*—As this fearful disease was contagious, and hereditary to the third and fourth generations, the separation of lepers from the camp and congregation, and the destruction of infected houses and clothes, were of the utmost importance to the preservation of public health. Moses thus acted respecting leprosy: I. He ordered every man attacked by a cutaneous disorder to show himself to the priest. II. He authorized the priests to examine the disease wherever it appeared. III. He gave the priests ample directions for distinguishing between leprosy and a harmless spot or scab, for deciding upon its progress or cure in man, and for eradicating the infection from walls and garments. IV. He prescribed the days that must expire, and the sacrifices and ceremonies to be performed, before the leper could be finally purified and restored to civil society and the participation in things holy. Lev. xiii.

---

* For a further account of purifications, etc., see Michaelis.

208. *Classification.*—LEPROSY was of three kinds—1st. LEPROSY IN MAN; 2d. LEPROSY IN HOUSES; 3d. LEPROSY IN CLOTHES—for each of which a purification was required. Lev. xiii.

209. *1st. Leprosy in Man: Character and Symptoms.*—This disease was of two species—viz. I. CONTAGIOUS LEPROSY, which rendered a person *unclean*, and was called *tsorat*, signifying "venom" or "malignity;" II. UNCONTAGIOUS LEPROSY, under which a person was still *clean*, and which was called *bohak*, or "dull white." Both *tsorat* and *bohak* were also called *berat*, signifying "bright spot," but *bohak* imported brightness in a subordinate degree.

210. *Laws for distinguishing Leprosy.*—When a person was attacked by either of the foregoing affections, he was immediately taken to the priest; and if the priest saw the bright-white scarlet surface depressed in the middle and the white patches, he immediately declared the person to be leprous and unclean, and sent him without the camp. If the priest had any doubt, he put the person under domestic confinement for seven days, and then examined him a second time, when, if it had spread, etc., he was declared leprous and unclean; if it had subsided, he was discharged; but if it was stationary, he was confined another seven days, after which the nature of the disease always exhibited itself. If leprosy spread over the entire frame without producing ulceration, it lost its contagious power or exhausted itself, and the patient was declared clean by the priest whilst the dry scales were yet upon him. Lev. xiii. 12, 13. If, on the contrary, the patches should ulcerate, and quick or fungous flesh spring up in them, the priest was at once to pronounce the case to be an inveterate leprosy, for which a temporary confinement was unnecessary; and the leper was unclean for life. Lev. xiii.

211. *Purification from Leprosy.*—When the priest was satisfied that the leper was healed, he was to take two birds, and kill one of them over an earthen vessel filled with river water, so that the blood might mingle with the water. He was then to dip the other bird into the blood and water and sprinkle the leper with it seven times with a stick of cedar upon which a bunch of hyssop was tied

with a scarlet thread; after which, he was to pronounce the leper clean and to let loose the living bird. The leper was then to wash and stay without the camp seven days, and on the seventh day to shave off all his hair and bathe. On the eighth day he was to take to the priest two male lambs and one ewe-lamb of the first year for a trespass-offering, sin-offering, and burnt-offering, together with a meat-offering, and one log [nearly two-thirds of a pint] of oil. If the leper was poor, he might take two turtle-doves for the sin-offering and burnt-offering. In offering the trespass-offering the priest was to sprinkle the blood upon the leper's right ear, thumb, and great toe. He was then to do the same with the oil after sprinkling it seven times before the Lord; and upon the completion of the sacrifices the leper was to be considered purified. Lev. xiv.

212. *2d. Leprosy in Houses.*—This exhibited itself in green or red spots on the walls, continually spreading, which the priest was to examine, and then order the house to be shut up for seven days. If after this the leprosy had not spread, the house was shut up for seven days more. If it was then dim or gone away, the part of the wall was to be taken away to an unclean place, and the house mended, scraped, and replastered. It was then shut up for another seven days; and if after this the plague broke out upon it anew, it was to be pulled down and carried away to an unclean place; but if it was pronounced clean, two birds were offered, as in the case of human leprosy. Lev. xiv.

213. *Third. Leprosy in Clothes.*—This also exhibited itself in green or reddish spots, which remained in spite of washing, and continued to spread. Suspected garments were to be examined by the priest; if he found them corroded, he burnt them; but if the spots were taken out by washing he pronounced them clean. Lev. xiii.

---

214. *Typical Intimations in Leviticus.*—(See sect. 169, *note,* and sects. 177, 196.) The Epistle to the Hebrews should be carefully read in connection with Leviticus, of which it forms an important illustration.

NUMBERS.

(*Numbering and Marshalling of the Israelites.*)

HISTORY OF THE ISRAELITES FROM THE DELIVERING OF THE LAW AT SINAI TO THE CONQUEST OF THE COUNTRY EAST OF THE JORDAN. B. C. 1490 TO 1451.—ABOUT 38 YEARS AND 9 OR 10 MONTHS.

ANALYSIS.
I. *Wanderings in the Wilderness.*

Review of the chronology.—Numbering of the people, and march from Sinai to Zin, 1490.—March to Taberah; murmurings at fatigue.—March to Kibroth-hattaavah; murmuring for flesh; quails and plague sent.—Council of LXX. appointed.—Sedition of Aaron and Miriam at Hazeroth.—ENCAMPMENT AT KADESH; spies sent to Canaan.—Ten spies destroyed; forty years' wanderings declared; Israelites defeated.—History of thirty-eight years' wanderings, 1490-1451.—Rebellion of Korah, Dathan, and Abiram, 1471.—Congregation murmur; 14,700 slain by a plague; blossoming of Aaron's rod, 1471.—Return to Kadesh; water from Meribah; Moses and Aaron sin, 1453 . . . . page 120.

II. *Conquest of the Country east of the Jordan.*

Israelites refused a passage through Edom; Aaron dies at Hor, 1452.—Defeat of the Canaanites at Hormah.—March from Hor to the Arnon; fiery serpents, and miracle of the brazen serpent.—Defeat of Sihon and Og, 1452.—Balak fails to persuade Balaam to curse Israel.—Israelites commit idolatry; Zimri and Cozbi slain by Phinehas.—Midianites defeated; Balaam slain.—Second mustering, 1451.—Census of 1491 and 1451 compared. Reuben, Gad, and half Manasseh's territory east of the Jordan, 1451.—Six cities of refuge; conclusion of Numbers.—Book of the Wars of the Lord.—Typical and prophetical intimations of the Messiah in Numbers.—Names, and meanings of the names of the principal persons mentioned in Exodus and Numbers . . . . page 124.

SUMMARY.
I. *Wanderings in the Wilderness.*

215. *Review of the Chronology.*—On the fourteenth day of the first month of the year, B. C. 1491, the Israelites kept the Passover and marched from Egypt. Ex. xii.

2, 3, 6, 18, 29–37. On the first day of the third month of the same year [B. C. 1491] they encamped at Sinai. Ex. xix. 1. On the first day of the first month of the next year [B. C. 1490] the tabernacle was completed. Ex. xl. 2, 17. On the first day of the second month of the same year [B. C. 1490] the numbering of the people commenced. Num. i. 1–4. And on the twentieth day of the second month of the same year [B. C. 1490] the Israelites marched from Sinai. Num. x. 11. The Israelites were therefore two months marching from Egypt to Sinai; and the whole encampment at Sinai lasted eleven months and nineteen days, during which the laws, tabernacle, and order of divine service were established, and the people numbered and mustered for the approaching war.

216. *Numbering of the People, and March from Sinai to Paran or Zin, 1490.*—Moses now, at the command of Jehovah, numbered the twelve tribes and marshalled them into a regular camp, each tribe by itself under its own captain or chief, and distinguished by its own peculiar standard; upon which the cloud left the tabernacle and rested in the wilderness of Paran. Two silver trumpets were also made according to God's direction—one to summon the princes, and the two to call together the camp and to be sounded at the national sacrifices. After this the whole twelve tribes marched forward through the desert of Zin or Paran in prescribed order, Moses taking with him his brother-in-law, Hobab, to mark out the ground for the several encampments. Num. i.; ii.; x.

217. *March to Taberah; Murmurings at Fatigue.*—Three days' journey from Sinai the people complained, and many were destroyed by fire from heaven, which was only quenched by the prayers of Moses, who called the place "TABERAH," "a burning." Num. xi. 1–3.

218. *March to Kibroth-hattaavah; Murmuring for Flesh; Quails and Plague sent.*—After the Israelites had left Taberah they wearied of manna and murmured for flesh. A wind from the sea then brought up abundance of quails, which the people rebelliously brought to the camp; but whilst the flesh was between their teeth a plague from Jehovah carried off the ringleaders, and

Moses called the place "KIBROTH-HATTAAVAH" ("the graves of lust"). Num. xi. 4–15, 18–23, 31–35.

219. *Council of LXX. appointed.*—Moses now found so much difficulty in governing the people that, at God's command, he appointed seventy elders to share the burden. These are supposed to have been the origin of the great national council of the Jews, called afterward the *Sanhedrim.* (See sect. 138.) Num. xi. 16, 17, 24–30.

220. *Sedition of Aaron and Miriam at Hazeroth.* —From Kibroth-hattaavah the Israelites journeyed to Hazeroth, where Aaron and Miriam murmured at Moses because of his marriage with an Ethiopian or Cushite woman, who is supposed by some to have meant Zipporah. The anger of Jehovah was kindled; he came down in the pillar of cloud and called Aaron and Miriam to the door of the tabernacle, and, having reproached them for their rebellious envy, he struck Miriam with a leprosy. Aaron entreated pardon of Moses, who then besought God to heal his sister, and she was healed after seven days. Num. xii.

221. *Encampment at Kadesh-barnea; Spies sent to Canaan.*—The Israelites had now advanced by short marches through the mountains into the great sand desert of Zin or Paran, as far as Kadesh-barnea. Here Moses sent twelve men to spy out Canaan, who returned after forty days' absence with favorable specimens of the grapes, pomegranates, figs, and other fruits of the Promised Land, but with such fearful accounts of the stature and strong positions of the inhabitants that they terrified a generation whose spirit had been broken by Egyptian slavery. Num. xiii.

222. *Ten Spies destroyed; Forty Years' Wanderings declared; Israelites defeated.*—Ten spies out of the twelve had thus reported unfavorably of the enemy; and in spite of the remonstrances of the other two, Caleb and Joshua, a most dangerous insurrection broke out. In vain these two faithful men represented that, with the assistance of Jehovah, the conquest would be easy; the people threatened to stone them, and prepared to return to Egypt. Then followed the awful sentence of God— that all the Hebrews who had been more than twenty years old on the exode from Egypt, except Joshua and

Caleb, should die in the desert and Canaan be conquered by the next generation; and the ten spies who had incited them to rebel were carried off by a plague. The Israelites were now sensible of their folly, and perversely advanced upon the Promised Land; but being repulsed by the Canaanites and Amalekites on the southern border of Palestine with great slaughter, they turned back, and spent nearly thirty-eight years in wandering about Mount Seir. Num. xiv.

223. *History of Thirty-eight Years' Wandering, 1490-1453; Rebellion of Korah, Dathan, and Abiram, 1471.*—The events of this period are but briefly recorded; some more laws were promulgated (see "LEVITICUS"), and in B. C. 1471 the rebellion of Korah, Dathan, and Abiram broke out, Korah aspiring to the priesthood, and Dathan and Abiram to the leadership of the people. It appears that Korah was a Levite, and one of the chiefs of the family of Kohath, the second son of Levi, who were especially employed in carrying the ark and Holy of Holies, and therefore the most nearly related to Aaron and next to his family in the sacred character of their functions. Num. iii. 27–31. Korah therefore rebelled, under the pretence that all the congregation were as holy as Aaron and his family, and had as much right to the priesthood. On the other hand, Dathan and Abiram were descended from Reuben, the first-born of Jacob, and therefore considered that their birth entitled them to greater pre-eminence in temporal matters than Moses, who was the great-grandson of Levi, the third son of Jacob. Moses now desired Korah and his party of two hundred and fifty men to assemble with censers and see whom the Lord chose to come near him, and then he desired the whole congregation to separate themselves from the tents and families of the three conspirators and their followers. At the command of Jehovah the earth then opened and swallowed up the families, tents, and goods appertaining to the rebels, whilst a fire consumed the two hundred and fifty men who presumed to offer incense, and the censers of the latter were collected and made into broad plates for a covering for the altar. Num. xvi. 1–40. St. Jude compares the doctrines of false teachers to this rebellion. Jude 11.

224. *Congregation Murmur; 14,700 slain by a Plague; Blossoming of Aaron's Rod, 1471.* —The next day the congregation murmured at this destruction of the rebels, and Jehovah sent a plague which carried off 14,700 of the murmurers. At the direction of God, the prince of each tribe then wrote his name on a rod, Aaron writing his name on the rod for the tribe of Levi. The twelve rods were then laid up in the tabernacle for one night, that it might be distinctly seen by all whom it was that the Lord had chosen as high priest. The next morning the rod of Aaron had blossomed, budded, and yielded almonds, and was ever afterward preserved in the ark as a testimony against the rebels. Num. xvi. 41–50; xvii.

225. *Return to Kadesh; Water from Meribah; Moses and Aaron sin, 1453.* —In the first month of this year the Israelites again returned to Kadesh, in the wilderness of Zin, where Miriam died and was buried. The congregation murmured for water, and Moses, having been directed by God to *speak* to the rock at Meribah, *struck* it twice with Aaron's rod and brought forth abundance of water. Before *striking* the rock Moses and Aaron said to the congregation, "Hear now, ye rebels; must we fetch you water out of this rock?" For this speech, in which they did not give the honor of the miracle to God, and for *striking* the rock instead of *speaking* to it, Jehovah punished them by refusing them the privilege of leading the Israelites into Canaan. Num. xx. 1–13.

II. *Conquest of the Country east of the Jordan.*

226. *Israelites refused a Passage through Edom; Aaron dies at Hor, 1452.* —The Israelites had been forbidden to molest either the Moabites or Edomites; accordingly, Moses sent messengers from Kadesh to entreat the Edomites to grant the Hebrews a free passage through their country to Southern Canaan. The descendants of Esau refused this request, and the children of Israel were accordingly compelled to take a circuitous route round the frontiers of Edom. From Kadesh the Hebrews marched to Mount Hor, in Moab, where it was intimated by Jehovah that Aaron should be gathered unto his people. Accordingly, Moses and Aaron and Aaron's son, Eleazar, ascended the mount, and, Moses having stripped the sacerdotal garments from Aaron and put them upon Eleazar, the old high priest died on the summit of the mount, and all Israel mourned for him thirty days. Num. xx. 14–21, 29.

227. *Defeat of the Canaanites at Hormah.*—The Israelites now attacked Arad, king of a Canaanite nation on the southern border of Palestine, who with the Amalekites had defeated them after the return of the twelve spies (sect. 222). On this occasion Israel utterly destroyed the Canaanite cities, and the place was called HORMAH ("utter destruction)." Num. xxi. 1–3.

228. *March from Hor to the Arnon; Fiery Serpents.*—The Israelites, having passed along the frontier of Edom, crossed the river Zared, and proceeded northerly through the Moabite territory to the river Arnon. On their way they again murmured at their fatigues and deprivations, and a plague of fiery serpents destroyed several; but at length they confessed their sin, and Moses, having interceded for them, was ordered to set up a brazen serpent, which healed all who looked upon it. Num. xxi. 4–9. These fiery serpents might have reminded the Israelites of the old serpent who brought sin into the world, whilst the brazen serpent was the type of the Messiah: "And as Moses lifted up the serpent in the wilderness, even so must the Son of man be lifted up." John iii. 14. This serpent was preserved to the time of Hezekiah, who broke it in pieces because the Israelites burnt incense before it. 2 Kings xviii. 4.

229. *Defeat of Sihon and Og, 1452.*—Upon reaching the river Arnon, Moses requested a free passage from Sihon, king of the Amorites, who refused and marched against the Israelites, but was utterly defeated. Og, king of Bashan, the last of the giants,* whose iron bedstead was nine cubits [16 feet 4 inches] long and four cubits [7 feet 3 inches] broad, followed the example of Sihon,

---

* One of the old race of Rephaim, who abode here in the time of Abraham, and were subjected by the Assyrian forces under Chedorlaomer.

and was also completely routed at Edrei. By these two victories the whole country east of the Jordan—from the river Arnon, which falls into the Dead Sea, to Mount Hermon, at the foot of the chain of Anti-Lebanon—fell into the hands of the Hebrews. Num. xxi. 10-35.

230. *Balak fails to persuade Balaam to curse Israel.*—The Moabites and Ammonites saw the defeat of their old enemies the Amorites with pleasure, but, being ignorant that the Israelites were forbidden to attack themselves, they regarded their new and powerful neighbors with suspicious dread. Balak, king of Moab, allied with some Midianites, a nomad race descended from Abraham and Keturah, who were then pasturing in the Amorite territory; and the elders of Midian and Moab went to Balaam, the son of Beor, an Edomite prophet living at Pethor, in Mesopotamia, on the Euphrates, to endeavor to persuade him by rewards to curse the Hebrews in the name of the Lord. But "God said to Balaam, Thou shalt not go with them; thou shalt not curse the people, for they are blessed;" upon which, Balaam dismissed the messengers. The next morning more honorable princes were sent to Balaam with more pressing entreaties for his presence; upon which, God permitted him to go, but "what I shall say unto thee, that shalt thou do." Balaam proceeded before the appointed time, when the angel of the Lord stood in the way and stopped his ass, who then miraculously spoke and rebuked his master; and the angel said to Balaam, "Only the word that I shall speak unto thee, that thou shalt speak." Upon arriving before Balak and offering up sacrifies, Balaam, instead of cursing, *blessed* the Israelites, and said, "There shall come a Star out of Jacob, and a Sceptre shall rise out of Israel, and shall smite the corners of Moab, and destroy all the children of Sheth." Num. xxii.; xxiii.; xxiv.

231. *Israelites commit Idolatry; Zimri and Cozbi slain by Phinehas.*—Subsequently, by the counsel of Balaam, the women of Moab and Midian tempted the Hebrews to fornication and the worship of Baal-peor. God ordered Moses to punish the offenders with death; a plague destroyed 24,000, but the evil seemed to in-

crease. Zimri, an Israelite, and the prince of a chief house among the Simeonites, had the audacity to bring a Midianitish woman of noble family, named Cozbi, into the camp before the whole congregation. Phinehas, the son of Eleazar the high priest, transfixed the guilty pair with a javelin, and his holy zeal pleased Jehovah and the plague ceased. God rewarded Phinehas by promising to him and his seed "the covenant of an everlasting priesthood;" which, however, must not be understood literally, for after a few successions the priesthood fell for a time into the hands of Eli, of the family of Ithamar, the youngest son of Aaron, B. C. 1181–1141. But in Solomon's reign it again reverted to the family of Phinehas, in which it continued as long as the priesthood lasted. Num. xxv.

232. *Midianites defeated; Balaam slain.*—The Lord now commanded the Israelites to avenge themselves on the Midianites. Every tribe accordingly sent in a thousand men, and the whole 12,000 marched against the enemy, under the command of Phinehas, and utterly routed them with great slaughter, but incensed Moses by saving the women alive, and he immediately ordered all the male children and female adults amongst the captives to be slain. Balaam, the son of Beor, was amongst the dead on the field of battle.* Num. xxxi.

233. *Second Mustering, 1451.*—The Jordan alone now separated the Hebrews from Canaan, and the new generation of soldiers, of twenty years old and upward, were mustered and reviewed by Moses and Eleazar in the plains of Moab previous to the conquering of the country. The punishment declared by God was now found to be completed; for none of the old generation that were reviewed at Sinai were found amongst the present mustering, save Joshua and Caleb. Num. xxvi.

---

* The conduct of this unprincipled prophet is alluded to by St. Jude, ver. 11, who accuses false teachers of "running greedily after the error of Balaam *for reward*"—*i. e.* corrupting Christ's doctrine for lucre's sake. St. Peter in his Second Epistle (ii. 15) says the same, but calls Balaam "*the son of Bosor.*" Bosor may be the Chaldaic spelling of Beor, or a second name, or it may be for Pethor, by changing, as is common in Syriac, *p* to *b* and *th* to *s;* hence *Besor, Bosor.*

234. *Census of B. C. 1491 and that of B. C. 1451 compared.—*

At the first census taken of the various tribes at Sinai, the number of males above twenty years of age was found to be 625,850

Whilst, according to the census of B. C. 1451, after about forty years' wanderings in the wilderness and the first generation had died, the number of males above twenty years old was 625,030

Net decrease in about forty years . . 820

The Levites are included in both enumerations. The whole population of the Israelites, including women and children, must have been at the exode from Egypt about 2,000,000 a wonderful increase from the seventy-five persons of Jacob's family who migrated to Egypt in the time of Joseph, B. C. 1706. (See sect 70.)

235. *Reuben, Gad, and half Manasseh's Territory east of the Jordan.*—
Moses was informed by God of his approaching death, and appointed Joshua as his successor. He gave to Reuben, Gad, and half Manasseh the country east of the Jordan, but ordered them to assist the other tribes previous to settling. Num. xxvii. 12-23; xxxii.

236. *Six Cities of Refuge; Conclusion of Numbers.*—
Moses appointed forty-eight cities to the Levites (see sect. 164), six of which were to be *cities of refuge*. These were easy of access to those who had accidentally committed murder, all cross-roads having a finger-post bearing the word "REFUGE" to direct the fugitive. There were three on each side of the Jordan—viz. EAST: Bezer, Golan, Ramoth-gilead; WEST: Kedesh, Hebron, and Shechem. Josh. xx. The history of Numbers concludes with a description of the territory to be subdued, a repetition of the injunctions to expel the inhabitants, and a list of the forty-two encampments of the Israelites in the wilderness. Num. xxxiii.; xxxv.

237. *Book of the Wars of the Lord.*—
In Num. xxi. 14 an allusion is made to this book, upon which there are many opinions. Some think it refers to either of the books of Numbers, Joshua, or Judges; others, to an authentic history of the conquests east of Jordan by the Amorites themselves; whilst Dr. Lightfoot thinks it was

a book written by Moses, containing directions to Joshua for conquering Palestine. (See Ex. xvii. 14.)

---

238. *Typical and Prophetical Intimations of the Messiah in Numbers.*—There are two types of the Messiah in this book. I. THE WATER THAT ISSUED FROM THE ROCK: "For they drank of that spiritual Rock that followed them; and that Rock was Christ." 1 Cor. x. 4. II. THE BRAZEN SERPENT: "And as Moses lifted up the serpent in the wilderness, even so must the Son of man be lifted up." John iii. 14. There is but ONE PREDICTION concerning the Messiah, which is placed in the mouth of Balaam: "I shall see him, but not now: I shall behold him, but not nigh: there shall come a Star out of Jacob, and a Sceptre shall rise out of Israel, and shall smite the corners of Moab, and destroy all the children of Sheth. . . . Out of Jacob shall come He that shall have dominion." Num. xxiv. 17, 19.

Names, and Meanings of the Names, of the principal Persons mentioned in Exodus and Numbers.

MOSES (*saved from the water*).
Pharaoh (*spreading abroad vengeance*), king of Egypt.
Miriam (*exalted*), sister of Moses.
Aaron, (*a teacher, a hill*), high priest and brother of Moses.

THE FOUR SONS OF AARON.

Nadab (*liberal vowing*).   Eleazar (*the aid of God*)
Abihu (*he is father*).   Ithamar (*woe to the hand*).

Korah (*baldness*), } the three rebellious leaders in the wilderness.
Dathan (*laws*),
Abiram (*deceit*),

Joshua (*saviour*), } the two faithful spies.
Caleb (*a dog, crow, basket*),
Balak (*who lays waste*), king of Moab.
Balaam (*ancient of the people*) an Edomite prophet.

DEUTERONOMY.

(Δευτερος νομος, "*the second law*"—*a repetition of the law.*)

REPETITION AND CONFIRMATION OF THE LAW. B. C. 1451—ABOUT TWO MONTHS.

ANALYSIS.

The last Acts of Moses.

Repetition and confirmation of the Law.—Death of Moses, 1451.
—Review of the life and character of Moses.—His mission.—Prophecies in Deuteronomy. — Authenticity of the last chapter of Deuteronomy. . . . . page 130.

§ *Canaan prior to its Conquest by the Israelites.*

Canaan.—Boundaries and bordering nations.—Description of the country.—Early inhabitants—viz. 1st. Canaanites of Arabia, or Amalekites; 2d. Canaanites of Sidon and its neighborhood, or Phœnicians; 3d. Canaanites who occupied Palestine.—The Philistines.—Palestine the highway between Egypt and the Asiatic empires. . . . . page 133.

SUMMARY.

The last Acts of Moses.

239. ***Repetition and Confirmation of the Law; Death of Moses, 1451.***—Moses now felt that his end was approaching, and his last act was to deliver to the magistrates a farewell address, which composes his fifth book, or Deuteronomy. In this he earnestly exhorted the people to obedience by alluding to the kindness, severity, and providence of God. He exhibited the sanctions of the law and repeated the most important statutes, and, as circumstances had changed, he made several additions and alterations to the code; and the laws were ordered to be subsequently engraved on stone pillars and solemnly erected at Shechem, on Mount Ebal. Deut. xxvii.; Josh.

viii. 32–35. Moses then minutely developed the conditions upon which Jehovah would govern his people, and how their destinies would depend upon their faithful adherence to the God of their fathers. He commissioned Joshua to be the military leader after his death, and delivered the book of the law to the priests, to be kept in the ark and publicly read at the feast of tabernacles every sabbatical year; and he left a song which was to be "taught to all Israel," in which he vividly represented the perverseness of the Hebrews, their future disobedience and punishment, repentance, and pardon. Finally, the venerable old lawgiver, "when his eye was not dim nor his natural force abated," ascended the height of Pisgah and viewed the land of promise; and then, when borne down by the weight of one hundred and twenty years, his bones were laid in a mysterious and unknown grave. Deut. i.; xxxiv. "And the Lord buried him in a valley in the land of Moab over against Beth-peor: but no man knoweth of his sepulchre unto this day." And the children of Israel mourned for him thirty days.

240. *Review of the Life and Character of Moses.*—The life of the great legislator and deliverer of the Hebrews is divided into three distinct but equal periods of forty years each: first, when he was a student in the Egyptian court; second, a shepherd in Midian; and third, the leader and lawgiver of the Israelites during their nomad state. He was born B. C. 1571, of Amram and Jochebed, of the tribe of Levi, and when an infant was exposed on the banks of the Nile, but rescued by the daughter of Pharaoh; and during the first period of forty years he became "learned in all the wisdom of Egypt, and was mighty in words and deeds." Acts vii. 22. In B. C. 1531, being forty years old, he slew an Egyptian and fled to Midian, where he led a shepherd's life for another forty years, and married Zipporah, daughter of Jethro, by whom he had two sons, Gershom and Eliezer. In B. C. 1491, being eighty years old, he was called by the angel of the Lord from a burning bush to deliver the chosen people of God. The aged shepherd now stood before Pharaoh, and, inspired and assisted by Jehovah, he achieved the deliverance of his brethren from their tyrannical oppressors, and led them through the waves of

the sea and the dangers of the wilderness to the land promised by the God of their fathers. The history of this period, his abode in the mount and breaking of the first tables of stone, the erection of the tabernacle and consecration of the priests and Levites, are too fully detailed in the preceding pages to require repetition.

His Mission.—The part assigned to Moses was that of a deliverer, a leader, a legislator, and a prophet. As a deliverer, he was commissioned to emancipate a people oppressed by centuries of Egyptian slavery, and thus to typify that glorious Messiah who should deliver the world from the darkness of sin and the bondage of Satan. As a leader, he was appointed to guide the Hebrews through the wilderness into the land of promise, and thus to represent those faithful ministers of God who in the latter times have preserved the Church against the dangers of the world and temptations of the devil. And, lastly, it was destined for him, as a legislator and a prophet, to promulgate to the seed of Abraham a mysterious and prophetic code of laws and ordinances which should purify their hearts from sin and idolatry, elevate their intellectual character, and prefigure that wondrous gospel scheme which could alone save man from paying the just penalty of his disobedience and fall.

241. *Prophecies in Deuteronomy.*—The following remarkable prophecy relative to the Messiah was fulfilled 1500 years after it had been delivered. The Lord said, "I will raise them up a prophet from among their brethren, like unto thee, and will put my words in his mouth; and he shall speak unto them all that I shall command him." Deut. xviii. 15–19. This is expressly applied to Jesus Christ in Acts iii. 22, 23, and vii. 37. Moses also plainly predicted the corruptions of the Hebrews, their subsequent calamities under their judges and kings, and the horrors of the Assyrian, Babylonian, and Roman dominion.

242. *Authenticity of the last Chapter of Deuteronomy.*—There are several passages in the Pentateuch, particularly some posthumous allusions, which many suppose to have been inserted by a more modern hand than Moses. Ezra is also thought to have added certain explanatory matter. The last chapter of Deuteronomy.

describing the death of Moses, must have been written by Joshua or Samuel, or some other later prophet, but Ezra admits it as authentic.

§ *Canaan prior to its Conquest by the Israelites.*

243. ***Canaan.***—Before entering upon the conquest of Canaan, it will be necessary to describe the country and bring together the scattered notices of its early history.

244. ***Boundaries.***—The *natural* boundaries* of Palestine Proper, or Canaan, as subsequently occupied by the twelve tribes, were as follows: NORTH, the highlands of Syria, terminating in Lebanon and Anti-Lebanon, occupied by the *Syrians*, who were divided into numerous small states or cantons, and the *Phœnicians*. EAST, the desert of Syria, inhabited by the *Ammonites, Moabites, Amorites,*† and *Midianites*. SOUTH, Arabia Petræa, peopled by the *Edomites* and *Amalekites*, who seem to have divided Palestine from Egypt. WEST, the Mediterranean Sea.‡

245. ***Description of the Country.***—The extreme length of Palestine is about one hundred and eighty miles; its width in the north scarcely exceeds twenty miles, whilst on the south it has been variously estimated at from forty-five to sixty miles. Two sets of highlands range north and south, between which is the valley of the river Jordan, a very remarkable depression. The principal mountains in the western highlands are Carmel, Tabor, Gilboa, and Ebal or Gerizim; those on the east of Jordan are Hermon and Gilead.§ The river Jordan seems like the natural centre of the country. It flows from the low grounds of Mount Hermon—the lofty peak which terminates Anti-Lebanon on the south—reaches

---

* The *political* boundaries of the Jewish territory varied considerably at different periods. The kingdoms of David and Solomon extended from the Euphrates to the Mediterranean, and from Phœnicia to the Red Sea; but the divided monarchies of Judah and Israel were unable to maintain the rule over this enlarged dominion.

† Prior to the Hebrew conquest, the Amorites had extended into the interior of Canaan westward toward the Mediterranean.

‡ For a description of these bordering nations, see the "Introductory Outline of the History and Geography of the Countries noticed in the Old Testament."

§ Mount Nebo, from which Moses viewed the land of promise, has not yet been satisfactorily identified.

first the waters of Merom and then the Sea of Chinneroth, called also the Sea of Gennesareth, from whence it precipitates itself down a succession of rapids into the Dead Sea, the waters of which are calculated to be more than 1300 feet below the level of the Mediterranean. From both sides of the western highlands several streams run into the Mediterranean and into the Jordan, but are nowhere navigable or of any magnitude. The most important of these is the river Kishon, which falls into the sea north of Carmel. On its eastern side the Jordan receives the river Yarmuk just below the Sea of Gennesareth, and the river Jabbok north of Mount Gilead; whilst still farther southward the river Arnon falls into the Dead Sea.

246. *Early Inhabitants.*—The descendants of Canaan, youngest son of Ham, appear to have originally settled in Arabia, but a branch of them seems to have migrated to Canaan some time before the arrival of Abraham. The Canaanites were thus divided into three distinct classes—viz.

247. *1st. Canaanites of Arabia—Amalekites.*— These comprehended those Canaanites who remained in Arabia and formed a numerous people, and of whom in the seventh century there were distinguished families still in existence. They are called *Amalekites* in the Scriptures, but could not be descendants of Amalek, grandson of Esau, as they are mentioned as having long before his time inhabited the southern boundaries of Canaan, and Balaam calls them one of the most ancient nations and their king the most powerful monarch that he knew. Num. xxiv. 20. They subsequently led a nomad life on the southern borders of Palestine.

248. *2d. Canaanites of Sidon—Phœnicians.*—These Canaanites took possession of the northern coasts of Canaan, together with a strip of land between Lebanon and the Mediterranean. They subsequently became the great merchants and navigators of the ancient world, and appear to have continued on terms of friendship with the Israelites.*

---

* Herodotus also says that the Phœnicians originally migrated from the coasts of the Erythræan or Red Sea. (i. 1.)

249. ***3d. Canaanites who occupied Palestine.*—**
These seem to have been divided into several races, and to have established at least thirty-one small kingdoms, which were, however, united in more than one confederacy by conquest or alliance. Between the period of Abraham and that of Moses they appear to have greatly degenerated, for we read of no successor to Melchizedek as priest of the most high God. (See sects. 25, 261.)

250. ***Philistines.*—**These were not Canaanites, but originally Egyptians from the Pelusiac branch of the Nile. They migrated from Caphtor [Cyprus], and expelled the Avim, or Hivites, from the low country in Southern Palestine, and there established five governments, or lordships, in five cities.

251. ***Palestine the Highway between Egypt and the Asiatic Empires.*—**A remarkable peculiarity of Palestine consisted in its being the highway for armies between Egypt and all the great countries of Western Asia. In the time of Jacob we find his sons selling Joseph to a caravan of Ishmaelite merchants who were passing through the country on their way to Egypt, and in the time of Josiah the army of Pharaoh-Necho was obliged to march through Palestine on the way to the Euphrates.

THE TWELVE
HISTORICAL BOOKS.

[THESE CONSIST OF JOSHUA, JUDGES, RUTH, 1 AND 2 SAMUEL, 1 AND 2 KINGS, 1 AND 2 CHRONICLES, EZRA, NEHEMIAH, AND ESTHER.—SEE INTRODUCTION.]

JOSHUA.

(*The Acts of Joshua, supposed to be partly written by Joshua.*)

HISTORY OF THE CONQUEST OF CANAAN AND SETTLEMENT IN THE COUNTRY UNDER JOSHUA. B. C. 1451 TO 1426.—ABOUT 25 YEARS.

ANALYSIS.

I. *Conquest of Canaan.*

Previous life of Joshua, 1536–1451.—Sends spies to Jericho, 1451.—Crosses the Jordan.—Circumcision re-established.—Manna ceases.—Jericho taken.—Ai taken; Achan's sin.—Gibeonites craftily persuade Joshua to an alliance.—Defeat of Adonizedek and his four allied kings; sun and moon stand still.—Defeat of the northern kings; Anakims destroyed.—Seven years' war; thirty-one kings subdued. . . . . page 136

II. *Settlement in Canaan.*

Tabernacle set up in Shiloh, 1444.—Division of the country amongst the twelve tribes.—Districts given to Caleb and Joshua. —Tribes east of the Jordan sent home; misunderstanding with their brethren.—Death of Joshua, 1426; burial of Joseph's bones; death of Eleazar.—Election of princes or elders.—Account of the "Book of Jasher." . . . . page 141

SUMMARY.

I. *Conquest of Canaan.*

252. *Previous Life of Joshua, 1536–1451.*— Joshua,* the son of Nun, of the tribe of Ephraim, was

---

* Joshua's first name was *Hosea*, or *Oshea*, but Moses changed it to *Jehoshua*, or *Joshua*. Num. xiii. 16. HOSEA signifies "a savior," or

born about B. C. 1536; he is commonly called the servant of Moses. His first exploit was defeating the Amalekites (sect. 105); he is soon afterward mentioned as having accompanied Moses up Mount Sinai (sect. 109); and he also seems to have had the care of the tabernacle, and to have dwelt in or near it. Ex. xxxiii. 11. He was subsequently sent with Caleb and ten others to spy out Canaan, and for their pious expression of confidence in Jehovah he and Caleb only of that generation were permitted to enter the Promised Land. After the death of Moses he took command of the Israelites, having been previously installed into it by the dying legislator at the command of Jehovah. Josh. i.

253. *Sends Spies to Jericho, 1451.*—Joshua now made immediate preparations for the conquest of Canaan. He led the Israelites to Shittim, on the eastern bank of the Jordan, from whence he sent two spies to Jericho to view the land. The king of Jericho heard of their coming, but Rahab, the harlot, hid them in her house under some flax-stalks, and at night let them down from her window by a rope, for her house was upon the town-wall. In return for this favor, the spies promised that if she would hang a scarlet line from her window when they took the city she and her household should be preserved. Josh. ii.

254. *Crosses the Jordan.*—On the return of the spies, Joshua and all the Israelites approached the Jordan, whilst the ark was borne by the priests 2000 cubits [1216 yards] in advance; and when the feet of the ark-bearers touched the water the Jordan rose up on a heap, so that the Israelites passed over on dry ground, and encamped at Gilgal, opposite Jericho. The priests remained with the ark in the centre of the river until all the people had passed over; after which twelve men, one from every tribe, took each a stone from the place where the priests stood, and the twelve stones were afterward pitched at Gilgal as a memorial of the miracle. The priests then passed over, and the waters immediately flowed on as before. This occurred within five

---

"he will save," but JEHOSHUA signifies "the salvation of God," or "God will save." He is also called JESUS in St. Luke and Ecclesiasticus, which has a similar meaning to "Jehoshua."

days of the forty years which had expired since they came out from Egypt. Josh. iii.; iv.

255. *Circumcision re-established; Manna ceases.* —At Gilgal, Joshua was ordered to circumcise all the Israelites, which rite had been neglected during the whole forty years' wanderings. The passover was now kept, and, the forty years being completed, the manna ceased to fall. It was about this time that an angel appeared to Joshua with a drawn sword in his hand, announced himself as the captain of the host of the Lord, and said to him the same words that Moses had heard from the burning bush at Horeb: "Loose thy shoe from off thy foot, for the place whereon thou standest is holy." And Joshua fell on his face and worshipped. Josh. v.

256. *Jericho taken, 1451.*—Joshua now proceeded to besiege Jericho, which lay about six miles from the Jordan, and about twenty miles north-east from Jerusalem. Having encompassed the city, it was at length taken by a miracle. At God's command, the whole of the people marched in solemn silence round the walls once a day for six days, accompanied by the ark and seven priests sounding seven trumpets of rams' horns. On the seventh day they marched round seven times in the same manner, but the seventh time the whole of the people suddenly shouted at the command of Joshua, when the walls fell flat down before the tremendous acclamations, and the multitude marched immediately into the city. Jericho was then taken and utterly destroyed, and all its inhabitants, except Rahab and her family (sect. 253), were put to the sword. Deut. vii. 2. The city itself was burnt with fire, and Joshua adjured the people, saying, "Cursed be the man before the Lord that riseth up and buildeth this city Jericho: he shall lay the foundation thereof in his first-born, and in his youngest son shall he set up the gates of it." Josh. vi. This prophecy was fulfilled in the reign of Ahab, king of Israel, about B. C. 925. Hiel the Bethelite rebuilt Jericho, and his first-born, Abiram, died whilst he was laying the foundation, and Segub, the youngest, died whilst his father was setting up the gates. 1 Kings xvi. 34.

257. *Ai taken; Achan's Sin.*—Joshua now despatched spies to Ai, which lay about ten or twelve miles from Jer-

icho, and, finding that the city was small, he sent only 3000 men against it, and these were defeated and thirty-six of them slain. Joshua prayed to God, and by casting lots he discovered that Achan, an Israelite of the tribe of Judah, had sinned against Jehovah; and Achan then confessed that he had hidden in his tent a Babylonian garment, with two hundred silver shekels [91 oz. = £22 15s. 4d.] and a wedge of gold weighing fifty shekels [22¾ oz. = £91 1s. 5d.], which he had taken from the spoils of Jericho. He and his family were stoned to death, and afterward burned in the valley of ACHOR—*i. e.* "trouble." Joshua afterward prepared to take Ai. He posted 5000 men in ambush west of the city, between Ai and Bethel, and then advanced with a larger force against the northern side. The king and citizens sallied out against Joshua, who, counterfeiting a flight, drew the enemy farther from the city, when the 5000 men in ambush entered Ai and fired it. Joshua then turned back upon the men of Ai and utterly defeated them; 12,000 were slain, the king was hung, and the city burnt and made a heap of desolation, but the cattle and spoils the Israelites were permitted to divide amongst themselves. Josh. vii.; viii.

258. *Gibeonites craftily persuade Joshua to an Alliance.*—The Gibeonites, whose city lay only about eight miles south-west of Ai, were now alarmed at the reports of Joshua's successes. Accordingly, knowing that the Israelites would not ally with the inhabitants of Canaan, they sent ambassadors disguised as men who had travelled from a far country. These envoys assured Joshua that they came from a distant people, who, having heard what wonders God had wrought for the Hebrews, desired the friendship and alliance of so favored a nation; and for the truth of this statement they appealed to their dry and mouldy bread, to the rent skins which contained their wine, and to their worn-out clothes and sandals, all of which they vowed to have been new when they commenced their journey. Accordingly, Joshua and the princes of the congregation—*i. e.* the national assembly (see sect. 134)—leagued with the Gibeonites "to let them live," without asking counsel "at the mouth of the Lord." Three days afterward the Israelites came to their four cities, Gibeon, Chephirah, Beeroth, and Kir-

jath-jearim, and discovered the falsehood. The Israelites now murmured, but their princes would not break their word, and Joshua reduced the Gibeonites to bondage and made them hewers of wood and drawers of water to the tabernacle. (See "Nethinim," sect. 165.) Josh. ix.

259. *Defeat of Adonizedek and his four allied Kings; Sun stands still.*—The princes of the numerous small states of different races who occupied Southern Palestine now saw the necessity for energetic measures. Adonizedek, king of Jerusalem, having heard of Joshua's victories and league with the Gibeonites, sought to dissolve this powerful alliance, and accordingly sent to four auxiliary or vassal kings—viz. Hoham, king of Hebron, Piram, king of Jarmuth, Japhia, king of Lachish, and Debir, king of Eglon, to assist him in attacking Gibeon. The Gibeonites sent to Joshua, who immediately marched with his victorious Hebrews to their assistance. The army of the five kings was routed with a great slaughter; a hailstorm from heaven cut off more of the enemy than fell by the sword, and the day was prolonged—or, in the words of the inspired historian, "the sun and moon miraculously stood still"—for twelve or fourteen hours, to enable the Israelites to prolong the pursuit. The five kings fled to the cave at Makkedah, where they were taken prisoners and slain and hung upon five trees, and their cities and territories were soon afterward taken and desolated. This brilliant victory was followed by the reduction of Libnah, Lachish, Eglon, Debir, and Hebron in rapid succession, together with the Anakims in the neighborhood; and thus was completed the conquest of nearly all Southern Palestine. Josh. x.*

260. *Defeat of the Northern Kings.*—The northern kings were now aroused by the successes of these terrible and mysterious invaders. Jabin, king of Hazor, organized a powerful league amongst the surrounding princes, and assembled an immense host, provided with chariots and cavalry, by the Waters of Merom, north of the Sea of Chinneroth or Galilee. But Joshua penetrated to Upper Galilee by rapid marches, and, falling upon the

---

* The writer of the book of Joshua quotes the *Book of Jasher* in confirmation of the miracle of the sun's standing still. (See sect. 269.)

combined forces by surprise, he routed them with immense slaughter and burnt their chariots and hamstrung their horses. The reduction of their cities quickly followed, and thus the Israelites became the predominant power in Northern and Southern Palestine. Josh. xi.

261. *Seven Years' War; Thirty-one Kings subdued, 1451-1445.* — For seven years Joshua proceeded with his conquests, during which he subdued thirty-one kings belonging to seven nations—viz. Amorites, Canaanites, Girgashites, Hittites, Hivites, Jebusites, and Perizzites. A list of the thirty-one kings may be found in Josh. xii. 9-24. A desultory war had yet to be carried on with some scattered cities and tracts still occupied by the Canaanites, Jebusites, Philistines, Sidonians, Geshurites, Maachathites, and others, but the country was soon divided by lot amongst the several tribes, and each was left to expel its own enemies. Josh. xii.

II. *Settlement in Canaan.*

262. *Tabernacle set up in Shiloh, 1444.*—The tabernacle was now removed from Gilgal, and the whole congregation of Israel assembled at Shiloh, a city of Ephraim, to which tribe Joshua belonged, and fixed it there as a sign of rest. Josh. xviii. 1. The tabernacle remained at Shiloh for three hundred and fifty years, when it was taken by the Philistines in the time of Eli. 1 Sam. iv. 10, 11. God had previously commanded this setting up of the tabernacle: " When ye go over Jordan, and dwell in the land, . . . then there shall be a place which the Lord your God shall choose to cause his name to dwell there; thither shall ye bring all that I command you; your burnt-offerings, and your sacrifices, your tithes, and the heave-offering of your hand, and all your choice vows which ye vow unto the Lord." Deut. xii. 10, 11. Jeremiah afterward in prophesying against Judah, after Israel had been desolated by the Assyrians, says, " Then will I make this house [the temple] like Shiloh, and will make this city [Jerusalem] a curse to all the nations of the earth." Jer. vii. 14; xxvi. 6.

263. *Division of the Country amongst the Twelve Tribes.*—Joshua now divided the newly-conquered terri-

tory, *by lot*, into twelve parts; for, though the descendants of Joseph were divided into the two tribes of Ephraim and Manasseh, yet no territory was assigned to Levi; the tithes alone were their inheritance, and forty-eight cities taken by lot from the districts of their brethren were appointed for their abode. The twelve tribes occupied the following portions of territory—viz.:

East of the Jordan.

1. REUBEN, the southernmost portion, being bounded on the south by Moab and the river Arnon, on the east by the Ammonites, and on the west by the Jordan and Salt Sea.

2. GAD, north of Reuben.
3. MANASSEH (*half*), north of Gad.

} These two tribes were situated between the Jordan and the Ammonite and Syrian territories.

West of the Jordan.

4. JUDAH, the southernmost portion, being bounded on the east by the Salt Sea, on the south by Edom and the desert of Shur, on the west by Simeon and Dan, and on the north by Benjamin.

5. SIMEON, south-west of Palestine, and between Judah and the Mediterranean Sea.

6. DAN, north of Simeon, and also between Judah and the Mediterranean.

7. BENJAMIN, an inland territory, north of Judah.
8. EPHRAIM, north of Benjamin.
* MANASSEH (*half*) north of Ephraim.
9. ISSACHAR, north of Manasseh.
10. ZEBULUN, north of Issachar.
11. NAPHTALI, north of Zebulun, between Asher and the Jordan.
12. ASHER, north of Zebulun, between Naphtali and the Mediterranean. Josh. xii.; xiii.; xv.–xix.; xxi.

264. ***Districts given to Caleb and Joshua.***—Caleb, the son of Jephunneh, who, with Joshua, had been pre-

---

* For the other half of Manasseh see " Tribes East of the Jordan."

served for his pious conduct after spying out Canaan, was now presented with Mount Hebron, as Moses had sworn to him that the land on which his feet trod when he spied out Canaan should be the inheritance of himself and his children for ever. Caleb then drove out the three sons of Anak—Sheshai, Talmai, and Ahiman—from Hebron, and gave his own daughter Achsah to be wife of his nephew Othniel, because the latter took the city of Debir or Kirjath-sepher. The Israelites also gave Timnath-serah in Mount Ephraim to Joshua for an inheritance. Josh. xiv. 6–15; xv. 13–19; xix. 49–51.

265. *Tribes east of the Jordan sent Home; misunderstanding with their Brethren.*—The tribes of Reuben, Gad, and the half-tribe of Manasseh now returned to the country assigned them east of the Jordan. On the banks of the river they erected an altar as a memorial of their connection with the other nine and a half tribes; but the latter, suspecting that the altar was built for sacrifice, followed them, and a civil war would have commenced had not the affair been at once explained. Josh. xxii.

266. *Last Days of Joshua.*—The military career of Joshua was now concluded. The remainder of his life was devoted to the settlement of the theocratic policy and preservation of the worship of Jehovah. He convened two general assemblies, in the first of which he exhorted the elders to be faithful to God and obedient to his law; and in the second he proclaimed the might of the God of Israel, and called upon the people to elect him for their King and cast away idolatry. He then set up a stone as a testimony of their homage, and wrote the covenant in the book of the law. Josh. xxiii.; xxiv. 1–28.

267. *Death of Joshua, 1426; Burial of Joseph's Bones; Death of Eleazar.*—Joshua the son of Nun died B. C. 1426, at the supposed age of one hundred and ten years,[*] and was buried in his inheritance on Mount Ephraim. "And Israel served the Lord all the days of Joshua and all the days of the elders that over-lived him." The bones of Joseph, which had been brought up from

---

[*] The difficulty of ascertaining the precise chronology here renders any statement of the exact age of Joshua uncertain.

Egypt, were also buried in the field which Jacob had bought of the sons of Hamor, the father of Shechem. About this time also Eleazar the son of Aaron died (cir. B. C. 1420), and was buried in a field belonging to his son Phinehas. Josh. xxiv. 29-33.

268. ***Election of Princes or Elders.***—After the death of Joshua each tribe chose a prince or elder to govern them, according to the injunction of Moses. Ex. xviii. 13-26; Deut. i. 13. (See sect. 133.)

269. ***Book of Jasher.***—The writer of the book of Joshua, in confirmation of the truth of the sun and moon's standing still, refers to the book of Jasher (Josh. x. 13), a work which is also quoted in 2 Sam. i. 18. Some think that this book is the same as the "Book of the Wars of the Lord," mentioned in Numbers; others, that it is the book of Genesis; and others, that it is the Pentateuch. It is probable that from the beginning persons were employed among the Hebrews to write the national annals, which were then lodged in the tabernacle or temple, and respectively called the "Book of the Wars of the Lord," the "Book of Jasher" ($Εὐθος$, or the *upright*), and when they referred to the times of the kings were called the "Book of the Chronicles of the Kings of Israel or Judah." The book of Jasher has been thought to have been a collection of poetical compositions. Jasher— "the upright"—may signify the *standard, authentic* book, or it may merely imply that it is a record of *upright* men. (See *Calmet*, art. "Bible.")

# JUDGES.

(Supposed to be written by Samuel.)

HISTORY OF THE JEWS AS A FEDERATIVE REPUBLIC. B. C. 1425 TO 1095.
ABOUT 330 YEARS.

[The book of Judges does not contain the judgeships of Eli and Samuel and his sons, but concludes about B. C. 1112, extending over a period of three hundred and thirteen years; but it has been thought advisable to include in this portion the first ten chapters of 1 Samuel, which will complete the HISTORY OF THE JUDGES. (See pp. 158–161.) It is stated (Acts xiii. 20) that this period—viz. from the death of Joshua to the anointing of Saul—extended to four hundred and fifty years; which calculation is thought to include the one hundred and twenty years under Saul, David, and Solomon. But certain inaccuracies have crept into the chronology of the time of the Judges which it is impossible to correct.

The whole chronology of the time of the Judges is more obscure than that of any other period of Scripture history, which can, however, be somewhat explained by the supposition that in many cases the servitudes and judgeships extended over only a portion of Palestine, and therefore contemporary judges and tyrants were by no means unfrequent. As this theory has been generally adopted by chronologers, it is illustrated in the table on p. 148.]

ANALYSIS.

I. *Period prior to the Judges.*

Prosecution of the conquest of Canaan by the separate tribes, 1425.—Introduction of idolatry, 1425–1406.—Idolatry of Micah, 1406.—War with Benjamin.—Six hundred Benjamites forcibly obtain wives. . . . . page 145.

SUMMARY.

I. *Period prior to the Judges.*

270. *Prosecution of the Conquest of Canaan by the Separate Tribes, 1425.*—After the death of Joshua the conquest of Canaan was prosecuted by the separate tribes, and that of Judah, having been chosen by lot to attack the Canaanites, joined itself to that of Simeon.

The two tribes slew 10,000 men of Bezek and utterly defeated Adonibezek the king, and cut off his thumbs and great toes and brought him to Jerusalem, which city had been previously taken from the Jebusites, by whom it had been called Jebus. Adonibezek acknowledged having deprived seventy other kings of their thumbs and great toes and obliged them to gather their meat under his table. The other tribes were equally successful against other Canaanite nations, but they made the idolaters tributary instead of utterly expelling them, as they had been expressly commanded, and they gradually suffered their children to intermarry with them, which had been as expressly forbidden. Judg. i.; iii. 7, 8.

271. *Introduction of Idolatry, 1425-1406.*—The consequences of this ill-judged lenity to their enemies were ruinous alike to the religion and liberties of the next generation of Israelites. Their connections with the Canaanites naturally prevented them from expelling their idolatrous relatives; it led them to festivals where not only lascivious songs were sung in honor of the gods, but where gross debaucheries were part of the divine service, until at length a vile idolatry which chiefly recommended itself by pandering to sensual appetites and depraved tastes spread through the land like a deadly plague, and weakened the energy and quenched the spirit of the seed of Abraham. The infatuated Hebrews transferred to Baal and Ashtaroth the honors due to Jehovah, and a most gross example of idolatry is recorded as having taken place within twenty years of the death of Joshua. Judg. ii.

272. *Idolatry of Micah, 1406.*—Micah, a native of Mount Ephraim, had stolen eleven hundred silver shekels [500 oz., or £125] from his mother, but subsequently restored her the money, upon which she gave two hundred of the shekels (91 oz. = £22 15s.) to a founder to make a graven and a molten image. Micah, then, "had a house of gods, and made an ephod and teraphim," and first consecrated one of his sons to be priest, but afterward hired a young Levite. Soon after this the Danites sent five men to spy out Laish, in Northern Palestine, who in passing lodged at the house of Micah. Their report of Laish being favorable, six hundred Danites marched on to conquer it, and, passing by

Micah's house, the spies told them of his idols, upon which they forcibly carried off both images and Levite, and, having taken Laish and called it Dan, they carried on there the worship of the stolen gods. Judg. xvii.; xviii.

273. *War with Benjamin, 1406.*—The same year all Israel was aroused by a horrible tragedy enacted in the country of Benjamin, which but too plainly indicated the fearful increase of idolatry and debauchery. A woman was murdered in the streets of Gibeah amid circumstances of the most revolting barbarity, and her injured husband divided the corpse into twelve portions and sent one to each tribe. The people assembled from Dan to Beersheba to avenge the outrage, but Benjamin refused to give up the perpetrators, and three bloody battles were the result. Twice were the other eleven tribes defeated with immense slaughter before Gibeah; but on the third day they placed an ambush beside Gibeah, who entered and burnt the city whilst the Benjamites were drawn from it to engage their main army. The eleven tribes thus gained a complete victory. Gibeah was burnt to the ground* and 25,000 Benjamites were slain, whilst only six hundred of their number escaped from the field of battle. Judg. xix.; xx.

274. *The Benjamites forcibly obtain Wives.*—The six hundred Benjamites now fled to the Rock Rimmon and abode there four months, whilst the Israelites destroyed all their cities and possessions. The eleven tribes also swore not to give their daughters in marriage to the survivors; but soon repented their oath, by which the tribe of Benjamin must soon cease to exist. Soon after, 12,000 of their number fell upon Jabesh-gilead, destroyed the inhabitants, but saved four hundred of their virgins and sent them to be wives to the Benjamites on Rock Rimmon; and, as the number was found to be insufficient, they subsequently directed the Benjamites to lie in wait in the vineyards round Shiloh, where there was to be a feast; and whilst the daughters of Shiloh were dancing the Benjamites rushed in and carried them off to be wives for the remainder. The Benjamites then returned to their own territory and rebuilt all their cities. Judg. xxi.

---

* Gibeah was subsequently rebuilt, and became the residence of Saul.

JUDGES.

THE SEVEN SERVITUDES OR TYRANNIES, AND THE FIFTEEN JUDGESHIPS.

CANAAN GENERALLY.

	B.C.	yrs.
1. *Cushan-rishathaim, king of Mesopotamia, tyrant*	1402–1394	8
1. **Othniel**, nephew of Caleb and married his daughter, judged,	1394–1354	40

SOUTHERN CANAAN. / NORTHERN CANAAN.

SOUTHERN CANAAN		NORTHERN CANAAN	
	B.C. yrs.		
2. *Eglon of Moab, tyrant*	1354–1336 18	4. *Jabin of Hazor, with nine hundred iron chariots, tyrant*	1316–1296 20
2. **Ehud**, stabbed Eglon	1336–1296		
3. *Philistines, tyrants*	1296	4. **Deborah and Barak**, defeated Sisera, who was slain by Jael the Kenite; judged	1296–1256 40
3. **Shamgar**, slew six hundred Philistines with an ox-goad	1206–1256		
Under Ehud and Shamgar the land rested	80		

CANAAN GENERALLY.

5. *Midianites, Amalekites, and others; tyrannized* . . . 1256–1249 7
5. **Gideon**: called by God; throws down Baal's altar; gains a victory with three hundred men, each bearing a trumpet, pitcher, and torch; 120,000 slain; Oreb and Zeeb beheaded; Zebah and Zalmunna slain; makes an ephod; judged . 1249–1209 40
6. **Abimelech** slays his seventy brethren; Jotham's apologue of the trees; Shechemites rebel; burns Berith's temple; killed by a millstone; judged 1209–1206 2
7. **Tola**, judged 1206–1183 23
8. **Jair**, judged 1183–1161 23

EAST OF JORDAN. / SOUTHERN CANAAN.

EAST OF JORDAN.		SOUTHERN CANAAN.	
	B.C. yrs.	(History continued from 1 Sam. i.–x., which completes the Judges.)	
6. *Ammonites, tyrants*	1161–1143 18		
9. **Jephthah**, defeated the Ammonites; slew 42,000 Ephraimites, who said *Sibboleth for Shibboleth*; vows his daughter; judged	1143–1137 6	7. *Philistines, tyrants, during Samson and part of Eli and Samuel.* (See 13.)	
		14. **Eli**, judged, previous to Samson and contemporary with *Jair* and *Jephthah*. His two sons slain.	1181–1141 40
10. **Ibzan**, judged	1137–1130 7		
11. **Elon**, judged	1130–1120 10		
12. **Abdon**, judged	1120–1112 8		
SOUTH-WESTERN CANAAN.		15. **Samuel**, born 1171; judged Contemporary with *Jephthah*, *Ibzan*, *Elon*, and *Abdon*, east of Jordan, and with *Samson*, who appears to have been more of a border chieftain against the Philistines than a judge.	1141–1112 29
13. **Samson**, born 1161; marries a woman of Timnath; his riddle; burns Philistine corn with three hundred fox-tails; slays one thousand men with jaw-bone of an ass; carries off the gates of Gaza; treacherously given up by Delilah; pulls down Dagon's temple; judged	1141–1120 20		

Samuel's Sons judged the land, but exasperated the people by their cupidity 1112–1095
The people at length forced Samuel to anoint Saul as king . 1095

N.B.—In the above table the *Tyrants* are printed in Italics, and the numbers of their succession in Roman; the **Judges** in bold.

II. *The Seven Servitudes, or Tyrannies, and Fifteen Judgeships.*

CANAAN GENERALLY, 1402–1354.

275. ***First Judgeship: Othniel, forty years, 1394–1354.***—Jehovah now prepared to punish the national treachery of Israel with national misfortunes. Cushan-rishathaim, king of Mesopotamia—*i. e.* Padan-aram, a territory lying east of the Euphrates, and perhaps at this time including Syria—advanced to Canaan and made the Hebrews tributary. They endured the yoke for eight years, when they cried unto the Lord, and Othniel, a nephew of the celebrated Caleb (sect. 264), overthrew the Mesopotamian king and judged the people for forty years. Judg. iii. 1–11.

_{First Servitude: Cushan-rishathaim of Mesopotamia. Eight years, 1402–1394.}

SOUTHERN CANAAN, 1354–1256.

276. ***Second Judgeship: Ehud, eighty years, 1336–1256.***—After the death of Othniel the Hebrews again fell into idolatry, when Eglon, king of Moab, having allied with the Ammonites and Amalekites, succeeded in defeating them, and established himself in Jericho—*i. e.* the city of palm trees—and oppressed the land for eighteen years. The deliverer on the present occasion was Ehud, a left-handed Benjamite, who being sent with a present to Eglon, assassinated the king in his summer parlor, and, assembling the people by the sound of the trumpet, delivered Israel by the slaughter of 10,000 Moabites. The land now rested for eighty years. Judg. iii. 12–30.

_{Second Servitude: Eglon of Moab. Eighteen yrs., 1354–1336.}

277. ***Third Judgeship; Shamgar.***—During the last-mentioned period of eighty years' rest the Philistines attacked the southern tribes, but were repulsed with great slaughter by Shamgar, son of Anath, who slew six hundred of them with an ox-goad.* Judg. iii. 31.

_{Third Servitude: the Philistines.}

---

* The Philistines were not Canaanites, but originally Egyptians from the Pelusiac branch of the Nile, and they had migrated from Caphtor [Cyprus] before the arrival of the Hebrews, and expelled the Avim [Hivites] from the low country in Southern Palestine, and there

NORTHERN CANAAN, 1316-1256.

Fourth Servitude: Jabin.
Twenty years, 1316-1296.

278. Fourth Judgeship: Barak and Deborah, forty years, 1296-1256,—During the same period of eighty years' partial rest, the northern Canaanites had regained their power, and were commissioned by Jehovah to punish the idolatry of the neighboring Hebrews. A new Jabin, king, like his predecessor, of Hazor (sect. 260), was enabled by a numerous army and nine hundred chariots of iron to oppress the northern Israelites for twenty years. At length Deborah the prophetess, and wife of Lapidoth, sat under a palm between Ramah and Bethel and judged Israel. She aroused the courage of Barak, and sent him at the head of 10,000 men against Sisera, general of Jabin's army, who had posted his chariots and troops between Harosheth and the river Kishon. Barak refused to march unless Deborah accompanied him; accordingly, she herself animated his army by her presence, and strengthened it by her promises of victory. The army of Barak poured down the sides of Mount Tabor and routed the forces of Jabin with immense slaughter. The Canaanites never recovered from the blow, and their general, Sisera, on taking refuge in a tent from the field of battle, fell asleep, and was slain by Jael, wife of Heber the Kenite, who drove a nail through his temples. Deborah afterward composed a song of thanksgiving, which she and Barak sang, and in which she gave due honor to God and blessed the action of Jael. After this the land had rest forty years. Judg. iv.; v.; Ps. lxxxiii. 9.

CANAAN GENERALLY, 1256-1161.

Fifth Servitude: Midianites, Amalekites, etc.
Seven years, 1256-1249.

279. Fifth Judgeship: Gideon, forty years, 1249-1209.—During the seven years following the eighty years' rest the Midianites united with the Amalekites and other nomad Arabs, and entered Palestine in great numbers and plundered and rioted without restraint, whilst fields, gardens, and vineyards were trampled and destroyed by their

---

founded five governments or lordships—viz., at Ekron, Gath, Askelon, Ashdod, and Gaza.

countless herds. The suffering Israelites again cried unto the Lord, and a deliverer was sent.

280. *Throws down the Altar of Baal.*—Gideon, the son of Joash the Abi-ezrite, and a native of Ophrah in Manasseh, was threshing wheat by the winepress to hide it from the invaders when an angel appeared and called upon him to deliver Israel in the name of the Lord. A miraculous fire, which burnt up a kid and unleavened bread, proved the divine origin of the mission, and Gideon threw down the altar of Baal, which procured him the name of Jerubbaal—*i. e.* "let Baal plead"—and prepared to levy an army. A fleece, at first wet with dew whilst the earth was dry, and then the next night dry whilst the earth was wet, furnished another proof of the determination of Jehovah to deliver his people.

281. *Defeats the Midianites, etc. with three hundred men bearing Trumpets, Pitchers, and Torches.*—Gideon immediately advanced on the enemy with 32,000 men, whom, by the direction of God, he reduced to 10,000 by sending home all who were fearful, and again to three hundred by selecting only those who in drinking lapped water with their tongues. He now directed each of the three hundred to carry a trumpet in one hand and a pitcher containing a lighted torch in the other; and, dividing his small band into three companies, he approached the Midianite host, who were encamped like a vast army of grasshoppers in the valley of Jezreel. The three divisions then blew their trumpets and broke their pitchers, and with loud cries of "The sword of the Lord and of Gideon!" they fell upon the enemy whilst the darkness of midnight was broken by the glare of torches. The invaders were smitten with an uncontrollable panic. They fled in the utmost trepidation, and slew each other in their confusion. Fresh forces of the Israelites joined in the pursuit or guarded the fords of the Jordan, and 120,000 of the enemy were slain, and their two princes, Oreb and Zeeb, taken and beheaded by the Ephraimites—Oreb on the rock Oreb, and Zeeb at the winepress of Zeeb—and their heads were taken beyond Jordan to Gideon. Meantime, Gideon crossed the Jordan with his three hundred, and pursued a flying remnant of 15,000 under the two Midianite kings Zebah

and Zalmunna. At Succoth* the elders refused him refreshment, but he defeated the 15,000, took Zebah and Zalmunna, and, finding that they had murdered his own brethren at Tabor, he slew them with his own hand. On his return he chastised the seventy-seven Succoth princes with thorns and briers. An allusion is made to the two kings of Midian in Ps. lxxxiii. 11.

282. *Refuses to be King.*—The grateful Hebrews now desired to make Gideon king, but he rejected the proffer in the true spirit of theocratic policy. "No!" cried the magnanimous warrior, "not I, nor my son, but Jehovah, shall reign over you." One stain remains on the character of this dauntless chieftain. With the spoils of Midian he made an ephod, which subsequently tempted the Israelites to idolatry and became a snare to his own house. Gideon died forty years after the defeat of the Midianites, during which period the land had rest. Judg. vi.–viii.

283. *Sixth Judgeship: Abimelech, three years, 1209–1206.*—After the death of Gideon (Jerubbaal), Abimelech, son of Gideon by a concubine, persuaded his mother's family to win over the Shechemites† to his interest by saying it was better that they should be ruled by one man (Abimelech) than by the seventy men who were Abimelech's brethren. The Shechemites then inclined to Abimelech, and gave him money, with which he paid men to follow him to his father's house, where he slew all his seventy brethren, Jotham, the youngest, only escaping. Abimelech was then made king, but when Jotham heard of it, he addressed to the Shechemites from Mount Gerizim the following apologue, which is the earliest recorded in Scripture. Judg. ix. 1–7.

284. *Parable of the Trees.*—"The trees went forth on a time to anoint a king over them, but the olive refused to leave its oil, the fig tree its sweetness, and the vine tree its wine [thus intimating the refusal of Gideon's sons]; but the upstart bramble [Abimelech] accepted the honor, saying, If ye anoint me king, you may put your trust in my shadow [*i. e.* rely upon my protection]; otherwise let fire come out of the bramble and devour the cedars

---

* This city lay near the banks of the river Jabbok. (See note to sect. 100.)

† Shechem, or Sichem, was in Samaria, and in the beginning of the divided monarchy of Judah and Israel it formed the capital of the latter kingdom.

of Lebanon [*i. e.* if ye act faithlessly, Abimelech will be revenged even upon the most powerful of his enemies]. If then ye have dealt truly with Gideon and his sons, rejoice in Abimelech, and let him rejoice in you; but if not, let fire come out of Abimelech and devour the men of Shechem, and let fire come out of the men of Shechem and devour Abimelech."

Jotham then fled to Beer, but his subsequent history is unknown. Judg. ix. 8–21.

285. *Abimelech killed by a Millstone, 1206.*—After three years the Shechemites repented of the murder of Gideon's seventy sons, and revolted from Abimelech and followed Gaal, the son of Ebed; but Zebul, the governor of Shechem, having become disgusted with Gaal's presumption, sent notice to Abimelech that Gaal and the Shechemites had fortified their city against him. Abimelech immediately marched against Shechem, defeated Gaal, beat down the city, and sowed it with salt; and as many of the besieged had escaped to a hold in the house of the god Berith, he and his men cut down trees and placed them round the hold and fired them, and thus burnt a thousand men and women to death. [Immediately after Gideon's death the people had begun the worship of Berith. Judg. viii. 33.] Abimelech then besieged Thebez, but, in approaching to burn the door of the tower, a woman cast a piece of millstone upon his head, and he said hastily to his armor-bearer, "Draw thy sword and slay me, that men say not of me, A woman slew him." The armor-bearer then thrust him through, and he died. Judg. ix.

286. *Seventh Judgeship: Tola, twenty-three years, 1206–1183.*—Dwelt in Mount Ephraim. Judg. x. 1, 2.

287. *Eighth Judgeship: Jair, twenty-two years, 1183–1161.*—A Gileadite who had thirty sons who rode on thirty ass-colts, and had thirty cities called Havoth-jair—*i. e.* "the villages of Jair"—in Gilead. Judg. x. 3–5.

EAST OF JORDAN, 1161–1112.

288. *Ninth Judgeship: Jephthah, six years, 1143–1137.*—The Israelites again fell into idolatry and worshipped Baalim, Ashtaroth, and the gods of Syria, Zidon, Moab, Ammon, and the Philistines. For eighteen years

Sixth Servitude: Ammonites. 18 yrs., 1161–1143.

the Ammonites oppressed the tribes east of the Jordan and made frequent incursions upon Judah, Ephraim, and Benjamin, who at the same time had to defend themselves from the growing power of the Philistines. (See sect. 298.) The Israelites again cried to the Lord for deliverance, and the Lord heard them.

289. *Captain of a Band of Men in Tob.*—Jephthah, son of Gilead by a harlot, having been expelled from his father's house by his more legitimate brethren, had collected a band of vain men in the land of Tob, a small district east of Jordan, and lying to the north of the half tribe of Manasseh. In that age of anarchy Jephthah had distinguished himself by his valor, and probably by his predatory exploits; and the elders of Gilead now applied to him for assistance, and covenanted to atone for former insults by making him their head.

290. *Sends Envoys to the King of Ammon.*—Jephthah immediately sent to the Ammonite king to demand the reason of his invasion. The Ammonite replied by laying claim to the region from the Arnon to the Jabbok and from the Jordan to the wilderness, which had been occupied by the Israelites since their conquest of Sihon, king of the Amorites, but which Sihon had wrested from the Ammonites before the time of Moses. (See sect. 229.) This preposterous claim was explicitly opposed by the Gileadite chieftain. His messenger repeated his words to the king of Ammon: "Thus saith Jephthah, The Israelites took not the lands of Moab or Ammon, but conquered the dominions of Sihon, who refused them a passage through his territories. This land they have occupied for three hundred years: therefore the Lord shall be our judge."

291. *Defeats the Ammonites; his Rash Vow.*—The Ammonite king refused to hear the message, but Jephthah, after vowing, in case of victory, to offer as a burnt-offering to God whoever should meet him on his return, invaded the dominions of Ammon, destroyed twenty cities between Aroer and Minnith, and effectually subdued the Ammonites by an immense slaughter. On returning to his house at Mizpeh he met his only daughter, who had come out to welcome him with timbrels and dances; but the issue of his rash vow is still a subject of controversy

amongst critical commentators.* The Ephraimites afterward quarrelled with Jephthah, and threatened to burn his house for not permitting them to share the booty of his expedition and the glory of his victories. A battle was the result, but Jephthah, at the head of his conquering Gileadites, speedily routed the children of Ephraim; and then, guarding the passes of the Jordan, he slew every fugitive who pronounced the word "Shibboleth" as "Sibboleth," and thus completed the slaughter of forty-two thousand of the enemy. Jephthah died after judging Israel six years. Judg. x. 6–16; xi.; xii. 1–7.

292. *Tenth Judgeship: Ibzan, seven years, 1137–1130.*—A Bethlehemite, who seems to have been only a civil judge in the north-east of Israel. Judg. xii. 8–10.

293. *Eleventh Judgeship: Elon, ten years, 1130–1120.*—A Zebulunite, who appears to have been also only a civil judge in the north of Israel. Judg. xii. 11, 12.

294. *Twelfth Judgeship: Abdon, eight years, 1120–1112.*—A Pirathonite, who had forty sons and thirty nephews, who rode on seventy ass-colts. He seems to have been only a civil judge in the north of Israel, like the two former. Judg. xii. 13–15.

SOUTH-WESTERN CANAAN, 1161–1120.

295. *13th Judgeship: Samson, twenty years, 1140–1120.*—During the judgeships of Jephthah, Ibzan, and Elon in the north and eastern districts, the continued idolatry of the south-western Israelites was punished by forty years of Philistine oppression. The latter half of this period has been rendered memorable by the exploits of Samson, whose life may be thus briefly sketched. Judg. xiii. 1.

Seventh Servitude: the Philistines. 40 years, 1161–1120.

296. *Life and Exploits of Samson; born 1161; became judge 1140; judged twenty years, 1140–1120.*—The wife of Manoah, a Danite, was barren,

---

* Modern critics have ingenuously supposed that Jephthah's daughter was only devoted to perpetual virginity. See the different *Commentaries*, and a curious article on Jephthah's vow, in Sir Thomas Browne's *Vulgar Errors*, upon this point. Their arguments, however, are scarcely sufficient to set aside the plain words of the sacred writer: "And Jephthah did with her according to his vow."

when an angel appeared to her and promised her a son who should be a Nazarite from his birth, and Samson was born in B. C. 1161. Having attained the age of twenty in B. C. 1141, Samson saw a Philistine woman at Timnath whom he desired for a wife, and his parents, after some opposition, went with him to the abode of her father. On the journey, whilst Samson was alone and unarmed near the vineyards of Timnath, a young lion roared against him; but the muscular Nazarite rent the beast as he would a kid, and visited his intended bride without revealing his exploit. Shortly after this visit Samson returned to marry the fair Philistine, and on his way he saw that a swarm of bees had established themselves in the lion's carcass, and accordingly carried off a portion of the honey. The marriage was soon arranged, and at the feast Samson propounded the following riddle: "Out of the eater came forth meat, and out of the strong came forth sweetness;" and he promised that if his thirty guests could solve it within seven days, he would give them thirty sheets and changes of garments, but if not, that they must give him the same. The thirty guests totally failed in discovering the solution, but obtained the answer on the seventh day by threatening the wife of Samson, who cajoled her husband out of the secret. Samson saw their treachery, and paid them with the spoils of thirty Philistines whom he slew at Askalon, but left his wife in anger and returned to his father's house. Soon afterward he visited his wife with a kid, but his father-in-law would not suffer him to see her, and admitted that in his absence she had been given to a companion of Samson's. The infuriated husband now determined on revenge. He affixed burning firebrands to the tails of three hundred foxes and let them loose in the standing corn of the Philistines; and though the latter, upon learning the cause, burnt both his Timnath wife and his father-in-law, yet Samson smote them with great slaughter, and then retired to the rock Etam. The Philistines now encamped in Lehi, whilst three thousand men of Judah ascended the rock to take Samson; and as the three thousand promised not to kill him, he suffered himself to be bound with two new cords and taken to Lehi. The Philistines approached their captive enemy with shouts of exultation, when Samson suddenly burst his bonds, and, finding the new jaw-bone of an ass, he slew with it one thousand men. After the battle he was fainting with thirst, when the same weapon which had delivered him from his enemies miraculously furnished him with water. "And Samson judged Israel [*i. e.* the south-western districts] in the days [*i. e.* servitude] of the Philistines twenty years." Judg. xiii. 2–25; xiv.; xv.

297. *Samson's Capture and Heroic Death, 1120.* —The name of Samson now became a terror to the Philistines, and they used every effort to take him prisoner. At one time, when he had gone to Gaza to visit a harlot, the Gazites encompassed the city and guarded the gates, thinking to take him on the morning; but Samson arose at midnight, took the city gates with the two posts, bar and all, and carried them away on his shoulders to the summit of the hill before Hebron. Samson was at length taken by treachery. He loved a woman in the valley of Sorek named Delilah, who was promised eleven hundred pieces of silver by the Philistine lords if she could discover a foil to his great strength. Three times Samson evaded her questions. First he said that green undried withs could overcome him, and with these Delilah bound him whilst Philistine lords were stationed in her chamber; but when she suddenly cried, "The Philistines be upon thee, Samson," the withs were broken like a thread of tow touched with fire. She afterward, in accordance with his replies, bound him with new ropes, but with the same result; and again she wove the seven locks of his head with a web and fastened it with the pin of the beam, but he arose and carried away both pin and web, and she still found herself mocked. At last, by constant pressing, Delilah obtained the secret from Samson—namely, that if he was shaved his strength would leave him. She immediately sent again for the Philistine lords, and Samson was shaved whilst sleeping on her knees, taken prisoner, carried to Gaza, and bound with brazen fetters, whilst his savage captors put out his eyes and made him grind in his prison-house. After a time Samson's hair began to grow, and the moment for revenge arrived. The Philistines held a great feast in the temple of Dagon to celebrate their victory, and sent for Samson to make them sport. All the Philistine nobles were assembled, whilst three thousand people crowded the roof, when the blind warrior begged the lad who led him to take him to the supporting pillars. Then Samson called upon the Lord, and, seizing the two middle pillars, he bowed with all his might, until the vast building fell in and buried alike the nobility and populace of Philistia in the temple of their idol. The hero fell with his enemies, but his death was attended by a greater slaughter than his whole lifetime had achieved; and his brethren obtained his body and buried it in the tomb of his father, B. C. 1120. Judg. xvi.

SOUTHERN CANAAN, 1181–1095.

Philistine tyrants. **298.** ***Obscure Chronology; Fourteenth Judgeship: Eli, forty years, 1181–1141.***—The chronology of the principal events in the time of the judges is exceedingly confused, and it is impossible to review the history in strictly chronological order, from the fact of the northern and southern districts being judged by different but contemporary judges. We now come to the history of Samuel, who was born about B. C. 1171, began to judge B. C. 1141, and died B. C. 1060, a series of years which commences in the judgeship of Jair, continues in that of Samson, and concludes only in the twenty-fifth year of the reign of Saul. For ten years previous to the birth of Samuel, and until Samuel was thirty years of age, B. C. 1181–1141 (a period just prior to the judgeship of Samson), Eli had ruled the south-western districts of Canaan. Eli was high priest, and descended from Ithamar, fourth son of Aaron, and was the first of that branch who enjoyed the high priesthood; why it was transferred from the family of Eleazar is unknown. (See sect. 231.) During his judgeship, Elkanah, a native of Mount Ephraim, had two wives, Peninnah and Hannah; Peninnah was a mother, but Hannah was barren. In B. C. 1171, Hannah vowed in the tabernacle that if a son was granted her, she would devote him to the service of Jehovah; and, Eli having promised that God would answer her petition, she returned home and gave birth to Samuel, who was then devoted to the service of God as a

Nazarite from his infancy, and when the lad was weaned his mother took him to the tabernacle at Shiloh, where he was brought up under the care of Eli. 1 Sam. i.; ii. 1–11.

299. *Misconduct of Eli's Sons.*—Meanwhile, the flagrant misconduct of Hophni and Phinehas, the two sons of Eli, called down the vengeance of God. These two men were priests, and instead of being satisfied with the priest's portion, the right shoulder and breast of peace-offerings, etc. (see sect. 170), they thrust a flesh-hook with three teeth into the seething-kettle and took all that was brought up for themselves; they demanded all the choicest parts for themselves before God was served and the fat burnt, and, moreover, debauched the women of the congregation. Eli, instead of punishing his sons, simply reprimanded them, and a prophet was sent to reprove him for his criminal leniency as a parent, and to foretell the destruction of his house and advent of a more faithful priest; and as a sign that the message was from God, it was declared that Eli's two sons should be cut off in one day. 1 Sam. ii. 12–36.

300. *Prophecy of Samuel.*—When Samuel was yet a youth the Lord called him by name one night whilst he was sleeping near the tabernacle. Samuel immediately thought that Eli had called, and ran to him; but when this had occurred three times, Eli perceived that the Lord had called the boy, and directed Samuel, if called again, to reply, "Speak, Lord, for thy servant heareth." Samuel did as he was directed, and the Lord, calling to him again, announced the forthcoming destruction of the family of Eli. The next morning Eli learnt the awful sentence from the trembling boy, "and all Israel, from Dan to Beersheba, knew that Samuel was established to be a prophet of the Lord." 1 Sam. iii.

301. *Philistines defeat the Israelites; Eli and his two Sons slain, 1141.*—In B. C. 1141, the Israelites were defeated by the Philistines at Ebenezer and four thousand slain. A second time the Israelites marched against the enemy, whilst Hophni and Phinehas bore the ark of God; but they were again defeated with the loss of 30,000 men, the ark was taken, and the two sons of Eli were slain. The fearful news was brought to the old man, bending

beneath the weight of ninety-eight years. The accumulated disasters were too much for the father, priest, and judge; and, falling back from his seat by the gate of Shiloh, he dislocated his neck and died. Eli was succeeded in the priesthood by his third son, *Ahitub*—or as some say *Ahiah*—and in the government by Samuel. 1 Sam. iv.

302. *Fifteenth Judgeship: Samuel, 1141–1112.*— After their victory the Philistines carried the ark from Ebenezer to Ashdod and placed it in the temple of Dagon, but their idol was thrown down and themselves were smitten with hæmorrhoids. They then carried the ark first to Gath, and afterward to Ekron, but the same disease attacked the inhabitants of both cities, and after keeping the holy chest for seven months they were compelled to send it back to the Israelites with five golden emerods and mice,* according to the number of their lords and cities, as a trespass-offering for their sin. The Philistines carried the ark and gifts to the field of Joshua the Bethshemite, who offered up the kine on the wood of the cart which conveyed them as a burnt-offering to God; but the wrath of Jehovah slew 50,070† Bethshemites for looking into the ark, and the mourners sent to the inhabitants of Kirjath-jearim to take it to their city, where it remained in the house of Abinadab till B. C. 1042, when it was fetched by David. In B. C. 1120, being twenty years after the victory of the Philistines, Samuel assembled all Israel at Mizpeh, and called upon the people to put away Baal and Ashtaroth and worship God only; and he then offered up a sucking lamb as a burnt-offering. During the ceremony the Philistines fell upon the assembly, but, with the assistance of a thunderstorm, the Israelites gained a complete victory and recovered their cities from Ekron to Gath, whilst Samuel set up a stone between Mizpeh and Shen and called it Ebenezer, saying, " Hitherto hath the Lord helped us." Samuel now judged Israel in Bethel, Gilgal, and Mizpeh, to which places he made yearly circuits from his residence at Ramah; but in B. C. 1112, having become

---

* The LXX. add to 1 Sam. v. 6 that whilst the Philistines were tormented with hæmorrhoids their country was afflicted with mice.— *Patrick.*

† Josephus says seventy persons only were slain, which appears to be the true reading of the sacred text.

very old, he made his sons, Joel and Abiah, judges in Beersheba. 1 Sam. v.-viii. 1, 2.

303. *Judgeships of Samuel's Sons, 1112-1095; Hebrews desire a King.*—The sons of Samuel judged the land till B. C. 1095, when all the elders of Israel (or the legislative assembly of the nation; see sect. 133) gathered together and complained to the father of the cupidity of his children, and, as the country was threatened by the Ammonites, they begged him to grant them a king. Samuel represented to them the evils of a monarchy, but in vain, and at length the Lord desired him to accede to their wishes. About this time a Benjamite named Kish lost his asses, and sent his son Saul, who was the tallest and handsomest young man in Israel, to seek for them. Saul was unsuccessful, but by the advice of his servant he inquired of Samuel, who was still residing at Ramah, and to whom his coming and royal destiny had been previously revealed by God. Samuel satisfied Saul respecting the asses, set him in the chief place amongst thirty other guests, and gave him a portion of the feast which had been set aside in expectation of his coming. In the morning Samuel accompanied him to the end of the city, where he anointed him king and confirmed it by three signs: 1st. That he should meet two men by Rachel's sepulchre who would acquaint him with the recovery of the asses; 2d. That after that he should meet three men in the plain of Tabor with three loaves, three kids, and one bottle of wine; 3d. That a company of prophets should meet him with instruments of music, and the Spirit of the Lord should descend upon him. These events took place as Samuel had foretold, and, having assembled the whole mass of the people at Mizpeh and taken out Saul from the family of Matri and the tribe of Benjamin, he declared him to be king amid the acclamations of the multitude, B. C. 1095. 1 Sam. viii. 3-22; ix.; x.

RUTH.

(Supposed to have been written by Samuel.)

AN EPISODE IN THE HISTORY OF THE JUDGES.—ABOUT B. C. 1320.

---

304. *Character of the Book of Ruth.*—The book of Ruth forms an episode in the history of the judges, and the events it records probably took place during the judgeship of Shamgar, about B. C. 1322–1312. Whilst this book is useful in exhibiting the providence of God over individuals, and interesting as an illustration of life and manners in those ancient times, it is more especially valuable as containing the descent of David in a direct line from Judah, to which tribe the promise of the Messiah belonged. Moreover, the adoption of Ruth, a heathen Moabitess, into the line of the Messiah seems to intimate that mystery which was revealed under the gospel—that the Gentiles should be fellow-heirs and partakers of God's promises in Christ. Eph. iii. 6–9.

305. *Story of Ruth, cir. 1322.*—Elimelech, a native of Bethlehem-judah, had been driven by a famine to the land of the Moabites, east of the Dead Sea. Here he died, leaving his wife, Naomi, with two sons, but the latter subsequently married two Moabite women, Orpah and Ruth. After ten years Naomi's two sons died also, and the bereaved widow desired to send her two daughters-in-law each to her mother's house, whilst she herself returned to Bethlehem-judah. Orpah then affectionately kissed Naomi and departed, but Ruth refused to go, saying, " Whither thou goest, I will go ; and where thou lodgest, I will lodge : thy people shall be my people, and thy God my God." The two women then proceeded to Bethlehem, where Naomi sent Ruth to glean in the field of Boaz, a kinsman, who behaved kindly to her and invited her to take refreshment with his reapers. When Naomi heard this she directed Ruth how to remind Boaz of their close relationship, which Boaz immediately acknowledged, and soon after married her according to the law of Moses (sect. 122). Boaz and Ruth then had a son named Obed, who was the father of Jesse and grandfather of David, from whom was descended the Messiah. Matt. i. 5. Boaz was descended from Judah through Pharez (sect. 62).

1 AND 2 SAMUEL; 1 AND 2 KINGS.

HISTORY OF THE JEWS UNDER A MONARCHY. B. C. 1095 to 588—508 YEARS.

[**1 Samuel** records the judgeships of Eli and of Samuel and his sons,* and the reign of Saul, B. C. 1181–1055, about one hundred and twenty-six years. **2 Samuel** records nearly all the reign of David, B. C. 1055–1015, about forty years. The two books derive their name from being in part written by Samuel. He wrote the first twenty-four chapters of the first book, but the remainder is supposed to have been written by the prophets Gad and Nathan: "Now the acts of David, first and last, behold, they are written in the book of Samuel the seer, and in the book of Nathan the prophet, and in the book of Gad the seer." 1 Chron. xxix. 29. Samuel could not have written the whole, because his death occurs in the twenty-fifth chapter of the first book, and the remainder of the first and whole of the second book relate events which took place after his death. The two books were considered as one in the Hebrew canon, and are termed the first and second Books of Kings in the Vulgate.

1 Kings begins in the last year of David's reign, and ends with the death of Jehoshaphat, B. C. 1015–889—one hundred and twenty-six years—including the reign of Solomon, and the reigns of Rehoboam, Abijah, Asa, and Jehoshaphat over Judah, and of Jeroboam, Nadab, Baasha, Elah, Zimri, Omri and Tibni, and Ahab over Israel. **2 Kings** extends from the death of Jehoshaphat to the destruction of Jerusalem by Nebuchadnezzar, B. C. 889–588—about three hundred years—including the continuation of the contemporaneous history of the kingdoms of Israel and Judah till the former was subverted by the Assyrian captivity, B. C. 721, and the latter by the Babylonian captivity, B. C. 588. The two books are generally ascribed to Ezra, although some have imputed them to Jeremiah, and others to Isaiah. They were considered as

---

* See Table of "Seven Servitudes," etc., p. 148.

one book in the Hebrew canon, and are termed the third and fourth Books of Kings in the Septuagint and Vulgate.]

ANALYSIS.

History of the Single Monarchy.

1. Saul, 1095-1056.—Defeat of the Ammonites, 1095.—Defeat of the Philistines; gallantry of Jonathan, 1093.—Defeat of the Moabites, Edomites, kings of Zobah, and Amalekites, 1079.—David anointed king, 1063.—Slays Goliath.—Excites the jealousy of Saul.—Flies from court, 1062.—His covenant with Jonathan.—Goes to the Philistines, but at length returns to Judah.—Saul massacres the priests at Nob, 1062.—David rescues Keilah, and flees from Saul to Ziph, Maon, and Engedi.—Forbears to slay Saul at Engedi, 1061.—Death of Samuel, 1060.—David marries Nabal's wife.—Forbears to slay Saul at Ziph, 1060, but flies to the Philistines, 1058.—Philistine invasion; Saul consults the witch of Endor, 1056.—Defeat and suicide of Saul.—His character.—*Reigned forty years.* . . . . page 169.

2. David, 1056-1015.—Defeats the Amalekites, and is proclaimed at Hebron, 1056.—Abner joins David, but is slain by Joab, 1048.—Ishbosheth slain; David rules all Israel, 1048.—Takes Jerusalem from the Jebusites.—Defeats the Philistines, 1043.—Removes the ark from Kirjath-jearim to Jerusalem, 1042.—Conquers the Philistines, Moabites, Edomites, and Syrians.—Adopts Mephibosheth, 1040.—Defeats the Ammonites and Syrians, 1037-1035.—Adultery with Bathsheba, 1035.—Death of his child, 1034.—Solomon born, 1033.—Rabbah taken, 1033.—Tamar abused by Amnon, 1032.—Amnon slain and Absalom exiled, 1030.—Return of Absalom, 1027.—Absalom's revolt, 1023.—David leaves Jerusalem.—His concubines insulted.—Ahithophel's counsel rejected.—David prepares for battle.—Absalom's defeat and death.—David returns to Jerusalem.—Dissensions between Judah and Israel; revolt of Sheba, 1022.—Amasa and Sheba slain.—Famine for three years, 1022-1019.—Atonement for Saul's slaughter of the Gibeonites, 1019.—David's last expedition against the Philistines, 1018.—Numbering of the people, and 70,000 slain by pestilence, 1017.—Revolt of Adonijah, 1015.—Solomon declared successor.—Death of David, 1015.—Character of David.—*Reigned forty years.* . . page 178.

3. Solomon, 1015-975.—Extent of the kingdom.—Joab and Adonijah slain, and Abiathar banished, 1014.—Character of Joab.—Shimei slain, 1011.—Solomon's marriage with Pharaoh's daughter, 1014; his singular wisdom.—Commerce of Solomon.—Building of the temple and palaces, 1012-992.—Description of the temple.—Its dedication, 1005.—Glory of Solomon; visits of the queen of Sheba, etc.—Kingdom disturbed by idolatry and faction.—Death and character of Solomon, 975.—*Reigned forty years.* . . . . page 191.

§ Accession of Rehoboam; revolt of the ten tribes, 975. page 198.
§ Prefatory review of the history of the divided monarchies.—Contracted frontiers.—Reciprocal relations of the two monarchies.—Causes which led to their destruction.—Idolatry of Israel.—Idolatry of Judah. . . . . page 199.

SYNCHRONISTICAL TABLE OF THE

JUDAH.

First Period.
B. C. 975–884.
From the revolt of the ten tribes until Jehu destroyed the dynasty of Ahab in Israel and slew Ahaziah in Judah.

1. **Rehoboam, 975.**—Warned by Shemaiah not to war against Israel; built fenced cities. *Shishak* invades Judah and plunders the temple.
2. **Abijah, 958.**—Defeats Jeroboam; heart not perfect.
3. **Asa. 955.**—Suppresses idolatry; defeats *Zerah* the Ethiopian; leagues with *Benhadad* I. of Syria, to attack *Baasha* of Israel; dies of diseased feet; seeks physicians more than the Lord.
4. **Jehoshaphat, 914.**—Upholds the worship of Jehovah; organizes national education; fortifies Judah; levies an army; appoints judges; flourishing state of the kingdom; marries his son *Jehoram* to *Athaliah*, Ahab's daughter; joins Ahab against Ramoth-gilead; rebuked by Jehu; tries to revive the commerce of Solomon, on the Red Sea, to Ophir; defeats confederacy of Moabites and Ammonites; allies with Jehoram of Israel to put down Moabite revolt; his son shares the throne.
5. **Jehoram, 889.**—Sins like his father-in-law, Ahab; establishes idolatry; *Idumæa* secedes wholly from Judah.
6. **Ahaziah, 885.**—Sins like Ahab; allies with Jehoram of Israel; slain by Jehu.

Prophetical schools established in Judah and Israel from the time of Samuel.

Celebrated Prophets of Israel.

Elijah, 910–896.—Predicted three years' drought; fed by ravens and exhaustless oil and meal; restores widow of Zarephath's son; proves the superiority of Jehovah to Baal at Carmel; flies to Horeb; ordered to anoint Hazael, Jehu, and Elisha; denounces Ahab; predicts Ahaziah's death; divides Jordan; ascends in a chariot of fire.

Elisha, 896–838.—Receives mantle of Elijah; divides Jordan; heals waters at Jericho; slays forty-two children by two she-bears; supplies allied armies with water; promises the Shunammite a son; heals Naaman; Gehazi leprous; makes iron axe swim; discloses Benhadad's counsels to Jehoram; blinds Syrian host; promises provisions at siege of Samaria; heals deadly pottage; feeds one hundred men with twenty loaves; restores Shunammite's son; foretells seven years' famine, death of Benhadad and accession of Hazael; sends to anoint Jehu; promises three victories to Joash; a corpse revived in his tomb.

Second Period.
B. C. 884–721.
From the simultaneous accession of Jehu in Israel and usurpation of Athaliah in Judah, until Israel was carried away captive by the Assyrian power.

7. **Athaliah's usurpation, 884.**—Joash saved; educated by Jehoiada the priest; Athaliah slain; Joash anointed king.
8. **Jehoash, or Joash, 878.**—Jehoiada regent; worship of Jehovah restored; death of Jehoiada; re-establishment of Baal; part of the kingdom ravaged by Hazael; Joash slain by his servants.
9. **Amaziah, 839.**—Begins well; defeats the Edomites; worships the Edomite gods; challenges *Joash* of Israel, but is defeated; slain at Lachish.
10. **Uzziah, 810.**—Influence of Zechariah; kingdom flourishes; Uzziah smitten with leprosy.
11. **Jotham, 758.**—Reigned righteously and prosperously; *decline of the Syrian power.*

    Joel prophesied, cir. 800.
    Isaiah prophesied, cir. 760–698.
    Micah prophesied, cir. 750–710.
12. **Ahaz, 742.**—Worships Baal and Molech; first invasion of *Pekah* of Israel and *Rezin* of Syria; Isaiah gives to Ahaz the sign of a virgin's conception; second invasion of Pekah and Rezin; Ahaz applies to **Tiglath-pileser,** king of Assyria; worships the gods of Damascus.
13. **Hezekiah, 726.**—Breaks the brazen serpent, and destroys idolatry; restores the worship of Jehovah; celebrates the passover; rebels against Shalmaneser, 725; defeats the Philistines.

    Explan. Tiglath-pileser had made Ahaz tributary, but Hezekiah now refused to pay this tribute to *Shalmaneser,* who was the son and successor of Tiglath.

HISTORY OF JUDAH AND ISRAEL.

ISRAEL.

From the revolt of the ten tribes until Jehu destroyed the dynasty of Ahab in Israel and slew Ahaziah in Judah.   First Period. B. C. 975-884.

1. **Jeroboam, 975.**—Fortifies Shechem. Establishes golden-calf worship and profane priesthood. Man of God sent to Bethel. Ahijah's prophecy. Defeated by Abijah. **Made Israel to sin.**
2. **Nadab, 954.**—Worships the calves.
3. **Baasha, 953.**—Worships the calves. Allies with Benhadad I. Fortifies *Ramah*, but stopped by *Asa's* interference.
4. **Elah, 930.**—Assassinated by Zimri his captain.
5. **Zimri, 929.**—Reigned seven days; burnt himself at Tirzah.
6. **Omri. 929.**—Factions of Omri and Tibni. Omri reigns wickedly.
7. **Ahab, 918.**—Marries *Jezebel*, a Phœnician princess; worships Phœnician gods, *Baal* and *Astarte*; three years' famine; Jezebel persecutes the prophets; grand trial on *Carmel* between **Elijah** and priests of *Baal:* ELIJAH ordered to anoint *Elisha, Hazael*, and *Jehu*. War with Syria. First campaign of Benhadad II.; siege of Samaria; second campaign; Benhadad defeated at Aphek; unholy alliance between Syria and Israel; Ahab seizes Naboth's vineyard; *Elijah's fearful prophecy;* unites with Jehoshaphat against Ramoth-gilead; killed by a random arrow; Jericho rebuilt.
8. **Ahaziah. 897.**—Worships both Baal and the calves; revolt of the Moabites; Ahaziah sick; sends to Baal-zebub.
9. **Jehoram. 896.**—Worships the calves; *death of Elijah:* allies with Jehoshaphat to put down Moabite revolt; saved by Elisha; Elisha heals Naaman; other miracles; Benhadad II. again besieges Samaria; fearful famine; Elisha restores the Shunammite's son; foretells the accession of Hazael; anoints Jehu; destruction of the reigning dynasty. [**Elijah and Elisha,** *see opposite page*.]

Rise of the kingdom of Syria.—Syria was anciently divided into small independent states, but *David* reduced them to a province. In Solomon's reign *Rezon* seized *Damascus* and erected a kingdom. *Monarchs.*—Rezon, 980; Benhadad I., 940; Benhadad II., 910; Hazael, 885; Benhadad III., 839; Rezin, 742. Kingdom overthrown by Assyria, 740.

From the simultaneous accession of Jehu in Israel and usurpation of Athaliah in Judah until Israel was carried away captive by the Assyrian power.   Second Period. B. C. 884-721.

10. **Jehu, 884.**—Slays Jezebel and destroys the house of Ahab; worships the calves; destroys Baal's worshippers; *Hazael* seizes all Israel east of the Jordan.
11. **Jehoahaz, 856.**—Worships the calves; oppressed by *Hazael* and Benhadad III. | **Jonah** prophesies, cir. 862.
12. **Joash. 839.**—Worships the calves; promised three victories by Elisha; defeats Syrians three times; defeats *Amaziah* of Judah.
13. **Jeroboam II.. 825.**—Decline of the Syrian power; brilliant successes against Syria. . . . **Flourishing period of Israelite history.**
Interregnum, 784-773.   [by Shallum. | **Amos** prophesies, 787.
14. **Zechariah, 773.**—Reigned six months; slain | **Hosea** prophesies, 785.
15. **Shallum, 772.**—Reigned one month; assassinated by Menahem.
16. **Menahem, 772.**—First Assyrian invasion under Pul.
17. **Pekahiah, 761.**—Assassinated by Pekah.
18. **Pekah, 759.**—Allies with Rezin, king of Syria, and invades Judah; makes a second invasion; second Assyrian invasion: **Tiglath-pileser** transplants the Syrians and all the tribes east of the Jordan to Media.

Rise of the Assyrian Power.—Prior to PUL the history of this empire is uncertain. *Monarchs.*—Pul. 770; Tiglath-pileser, 750; Shalmaneser, 730; Sennacherib, 715; Esarhaddon, Saosduchinus, Chyniladanus. Empire at length overthrown by Medes and Chaldeans, about B. C. 606.

Interregnum, 739-730.
19. **Hoshea. 730.**—Better than his predecessors; third Assyrian invasion: Shalmaneser makes Hoshea tributary; Hoshea rebels and is imprisoned, 725; siege of Samaria and captivity of Israel, 721; inhabitants transplanted to Media and Inner Asia.
§ Colonization of Samaria by Esarhaddon; origin of the Samaritans.

TABLE OF KINGS OF JUDAH—*Continued.*

Third Period. *From the Assyrian captivity of Israel to the Babylonian captivity of Judah.*
B. C. 721–588.

13. **Hezekiah, continued.**—First Assyrian invasion of Judah: Hezekiah submits to **Sennacherib**, 713; Sennacherib takes Ashdod, and again invades Judah; called away by the invasion of Tirhakah the Ethiopian; miraculous destruction of his army; Hezekiah's sickness, 712; messengers from *Merodach-Baladan*, king of *Babylon*; Isaiah foretells the Babylonian captivity; peaceful state of Judah.

    The Medes and Babylonians had revolted from Assyria after the destruction of the army of Sennacherib, but the *Babylonians* were subsequently reduced by *Esarhaddon*.

    Contemporary Events in Egypt.—The Ethiopians had now for more than two hundred years contested the possession of Egypt. According to Herodotus, Sabaco the Ethiopian abandoned Egypt about B. C. 715, and was succeeded by Sethon, or So, an Egyptian priest, whose power was weakened by the disaffection of the military caste. Probably *Sethon* reigned only in *Lower Egypt*, whilst *Tirhakah*, an Ethiopian, successor of Sabaco and a powerful warrior, reigned in *Upper Egypt*.

14. **Manasseh, 698.**—Restores idolatry and necromancy; carried into Assyrian captivity by Esarhaddon, 677; humbles himself.
15. **Amon, 643.**—Restores idolatry; slain by his servants.
16. **Josiah, 641.**—Seeks God in his youth; purges Judah and Israel from idolatry; repairs the temple, 624; book of the law found by *Hilkiah* and confirmed by *Huldah*; the altar of Jeroboam thrown down. Celebration of a solemn passover, 623; decline of the Assyrian empire under Esarhaddon, Saosduchinus, and Chyniladanus; invasion of Pharaoh-Necho; Josiah slain at Megiddo, 610.

    Egypt increases in strength, whilst the Assyrian power is declining. After Sethon, Egypt was divided by civil war into twelve states, which at length merged into a single kingdom under *Psammetichus* (B. C. 650), and flourished under Greek influence. *Necho*, son of Psammetichus, succeeded, B. C. 617, and fostered commerce, and defeated the Assyrians, but was at length overcome by the Chaldee-Babylonians under Nebuchadnezzar.

    Zephaniah prophesied, cir. 630.
    Jeremiah began to prophesy, 629.
    Habakkuk prophesied, cir. 626.

17. **Jehoahaz, 610.**—Reigns wickedly; deposed by Pharaoh-Necho.
18. **Jehoiakim, 610.**—Reigns wickedly; Jeremiah and Urijah prophesy against him. Charged by Jeremiah with the murder of Urijah. Jeremiah publicly foretells the seventy years' captivity, 607. Pharaoh-Necho defeated by NEBUCHADNEZZAR, *who soon after ascends the throne of the Chaldee-Babylonian kingdom.* Nebuchadnezzar takes Jerusalem; makes Jehoiakim tributary; carries off Daniel and the three pious Jews, 606. Jeremiah's prophecies publicly read a second time. Jehoiakim seeks

    Overthrow of the Assyrian Power; rise of the Medo-Persian and Chaldee-Babylonian Empires.—The MEDES, who had revolted from the Assyrians B. C. 712, conquered the Persians and established an empire. The CHALDEES, about a century later, also revolted from Assyria under *Nabopolassar*, father of NEBUCHADNEZZAR, and seized Babylonia. Nabopolassar then allied with *Cyaxares*, king of the Medes, and the two powers took Nineveh, about B. C. 606. The Medes then possessed Assyria Proper, and the Chaldees all Babylon and its dependent provinces. Nabopolassar was succeeded by **Nebuchadnezzar** very shortly after.

    to destroy him, 605. Jehoiakim revolts from Nebuchadnezzar, 603. Jerusalem blockaded; Jehoiakim slain, 599.
19. **Jehoiachin, or Coniah, 599.**—Nebuchadnezzar besieges Jerusalem in person; carries away Jehoiachin and 10,000 captives, 599.

    Daniel begins to prophesy, cir. 600.

20. **Zedekiah, 599.**—False prophets predict the speedy return from captivity. Zedekiah allies with *Pharaoh-Hophra* (called *Apries* by the Greeks), and rebels, 593. Nebuchadnezzar be-

    Ezekiel begins to prophesy, 595.

TABLE OF KINGS OF JUDAH—*Continued.*
sieges Jerusalem; retreat of Hophra, 590. Zedekiah secretly applies to Jeremiah; the princes throw the prophet into a pit, 589. Jerusalem taken, 588. *Nebuzaradan* sacks the city. *Gedaliah* appointed governor; slain by *Ishmael*. Jeremiah and Baruch go to Egypt; remnant of the people carried to Babylon.
(For the history of Syria see sect. 493, *note*, and of Assyria, see sect. 554. For the life of Elijah see sect. 428, *note*, and of Elisha, see sect. 463, *note*.)

SUMMARY.

I. *History of the Single Monarchy.*

SAUL, 1095—1056. ABOUT FORTY YEARS.

Prophets—Samuel and Gad.

306. ***Defeat of the Ammonites, 1095.*** — Scarcely had Saul ascended the throne when Nahash, king of the Ammonites, marched into the territory east of the Jordan and besieged Jabesh-gilead. The inhabitants offered to surrender, but Nahash declared that he would only come to terms on condition of thrusting out the right eye of each of the besieged. The elders of the city obtained seven days' respite, and their messengers reached Saul, who immediately hewed a yoke of oxen to pieces and sent them throughout Israel, saying, "Whosoever cometh not forth after Saul, and after Samuel, so shall it be done unto his oxen." The people obeyed the summons, to the number of 300,000 Israelites and 30,000 men of Judah. The messengers returned to Jabesh-gilead with promise of help on the morrow, being the very day appointed for the surrender. Saul now divided his army into three divisions, and falling upon the Ammonites at morning watch he routed them by noon. The victory was followed by a national assembly at Gilgal, where Samuel confirmed the election of Saul by sacrifices and rejoicings, testified his own integrity, reproved the people for ingratitude to Jehovah in demanding a king, punished their wickedness by calling down thunder and lightning upon the wheat harvest, and lastly reassured them by declaring that the Lord would not forsake them so long as they served him. 1 Sam. xi.; xii.

307. ***Defeat of the Philistines; Gallantry of Jonathan, 1093.***—Saul had now dismissed all his numerous

army except 3000 men, 2000 of whom he retained at Michmash and Bethel under his own immediate orders, and placed the remaining 1000 under the command of his son Jonathan at Gibeah. At this time the country, or at least the southern tribes, was in subjection to the Philistines, and the latter had garrisons in the land and had deprived the Israelites of smiths,* so that only Saul and Jonathan possessed a sword or spear. Jonathan, however, with his thousand men (probably bowmen and slingers), attacked and overcame a Philistine garrison stationed at Gibeah, upon which the Philistines assembled a host of 30,000 chariots and 6000 cavalry at Michmash, while Saul summoned a fresh army, and, in obedience to the command of Samuel, awaited the prophet's coming at Gilgal. Saul waited for seven days, being the time appointed, but Samuel never came, and the impetuous monarch, seeing that the country was panic-struck and his army leaving him, commenced offering the sacrifices with his own hand. Samuel arrived during the ceremony, rebuked Saul for his presumptuous disobedience, and threatened him with the loss of his kingdom. Saul now joined his son at Gibeah with an army dwindled to six hundred men, but a victory was obtained by the gallantry of Jonathan. The Philistines were securely encamped on the summit of a precipice, whence they descended in three companies and ravaged the country. The young prince and his armor-bearer climbed up the rocks, took the camp by surprise, and slew twenty of the garrison single-handed. A fearful panic seized the enemy; they fled in the utmost confusion, slaying each other in their disorder; whilst Saul and his army, strengthened by re-inforcements and deserters, fell upon the Philistines in their retreat and completed the victory. The defeat would have been decisive, but Saul had weakened his ranks by solemnly saying, "Cursed be the man that eateth before the evening!" and the stern monarch would have slain his own son for having inadvertently partaken of honey had not the heroic prince been rescued by the voice of the people. 1 Sam. xiii.; xiv. 1–46.

---

* A similar prohibition of iron was laid upon the Romans by Porsenna amongst the conditions of peace after Mucius Scævola had attempted to assassinate him.

308. *Defeat of the Moabites, Edomites, Kings of Zobah, and Amalekites, 1079*.—These brilliant successes were speedily followed by the conquest of the Moabites, Edomites, and kings of Zobah;* and in B.C. 1079, Saul was sent by Samuel to destroy Amalek utterly. He accordingly levied an army of 200,000 Israelite infantry and 10,000 men of Judah, and defeated the Amalekites from Havilah† to Shur, on the borders of Egypt, but saved their king, Agag, alive, together with the choicest flocks. Samuel met him on his return and bitterly reproved him for his disobedience, assured him that the kingdom was rent from him, and slew Agag with his own hand. "And Samuel came no more to visit Saul until the day of his death." 1 Sam. xiv. 46–52; xv.

309. *David anointed King, 1063*.—In B.C. 1063, Samuel was sent by God to anoint a son of Jesse to be king in the room of Saul. Having gone to Bethlehem to sacrifice, he sanctified Jesse and his sons, and first looked at Eliab the eldest, but rejected him because the Lord said, "Look not on his countenance nor on the height of his stature, because I have refused him; for the Lord seeth not as man seeth; for man looketh on the outward appearance, but the Lord looketh on the heart." Samuel also rejected Jesse's other sons, Abinadab, Shammah, Nethaneel, Raddai, and Ozem; and, learning of Jesse that the youngest was left behind to keep the sheep, he sent for him, and found him to be a ruddy youth of a beautiful countenance; and God said, "Arise, anoint him; for this is he;" and shortly afterward the young shepherd was called to court to charm away the evil spirit of the monarch by the melody of his harp. 1 Sam. xvi.

310. *Slays Goliath*.—Twenty-six years had now passed since the overthrow of the Philistines at Michmash (sect. 300), and the latter again invaded the territory of Judah. Saul marched against them, and the two armies encamped

---

* **Zobah** was one of the cantons or petty states that existed in Syria before the erection of the kingdom of Damascus by Rezon. (See sect. 362.)

† This *Havilah* must have been situated near the south coast of the Dead Sea. It is impossible that the army of Saul could have penetrated to the junction of the Euphrates and Tigris, where Bochart and Calmet place it.

in the face of each other, on the sides of two opposite mountains separated by a valley. A Philistine named Goliath of Gath, six cubits and a span [11 feet 10 inches] in height, stood forth and proposed that the question of servitude should be decided by single combat, but no Israelite would accept the challenge. At this time David was with his father, whose three sons were in the Israelite army. Forty days having elapsed, Jesse sent David with a present of provisions to the captain of the thousand in which his sons were serving. Here David heard of Goliath's challenge, and learnt that whoever could overcome the Philistine would be rewarded with great riches and the hand of Merab, the king's eldest daughter. Accordingly, though reproved by his brother, he presented himself before Saul and offered to fight the giant, modestly observing that the same Jehovah who had delivered him from the lion and the bear would preserve him from the Philistine. He then, after declining the use of Saul's armor, set out to meet Goliath with only a staff, a sling, and five smooth stones from the brook. The gigantic warrior declared that he would give the flesh of David to the birds of the air and beasts of the field; but the intrepid youth replied, "I come to thee in the name of the Lord of hosts, the God of the armies of Israel, whom thou hast defied: this day will the Lord deliver thee into my hand." A stone from the sling of David struck Goliath in the forehead, and the Philistine was decapitated with his own sword. The enemy fled, and were pursued to the gates of Ekron;* and David was taken to the king's house, and the celebrated friendship commenced between him and Jonathan. 1 Sam. xvii.; xviii. 1–4.

311. *Excites the Jealousy of Saul.*—But the songs in honor of the victory, that "Saul had slain his thousands and David his ten thousands," alarmed the jealousy of the Hebrew king. Thrice the monarch threw a javelin at the warrior, but afterward attempted his death by more secret means. He made him captain† of a thousand, and by repeated promises of his eldest daughter

---

* One of the five townships into which the Philistine power was divided.

† This was a military office, and neither the head nor the judge of a thousand, mentioned in sect. 133.

Merab, whose hand David had won by the slaughter of Goliath, he induced him to engage in hazardous enterprises against the Philistines. The designs of Saul were frustrated and he gave Merab to another, but again hoped to accomplish his end by promising David a younger daughter, Michal, upon his slaying one hundred Philistines. This definite proposal was accepted; David returned with trophies of the slaughter of two hundred of the enemy, and Saul was compelled to fulfil his promise. 1 Sam. xviii. 5–30.

312. *Flies from Court, 1062.*—This new alliance rendered David yet more illustrious, and Saul determined to destroy him at all hazards; but the very efforts he made to secure the crown to his posterity endangered the succession and riveted the public attention on David. For some time Jonathan, the heir-apparent, who loved David as his own soul, preserved a friendly feeling between his father and brother-in-law; but some fresh exploits of the latter against the Philistines brought back the evil spirit to Saul, and whilst David was endeavoring to restore the monarch by his harp he narrowly avoided a javelin from the royal hand, and the same night only escaped with his life by being let down from his window by Michal and having his place supplied by an image. David fled to Ramah, where Samuel resided, and the prophet took him to Naioth.* Three times Saul sent messengers to bring him back, but when the latter saw the company of prophets prophesying with Samuel at their head, they prophesied in like manner, and Saul, who subsequently went in person to enforce his commands, was similarly affected. 1 Sam. xix.

313. *His Covenant with Jonathan.*—David now left Samuel and sought Jonathan at Gibeah, and asked in what way he had sinned, that Saul should seek his life. Jonathan could not believe that his father had entertained such a design, but the two friends at length agreed that David should absent himself from the approaching festival of the new moon,† in order to try the king's tem-

---

* **Naioth** appears to have been a college of prophets near Ramah, over which Samuel presided.

† At this festival (see sect. 186) it appears to have been customary for the king to entertain his principal officers.

per, and that Jonathan should report the result, and a solemn covenant was then made between them. On the second day of the feast Saul missed David, and Jonathan excused his absence by saying that by his permission David had gone to sacrifice with his own family at Bethlehem. Saul then grossly abused Jonathan, and assured him that his succession to the throne could never be secured whilst David lived, and that the latter should surely die. Jonathan ventured to remonstrate, but he narrowly escaped a javelin from the hand of his father. He now saw that David's life was in danger, and next morning went to the field where he was concealed. It had been settled between them that the manner in which Jonathan should shoot three arrows, and the expressions he should use to his attendant lad, were to intimate to David the course to pursue. The unfavorable sign was now given, and the two friends at length parted with many tears. 1 Sam. xx.

314. *Goes to the Philistines, but at length returns to Judah.*—After leaving Jonathan, David, and a few young men who were with him, went to Nob, a sacerdotal city about twelve miles from Gibeah. Here he told the high priest, Ahimelech, that he had been sent by Saul on a private mission, and, having obtained some shew-bread and the arms of Goliath, he fled to Achish, king of the Philistines, at Gath. Here he aroused the jealousy of the Philistine princes, but escaped by feigning himself insane. The cave of Adullam in Judah next afforded him concealment, where he was joined by his relatives and many who were discontented, and thus possessed a force of four hundred men. He now consigned his parents to the care of the king of Moab, and by the direction of the prophet Gad he retired from Adullam to the forest of Hareth. 1 Sam. xxi.; xxii. 1-5.

315. *Saul massacres the Priests at Nob.*—Saul was dwelling at Gibeah when he heard of David's return and place of retreat, and whilst standing under a tree with his spear in his hand he indignantly cried to his officers around him, "Will the son of Jesse give you fields and vineyards, and make you captains of thousands and of hundreds, that you all conspire against me?" Doeg the Edomite then told the king of the assistance David had

received from Ahimelech at Nob. Saul immediately summoned the high priest and all the priests of his family, and charged them with having conspired with David against him, and, without listening to their excuses, he commanded his body-guard to slay them. No one moved to obey the order, when the king turned to Doeg, who fell upon them and slew eighty-seven in that day. Doeg then marched against Nob and massacred alike the priests and women with their families and flocks, but Abiathar, the son of Ahimelech, escaped to David. 1 Sam. xxii. 6-23.

316. *David rescues Keilah, and retires to Ziph, Maon, and Engedi, cir. 1061.*—About this time David heard that the Philistines had come up to carry away the harvest from the threshing-floors in Keilah, and he immediately marched against the enemy, defeated them with great slaughter, and relieved the town. Saul, hearing that David was still in Keilah, exclaimed, "God hath delivered him into my hand, for he is shut in, by entering into a town that hath gates and bars;" and he immediately prepared to besiege the city. David, however, was soon apprised of the threatened danger, and, being informed by the sacred oracle that the inhabitants of Keilah would deliver him up, he withdrew with his six hundred men to the wilderness of Ziph, in the eastern part of Judah, toward the Dead Sea. Saul sought him every day, but without success. Jonathan, however, met him in a wood, and said, "Saul, my father, shall not find thee, and thou shalt be king over Israel." Some Ziphites at length acquainted Saul with David's retreat, and the king, having blessed the informers, commenced a fresh pursuit. David withdrew southward into the wilderness of Maon, but was still followed by Saul; and the latter reached one side of a mountain, whilst David was encamped on the other, when he was suddenly called off by the news of a Philistine invasion. 1 Sam. xxiii. 6-28.

317. *Forbears to slay Saul at Engedi, 1061.*— David now sought refuge in the rocky heights in the wilderness of Engedi, but his movements were betrayed, and Saul, having returned from the Philistine war, commenced scouring the mountains with 3000 men. It was at this period that the king happened to repose in a cave at noon, whilst David and his men were hidden by the darkness

of the inner extremity. The band of outlaws joyfully congratulated their captain upon having his enemy in his power, and David arose and cut off the skirts of Saul's robe; but his heart soon smote him, and his habitual self-command stifled the desire for revenge. "The Lord forbid," said the pious son of Jesse, "that I should stretch my hand against the Lord's anointed!" He restrained his soldiers and aroused the monarch to a sense of his danger. The heart of Saul was touched; the forbearance of David seemed to him like an act of superhuman virtue; and he burst into tears and remorsefully confessed that the crown of Israel was indeed designed for a nobler and better man. Before they parted David took an oath that he would not destroy the family of the king, and Saul then returned to Gibeah. 1 Sam. xxiii. 29; xxiv.

318. *Death of Samuel, 1060; David marries Nabal's wife.*—In B. C. 1060, Samuel died, and was buried by all Israel at Ramah. The same year David left Engedi for the wilderness of Paran, where Nabal churlishly refused to supply him with provisions.* David prepared to inflict summary punishment, but was stopped by Abigail, wife of Nabal, who pacified him by presents and conciliatory speeches. Ten days afterward Nabal died, and David sent for Abigail and married her; at the same time he married Ahinoam of Jezreel, for Saul had given Michal to Phalti, son of Laish. 1 Sam. xxv.

319. *David forbears to slay Saul at Ziph, 1060, but flies to the Philistines, 1058.*—David then returned to the wilderness of Ziph, but his retreat was again betrayed to Saul, who, forgetting his former repentance, once more scoured the country with 3000 men. Here the king was again reproved by the forbearance of David, who entered his camp at night and carried off the spear from his bolster and the cruse of water from his side, without inflicting on him the slightest personal injury. Saul once more confessed his own wickedness and the righteousness of his son-in-law. But David could not trust in his sincerity, and retired again in B. C. 1058 to

---

* It is probable that David's forces had been of the utmost service to Nabal in protecting his flocks and shepherds from the depredations of the Arab races who roved about the southern borders.

Achish at Gath, who gave him Ziklag* as a residence for himself and band. Here he remained until the death of Saul, a period of one year and four months, making occasional excursions against the Geshurites, Gezrites, and Amalekites,† and at the same time won the confidence of Achish by declaring that his expeditions had been directed against Judah. 1 Sam. xxvi.; xxvii.

320. *Philistine Invasion; Saul consults the Witch of Endor, 1056.*—The time of Saul's death now approached, and a presentiment of evil oppressed his spirit. The Philistine armies under Achish had again invaded Palestine and encamped on Mount Gilboa, but Saul was no longer animated by military enthusiasm or confidence in Jehovah. He gazed upon the enemy's host with a trembling heart; and when he inquired of the Lord, the Lord answered neither by dreams, nor by Urim, nor by the prophets. In this extremity he sought the witch of Endor in disguise, for he had previously cut off all wizards and those who had familiar spirits, and he now desired the woman to call from the grave his deceased friend and early counsellor, Samuel. The witch and the king were soon astonished by the actual appearance of the prophet from his tomb, but in the place of friendly consolation they heard nothing but fearful prophecies and mysterious denunciations. "The Lord," cried the terrible spectre, "will deliver thee and Israel into the hands of the Philistines, and to-morrow thou and thy sons shall be with me." 1 Sam. xxviii.

321. *Defeat and Suicide of Saul, 1056.*—The broken-hearted monarch returned to the fated field. The Israelites were defeated on the mountains of Gilboa; the three sons of Saul, including Jonathan, were slain; and he himself, after begging his armor-bearer to thrust him through, fell upon his sword, and his faithful servant followed his example. The Philistines stripped the bodies

---

* Whilst David was at Ziklag he received most important reinforcements from his own countrymen, and a long list has come down to us of more or less eminent persons who, through dissatisfaction with Saul, became voluntary exiles and staked all their prospects on David's cause. 1 Chron. xii. 1–22.

† These were nomad races on the southern borders of Palestine. *Geshur* was also the name of one of the early petty Syrian kingdoms. (See sect. 335.)

of Saul and his sons. The head and armor of Saul they sent into Philistia, and the armor was subsequently placed in the temple of Ashtaroth; but they fastened the corpses on the wall of Bethshan, a town west of the Jordan (afterward called Scythopolis). The Jabesh-gileadites,* from the east of the Jordan, afterward recovered the bodies, burnt them, and buried them beneath a tree and fasted seven days. 1 Sam. xxix.-xxxi.; 1 Chron. x.

322. *Character of Saul.*—The character of Saul may be briefly drawn. Though distinguished as a warrior, yet he never neglected the internal affairs of his kingdom, and severely punished all idolatrous acts and rebellion against Jehovah. Though he incessantly labored to secure the succession to his family, he seems to have discharged the trust reposed in him for the good of the state; no complaints were uttered against him after his death, but eleven tribes remained faithful to his son Ishbosheth. His great error consisted in refusing to rule in the spirit of theocracy—in forgetting that he was a vassal of Jehovah and bound to follow the divine commands in opposition to his own views. He thus rendered himself unfit to become the founder of a royal house, as he could not be regarded as a worthy example for his successors. In person he was tall, and, when young, eminently handsome, but his appearance probably changed with his years, for we can only recall him as a gloomy, stern, and suspicious monarch.

DAVID: OVER JUDAH, 1056–1048; OVER JUDAH AND ISRAEL, 1048–1015.—ABOUT FORTY YEARS IN ALL.

Prophets, Nathan and Gad.

323. **Defeats the Amalekites and proclaimed at Hebron, 1056.**—David was at Ziklag at the time of Saul's death. He had accompanied Achish in his expedition against Israel, but the Philistine princes were fearful lest their ancient enemy should prove a faithless ally, and Achish was compelled to dismiss both him and his band. On returning to Ziklag, David found that the Amalekites had pillaged and burnt the city and carried

---

* The Jabesh-gileadites were probably grateful to Saul for having delivered them from the Ammonites. (Sect. 306.)

away the women and families. In the madness of grief his band talked of stoning him, but David having inquired of God, and learnt the course of the ravagers from a sick Egyptian slave whom they had left behind, he fell upon the Amalekites the next evening, recovered the captives and plunder, and seized so much additional booty that he was enabled to send presents to all the elders of Judah who had favored his cause. Two days after returning from the slaughter an Amalekite brought him the crown and bracelets which had been stripped from the corpse of Saul, and boasted that he himself had slain the king. David executed the messenger as a regicide, and lamented the death of Saul and Jonathan in a most affecting elegy. He then, in obedience to the sacred oracle, went up to Hebron, where the elders of Judah anointed him king. David was now thirty years old; he reigned over Judah at Hebron for seven years and six months, B. C. 1056–1048, whilst Ishbosheth, son of Saul, had been established over the remaining eleven tribes through the influence of Abner. 1 Sam. xxx.; 2 Sam. i.; ii. 1–11.

324. *Abner joins David, but slain by Joab, 1048.*—In B. C. 1053, Abner, who was now the commander of Ishbosheth's army, marched against Joab,* the commander under David, to reduce Judah to obedience. The two armies met at Gibeon, and twelve men from each side engaged in combat, but were all slain in the struggle. The battle then became general; the army of Ishbosheth was defeated, and Abner only escaped by slaying Asahel, the brother of Joab, who pertinaciously pursued him. Some time afterward Ishbosheth quarrelled with Abner for being too free with Saul's concubine, Rizpah, and the indignant general immediately made arrangements for bringing over the eleven tribes to David. He went to Hebron and communicated with the elders of Israel—*i. e.* the national assembly (sect. 134)—and restored to David his former wife, Michal; but his career was sud-

---

* Joab was one of the three sons of Zeruiah, sister of David. Of these, *Joab* was slain at the horns of the altar, in the beginning of Solomon's reign, for his share in the rebellion of Adonijah (sect. 353). *Asahel* was slain by Abner, as recorded in the present section. The fate of *Abishai*, the third, is unknown.

denly closed by Joab, who treacherously assassinated him in revenge for the death of Asahel. 2 Sam. ii. 12–32; iii.

325. *Ishbosheth slain; David rules all Israel, 1048.*—The death of Abner called forth the tears of David, but heralded the downfall of his enemy. Whilst Ishbosheth was sleeping at midday he was murdered by his two captains, Baanah and Rechab, who carried his head to David in expectation of reward, but were summarily executed for their treachery. The elders of the eleven tribes—*i. e.* the national assembly (sect. 134)—then went to Hebron and anointed David to be their king; "Because," they said, "under Saul thou wast our general, and Jehovah hath said of thee, Thou shalt rule my people." And David made a league with them in Hebron.* 2 Sam. iv.; v. 1–5.

326. *Takes Jerusalem from the Jebusites.*—After this David marched against Jebus, or Jerusalem,† which in consequence of its natural strength had been retained by the Jebusites in the centre of the Israelite population. The Jebusites defied his power, but David declared that

---

* This was equivalent to a coronation oath, and denoted that David was a constitutional, and not an arbitrary, monarch.

† **Description of Jerusalem.**—Jerusalem is built on four hills—Zion, Millo or Acra, Moriah, and Bezetha—and is surrounded by a valley, again encompassed by high ground. The stronghold of the Jebusites was on the southern and larger hill of Zion, on which was subsequently built the City of David; but their town was built on the northern hill, called Millo in the Hebrew and *Acra* (or "citadel") in the Greek. Zion was subsequently called the Upper City, and Acra the Lower City, and the depression between the two mountains was filled up by Solomon. East of Millo and Zion was the flat-topped hill of Moriah, on which Solomon built the temple. The same king united Zion and Moriah by a causeway, and the Maccabees filled up the valley between Moriah and Millo. At a later period a fourth hill was included on the north of Moriah, called Bezetha. The brook Kidron winds round Jerusalem on the north and east along the valley of Jehoshaphat. On the south of Zion lies the narrow valley of Hinnom or Tophet. The ravines on three sides of the ancient city form a natural defence. On the west the descents are more gradual, but are protected by depressions of moderate depth, which might have been easily fortified against the simple forms of attack known to the Hebrews. The hills which look down on Jerusalem, and lay it open to destructive attack from modern artillery, probably explain the abundance of spring-water for which the city has been celebrated; for in the numerous blockades which it has endured the besiegers are said to have been often distressed for want of water, the besieged never.

whoever first scaled the wall and drove off the defenders should be made his chief captain. The feat was accomplished by Joab, and the king took the stronghold of Zion and made the city his metropolis; and, with the assistance of artisans sent him by Hiram, king of Tyre, he built a palace on Mount Zion, which gave it the name of the City of David. 2 Sam. v. 6–16; 1 Chron. xi. 4–9.

327. *Defeats the Philistines, 1043.*—In B.C. 1043 the Philistines twice encamped in the valley of Rephaim, south of Jerusalem, but each time were routed by David. 2 Sam. v. 17–25; 1 Chron. xi. 12–20; xiv. 8, 17.

328. *Removes the Ark from Kirjath-jearim to Jerusalem, 1042.*—In B.C. 1042, David removed the ark from Kirjath-jearim to Jerusalem, but on the way Uzzah was slain by God for sacrilegiously touching it, and the king left it without the city, in the house of Obed-edom. Three months afterward, David, having seen that the Lord blessed the household of Obed-edom, brought it to his own house with sacrifices and rejoicings. On this occasion Michal sharply taunted David with his unkingly dancing, but he answered her with humility and zeal, and perpetual barrenness was the punishment for her presumption. David would now have built a temple for the ark, but was commanded by the prophet Nathan to relinquish the design to his successor; but Nathan at the same time predicted the glory of his posterity, saying, "I will raise up thy seed after thee, which shall be of thy sons; and I will establish his kingdom. He shall build me an house, and I will establish his throne for ever." 2 Sam. vi.; vii.; 1 Chron. xiii.; xv.–xvii.

329. *Conquers the Philistines, Moabites, Syrians, and Edomites, 1040.*—In B.C. 1040, David prepared for an extensive war upon the bordering nations, and the most brilliant successes followed the progress of his armies. The Philistines were first vanquished, and Gath and its dependencies were taken by the Hebrews. David then conquered Moab, and, measuring the whole country with a line, he slew one half the nation and rendered the other half tributary. He next invaded the dominions of Hadadezer, king of Zobab (a Syrian state), and advancing to the Euphrates, he took from him one hundred chariots, seven hundred cavalry, and 20,000 infantry;

whilst the Syrians of Damascus, who marched to the assistance of the enemy, were defeated with the loss of 22,000 men. David hamstrung the chariot-horses, reserving a sufficient number for one hundred chariots; he garrisoned Syria and made the people tributary, and returned to Jerusalem with shields of gold and an immense quantity of brass. This victory was followed by a visit from Joram, son of Toi, king of Hamath (a Syrian state), who brought presents to David and congratulated him on his conquest. After the Syrian campaign the Israelite army turned southward and invaded Edom. The conquering Hebrews slew 18,000 Edomites in the Valley of Salt, and garrisoned the whole country and made the people tributary. By these conquests the dominions of David were extended to the Euphrates on the north and east, and to the Red Sea on the south. 2 Sam. viii.; 1 Chron. xviii.

330. *Adopts Mephibosheth, 1040.*—David, being now firmly established, fulfilled his former covenant with Jonathan by sending for his son Mephibosheth, whom he placed under the care of Ziba, an old servant of Saul's, and entertained at his own table. Mephibosheth had been lamed by his nurse in both feet during the flight from Jezreel on the arrival of the tidings of the deaths of Saul and Jonathan. 2 Sam. ix.

331. *Defeats the Ammonites and Syrians, 1037-1035.*—In B. C. 1037, Nahash, king of the Ammonites, died, and David sent ambassadors to condole with his son Hanun. The Ammonite princes persuaded their new king that their messengers were sent as spies, and Hanun accordingly shaved off half their beards, cut off their garments, and sent them back to David; and, seeing that a war would be now inevitable, he hired 20,000 infantry from the two Syrian states of Beth-rehob and Zoba; 1000 men of King Maacah, in the immediate north of Palestine; and 12,000 men of Tob, a small territory north of Manasseh and east of the Jordan. Joab was immediately sent by David against the combined forces. He divided his army into two divisions; with the first, consisting of chosen men, he fell upon the Syrians, whilst he sent the other, under his brother Abishai, against the Ammonites. The enemy were routed on all sides, and the conquering Hebrews returned to Jerusalem. The

next year, B. C. 1036, a fresh army of Syrians were collected by Hadadezer, but David quickly reassembled his forces, crossed the Jordan, and defeated him at Helam; the fighting-men of seven hundred chariots and 40,000 cavalry fell upon the field of battle, and Shobach, the commander-in-chief, was slain. This decisive victory prevented the Syrians from affording any further aid to the Ammonites, and the next year, B. C. 1035, David sent Joab to destroy Ammon and besiege Rabbah—*i. e.* " chief city"—whilst he himself remained at Jerusalem. 2 Sam. x.; 1 Chron. xix.

332. *Adultery with Bathsheba, 1035.*—During the siege David was attracted by the beauty of Bathsheba, wife of Uriah, and sent for her to his palace whilst her husband was serving under Joab at Rabbah. The natural result followed the intercourse, and David sought to veil his guilt by sending for Uriah to Jerusalem, but the gallant soldier refused to sleep in his house whilst his companions-in-arms were encamped in the open fields. The disappointed monarch sent him back with directions to Joab to compass his death by placing him "in the forefront of the hottest battle," and the adultery of David was quickly followed by the murder of Uriah. Scarcely was the mourning of Bathsheba completed when David made her his wife and she bore him a son. The anger of the Lord was now aroused, and Nathan was sent to David, and by the parable of the poor man's ewe lamb forced the king to become his own judge. He then assured David that in punishment for his crime the sword should never depart from his house, that evil should be raised up against him in his own family, that his own wives should be openly abused, and that the child of Bathsheba should die. 2 Sam. xi.; xii. 1-12.

333. *Death of his Child, 1034; Solomon born, 1033; Rabbah taken, 1033.*—David confessed and repented of his crime, but scarcely had Nathan left his presence when his child by Bathsheba was seized with sickness, and though he prayed and fasted before God, yet it died on the seventh day after. The bereaved parents were at length comforted, and Bathsheba bore Solomon in B. C. 1033. Meanwhile, Joab had reduced Rabbah to extremities, and sent to David to come in

person and take the honors of the capture. David then went down and took the city; the royal crown, rich with jewels, and weighing a talent of gold [170 oz. = £680],* was transferred to his head, and the inhabitants were either slain or made to labor in brick-kilns or with saws, axes, and harrows. 2 Sam. xii. 13–31; 1 Chron. xx. 1–3.

334. *Tamar abused by Amnon, 1032.*—The fearful prophecies of Nathan were now to be accomplished in the family of David, and a revolting outrage divided the royal household, and ultimately led to fratricide and rebellion. Amnon, son of David by Ahinoam, being in love with his half-sister Tamar, incestuously abused her. The injured princess rent her garments and put ashes on her head, when her brother Absalom met her, learnt the cause of her grief, enjoined her to secrecy, and received her into his own house. 2 Sam. xiii. 1–20.

335. *Amnon slain, and Absalom exiled, 1030.*— For two years Absalom never spoke to his brother Amnon; but in B. C. 1030 he invited all his brothers to his sheep-shearing, and Amnon amongst them. During the feast Amnon was assassinated by the servants of Absalom, who instantly fled to the king of Geshur, whilst his remaining brothers returned to weep with their sorrowing father. 2 Sam. xiii. 20–38.

336. *Return of Absalom, 1027.*—After three years David forgot the murder of Amnon and mourned for the return of Absalom; and Joab, by means of a wise woman of Tekoah, persuaded the king to send to Geshur for the refugee. Absalom then returned to Jerusalem, and was praised throughout Israel as the most beautiful man in the kingdom; and his hair, which was annually polled, is said to have weighed two hundred royal shekels [91 oz.]. For two years longer David refused to see his favorite son, and Joab, who had been twice sent for by Absalom to effect a reconciliation, persisted in declining to come. At length, in B. C. 1025, Absalom obtained an interview with the commander-in-chief by the ingenious device of firing his field of barley, and Joab mediated between the

---

* The Syriac talent weighed fifteen Attic minæ, or one-fourth of the common Attic talent.

father and son, and "the king kissed Absalom." 2 Sam. xiii. 39; xiv.

337. *Absalom's Revolt, 1023.*—The last and severest calamity threatened by Nathan was now to be inflicted upon David, but the aged monarch was prepared to endure the affliction with a submissive humility which proved the depth of his piety and sincerity of his repentance. His son Absalom had won the hearts of all Israel by fair speeches and courteous behavior. In B. C. 1023 he obtained the permission of David to go to Hebron under the pretence of performing a vow; but he sent spies throughout all the tribes, saying, "As soon as ye hear the sound of the trumpet ye shall say, Absalom reigneth in Hebron." He then left Jerusalem with two hundred men totally ignorant of his design, and on arriving at Hebron he sent for Ahithophel the Gilonite, David's counsellor, whilst fresh adherents rapidly poured in and strengthened the conspiracy. 2 Sam. xv. 1–12.

338. *David leaves Jerusalem.*—Directly David heard of this formidable revolt he retired from Jerusalem to avoid a sudden attack, and left ten concubines to keep his house. All his servants followed him, with the Cherethites, Pelethites, and six hundred Gittites* from Gath, under Ittai; and though David especially advised Ittai to return because he was an exile, the latter declared his determination to follow him until death. Zadok and Abiathar the priests had also borne the ark after the king, but David ordered them to carry it back to the city and send him an account of future proceedings by their two sons, Ahimaaz, son of Zadok, and Jonathan, son of Abiathar. David and his followers, weeping and barefoot, then ascended Mount Olivet, where he heard that Ahithophel—"whose counsel," says the sacred record, "was like the oracle of God"—had joined Absalom in the revolt. David prayed that his advice might be turned into foolishness, and shortly afterward was joined by Hushai the Archite, whom he desired to join Absalom and endeavor to defeat Ahithophel and communicate through

---

* These Cherethites, Pelethites, and Gittites appear to have been foreign troops from Philistia and the neighborhood, whom David had taken into his pay.

Jonathan and Ahimaaz. After passing the summit of Olivet, David was met by Ziba, the servant of Mephibosheth, with two asses laden with provisions. On being asked for his master, Ziba falsely replied that he stayed at Jerusalem to receive Absalom, upon which the king transferred to him all that he had previously given to Mephibosheth. At Bahurim, Shimei, a member of Saul's house, came forth and cursed and threw stones at David and his people; but though Abishai, son of Zeruiah and brother of Joab, begged permission to slay the rebel, David indignantly refused, choosing rather to bear with an indignity which he considered to be a chastening from Jehovah. 2 Sam. xv. 13–37; xvi. 1–14.

339. *David's Concubines Insulted.*—Meanwhile, Absalom had reached Jerusalem with Ahithophel and been joined by Hushai. His first act was in accordance with the advice of Ahithophel, and, whilst it proved the consummate wisdom of the counsellor, it fulfilled the most mysterious prophecy of Nathan. To assure the people that the breach between himself and his father was irreparable, and that no sacrifice of his adherents would obtain a pardon for himself, he publicly abused his father's ten concubines. 2 Sam. xvi. 15–23.

340. *Ahithophel's Counsel Rejected.*—Ahithophel then advised Absalom to send him at the head of 10,000 men to pursue David and smite him whilst his people were weary; but Hushai opposed this by saying that David was a valiant man, and recommending that they should wait until all Israel were on their side, and thus be certain of victory before they ventured on a battle. This foolish proposal was immediately accepted by Absalom, and Hushai forwarded the news to David through the sons of Zadok and Abiathar. The two messengers narrowly escaped apprehension. They had waited at the Pool of Siloam, without Jerusalem, where a wench brought them the message, but a lad saw them, and told Absalom, who instantly ordered them to be pursued; and they would have been taken at Bahurim, where Shimei cursed David, had not a woman hid them in a well and misdirected the pursuers. 2 Sam. xvii. 1–20.

341. *David prepares for Battle.*—Upon learning that Hushai's advice was taken, David crossed the Jor-

dan and marched to Mahanaim, where his army were refreshed and strengthened by the generous hospitality of Shobi, son of Nahash the Ammonite, Barzillai the Gileadite, and Machir, son of Ammiel. David then divided his forces into three divisions, the first under Joab, the second under Abishai, and the third under Ittai the Gittite; and after reviewing the soldiers and strictly charging the generals to deal gently with Absalom, he sent them to the battle, whilst he himself remained in the city. 2 Sam. xvii. 22, 24, 26-29; xviii. 1-5.

342. *Absalom's Defeat and Death, 1023.*—Meantime, the party of Absalom had lost its best supporter, for Ahithophel was so hurt at the rejection of his advice that he returned home, set his affairs in order, and committed suicide. Absalom now made Amasa commander of his host, and, crossing the Jordan in pursuit of David, he encamped in Gilead. The battle was fought in the wood of Ephraim,* but became quickly scattered over the whole country, for the army of Absalom was soon divided and routed by the veterans of David. Whilst Absalom was riding on a mule during the engagement, his hair caught in the branches of an oak and kept him hanging. This being told to Joab, he hurried to the place and thrust three darts through the heart of Absalom, whilst ten young men who bore his armor completed the murder, threw the body into a pit, and covered it with stones. The news was carried to David by Ahimaaz and Cushi, but the agony of the father overcame the exultation of the king, and in the bitterness of grief he cried, on the eve of victory, "O Absalom, my son, my son! would God I had died for thee!" 2 Sam. xvii. 23, 25; xviii. 6-33.

343. *David returns to Jerusalem.*—The remonstrances of Joab and discontent of the people at length aroused David to a sense of his regal duty. He sent to Zadok and Abiathar to call upon the elders of Judah to bring back their monarch, and to reassure Amasa, the late commander-in-chief of Absalom, by a promise of the generalship of his own army in the room of the murderer of his son. All Judah now assembled at Gilgal to attend their king over Jordan and welcome his return. Amongst

---

* This forest was on the east of Jordan, in the tribe of Gad.

others was Shimei, who had cursed David at Bahurim, but who now prayed for forgiveness, and was pardoned in spite of the remonstrances of Abishai. Ziba also came with his fifteen sons and twenty servants, and Mephibosheth, who testified his own loyalty and complained of the treachery of his servant; and David now divided between the two the possessions which he had formerly given to Mephibosheth and afterward transferred to Ziba. Barzillai the Gileadite also came to congratulate David, for whom he had provided provisions at Mahanaim. He was eighty years old, and the king blessed and kissed him, and, as he declined going farther on account of his age, David took his son Chimham and rewarded him as he would have done his father. 2 Sam. xix. 1–40.

344. *Dissensions between Judah and Israel; Revolt of Israel under Sheba, 1022.*—When David reached his palace he imprisoned the ten concubines whom Absalom had abused, and condemned them to perpetual widowhood. Meantime, the kingdom was shaken by a fierce dispute which ended in a revolt. The Israelites complained that the men of Judah had not consulted them in bringing back David; to which Judah replied at first with sarcastic taunts, and afterward with fierce recrimination. Whilst the quarrel was at its height, Sheba, a Benjamite, blew a trumpet and cried in the language of rebellion, "We have no part in David, nor inheritance in the son of Jesse: to your tents, O Israel!" David immediately ordered Amasa, his new commander-in-chief, to assemble the warriors of Judah within three days to put down the revolt; but Amasa did not return at the appointed time, and David, getting alarmed, sent Abishai, brother of Joab, to seize Sheba before he could take any fenced cities. 2 Sam. xix. 41–43; xx. 1–6.

345. *Amasa and Sheba slain, 1022.*—Abishai instantly marched against the rebels with Joab's men and the Cherethites and Pelethites (see note to sect. 338); but at Gibeon he overtook Amasa, and the latter was then treacherously assassinated by Joab for having superseded him in the command of the army. All the people now followed Joab, who with his accustomed energy marched through all the tribes until he came to Abel of Bethmaachah, where Sheba was abiding; and when he had

cast up a bank and battered the wall, a wise woman saved the city by persuading the inhabitants to cut off the head of Sheba and send it to Joab. 2 Sam. xx. 6-20.

346. *Famine for Three years, 1022–1019; Atonement for Saul's Slaughter of the Gibeonites, 1019.*— Scarcely had peace been established when the land was visited by a three years' famine, and David learnt from God that it was caused by the previous slaughter of the Gibeonites by Saul. These Gibeonites were a remnant of the Amorites, but had artfully obtained an alliance with the Hebrews in the time of Joshua (see sect. 258); and many of the present race had been slain by Saul in his zeal against the enemies of Israel. David asked the Gibeonites what atonement they required, upon which they refused a blood-fine of silver or gold, but demanded that seven of Saul's remaining sons should be delivered up to them for execution. David then spared Mephibosheth, but gave them the two sons of Rizpah, Saul's concubine, and the five sons of Merab, Saul's eldest daughter, who had been promised to David, but given to Adriel. The Gibeonites hung the victims on a hill, but Rizpah clothed herself in sackcloth and guarded their bodies. David then fetched the bones of Saul and Jonathan from the Jabesh-gileadites, who had carried them off from the walls of Beth-shan, where they had been exposed by the Philistines as victorious trophies (sect. 321). They were now buried by David in the sepulchre of Kish, father of Saul, in the tribe of Benjamin. 2 Sam. xxi. 1-14.

347. *David's last Expedition against the Philistines, 1018.*—In B. C. 1018 the Philistines again declared war, and David marched against them, but it was his last expedition. During the fight the aged monarch was attacked by Ishbi-benob, a gigantic Philistine, and would have fallen but for the aid of Abishai, who slew the formidable enemy; and the army then declared that the light of Israel should no more be risked in battle. The war was concluded after three other Philistine giants of the family of Goliath had been slain by three heroes of Israel. 2 Sam. xxi. 15-22; xxii.; xxiii.

348. *Numbering of the People, and 70,000 slain by Pestilence, 1017.*—In B. C. 1017, David, in opposition to the divine command and the remonstrances of

Joab, ordered the latter to number the people, upon which there was found to be 800,000 fighting men of Israel and 500,000 of Judah. Scarcely had David learnt the result when he repented of the crime, and God sent the prophet Gad to offer him the choice of three punishments— viz. three years' famine, three months' destruction from the enemy, or three days' pestilence. David chose the latter, and 70,000 people were slain by a plague, but Jerusalem was saved, and the Lord stayed the hand of the destroying angel by the threshing-floor of Araunah the Jebusite on the summit of Moriah. David immediately bought the threshing-floor and oxen for fifty silver shekels [22¾ oz. = £5 13s. 8d.]*, and, erecting an altar on the spot, he showed his gratitude in burnt-offerings and peace-offerings to Jehovah. 2 Sam. xxiv.; 1 Chron. xxi.

349. *Revolt of Adonijah, 1015; Solomon declared Successor.*—David was now extremely old, and required the attendance of a Shunammite virgin named Abishag. Adonijah, son of David by Haggith, seeing the monarch's decrepitude, and having conferred with Joab the commander-in-chief and Abiathar the high priest, chose this moment for declaring himself king in opposition to Solomon, whom David had appointed to be his successor. Nathan immediately brought the news to Bathsheba, and advised her to carry it to David, and he would follow and confirm it. Bathsheba then entered the king's presence, and whilst telling him of the rebellion Nathan went into the royal chamber and requested to know whom he had appointed to be his successor. David signified before them both his desire that Solomon should reign after him, and ordered Nathan, Zadok, and Benaiah to proclaim him king. Solomon was accordingly anointed; the trumpet was blown and the people cried, "God save King Solomon!" and the tidings was carried to Adonijah whilst feasting his adherents. All the guests were struck with a panic, and Adonijah fled to the horns of the altar, but being reassured by Solomon, he gave himself up and was pardoned. 1 Kings i.

---

* In 1 Chron. xxi. 25 it is said that David gave Araunah six hundred shekels of gold. It is therefore supposed that subsequently, when David knew that this spot was chosen as a site for the temple, he made Araunah a further remuneration.

350. *Death of David, 1015.*—The dying hour of the old king soon arrived, and his last moments appear to have been employed in counselling his son and successor. He strictly charged him to walk in accordance with the laws of God, and to build the temple to Jehovah; and he warned him to punish the crimes of Joab and Shimei, but to show kindness to the family of Barzillai the Gileadite. So David slept with his fathers, and was buried in the City of David, B. C. 1015. 1 Kings ii. 1–11; 1 Chron. xxii.; xxviii.; xxix.

351. *Character of David.*—As a man David was a true Israelite, and as a king he was a faithful vassal of Jehovah. The piety, courage, and humility of his youth prepared him for that severe discipline of body and mind which he underwent in his persecuted wanderings; and whilst his genius as a king drew around him the great and distinguished spirits of his age, it led him to deal wisely and cautiously with the crafty and ambitious. He governed as the vice-regent of Jehovah, and though in two notable instances he fell into grievous sin and incurred the just punishment of God, yet his humble confession and sincere repentance are held out as a warning to all future generations. By his strict adherence to duty and confidence in God he set a worthy example to his successors; and, to crown all, he was an eminent type of that glorious Messiah who was to be born of his lineage and sit upon his throne for ever.

David was an affectionate friend, a generous enemy, a brave warrior, and a wise monarch. The fame of his youthful harp reached the ears of the court, and his melodies charmed the evil spirit from Saul, whilst the glowing poetry, lofty imagery, and fervent piety of his Psalms have elevated the devotions of all Jews and Christians for 3000 years, and earned for the glorious inspiration of their author a universal and undying popularity.

SOLOMON, B. C. 1015–975 = 40 YEARS.

Prophet—Ahijah.

352. *Extent of the Kingdom.*—The reign of Solomon is the most splendid period of Hebrew history. His kingdom was the ruling monarchy in Western Asia, and extended from the Euphrates to the Mediterranean and from Phœnicia to the Red Sea; whilst the warlike and civilized Philistines, the Edomites, Moabites, and Ammonites, the nomad Arabians of the desert, and the Syrians of Damascus, were alike tributary to the successor of David. 1 Kings iv. 20, 21.

353. *Joab and Adonijah slain, and Abiathar banished, 1014; Shimei slain, 1011.*—Solomon ascended the throne at the age of eighteen, and his first acts were in accordance with the dying advice of his father. His eldest brother, Adonijah, had persuaded Bathsheba to ask from Solomon permission to marry Abishag, the attendant of David; but the king was so enraged at the deep scheme which dictated this request that he slew Adonijah by the hand of Benaiah and punished his two principal adherents. Abiathar, in remembrance of former services to David, was only banished to Anathoth, but Joab, who, with conscious guilt, had fled to the horns of the altar, met with the fate of Adonijah. 1 Kings ii. 11–35.

354. *Character of Joab.*—The character of Joab demands a passing notice. He was the son of Zeruiah, David's sister, and was made commander-in-chief because he had been the first to mount the walls of Jebus and beat off the Jebusites. (See sect. 326.) The success of his arms and energy of his movements soon proved that he possessed military talents of the highest order, but he was cruel and unscrupulous in the attainment of his ends. He had avenged the death of his brother Asahel by the assassination of Abner and gratified his jealousy by the slaughter of Amasa. He had mortally offended the old monarch by compassing the death of Absalom, and aroused the fears of his successor by joining in the rebellion of Adonijah; and the genius of the commander would not atone for the treacheries of the assassin, nor a long service for a base desertion.

355. *Shimei slain, 1011.*—Shimei, another suspicious character, met with a similar fate. He had not followed Adonijah, but had cursed David at Bahurim, and at first was suffered to live in peace upon promising not to leave Jerusalem. Three years afterward two of his servants fled to Achish, and he followed them to Gath and

brought them back, upon which Solomon reproached him with his guilt, and he fell by the hand of Benaiah. 1 Kings ii. 36–46.

356. *Solomon's Marriage with Pharaoh's Daughter, 1014; his Singular Wisdom.*—In B. C. 1014, Solomon married the daughter of Pharaoh, and brought her to the city of David until he should have built a palace for himself, a temple for the Lord, and a wall around Jerusalem. He loved the Lord and walked in the statutes of his father, but the people, having no temple, sacrificed in high places, of which Gibeon was the chief. On one occasion, whilst staying at this place, the Lord appeared to Solomon at night in a dream and bade him ask what most he desired. Solomon begged for an understanding heart, when Jehovah not only granted his prayer, but promised him riches and honor above all contemporary kings, together with length of days, if he kept the statutes of the God of his fathers. The wisdom of the young king soon excited the astonishment and admiration of the whole nation. Two mothers, living alone in one house, came before him. One complained that the other, having had her child die in the night, had exchanged its corpse for the living child of the complainant. The other denied the charge, and no witnesses could be brought to prove the identity of the infants. Solomon elicited the truth by preparing to divide the living child, when the false mother discovered herself by the unconcern she showed for its life, whilst the real parent begged that it might be preserved, even if given up to the other. 1 Kings iii.; 2 Chron. i. 1–12.

357. *Commerce of Solomon.*—The profoundest peace was soon established throughout the dominions of Solomon. Every man dwelt in safety under his own vine and his own fig tree from Dan to Beer-sheba. An alliance with Egypt and Phœnicia enabled the wisest king to carry on an extensive commerce by land and sea. He built the magnificent city of Tadmor,* afterward called Palmyra, in Syria, on an oasis in the desert, for the convenience of caravans which traded with Babylon. He formed a navy,

---

* 2 Chron. viii. 4; Josephi, *Ant. Jud.* VIII. vi.; Heeren's *Asiatic Researches*, ii. 393; Wood's *Palmyra and Baalbec*, etc.

which was partly manned by Phœnician sailors, and his ships traversed the Mediterranean to the Pillars of Hercules, or sailed from Elath and Ezion-geber, on the Red Sea, to the golden regions of the far East. Horses, charriots, and linen yarn were brought from Egypt; gold and silver, ivory, apes, and peacocks from Tarshish, or Tartessus, on the southern coast of Spain; gold, jewels, and spices from the mysterious realms of Ophir on the coast of Arabia, Eastern Africa, or the southern peninsula of India; and cedars and firs were floated on the Mediterranean by the Phœnician king, Hiram, and carried from the heights of Lebanon to the metropolis of Palestine. Whilst David had vanquished the surrounding monarchs, Hiram, king of Tyre, was allied to him by a close friendship, which was now continued to Solomon to their mutual advantage. The mountainous territory of the Phœnicians was but little adapted for agriculture, and Palestine became their granary. The corn of Judæa, which excelled that of Egypt; the vine, which was indigenous to the soil; the oil, which is superior to that of Provence; the balm, which was collected in the lands round Lake Gennesareth, and is still famous under the name of balsam of Mecca,—were all exchanged by Solomon for the luxurious riches of distant climes.* 1 Kings iv.; v.; ix. 26–28; x. 22–29; 2 Chron. i. 13–17.

358. *Building of the Temple and Palaces, 1012–992.*—In B. C. 1012, after reigning three years, Solomon commenced building his celebrated temple; after which he erected a palace for himself, another of cedar in the forest of Lebanon, and a third for the daughter of Pharaoh. The whole were completed in twenty years; of this period, between three and four years were spent in collecting materials for the temple, and seven years and six months were employed in raising and decorating it. Upon this sacred structure the boundless genius of a magnificent king lavished all that wealth could purchase or art could execute; 70,000 proselytes, descendants of the Canaanites, were employed in carrying burdens; 80,000 in cutting stone out of the quarries; 3600 as overseers; to-

---

* Heeren's *Asiatic Researches*, i. 362.

gether with 30,000 Israelites in the quarries of Libanus. 1 Kings vi.; vii.; 2 Chron. ii.

359. *Description of the Temple.*—The temple was built on the summit of Mount Moriah, near Mount Zion, in Jerusalem, where Abraham had prepared to offer Isaac, and where the angel had appeared to David when the pestilence was stayed over the threshing-floor of Araunah. The site was enlarged by the erection of a strong wall of square stone around the mountain, with the intervening space filled up with earth. Another wall, with an interior colonnade, surrounded the whole structure, thus forming two courts; the inner one being called the court of the temple, and containing the sacred furniture and vestments of the priests and Levites; whilst in the outer one were erected the magazines for the wine, corn, oil, and wood used in the divine service. The temple itself is supposed to have been 70 cubits [128 feet] long, 20 cubits [36 feet] broad, and 30 cubits [54 feet] high, with a portico or porch 20 cubits [36 feet] broad like the main building, but 120 cubits [216 feet] high. The Holy Place was 40 cubits [72 feet] long, and the Holy of Holies 20 cubits [36 feet]. The interior edifice was built upon the plan of the tabernacle, but of much larger dimensions. The internal decorations are difficult to comprehend, and the reader of the sacred volume is bewildered and astonished by elaborate descriptions of cedar walls and golden roofs richly carved with flowers and cherubim; carved floors overlaid with gold; golden altar, shew-bread table, and cherubim; golden doors, chains, candlesticks, censers, basins, lamps, tongs, and hinges; veils of blue, purple, and crimson; brazen seas, lavers, wheels, oxen, and lions; brazen pillars thirty-two feet high and twenty-one feet round, and with chapiters or capitals nine feet higher, all richly carved with network, chain-work, pomegranates, and lilies; and such was the rich profusion of metal that its weight was never ascertained. 1 Kings vi.; vii.; 2 Chron. ii.–iv.

360. *Dedication, 1005.*—In the seventh month of the tenth year of the reign the temple was solemnly dedicated to Jehovah. The priests, Levites, and singers were all arrayed in their sacred vestments; the trumpets and cymbals were sounded; and the sacred ark, containing

the tables of stone which Moses had placed there at Horeb, was carried by the priests and set beneath the cherubim. Then the glory of the Lord filled the house of the Lord, and the youthful king stood before the altar in the presence of all Israel, and offered up an affecting and appropriate supplication to the God of Abraham. The service was concluded with sacrifices and rejoicings; and, the Lord appeared to Solomon a second time at Gibeon, and promised to protect his chosen people as long as they walked in his statutes, but to reject them utterly should they forsake his way.* 1 Kings viii.; ix. 1–25; 2 Chron. v.–vii.

---

* **Subsequent History of the Temple, B. C. 1005–588.**—After the consecration or dedication of Solomon's temple it underwent many revolutions.

B. C. 972. Only thirty-three years after its dedication it was plundered by Shishak, king of Egypt.

B. C. 856. Joash, king of Judah, collected money for repairing it, and the work was commenced in earnest.

B. C. 740. Ahaz, king of Judah, robbed it of its gold and treasures to bribe Tiglath-pileser, king of Assyria, to attack the kings of Israel and Syria. He afterward took away the brazen altar and replaced it by a copy of one he had seen at Damascus, and subsequently pillaged it, broke the sacred vessels, and shut it up.

B. C. 726. Hezekiah, son of Ahaz, reopened the temple, and purified and repaired it, but in B. C. 713 he was forced to take its riches and bribe Sennacherib to leave his dominions.

B. C. 698. Manasseh, son of Hezekiah, set up altars and idols in the courts of the temple, but afterward repented and removed them.

B. C. 624. Josiah repaired the temple and replaced the priests.

B. C. 606. Nebuchadnezzar plundered it in the reign of Jehoiakim.

B. C. 599. Nebuchadnezzar carried away others of its vessels in the reign of Jehoiachin or Jeconiah.

B. C. 588. Nebuchadnezzar entirely destroyed it in the eleventh year of Zedekiah's reign.

The Second Temple, B. C. 535.—Zerubbabel, the grandson of King Jehoiachin, and Jeshua, grandson of Seraiah, the high priest, laid the foundation of the second temple in B. C. 535, but were impeded in the building by the machinations of the Samaritans, and it was not completed until the reign of Darius Hystaspis, B. C. 515. (See sect. 580.) It was twice the size of Solomon's temple, both in breadth and height, but it wanted five things—viz. 1. The ark and mercy-seat. 2. The visible glory of the Shechinah or divine presence. 3. The holy fire of the altar. 4. The Urim and Thummim (sect. 162). 5. The spirit of prophecy. This temple was plundered and profaned by Antiochus Epiphanes, B. C. 170, and the idol of Jupiter Olympius was set up near the altar, and the sacrifices discontinued for three years, when it was restored by Judas Maccabeus. 1 Macc. iv. 52.

Temple of Herod, B. C. 17 to A. D. 70.—Herod, having been for two years preparing materials for building a new temple, pulled down the

361. *Glory of Solomon.*—The other works of Solomon display the same munificent splendor as his temple. The three hundred targets and three hundred shields of beaten gold; an ivory throne overlaid with gold, with a golden footstool and twelve golden lions; the golden vessels of his household; 12,000 cavalry and 40,000 stalls for chariot-horses; the administration of the government and the service of the court,—all excited as much wonder and applause as his own 3000 proverbs and 1005 songs, his knowledge of trees from the cedar to the hyssop, of beasts, birds, fishes, and creeping things. Many royal strangers were attracted to Jerusalem by the fame of Solomon; and the queen of Sheba is particularly mentioned as having been struck alike with astonishment and admiration at the grandeur of his works and the wisdom of his words. 1 Kings x.; 2 Chron. ix.

362. *Kingdom disturbed by Idolatry and Faction.*—The latter part of Solomon's reign was disgraced by voluptuousness and stained by idolatry. The royal harem of seven hundred wives and three hundred concubines included many women from the surrounding countries, who tempted the king to worship their national deities; and the monarch who had built so glorious a temple to Jehovah on Mount Moriah now erected high places for Chemosh, Molech, and Ashtoreth on the Mount of Olives. Then the Lord threatened to rend away the kingdom of Israel from the son of Solomon, leaving, however, one tribe for the sake of David and Jerusalem. The remain-

---

old one in B. C. 17, and began erecting a new one about forty-six years before the first passover of Christ's personal ministry. John ii. 20. Upon this work 1000 wagons and 10,000 artificers were engaged under the superintendence of 1000 priests. In nine and a half years the temple was fit for divine service, but additions continued to be made until A. D. 64. It was larger than the others, and the sanctuary, or *temple* strictly so called, was constructed of white marble, and, with the altar, was placed in a quadrangular area, called "The Court of the Priests," which was surrounded by three courts, each one of which was situated above the other. The inner court was called "The Court of the Israelites," the middle one, "The Court of the Israelite Women," and the outer one, "The Court of the Gentiles." This temple was at length completely demolished by Titus, A. D. 70, on the same day of the same month on which Solomon's temple had been destroyed. It was the presence of Christ in the second temple that fulfilled the prophecy of Haggai: "The glory of this latter house shall be greater than of the former." Hag. ii. 9.

der of the reign was darkened by intestine war. Hadad, a prince of Edom, who had fled to Egypt on the conquest of his country by David, and married the sister of Pharaoh's queen, now returned to Idumæa. Rezon, son of Eliadah, a servant of Hadadezer, king of Zobah (sect. 329), collected a band of men, seized Damascus, and founded a kingdom which soon became formidable (sect. 493, *note*); whilst Jeroboam, son of Nebat, an Ephrathite, who for his bold and enterprising conduct had been commissioned by Solomon to levy the taxes of Ephraim and Manasseh, was promised by Ahijah, the Shilonite prophet, the government of ten tribes, together with the further encouragement that if he kept the commandments and statutes as David had done, the Lord would be with him and build him a house equally sure. Solomon then sought to slay Jeroboam, who, however, escaped to Egypt, where he was protected by Shishak, until the death of Solomon released him from exile. 1 Kings xi.; 2 Chron. ix. 31.

363. ***Death and Character of Solomon, 975.***—Solomon died B. C. 975. His character, unlike that of his father David, was peaceful, learned, and luxurious. Called to the throne while yet a youth, he became deeply sensible of his great responsibilities, and sought for wisdom under divine encouragement. He was early celebrated for decision and righteous judgment, and his extensive acquaintance with natural history and physical science was the wonder of his age. He next prepared himself to fulfil the pious designs of his father in erecting a temple to Jehovah; and whatever subsequent ages may boast of the sublime and magnificent, this monument of art and piety remains unrivalled, and still flourishes in the pages of Holy Writ. His luxuries and sinful compliance in countenancing idolatrous practices will ever remain a stain on his memory; but his wisdom, learning, and taste were of the highest order, while his maintenance of the laws and patronage of useful arts secured the prosperity of his reign and formed the golden period of Jewish history.

REHOBOAM.

364. ***Revolt of the Ten Tribes, 975.***—Rehoboam, son of Solomon by Naamah an Ammonitess, succeeded

his father at the age of forty-one. He convened a general meeting of all the elders of Israel (sect. 133, 134) at Shechem, that he might be formally invested with the royal dignity. But Jeroboam had now returned from Egypt, and through him the assembly stipulated that the new king should remit the excessive taxation which had been exacted by Solomon. Rehoboam took three days to consider, and then, forsaking the old counsellors of his father and following young men's advice, he said to his subjects, "My father made your yoke heavy, and I will add to your yoke; my father also chastised you with whips, but I will chastise you with scorpions." The ten tribes of Israel then revolted from Judah, as God had predicted, stoned Adoram, who was over the tribute, forced Rehoboam to fly to Jerusalem, and made Jeroboam king. 1 Kings xii. 1–20; 2 Chron. x.

§ *Prefatory Review of the History of the Divided Monarchies.*

365. **Contracted Frontiers.**—The kingdom established by David was now contracted as well as divided, and the Euphrates and desert ceased to be its frontiers. ISRAEL lost her Syrian possessions by the rise of Rezon in Damascus; the Ammonites threw off her yoke, and the Moabites alone continued tributary. JUDAH still retained a supremacy over the Philistines, and received a homage, which was, however, merely nominal, from the Edomites; but being cut off from the Tyrians and maritime Israelites, and having lost the superfluous produce arising from the Israelite territory, her kings must have found the ports of Solomon on the Red Sea a barren possession.

366. **Reciprocal Relations of the Two Monarchies.**—JUDAH was the richest of the two kingdoms, from the possession of Jerusalem and the treasures of Solomon. She also enjoyed a compact dominion and a completeness of organization as the old centre of government; and Rehoboam, as the grandson of David, must have been more secure of the loyalty of the tribes which remained faithful to his rule. But, on the other hand, ISRAEL possessed four times the territory of Judah and a much larger population. Thus the power of the two states was

nearly balanced, and consequently the struggle between them was the more obstinate; and this continued rivalry led to alliances with Syria, Egypt, and Assyria which ultimately conduced to the downfall of the two nations.

367. *Causes which led to their Destruction.*—From the time of Moses, Jehovah had always governed his people according to the promises and threatenings which he delivered from Mount Horeb. If they deviated from their allegiance, he brought them back by suitable chastisements; and the same course was pursued in the government of the two kingdoms. If the monarchs of both had viewed the sundering of the empire as a consequence of Solomon's idolatry, and as a warning to them to govern their subjects according to the book of the Law, their kingdoms might have enjoyed uninterrupted prosperity. Even Jeroboam had been assured that if he kept the Law as David had done his house should be equally sure. But the kings of both states rebelled against Jehovah and worshipped other gods, and allied with their idolatrous neighbors; and after a succession of prophets had reminded both rulers and subjects of their duties to Jehovah, and threatened them with punishment in case of disobedience, there followed calamity after calamity to bring the nation to reflection.

368. *Idolatry of Israel.*—In spite of the promise of Jehovah through Ahijah (sect. 362), Jeroboam pursued a mere human policy, and in order to restrain his subjects from worshipping at Jerusalem he set up two golden calves in his own dominions. His example was but too well followed by his successors, and at length Ahab, after his Phœnician marriage, introduced a still viler idolatry, with all its concomitant vices. One after another the reigning families were removed, after their extermination had been announced by a prophet, and a successor appointed. At last, after all milder punishments had proved fruitless, the kingdom was destroyed and the people carried into the threatened captivity.

369. *Idolatry of Judah.*—In Judah the same Providence was favorable or adverse to the kingdom according as the people obeyed or transgressed the law, only the royal family remained unchanged, in accordance with the promise given to David. Though many of her kings were

rebellious and idolatrous, yet they were always succeeded by those of purer mind, who put a stop to idolatry, re-established theocracy in the hearts of their subjects, and by the aid of prophets, priests, and Levites and the services of the temple restored the knowledge and worship of God. Judah, therefore, though much smaller than Israel, continued her national existence one hundred and thirty-four years longer; but at last, as no durable reformation was produced, she experienced the same fate as her sister kingdom.

II. *History of the Divided Monarchies of Judah and Israel.**

JUDAH.

TRIBES—*Judah and Benjamin.*

Capital—**Jerusalem;** called Salem in the time of Abraham, Jebus in the time of Joshua, and afterward *Jebusalem* or *Jerusalem.*

ISRAEL.

TRIBES—*Asher, Naphtali, Manasseh, Zebulun, Issachar, Gad, Reuben, Ephraim, Dan,* and *Simeon.*

Capital—**Shechem** during the reigns of Jeroboam and Nadab. Baasha removed it to **Tirzah;** and Omri, in B. C. 925, to **Samaria.**

FIRST PERIOD—*from the Revolt of the Ten Tribes until Jehu destroyed the dynasty of Ahab in Israel and slew Ahaziah in Judah,* B. C. 975–884 = 92 *years.*

Judah—*Rehoboam.*

370. **1. Rehoboam; 975–958.** —Son of Solomon. Reigned seventeen years. Prophet—*Shemaiah.*

372. **Not to war against Israel; Fenced Cities.**—Rehoboam now assembled an army of 180,000 to recover Israel, but was forbidden the war by the

Israel—*Jeroboam.*

371. **1. Jeroboam, 975–954.** —Son of Nebat. Reigned twenty-two years. "Who made Israel to sin." PROPHETS—*Ahijah the Shilonite and a man of God sent to Bethel.*

373. **Fortified Shechem.**— Jeroboam built and fortified Shechem in the tribe of Ephraim,

---

* For analytical table of the history of the two kingdoms see pp. 166–169.

Judah—*Abijah.*

prophet Shemaiah. He then built fenced cities, and his kingdom was strengthened by the priests, Levites, and pious men who fled from the idolatry of Jeroboam. 1 Kings xii. 21-24; 2 Chron. xi. 1-17.

375. **Shishak's Invasion, 972.**—Three years after his accession both the king and the people fell into idolatry, and Shishak, king of Egypt, ravaged Judah and plundered the temple. Rehoboam and the princes of Judah were now rebuked by the prophet Shemaiah, and humbled themselves before the Lord. 1 Kings xiv. 25-28; 2 Chron. xii. 1-12.

376. *All the subsequent kings of Judah were descendants of David through Rehoboam, as God had promised.*

378. **2. Abijah, or Abijam, 958-955.**—Son of Rehoboam. Committed evil like his father, and had fourteen wives, by whom he had twenty-two sons and sixteen daughters. Reigned three years. 1 Kings xv. 1-5; 2 Chron. xiii. 1, 2, 21.

379. **Defeats Jeroboam, 957.** —Abijah with 400,000 men opposed Jeroboam with 800,000* on Mount Zemaraim, on the borders of Ephraim, and whilst the latter was plotting to hem him in, Abijah's people shouted and the priests blew their trumpets, which so terrified Jeroboam's army that they fled, and 500,000 of them were killed. 2 Chron. xiii. 3, 13-20.

Israel—*Jeroboam.*

which city Abimelech had destroyed two hundred and fifty-eight years previously (see sect. 385), and dwelt there. 1 Kings xii. 20, 25.

374. **Establishes Calf-worship and Profane Priesthood.** —Being afraid that Israel would return to the house of David if suffered to sacrifice at Jerusalem, he set up two golden calves—one in Bethel, the other in Dan, being the extremities of his kingdom. He then made priests of the lowest of the people, and ordained an idolatrous feast corresponding to the "Tabernacles," and sacrificed in person at Bethel. 1 Kings xii. 26-33.

377. **Man of God comes to Bethel.**—The Lord now sent a man to Jeroboam at Bethel, who, seeing him at the altar, cried, "O altar, altar! thus saith the Lord, A child shall be born to the house of David, Josiah by name, and upon thee shall he offer the priests of the high places that burn incense upon thee, and men's bones shall be burnt upon thee." Jeroboam stretched out his hand to seize the man, when the hand dried up, but was restored by the messenger's prayers. The prophecy was fulfilled three hundred and fifty years afterward, in *Josiah's reign* (sect. 525). Jeroboam invited the man of God to his house, but the latter declined, as God had commanded him neither to eat nor drink, nor return the same way he came. An old prophet of Bethel then followed the man of God, and said he had been ordered by an

---

* Owing to the mistakes of transcribers in copying numerals, we cannot answer for the correctness of the great numbers of men which are mentioned here and in the sequel.

Judah—*Asa.*

Israel—*Nadab, Baasha.*

angel to bring him to his house. This was false, but the man turned back, and whilst sitting at table the Lord told him, through the mouth of the old prophet, that for his disobedience his corpse should not come into the sepulchre of his fathers. The man then returned home and was killed by a lion, but not devoured; and the old prophet found his body and buried it in his own tomb. 1 Kings xiii. 1-32.

380. **His son Abijah sick; Ahijah's Prophecy.**—Abijah, son of Jeroboam, now fell sick, and the king sent his wife in disguise to consult Ahijah the prophet at Shiloh. Ahijah was blind, but discovered the queen, and denounced God's judgment against Jeroboam's whole family, and foretold the immediate death of his son; and added that the latter should be the only one of the family that should be buried. (See also sect. 362.)

381. **2. Nadab, 954, 953.**—Son of Jeroboam. Reigned two years.

382. **3. Asa, 955-914.**—Son of Abijah. Reigned forty-one years. PROPHETS—*Azariah and Hanani.*

384. **Suppresses Idolatry.**—Asa destroyed the idols, groves, and high places, and deposed his mother [*i. e.* grandmother] Maachah from being queen for practising idolatry. He also restored the national worship, built fenced cities, and levied a large army. 1 Kings xv. 9-13; 2 Chron. xiv. 1-8.

387. **Defeats Zerah the Ethiopian.**—Asa defeated Zerah the Ethiopian, who invaded Judah with 1,000,000 men and three hundred chariots. Encouraged by the prophet Azariah, he then made fresh efforts to eradicate

383. **Worships the Calves.**—Nadab followed in the sins of his father, and was at length slain at the siege of Gibbethon by his general, Baasha, who then slew all the house of Jeroboam. 1 Kings xv. 25-30.

385. **3. Baasha, 953-930.**—Reigned twenty-four years. PROPHET—*Jehu.*

386. **Worships the Calves.**—Baasha now usurped the throne, but walked in the ways of Jeroboam. He removed his capital from Shechem to Tirzah. 1 Kings xv. 33, 34.

388. **Allies with Benhadad I.**—The kingdom of Damascus, founded by Rezon (sect. 362),

Judah—*Asa.*

idolatry, and celebrated a solemn festival in which he and his people engaged to serve the Lord. 2 Chron. xiv. 9–15; xv.

390. Bribes Benhadad I. to attack Baasha.—In this reign Baasha king of Israel occupied and began to fortify Ramah, to prevent his people entering Judah, when Asa bribed Baasha's ally, Benhadad I., king of Damascus, to attack him. Benhadad did so, and took several cities of Naphtali, which obliged Baasha to give up the fortification. Hanani the prophet remonstrated with Asa for his Syrian alliance, but was imprisoned by the king. 1 Kings xv. 16-22; 2 Chron. xvi. 1–10.

391. Dies of Diseased Feet.—Asa was attacked with diseased feet, but sought the physicians [*i.e.* foreign magicians who practised sorcery and incantations] more than God, and died in B. C. 914. 1 Kings xv. 23, 24; 2 Chron. xvi. 11–14.

Israel—*Elah, Zimri, Omri.*

had now increased in power, and Baasha formed an alliance with the reigning monarch, BENHADAD. 1 Kings xv. 19; 2 Chron. xvi. 3.

389. **Fortifies Ramah.**—The next act of Baasha was to fortify Ramah, a town about six miles to the north of Jerusalem and in the heart of the tribe of Benjamin, in order to prevent his subjects from entering Judah.* But Asa, king of Judah, bribed Benhadad, king of Syria, to invade Israel, and Baasha was then obliged to give up the fortification.

Jehu, son of Hanani, prophesied to Baasha the extinction of his family on account of his wickedness. 1 Kings xv. 16-21; xvi. 1–7; 2 Chron. xvi. 1-5.

392. **4. Elah, 930, 929.**—Son of Baasha. Reigned two years.

393. **Assassinated by Zimri.**—Baasha was assassinated at Tirzah by Zimri, captain of half his chariots, whilst drinking in the house of Arza his steward. 1 Kings xvi. 8-10.

394. **5. Zimri, 929.**—Reigned only seven days, during which he destroyed all the house of Baasha. 1 Kings xvi. 10-15.

395. **Burnt himself at Tirzah.**—Being closely besieged by Omri, captain of the host, he burnt the royal palace at Tirzah, and expired in the flames. 1 Kings xvi. 15-20.

396. **6. Omri, 929-918; Factions of Omri and Tibni.**—For six years after the death of

---

* **Ramah** was also probably intended for an offensive fortress from whence to make incursions into the enemy's country, and not unlike the forts of Decelea in Attica and of Pylus in Messenia, occupied during the Peloponnesian war.—*Thucydides,* iv. 3; vii. 19, 27, 28.

Judah—*Jehoshaphat.*

398. 4. Jehoshaphat, 914–889.—Son of Asa. Reigned twenty-five years. PROPHETS—*Jehu, Eliezer, and Jahaziel.*

400. Upholds the Worship of Jehovah.—Jehoshaphat feared God like his father Asa, and cleansed the land of groves and other traces of idolatry, though the people still burnt incense in high places, though probably only to Jehovah. 1 Kings xxii. 4–43; 2 Chron. xvii. 3–6.

402. Organizes the National Education.—Jehoshaphat also organized a system for the religious education of the whole nation. He appointed priests

Israel—*Omri, Ahab.*

Zimri, Israel was divided, half for Omri and half for Tibni. The Omri party at last prevailed, Tibni died, and Omri reigned. 1 Kings xvi. 21, 22.

397. Omri reigns wickedly.—Omri built Samaria and made it his capital, and died after a wicked reign of twelve years, six only of which he reigned alone. 1 Kings xvi. 23–28.

399. 7. Ahab, 918–897.—Son of Omri, and the most wicked king that ever ruled Israel. — Reigned twenty-two years. PROPHETS—*Elijah, Micaiah, and three anonymous.*

401. Marries Jezebel; worships Baal and Astarte, Phœnician Gods.—Ahab married Jezebel, daughter of Ethbaal,* king of the Zidonians, and introduced the worship of Baal† and Astarte,‡ or Ashtaroth; for which, about B. C. 910, God sent ELIJAH the prophet to reprove him, and punished him with a three years' famine. 1 Kings xvi. 29–33; xvii. 1.

---

* **Ethbaal** was apparently king of the Sidonians and Tyrians, or perhaps of the Phœnicians generally. The Tyrian line in which he, as well as Hiram, the ally of David and Solomon, were included, reigned about B. C. 1050–586. The names of the various monarchs are given by Josephus as an extract from Manetho. Besides Jezebel, who paganized Israel, two other remarkable females were related to this dynasty—viz. Athaliah, daughter of Jezebel and Ahab, who usurped Judah (sect. 443), and Dido, sister of Pygmalion, who founded Carthage.

† **Baal**, or Belus, was the supreme deity amongst all the Semitic races, and thus came to be identified with the Sun, the greatest divine manifestation in the Sabæan system. Hence there is much mythological confusion between Belus and Apollo. According to Sanchoniathon, as quoted in Cory's *Fragments*, the Phœnicians stretched their hand toward the Sun, the only Lord of heaven, calling him Beelsamin, which in Phœnician is "Lord of heaven," but in the Greek Zeus. Compare Layard's *Nineveh.*

‡ **Astarte**, or Ashtaroth, or Queen of Heaven, was the female form of Baal, and was identified with the moon, and corresponded to the Venus of the Greeks. She is said to have consecrated a star in the holy island, Tyre. Her worship was accompanied by the most infamous and degrading rites.—*Ibid.* and *Herod.*, i. 196.

Judah—*Jehoshaphat.*

and Levites to make circuits throughout the land, attended by the princes, in order to teach the book of the Law to the several cities of Judah. 2 Chron. xvii. 7-9.

404. Fortifies Judah, and Levies an Army.—Jehoshaphat built numerous fenced cities throughout Judah, with strong fortifications, ammunition, and garrisons. Besides these garrison troops he had an immense army under five great generals stationed at Jerusalem, and also concentrated a large force on his northern frontier, especially in the cities of Ephraim which Asa had taken from Baasha. 2 Chron. xvii. 1, 2, 12-19.

407. Appoints Judges.—Jehoshaphat also appointed judges in all the fenced cities, probably re-establishing the system of judicial administration which had been organized by Moses (sect. 133). 2 Chron. xix. 5-11.

408. Flourishing State of his Kingdom.—The government of Jehoshaphat seems to have inspired his subjects with confidence and their enemies with fear. The Edomites continued firm in their allegiance; the Philistines regularly remitted their presents and tribute-silver; and several Arabian tribes brought him large tributes or gifts of sheep and goats from their flocks. 2 Chron. xvii. 10, 11.

409. His Affinity with Ahab, 897.—The capital error of Jehoshaphat was in contracting an alliance with Ahab and marrying his eldest son, *Jehoram*, to *Athaliah*, daughter of Ahab and Jezebel. This took place in the thirteenth year of Jehoshaphat's

Israel—*Ahab.*

403. Three years' Famine, cir. 910-906.—During the three years' famine ELIJAH was miraculously fed by ravens at Cherith, and by an exhaustless vessel of meal and cruse of oil belonging to a widow at Zarephath (a Phœnician city between Tyre and Sidon), whose dead son he restored to life. 1 Kings xvii. 2-24.

405. Jezebel persecutes the Prophets.—About this time Jezebel killed all the prophets of Jehovah whom she could find, but Obadiah, the governor of Ahab's house, hid one hundred by fifty in a cave, and fed them with bread and water.

406. Grand Trial on Carmel between Elijah and the Priests of Baal.—After the three years, Elijah, with Obadiah's assistance, met Ahab by God's direction. Ahab accused him of troubling Israel, but he retorted the charge, and challenged the four hundred and fifty priests of Baal to appear at Mount Carmel before Israel, for Israel to decide between Baal and Jehovah, the test being the kindling by fire from heaven of the sacrifices laid on their respective altars. Baal's priests then prepared their altar and victim, but implored their god in vain. Elijah then ordered an old altar on the spot to be repaired with twelve stones, placed the victim upon it, and after causing the whole to be drenched three times with water, he prayed to Jehovah, and fire immediately descended and consumed the victim. The surrounding multitude were now convinced, and slaughtered Baal's prophets at the brook Kishon, and soon after rain de-

Judah—*Jehoshaphat.*

reign. 2 Kings viii. 18; 2 Chron. xviii. 1; xxii. 2.

Israel—*Ahab.*

scended and the famine ceased. 1 Kings xviii.

410. **Elijah ordered to Anoint Hazael, Jehu, and Elisha.**—Elijah was now threatened by Jezebel, and fled to Beer-sheba, where an angel gave him a cake which nourished him for forty days. He then went to Mount Horeb, where, after a wind, an earthquake, and a fire, the Lord appeared to him in a still small voice, and ordered him to anoint Hazael to be king of Syria, Jehu to be king of Israel, and Elisha to be prophet. 1 Kings xix.

411. **Campaign of Benhadad II.; Siege of Samaria, cir. 901.**—Benhadad II.—probably the son of Benhadad I. (sect. 389)—now entered Israel with three vassal kings, and laid siege to Samaria. Ahab at first was terrified into an offer of unconditional surrender and vassalage, but Benhadad threatened to send his servants to search the houses of Ahab and his court, and this insult roused the king of Israel to opposition. The national assembly of elders exhorted him to firmness and vigor, and a prophet of the Lord promised that the host of Syria should be delivered into his hand. Ahab sent out two hundred and thirty-two princes, followed by an army of 7000 men, who fell upon the enemy at noon, whilst Benhadad and his kings were carousing in the pavilions. The Syrian army with its host of cavalry and chariots was taken by surprise and quickly routed; Benhadad escaped with the horsemen, and Ahab himself issued from Samaria and assisted in the slaughter; but the prophet who promised the victory foretold that the next

Judah—*Jehoshaphat.* **Israel**—*Ahab.*

year the Syrians would return. 1 Kings xx. 1-22.

412. Second Campaign of Benhadad II.; defeated at Aphek.—The next year the Syrian captains said to Benhadad, "The gods of Israel are only gods of the *hills:* if therefore we fight them in the *plain,* we shall be the stronger." Benhadad accordingly raised another army, and invaded Israel on the side of Phœnicia, as far as Aphek, which was included in the broad plain of Esdraelon, or Jezreel. A prophet again promised victory to Ahab, because of the blasphemous expression of the enemy concerning the God of Israel. A battle ensued, 10,000 of the Syrians were slain, and Benhadad fled with the remainder into the city of Aphek, and then surrendered to Ahab. 1 Kings xx. 23-33.

413. Alliance with Syria.—Benhadad now agreed that the king of Israel should build streets in Damascus, as his father Benhadad I. had done in Samaria; and Ahab then covenanted with him, contrary to God's command, for which he was rebuked and threatened by a son of the prophets. 1 Kings xx. 34-43.

414. Ahab seizes Naboth's Vineyard; Elijah's fearful Prophecy, 899.—Ahab coveted the vineyard of Naboth of Jezreel, and, acting by the advice of his wife Jezebel, he got false witnesses to procure Naboth's death as a traitor, and seized his confiscated possessions. Elijah then assured Ahab, "Where dogs licked the blood of Naboth shall dogs lick thy blood, and thine house shall

Judah—*Jehoshaphat.*   Israel—*Ahab.*
be like the houses of Jeroboam and Baasha; the dogs shall eat Jezebel by the wall of Jezreel; and him that dieth of Ahab in the city the dogs shall eat, and him that dieth in the field shall the fowls of the air eat." Ahab now humbled himself in sackcloth, and the evil was postponed until his son's days. 1 Kings xxi.

415. Jehoshaphat and Ahab unite in an Expedition against the Syrians at Ramoth-gilead, 897.—Israel was now at peace with Syria, but Benhadad still held Ramoth in Gilead beyond Jordan, which Ahab was anxious to regain, and accordingly invited the assistance of Jehoshaphat to expel the Syrian garrison. Jehoshaphat hesitated to go before the Lord had been consulted, when Ahab assembled his false prophets to the number of four hundred, including Zedekiah. These all predicted success, but Jehoshaphat doubted their truth, and Micaiah, the prophet of the Lord, was sent for, who prophesied the contrary, and was thrown into prison by Ahab. The two kings, however, marched against Ramoth—Jehoshaphat in his royal robes, but Ahab in disguise. Benhadad had commanded his captains, "Fight not with small or great, save only with the king of Israel." Jehoshaphat nearly lost his life from being mistaken for Ahab, but the latter was mortally wounded by a random arrow, and carried back in his chariot to Samaria. 1 Kings xxii. 1–37; 2 Chron. xviii.

416. Jehoshaphat rebuked by Jehu.—On returning to Jerusalem, Jehoshaphat was reproved by Jehu, son of Hanani, for joining an idolatrous king. He still continued in his work of reformation, and made a tour through his dominions from Beer-sheba on the south to Mount Ephraim on the north, seeking to bring back the people more entirely to the God of their fathers. 2 Chron. xix. 1–4.

419. Tries to revive the Commerce of Solomon, etc.—Jehoshaphat attempted to revive the ancient traffic of Solomon by the Red Sea to the region of gold. Accordingly, he built a

417. Death of Ahab, 897.—At evening Ahab died, and his chariot and harness were washed in the pool of Samaria, and the dogs licked his blood, as Elijah had prophesied. "There was none like unto Ahab for wickedness." He introduced the worship of Baal and slew the prophets of the Lord. 1 Kings xxi. 37–39; 2 Chron. xviii. 34.

418. Jericho Rebuilt.—In Ahab's reign Jericho was rebuilt by Hiel the Bethelite; "he laid the foundation thereof in Abiram his first-born, and set up the gates thereof in his youngest son Segub." (See sect. 256.) 1 Kings xvi. 34.

Judah—*Jehoshaphat.*

navy at his port of Eziongeber on the Red Sea to go to Ophir and Tarshish; but in an evil day he consented to allow Ahaziah, the new monarch of Israel, to take a part in the expedition; and Eliezer prophesied against the enterprise, and the ships were wrecked and broken up. 1 Kings xxii. 48; 2 Chron. xx. 35-37.

422. **Defeats Confederacy of Moabites and Ammonites, 896.** — Jehoshaphat's unfortunate expedition with Ahab against Ramoth-gilead, seems to have lowered him in the estimation of his neighbors, and thus his alliance with the idolatrous king brought its own punishment. The Moabites, who had rebelled against Israel, were joined by the Ammonites and some Arabian tribes, and invaded Judah. Jehoshaphat then proclaimed a solemn fast, and, being encouraged by the prophet Jahaziel, he proceeded with his forces to Tekoah to meet the enemy. Here the army of Jehoshaphat remained stationary, singing the praises of God; and whilst they were thus employed the enemy madly destroyed each other and left a rich spoil. Three days were employed by Jehoshaphat in collecting the riches and jewels, and then, after praising God in the valley of Berachah, which is supposed to be the same as the valley of Jehoshaphat on the north and east of Jerusalem (sect. 326, *note*), the whole army returned to Jerusalem. 2 Chron. xx. 1-30.

Israel—*Ahaziah, Jehoram.*

420. **8. Ahaziah, 897, 896.** —Son of Ahab. Reigned two years. PROPHET—*Elijah.*

421. **Worships both Baal and the Calves.** — Ahaziah united the sins of his father to those of Jeroboam, for he adopted the policy of the latter in worshipping the golden calves, whilst he followed in the idolatry of Baal and the other Phœnician gods which had been introduced by Jezebel. 1 Kings xxii. 51-53; 2 Chron. xxii. 1-4.

423. **Revolt of the Moabites.**—Moab, which had hitherto been tributary to Israel, and paid a yearly revenue of 100,000 rams and 100,000 lambs, was encouraged by the victory of Benhadad over Ahab to rebel against Israel. 2 Kings i. 1.

424. **Ahaziah sick; sends to Baal-zebub.**—Shortly afterward Ahaziah fell through a lattice, and sent for help to Baalzebub ("lord of flies"), who was the god at the Philistine town of Ekron. Elijah met the messengers, and sent them back with a prediction of Ahaziah's death. 2 Kings i. 2-4.

425. **Elijah brings Fire from Heaven.** — When Ahaziah heard of Elijah's prophecy he sent three successive companies of fifty each to arrest him: the first two were destroyed by fire, but Elijah returned with the third and repeated his previous prediction. So Ahaziah died, after reigning two years. 2 Kings i. 5-18.

426. **9. Jehoram, or Joram, 896-884.**—Son of Ahab and brother of Ahaziah. Reigned twelve years. PROPHETS—*Elijah and Elisha.*

Judah—*Jehoshaphat.*

Israel—*Jehoram.*

427. Worships the Calves.
—Jehoram followed the idolatrous policy of Jeroboam, though not the sins of his father Ahab, for he put away Baal, though he worshipped the golden calves. 2 Kings iii. 1–3.

428. Elijah translated, 896.
—Elijah,* whilst in company with Elisha, divided the Jordan with his mantle, and was carried to heaven in a whirlwind, and Elisha was appointed his successor. Elisha now repeated Elijah's miracle of dividing the Jordan, and sent fifty of the sons of the prophets to seek Elijah, but they returned unsuccessful after three days' search. Elisha then healed the waters at Jericho, and cursed the children at Bethel who mocked him, after

---

* **Life of Elijah (prophesied, 910–896).**—Elijah was a native of Tisbe in Gilead beyond Jordan, and flourished in the reigns of Ahab and Ahaziah. In B. C. 910 he predicted the three years' drought to Ahab, during which he was fed by ravens by the brook Cherith, and afterward by the meal which did not waste and the oil which did not fail of the widow at Zarephath, and raised the widow's son to life. In B. C. 906 he proved the superiority of Jehovah to Baal at Mount Carmel, and ordered the slaying of the four hundred and fifty prophets of Baal; he then promised abundance of rain, which fell and ended the famine. Jezebel now threatened Elijah's life, and the prophet fled to Mount Horeb, or Sinai, in Arabia Petræa, and was miraculously supported for forty days on his journey. Here, after a tempest, an earthquake, and a fire, Jehovah commanded him in a still small voice to return and anoint Hazael to be king over Syria, Jehu son of Nimshi to be king over Israel, and Elisha to be his successor. About B. C. 899, Elijah denounced Ahab and Jezebel for murdering Naboth and seizing his vineyard; and about B. C. 896 he predicted Ahaziah's death for consulting Baal-zebub, and burnt up two captains of fifties who were sent to arrest him. The same year he divided the waters of Jordan in the presence of Elisha, and, being carried to heaven in a chariot of fire, he left his mantle and a double portion of his spirit to him. Malachi foretold the reappearance of Elijah " before the coming of the great and terrible day of the Lord." Mal. iv. 5. Our Saviour informs us that Elijah, or Elias, came in spirit in John the Baptist (Matt. xi. 14; xvii. 10–13); and Elijah and Moses both appeared and conversed with our Lord at the Transfiguration. Matt. xvii. 3; Mark ix. 4; Luke ix. 30. Many of the Jews in our Saviour's time believed him to be Elijah risen from the dead.

Judah—*Jehoshaphat.*

Israel—*Jehoram.*

which forty-two were slain by two she-bears. 2 Kings ii.

429. Jehoram allies with Jehoshaphat to put down the Moabite Revolt, 895.—The first act of Jehoram was to subdue the Moabites, who in the previous reign had rebelled against Israel. Accordingly, he allied with Jehoshaphat and the king of Edom, and the three armies proceeded to Moab through the wilderness of Edom. There they suffered from want of water, and Jehoram applied to Elisha, who, in consideration for Jehoshaphat, relieved them. Elisha ordered trenches to be dug, which the Lord filled with water during the night. Next morning the Moabites mistook this water for blood, and thinking that the three armies had been fighting each other, they attacked them, but were defeated with great loss. The confederate armies now ravaged Moab, and so closely besieged the king in Kir-haraseth, his capital, that after vainly trying to cut his way with seven hundred men through the Edomite camp, he sacrificed his eldest son as a burnt-offering upon the wall. 2 Kings iii. 4–27.

430. Elisha heals Naaman's Leprosy, 894.—Naaman, a Syrian general under Benhadad, was afflicted with leprosy, when an Israelite captive, handmaid to his wife, mentioned the power of the prophet in Samaria. Benhadad then sent Naaman with a letter and presents to the king of Israel, but Jehoram received him with suspicious dread, and rent his clothes, saying, "Am I God, to kill and make alive, that this man doth send unto me to recover a man of his leprosy?" Elisha heard of Jehoram's distress, and, sending for Naaman, said to him, "Go and wash in Jordan seven times, and thou shalt be clean." Naaman at first was wroth because the rivers of Damascus were not preferred, but was at length persuaded by his servant to follow Elisha's advice, and was then healed of his leprosy. Naaman offered presents to

Judah—*Jehoram.*

Israel—*Jehoram.*

Elisha, which were refused, and he then begged for two mules' burdens of earth out of Canaan, as he would thenceforth sacrifice only to the Lord. Gehazi, Elisha's servant, grudged his master's liberality, and, following Naaman, he deceitfully obtained two changes of raiment and a silver talent [1366 oz. = £341 10s.]; but Elisha discovered his guilt, and transferred to Gehazi and his descendants the leprosy of Naaman. 2 Kings v. 27.

431. Other Miracles, cir. 893.—Elisha made an iron axe's head, which a son of the prophets had dropped in the Jordan, to swim. He also disclosed Benhadad's counsel to Jehoram, and, being in Dothan, the Syrian king tried to take him by surrounding the place with chariots and cavalry; but Elisha smote the Syrian host blind, and then ordered Jehoram to give them provisions and set them at liberty. 2 Kings vi. 1-23.

432. Jehoram associated with his Father, 892.—Jehoram was made king whilst his father Jehoshaphat was yet alive. 2 Kings viii. 16.

434. 5. Jehoram, or Joram, 889-885.—Son of Jehoshaphat. Reigned six years alone, but eight years altogether.

435. Sins like Ahab.—Jehoram had married Athaliah, daughter of Ahab, murdered all his younger brethren, and established idolatry. For these offences a prophecy came against him from Elijah in writing (supposed to be Elisha, as Elijah was dead). 2 Kings viii. 16-19; 2 Chron. xxi. 1-4, 12-15.

433. Benhadad II. again besieges Samaria, cir. 892.—Benhadad besieged Samaria so closely that a famine ensued. Women were forced to eat their own children, and Jehoram, charging the evil on Elisha, sought to slay him. Elisha predicted an abundance of provision on the next day; and the same night four lepers discovered that the Syrians, terrified by miraculous noises, had hurriedly fled and left all their effects, which amply supplied the wants of the besieged; and a lord who had scoffed at the prophecy of Elisha was trodden to death by the crowd at the

Judah—*Ahaziah.*

436. Fulfilment of Prophecy against Jehoram.—This was fulfilled; 1st, In the revolt of Edom, which from this time chose its own king and ceased to pay homage to Judah, and of Libnah. 2d, In the invasion of the Philistines and Arabian Ethiopians, who carried off his wives and children. 3d, In being attacked with a bowel disease, of which he died. 2 Kings viii. 20-22; 2 Chron. xxi. 8-11, 16-19.

439. 6. Ahaziah, Azariah, or Jehoahaz, 885, 884.—Son of Jehoram by Athaliah, began to reign in B. C. 886, whilst his father was alive. 2 Kings ix. 29.

440. Sins like Ahab; allies with Jehoram.—Ahaziah, like his father Jehoram, fell into the idolatry of Ahab, and joined Jehoram, king of Israel, in attacking Hazael, king of Syria, who had stifled his master, Benhadad II., and ascended his throne, and was now at Ramoth-gilead, east of the Jordan. Here Jehoram was wounded, and returned to Jezreel, where Ahaziah visited him, and the two kings went to meet Jehu, who slew Jehoram. 2 Kings viii. 27-29; ix. 16-26; 2 Chron. xxii. 2-6.

442. Slain by Jehu.—Ahaziah was afterward pursued and slain at Megiddo, but buried at Jerusalem. His forty-two nephews and kinsmen were also slain. 2 Kings ix. 27, 28; x. 12-14; 2 Chron. xxii. 7-9.

Israel—*Jehu.*

gate of Samaria. 2 Kings vi. 24-33; vii.

437. Elisha restores the Shunammite's son, etc., cir. 891.—Elisha healed the deadly pottage at Gilgal, and fed one hundred men with twenty loaves, restored the Shunammite's dead son, and predicted seven years' famine, during which the Shunammite retired to the land of the Philistines. 2 Kings iv. 8-41; viii. 1, 2.

438. Foretells the Accession of Hazael, cir. 885.—Elisha went to Damascus and foretold the death of Benhadad and accession of Hazael. This year the seven years' famine ended, and Elisha obtained for the Shunammite woman the restoration of her inheritance. 2 Kings viii. 3-15.

441. Anoints Jehu; Destruction of the Dynasty of Ahab, 884.—Elisha sent one of the sons of the prophets to anoint Jehu, son of Nimshi, and Jehoram's captain at Ramoth-gilead, to be king of Israel, according to the command given by God to Elijah on Mount Horeb (sect. 410). Jehu was then acknowledged king by the soldiers, and went to Jezreel, where Jehoram and Ahaziah king of Judah happened to be. Jehoram, informed by a watchman of Jehu's approach, sent three successive messengers to inquire, "Is it peace?" but neither of them returned. Jehoram and Ahaziah then went in person to meet Jehu with the same question, but Jehu replied, "What peace, so long as the whoredoms and witchcrafts of thy mother Jezebel are so many!" and shot an

Judah—*Athaliah, Joash.* **Israel**—*Jehu.*

arrow through the heart of Jehoram, whose body was then cast into Naboth's field, as predicted by Elijah (sect. 414). Ahaziah was also slain. (See also the Life of Elisha, sect. 436, note.) 2 Kings ix. 1-29; 2 Chron. xxii. 7-9.

SECOND PERIOD—*from the simultaneous accession of* JEHU *in Israel and usurpation of* ATHALIAH *in Judah, until Israel was carried away captive by the Assyrian Power.* B. C. 884-721 = 163 *years.*

443. **7. Athaliah's Usurpation, 884-878.**—Daughter of Ahab, wife of Jehoram, and mother of Ahaziah, now destroyed all the seed royal, and usurped the throne for six years. 2 Kings xi. 1, 3; 2 Chron. xxii. 10, 12.

446. **Joash saved; educated by Jehoiada.**—Joash, son of Ahaziah, was, however, saved by his aunt Jehosheba, who was wife of Jehoiada the high priest. 2 Kings xi. 2; 2 Chron. xxii. 11.

447. **Athaliah slain; Joash anointed King.**—After six years the people grew tired of Athaliah's tyranny, and Jehoiada the high priest anointed Joash in the temple and proclaimed him king, and Athaliah, rushing there to know the cause of the disturbance, was slain at the outer gate. 2 Kings xi. 4-16; 2 Chron. xxiii. 1-15.

448. **8. Jehoash, or Joash, 878-839.**—Son of Ahaziah. Reigned forty years. PROPHET—*Zechariah, son of Jehoiada.*

449. **Jehoiada regent; Worship of Jehovah restored.**—During the minority of Joash the high priest Jehoiada appears to have been guardian of

444. **10. Jehu, 884-856.**—Son of Nimshi. Reigned twenty-eight years. PROPHETS—*Elisha and Jonah.*

445. **Slays Jezebel and destroys the House of Ahab.**—Jehu now proceeded to Jezreel, where Jezebel reproached him, saying. "Had Zimri peace, who slew his master?" alluding to Zimri's murder of Elah, by which he enjoyed the throne only seven days. (See sect. 393.) Some eunuchs then, by Jehu's order, threw Jezebel from a window, and she was trampled to death by horses and her carcass eaten by dogs, according to Elijah's prophecy (sect. 414). Jehu now ordered the people of Samaria to send him the heads of Ahab's seventy sons, and proceeding to Samaria, he met Ahaziah's forty-two brothers and killed them. He next met Jehonadab, the son of Rechab (founder of the Rechabites; see sect. 201, *note*), and received him into favor, and proceeding to Samaria he completed the destruction of Ahab's family. 2 Kings ix. 30-37; x. 1-17.

450. **Destroys Baal's Worshippers.**—At Samaria, Jehu assumed the character of a de-

Judah—*Joash.*

the young king and regent of the kingdom. He aroused the religious zeal of the priests, Levites, and people, threw down the temple of Baal, and slew Mattan the priest; and having then destroyed all the idolatrous temples, altars, and monuments throughout the land, he restored the true worship of Jehovah. 2 Kings xi. 17–21; xii. 1–3; 2 Chron. xxiii. 16–21; xxiv. 1–3.

452. **Joash repairs the Temple, cir. 856.**—Joash being grown up, caused the temple at Jerusalem to be repaired by collecting money from the people, as Moses had done for the building of the tabernacle. He reigned well during the whole life of Jehoiada, though the high places were not removed; but after the high priest's death he fell into idolatry. 2 Kings xii. 4–16; 2 Chron. xxiv. 4–14.

454. **Death of Jehoiada; Re-establishment of Baal, cir. 840.**—Jehoiada died, aged one hundred and thirty years; and Joash, listening to the princes of Judah, re-established the worship of Baal; and when Zechariah the priest and son of Jehoiada remonstrated, Joash commanded the people to stone him. 2 Chron. xxiv. 15–22.

456. **Syrian Invasion under Hazael.**—Hazael, king of Syria, now marched against Judah, but Joash, with the vessels of the temple, bribed him to depart. At the end of the year, however, a small company of Syrians defeated the host of Judah, destroyed the princes, and sent the spoil to Damascus. 2 Kings xii. 17, 18; 2 Chron. xxiv. 23, 24.

459. **Joash slain by his Servants, 839.**—Joash was

Israel—*Jehu, Jehoahaz.*

vout votary of Baal, and by a pretended sacrifice collected all the idolaters into Baal's temple. Jehonadab the Rechabite, with eighty men, then entered the building by his direction and slew all who were within, and the images were brought out and burnt, and the temple converted to the vilest of purposes. 2 Kings x. 18–28.

451. **Cir. 862.—Jonah** *prophesied.* See *Prophetical Books*—JONAH.

453. **Hazael seizes the Territory east of the Jordan, 860.**—Jehu had been conducting the war against Hazael, king of Syria, at Ramoth-gilead when the message of Elisha called him to the throne. Hazael seems to have taken advantage of his absence to seize all the Israelite territory east of the Jordan; and Jehu, who still practised the idolatry of Jeroboam, was not permitted to regain this dominion. 2 Kings x. 32–36.

455. **Worships the Golden Calves, 856.**—Jehu, though he destroyed Baal, yet followed in the sins of Jeroboam, by worshipping the two golden calves; but for his faithfulness in exterminating Ahab's family God promised the kingdom to his descendants to the fourth generation. 2 Kings x. 29–31.

457. **11. Jehoahaz, 856–839.** —Son of Jehu. Reigned seventeen years. PROPHET—*Elisha.*

458. **Worships the Golden Calves; oppressed by Hazael and Benhadad III.**—Followed in the sins of Jeroboam, and was accordingly oppressed by Hazael, king of Syria, and his son, Benhadad III., who suc-

B. C. 884–721. 2 KINGS.

Judah—*Amaziah.*

afflicted with disease, and at length slain in his bed by two of his servants. 2 Kings xii. 20, 21; 2 Chron. xxiv. 25, 26.

460. **9. Amaziah, 839–810.**—Son of Joash. Reigned twenty-nine years. PROPHET—*Elisha.* 2 Kings xiv. 1–8; 2 Chron. xxv. 1.

462. **Begins well.**—Amaziah slew his father's murderers, but spared their children in obedience to the law of Moses. He began his reign well, but did not remove the high places. 2 Kings xv. 3–6; 2 Chron. xxv. 2–4.

Israel—*Joash.*

ceeded him; but Jehoahaz repented, and his successor, Joash, was enabled to rescue Israel. 2 Kings xiii. 1–9.

461. **12. Joash, or Jehoash, 839–826.**—Son of Jehoahaz. Reigned two years whilst his father was alive—in all fourteen years alone; seventeen years altogether. PROPHET—*Elisha.*

463. **Worships the Golden Calves; promised Three Victories by Elisha.**—Joash walked in the sins of Jeroboam. Elisha fell sick and sent for Joash, who, at the prophet's command, shot an arrow from his window, but when desired to smite the ground did so only three times. Elisha then promised him three victories over the Syrians, but rebuked him for not smiting more. Elisha soon afterward died.* 2 Kings xiii. 1–21.

---

* **Life of Elisha, 896–838.**—Elisha, son of Shaphat of Abel-meholah, was ploughing with twelve pair of oxen when Elijah called him to the prophetic office by throwing his mantle over him and anointing him as prophet, B. C. 896, in the reign of Jehoram. The same year Elijah was taken up to heaven in a chariot of fire, and gave Elisha his mantle and a double portion of his spirit, which Elisha had previously asked for, and assured that he should receive if he were with Elijah at the time of his departure. Elisha was now the prophet in Israel in the room of Elijah, and the remainder of his life was a series of miracles— viz.:

B. C. 896. 1st, He smote the Jordan with Elijah's mantle and divided the stream. 2d, He healed the waters of Jericho by throwing in salt. 3d, He cursed the mocking children at Bethel, and forty-two were slain by two she-bears.

B. C. 895. 4th, He miraculously supplied the allied armies of Judah, Israel, and Edom with water when perishing in the wilderness of Edom in their expedition against the Moabites. 5th, He promised the Shunammite a son.

B. C. 894. 6th, He healed Naaman's leprosy. 7th, He transferred the leprosy to his servant Gehazi.

B. C. 893. 8th, He made an iron axe's head to swim. 9th, He disclosed the secret counsels of Benhadad II. to Jehoram, king of Israel. 10th, He blinded the Syrian host sent to take him.

B. C. 892. 11th, He promised abundance of provision during the siege of Samaria.

Judah—*Amaziah.*

464. Defeats the Edomites, 827.—Amaziah levied an army to attack the Edomites, and hired 100,000 Israelites, but being forbidden by a prophet to use the idolatrous mercenaries, he sent them back, which so exasperated the 100,000 that they ravaged Judah on their way and killed 3000. Meantime, Amaziah conquered the Edomites in the Valley of Salt, at the southern extremity of the Dead Sea, and took Selah [Petra]. 2 Kings xiv. 7; 2 Chron. xxv. 5-13.

466. Worships the Edomite Gods.—On his return after these splendid successes Amaziah was mad enough to worship the Edomite gods, and was threatened with destruction by a prophet. 2 Chron. xxv. 14-16.

Israel—*Joash.*

465. Defeats the Syrians Three times, 836.—Joash defeated the Syrians three times, as Elisha had promised, and recovered the cities west of the Jordan, which Hazael had taken from his father Jehoahaz.

About this time Israel was invaded by predatory bands of Moabites. 2 Kings xiii. 20, 22-25.

467. Amaziah defeated by Joash, 826.—Amaziah now challenged Joash, king of Israel, to battle, but the latter replied, "The thistle that was in Lebanon said to the cedar, 'Give thy daughter as a wife to my son;' but a wild beast passed by and trod down the thistle. Now, thou hast indeed smitten Edom, and thy heart hath lifted thee up to boast, but tarry at home, for why shouldest thou meddle to thine hurt and fall, and Judah with thee?"

B. C. 891. 12th, He healed the deadly pottage at Gilgal. 13th, He fed one hundred men with twenty loaves. 14th, He restored the Shunammite's son. 15th, He foretold seven years of famine when the Shunammite went to the land of the Philistines.

B. C. 885. 16th, He foretold the death of Benhadad and accession of Hazael.

B. C. 884. 17th, He sent to anoint Jehu, son of Nimshi, to be king.

B. C. 838. He promised to Joash on his deathbed three victories over the Syrians.

After Elisha's death a corpse was hastily thrown into his sepulchre, that the mourners might escape from the Moabites, who then infested Israel; but as soon as the corpse touched the bones of Elisha it was restored to life.

ELISHA was contemporary with *Joram, Jehu,* and *Joash,* kings of Israel, and with *Joram, Ahaziah, Athaliah,* and *Joash,* monarchs of Judah.

Amaziah would not, however, be thus warned, but marched against Joash, and was utterly defeated; and the king of Israel took Jerusalem, broke down the wall, and plundered the temple and palace. 2 Kings xiv. 8-15; 2 Chron. xxv. 17-24.

Judah—*Uzziah*.

468. Slain at Lachish, 811. —A conspiracy was formed against Amaziah at Jerusalem, and he fled to Lachish, but was slain there. 2 Kings xiv. 19, 20; 2 Chron. xxv. 27, 28.

470. **10. Uzziah, or Azariah, 810-758.**—Son of Amaziah. Reigned fifty-two years. PROPHETS—*Zechariah, Joel, and Isaiah.*

472. **Influence of Zechariah; Kingdom flourishes.** Uzziah was sixteen years old when he ascended the throne, and as long as Zechariah the prophet lived he reigned righteously and prospered. He subdued the Philistines and bordering Arabs, and made the Ammonites tributary. He recovered the port of Elath on the Red Sea; fortified Jerusalem with towers; built towers and wells in the desert; and strengthened his works by the erection of new and extraordinary engines for the discharge of arrows and large stones. He also enrolled a large army like that of Jehoshaphat, and provided ample stores of armor and weapons. It is moreover particularly stated that he was fond of agriculture, and that both by example and encouragement he fostered husbandry, planting, and the keeping of cattle. 2 Kings xv. 1-4; 2 Chron. xxvi. 1-16.

474. **Cir. 800.**—**Joel** *prophesied.* See *Prophetical Books*—JOEL.

475. **Smitten with Leprosy, cir. 765.**—Uzziah, elated with

Israel—*Jeroboam II.*

469. **13. Jeroboam II., 825 -784.**—Son of Joash, had been made king whilst his father was engaged in the Syrian war, but now reigned alone forty-one years. 2 Kings xiv. 23. PROPHETS—*Amos, Hosea, and Jonah.*

471. **Decline of the Syrian Power.**—The power of Damascus, which under Benhadad II. and Hazael appears to have extended over nearly the whole of Syria, was now on the decline. The cause is unknown. A civil war may have arisen between the states which had been united into one kingdom, or the growing might of Nineveh had begun to seize the provinces on the frontier. But the three victories promised by Elisha to Joash had procured the recovery of the cities west of the Jordan, which had been seized by Hazael (sect. 465); and the prophet Jonah now promised Jeroboam the recovery of Israel east of the river. 2 Kings xiv. 25, 26.

473. **Brilliant Successes against Syria; flourishing period of Israelite History, 822.**—Jeroboam II. now recovered all the territory east of the Jordan, from Hamath to the Dead Sea, which had been taken by Hazael (sect. 453), and marching into Syria he reconquered Hamath and Damascus. (See sect. 329.) Jeroboam, however, walked in the sins of Jeroboam I., and worshipped the golden calves. 2 Kings xiv. 24-28.

476. **Cir. 787.**—**Amos** *proph-*

Judah—*Jotham, Ahaz.*

prosperity, entered the temple to burn incense. Azariah and eighty other priests remonstrated with him in vain, and whilst the censer was in his hand an incurable leprosy rose in his forehead. Jotham his son was vice-regent. 2 Kings xv. 5; 2 Chron. xxvi. 16-21.

480. **B. C. 760-698.**—**Isaiah** *prophesied.* See *Prophetical Books*—ISAIAH.

481. **11. Jotham, 758-742.**—Son of Uzziah. Reigned sixteen years. PROPHETS—*Isaiah and Micah.*

483. **Reigned righteously and prosperously.**—Jotham reigned righteously, and continued the improvements and plans of his father. He built many fortresses, and erected the west gate of the temple, and obliged the Ammonites to pay tribute. 2 Kings xv. 32-35; 2 Chron. xxvii. 1-6.

485. **B. C. 750-710.**—**Micah** *prophesied.* See *Prophetical Books*—MICAH.

487. **12. Ahaz, 742-726.**—Son of Jotham. Reigned sixteen years. PROPHETS—*Isaiah and Micah.*

488. **Worships Baal and Molech.**—Ahaz was the most corrupt monarch that had hitherto belonged to the line of David. He adopted the idolatry of Ahab and made molten

Israel—*Zechariah-Pekahiah.*

esied. See *Prophetical Books*—AMOS.

477. **Cir. 785.**—**Hosea** *prophesied.* See *Prophetical Books*—HOSEA.

478. **INTERREGNUM, 784-773,** lasting eleven years, during which no king reigned.

479. **14. Zechariah, 773.** PROPHET—*Hosea.*—Son of Jeroboam II., walked in the sins of Jeroboam, and was assassinated by Shallum after reigning six months. 2 Kings xv. 8-12.

482. **15. Shallum, 772.**—Son of Jabesh, reigned one month, and assassinated by Menahem. 2 Kings xv. 13-15.

484. **16. Menahem, 772-761.**—Son of Gadi, from Tirzah, walked in the ways of Jeroboam I. in worshipping the golden calves. Reigned ten years. PROPHET—*Hosea.* 2 Kings xiv. 17, 18.

486. **First Assyrian Invasion under Pul.**—Pul, king of Assyria,* invaded Israel, but Menahem bribed him with 1000 silver talents [113,839 lbs., about £340,500] to return to his kingdom. This sum was raised by making the wealthy Israelites pay fifty shekels [$22\frac{3}{4}$ oz. = £5 13s. 10d.] a man. 2 Kings xiv. 19, 20; xv. 16-22.

489. **17. Pekahiah, 761-759.**—Son of Menahem. Reigned two years. PROPHET

---

* **Nineveh,** or *Nimroud,* as has been proved by the recent researches of Mr. Layard, was situated on the eastern bank of the Tigris and near its junction with the Zab, about twenty miles south-east of the modern town of Mosul. The history of Assyria prior to the present period is uncertain, but, to use the words of Mr. Layard, "to reject the notion of the existence of an independent kingdom of Assyria at the very earliest period would be almost to question whether the country were inhabited." It would be directly in opposition to the united testimony of Scripture and tradition; and though a doubt may be entertained as to the dynasties, there is none as to its existence.

Judah—*Ahaz.*

images for Baalim; he sacrificed in the vale of Hinnom and in groves on high places; and he made his son to pass through the fire in honor of Molech, and practised all the abominations of the heathen. 2 Kings xvi. 1–4; 2 Chron. xxviii. 1–4.

Israel—*Pekah.*

—*Hosea.* He walked in the ways of Jeroboam I., and was slain by one of his generals and successor. 2 Kings xv. 23–26.

490. **18. Pekah, 759-739.** —Son of Remaliah, and had assassinated Pekahiah. He worshipped the golden calves like Jeroboam I., and reigned twenty years. 2 Kings xiv. 27, 28. PROPHETS — *Hosea and Oded.*

491. **Pekah and Rezin ally; invade Judah, 742.**—Pekah, king of Israel, now formed an alliance with Rezin, who appears to have re-established the kingdom of Syria. The two kings then invaded the territory of Ahaz and besieged Jerusalem, with the intention of placing an individual alluded to as the son of Tabeal (Isa. vii. 6) on the throne of Judah. The enterprise was unsuccessful, but Rezin seems to have marched southward and taken and occupied the port of Elath on the Red Sea. Isaiah then prophesied to Ahaz the destruction of both Pekah and Rezin [which was afterward accomplished by the arms of Tiglath-pileser]; and he also delivered as a sign the well-known prediction,

"Behold a virgin shall conceive, and bear a son,
And shall call his name IMMANUEL." Isa. vii. 14.

2 Kings xvi. 5, 6.

492. **Second Invasion of Pekah and Rezin, 741.**—Next year Pekah and Rezin again invaded Judah, and defeated Ahaz with the slaughter of 120,000 men; and Rezin took a multitude of captives to Damascus, whilst Pekah carried away 200,000 women and children and a large quantity of plunder to Samaria. But the prophet Oded remonstrated with Pekah against enslaving the children of Judah, and the elders of the national assembly * positively declared that the captives should not be brought into the land; and accordingly Pekah relieved the prisoners out of the spoil and returned them to their own country. 2 Chron. xxviii. 5–15.

493. **Ahaz applies to Tiglath-pileser; Second Assyrian Invasion; Syria and east of Jordan enslaved, 740.**—The Edomites now invaded Judah and carried off numerous prisoners, and the Philistines plundered the cities on the southern borders, whilst

---

* In the text they are called the elders of Ephraim, but this name only appears to have been adopted by the ten tribes after their separation from Judah.

Ahaz was probably threatened by a third invasion of the kings of Israel and Syria. In this extremity the king of Judah sent gold and silver from the treasures of the temple and palace as a present to TIGLATH-PILESER [or TIGLATH-PUL-ASSUR—*i. e. the tiger lord of Assyria*] to come to his assistance. Tiglath-pileser, who had ascended the throne of Assyria in the room of his father *Pul*, then marched an army westward, defeated and slew Rezin, sent the inhabitants to Kir, or Assyria Proper, and thus put an end to the kingdom of Damascene Syria.* He also car-

---

* **History of Syria.**—Syria, or Aram (from *Aram*, fifth son of Shem), was now merged in the Assyrian empire. It was bounded on the east by the Euphrates, west by the Mediterranean, north by Cilicia, and south by Phœnicia, Judæa, and Arabia Deserta.

Cir. B. C. 1055.—Before the time of David, Syria was divided into cantons and governed by petty kings, each of whom reigned in his own city and territories. These petty kingdoms are frequently mentioned under the names of Zobah, Damascus, Hamath, Geshur, Rehob, Ishtob, Maachah, etc.

Hadadezer, 1040–1036, was king of ZOBAH, and conquered by David, who after two brilliant victories extended his dominions to the Euphrates. (See sect. 329.) Contemporary with Hadadezer were TOI, king of HAMATH, who sent his son Joram to congratulate David on his victories over Hadadezer; and TALMAI, king of GESHUR, whose daughter Maachah married David and became the mother of Absalom, and to whom Absalom fled after the murder of his brother Amnon. 2 Sam. viii. 9; xiii. 37. After the defeat of Hadadezer, Rezon, one of his captains, fled from him and reigned in Damascus. (See sect. 362.)

Rezon, or Hezion, cir. 975.—During Solomon's reign Rezon, supposed to be the same as Hezion (1 Kings xv. 18), seems to have thrown off the Jewish yoke and founded the Syrian kingdom.

Tabrimon, cir. 960.—Father of Benhadad I. and son of Hezion or Rezon.

Benhadad, 941.—Succeeded his father. He assisted Asa, king of Judah, ravaged Israel, and compelled Baasha to give up the building of Ramah (sects. 389, 390).

Benhadad II., 910–885.—Invaded Israel B. C. 901, accompanied by thirty-two petty kings, but was defeated by Ahab (sec. 411).

B. C. 900. Thought Jehovah was God only of the *hills*, and therefore attacked Ahab in the *valley* of Aphek, but was defeated with great slaughter. Fled to Aphek, but Ahab allied with him (sect. 412).

B. C. 894. Sent Naaman, the Syrian leper, to Jehoram, king of Israel, to be cured (sect. 430).

B. C. 893. Prepared to attack Israel, but his secret counsels were revealed to Jehoram by Elisha (sect. 431).

B. C. 892. Blockaded Samaria and caused a terrible famine, but, hearing a noise of chariots and horses, he and his army fled, and his campstores fell into the hands of the enemy (sect. 433).

B. C. 885. Stifled by Hazael, according to Elisha's prophecy (sect. 440).

Hazael, 885–839.—Ravaged Ramoth-gilead (sect. 440).

B. C. 861. Attacked the Israelites east of the Jordan (sect. 453).

B. C. 850–840. Oppressed Israel, captured Gath, and prepared to attack Jerusalem, but bribed to return back by Joash, king of Judah (sect. 456). B. C. 839. Died (sect. 458).

ried away the tribes east of the Jordan—Reuben, Gad, and half Manasseh—captives to Media, where they were planted in Halah, Habor, and on the river Gozan; and to these he added the other half of Manasseh, which was seated in Galilee. He thus relieved Ahaz, but we are subsequently told that he "distressed him, but strengthened him not." 2 Kings xvi. 7-9; 2 Chron. xxviii 16-21.

B. C. 753. Rome was founded, according to VARRO.

Judah—*Ahaz, Hezekiah.*

494. **Ahaz worships the Gods of Damascus.**—Ahaz now went to Damascus to meet Tiglath-pileser. Here he saw an idolatrous altar, and sent a model of it to Urijah the priest, with directions to build one like it; and upon his return to Jerusalem he sacrificed on this altar to the gods of Damascus, shut up the temple, broke up the sacred vessels, and established idolatry throughout Judah. 2 Kings xvi. 10-18; 2 Chron. xxviii. 22-25.

499. **Sun-dial of Ahaz.**—Allusion is subsequently made to the sun-dial of Ahaz (see the reign of Hezekiah), and this is the first mention in Scripture of the use of dials for measuring time. The first mention of hours as a division of the day is in Dan. iv. 19 and in Tobit xi. 14.

501. **13. Hezekiah, 726-698.**—Son of Ahaz. Reigned nineteen years. PROPHETS—*Isaiah and Micah.*

502. **Breaks the Serpent**

Israel—*Hoshea.*

495. **Pekah slain by Hoshea, 739.**—Hoshea, son of Elah, formed a conspiracy against Pekah and slew him, and ascended the throne in his stead. 2 Kings xv. 30.

496. **INTERREGNUM, 739-730.**—ANARCHY FOR NINE YEARS.

497. **19. Hoshea, 730-721.**—Son of Elah. Reigned nine years. PROPHET—*Hosea.*

498. **Better than his Predecessors.**—The regicide Hoshea seems to have reigned better than the kings before him, though he followed in many of their sins. He allowed Hezekiah of Judah to send messengers throughout Israel to invite the people to the passover at Jerusalem, and did not prevent his subjects from accepting the invitation. 2 Kings xvii. 1, 2; 2 Chron. xxx. 6-11.

500. **Third Assyrian Invasion; Shalmaneser makes Hoshea tributary, 728.**—

Benhadad III., cir. 839.—Joash, king of Israel, obtained three victories over him, and recovered the cities *west* of the Jordan taken by Hazael, according to Elisha's prophecy (sect. 465).

B. C. 822. Decline of the Syrian power. Jeroboam II. of Israel recovers all the territory *east* of the Jordan, and conquers Hamath and Damascus (sect. 471).

Rezin, cir. 742-740.—In B. C. 742 he joined Pekah, king of Israel, in an expedition against Ahaz, king of Judah, which failed (sect. 491).

B. C. 741. Renewed the war, and was successful (sect. 492).

B. C. 740. Tiglath-pileser was bribed by Ahaz, and, taking Damascus, he slew Rezin and carried the Syrians captive to Kir, or Assyria Proper (sect. 493).

Judah—*Hezekiah.*

and destroys Idolatry.—Hezekiah began to reign at the age of twenty-five years. His first acts were to thoroughly extirpate idolatry throughout his dominions, and even to remove the high places, which his predecessors had preserved. Amongst other things he destroyed the brazen serpent which Moses had elevated in the wilderness (sect. 228), and before which incense had been burned until his own time. 2 Kings xviii. 4.

504. Restores the Worship of Jehovah and celebrates the Passover.—Hezekiah now purified the temple, reinstated the priests and restored their courses, and caused the passover to be kept with great solemnity for fourteen days, assembling the people from the eleven tribes of Israel, which had not been done since the days of Solomon. 2 Kings xviii. 3, 5, 6; 2 Chron. xxix. 11-36; xxx.; xxxi.

506. Rebels against Shalmaneser: defeats the Philistines, 725.—Hezekiah now refused to pay the annual tribute to Shalmaneser which Tiglath-pileser had exacted from his father, Ahaz (sect. 493). He also invaded the Philistine territory, and subdued it as far as Gaza. 2 Kings xviii. 7, 8.

Israel—*Hoshea.*

SHALMANESER, who appears to have succeeded Tiglath-pileser on the throne of Assyria, now invaded Israel, and made Hoshea tributary. 2 Kings xvii. 3.

503. Hoshea rebels, and is Imprisoned, 725.—Hoshea now appears to have envied the freedom and success of Hezekiah, who had refused to pay tribute to Shalmaneser. Accordingly, he made a treaty with *So*, king of Egypt, and either the *Sabacon* or *Sethon* of Herodotus (xxx. 1-7), and refused to pay tribute, though Isaiah strongly reprehended the alliance. Shalmaneser then sent for Hoshea, and imprisoned him; and the king of Egypt made no attempt to come to the assistance of the latter. 2 Kings xvii. 4.

505. Siege of Samaria, and Captivity of Israel, 723-721.—Shalmaneser besieged Samaria, and took it after three years' siege, and carried away Israel captive beyond the Euphrates. 2 Kings xvii. 5-23; xviii. 9-12.

---

507. Colonization of Samaria; Origin of the Samaritans, 678.—ESARHADDON, who succeeded to *Sennacherib* on the throne of Assyria, carried off the remnant that still remained in Israel, and sent men from Babylon, Cuthah, Ava, Hamath, and Sepharvaim to colonize Samaria, who then took the name of Samaritans or Cuthæans. These colonists being afterward, on account of their idolatry, troubled with lions, Esarhaddon, at their request, sent them a priest to instruct them in the worship of Jehovah, whom they supposed to be the *local* god, and therefore the only one who could preserve them in Samaria. The colonists, however, set up the gods of the various nations to which they belonged, and mingled their worship with that of Jehovah.

Eventually, after many Israelites had been incorporated amongst them, and they had erected a temple on Mount Gerizim, they abandoned idolatry, and worshipped Jehovah only.

THIRD PERIOD.—*From the Assyrian Captivity of Israel until the Babylonian Captivity of Judah.* B. C. 721–588 = 134 *years.*

508. *First Assyrian Invasion of Judah; Hezekiah submits to Sennacherib, 713.*—Sennacherib—or Sargon, as he is called by Isaiah—succeeded his father, Shalmaneser, on the throne of Assyria, B. C. 715, and in B. C. 713 prepared to punish the disaffection of Hezekiah. The inhabitants of Judah were now alarmed, and though it does not appear that the king himself despatched any embassy to Egypt, yet his nobles, in spite of the remonstrances of Isaiah (xxx.-xxxii.), sent camels and asses laden with treasure to ask aid from Pharaoh [Sethon],* and especially to request a force of cavalry and chariots. The weak parts of the wall of Jerusalem were mended; a second wall was added, and towers and fortifications were erected, and the fountains in the neighborhood were stopped up. Hezekiah himself encouraged the people by his confidence in Jehovah. Whilst, however, Sennacherib was approaching Jerusalem, Hezekiah sent to offer him an unqualified submission, and a fine of three hundred talents of silver [34,151 lbs. 9 oz. = £122,455 5s.] and thirty talents of gold [3415 lbs. 2 oz. = £163,928] was imposed upon him. Hezekiah paid the sum, though he was compelled to exhaust the sacred treasures, and even to strip the gold from the doors and pillars of the temple; and Sennacherib then retired. 2 Kings xviii. 13-16.

509. *Sennacherib takes Ashdod and again invades Judah.*—Sennacherib now took Ashdod in Philistia, one of the keys of Egypt, and then appears to have thought it would be unsafe to invade the latter country whilst Judah remained still unsubdued in his rear. Accordingly, he again invaded the territories of Hezekiah; took all the fenced cities, except Libnah and

---

* We learn from Herodotus that Sethon was priest of Vulcan, and had neglected the military caste, who accordingly refused to obey his orders. This may account for his not marching to the assistance of Hezekiah.—*Herod.*, ii. 141.

Lachish, to which he laid siege; and sent by Rabshakeh and two other of his generals a haughty summons to Jerusalem, requiring its immediate surrender. The latter also uttered blasphemies and disparaging expressions respecting Jehovah; they alluded to the fallacy of expecting aid from Egypt; and they endeavored to persuade the Jews to give hostages and pay homage by presents to the king of Assyria, by promising to leave them in peace until Sennacherib should carry them away to a land of corn and wine, like their own land.* Rabshakeh, however, returned without success to his master, whom he found besieging Libnah, whilst Isaiah prophesied the destruction of the Assyrian host: "Behold, I will send *a blast* upon him." 2 Kings xviii. 17–37; xix. 1–8; 2 Chron. xxxii. 1–20; Isa. xxxvi.; xxxvii. 1–8.

510. ***Sennacherib called away by the Invasion of Tirhakah; Destruction of his Army.***—Just at this time the news arrived at Libnah that Tirhakah, king of Ethiopia,† was on his march to repel Sennacherib. The Assyrian king sent a boastful letter to Hezekiah, defying the God of Israel and threatening destruction on his return, but his message of defiance was met by a splendid piece of inspired eloquence from Isaiah, which we still read with interest and admiration. 2 Kings xix. 21–34. But the career of Sennacherib was almost closed, and the very next night the ANGEL OF JEHOVAH went out and smote in the camp of the Assyrians 185,000 men.‡ Sen-

---

* This was exactly the spirit in which Darius, son of Hystaspis, subsequently transplanted the Pæonians from the Strymon into Asia.—*Herod.*, v. 12-14.

† **This Ethiopia** appears to answer to the country called by the ancients *Meroe*, and by the moderns *Sennaar* and *Atbar*. It is a large triangle formed by the Nile on the west, the *Tacazze*, a tributary of the Nile, o the east, and the highlands of Abyssinia on the south. The desert of Nubia divides it from Egypt, but its monarchs often held possession of Upper or Southern Egypt. It is therefore probable that Tirhakah, who is also in Manetho's list of Ethiopian kings of Egypt, reigned in the Thebais, or the upper country, whilst So, or Sethon, reigned in Lower Egypt. (See also Herod., ii. 137.)

‡ **Destruction of the Assyrian Army.**—Respecting the means by which the Assyrian army was destroyed, the Targum and Babylonian Talmud say it was by lightning. Isaiah refers to a blast (xxxvii. 7), and probably it was effected by a hot wind, or simoom. Herodotus relates that at night multitudes of field-mice ate up the bow-strings, quivers, and shield-handles of the invaders, who were thus easily defeated on the

nacherib himself fled to Nineveh, and in revenge murdered many captive Jews, but was killed shortly afterward by his two eldest sons whilst he was worshipping in the temple of Nisroch;* and Esarhaddon his son reigned in his stead. This blow so weakened the Assyrian monarchy as not only to free the king of Judah from his apprehensions, but enabled the Medes and Babylonians to assert their independence. [Herodotus dates the revolt of the Medes B.C. 711.] 2 Kings xix. 9–37; 2 Chron. xxxii. 21, 22; Isa. xxxvii. 9–38.

511. *Hezekiah's Sickness, 712.*—Hezekiah fell sick, and Isaiah predicted his death, but the king prayed to God, and Isaiah promised him fifteen years additional life, and confirmed it by the miracle of the sun's going back ten degrees on the dial of Ahaz. 2 Kings xx. 1–11; 2 Chron. xxxii. 24; Isa. xxxviii.

512. *Messengers from Merodach-Baladan, king of Babylon.*—MERODACH-BALADAN, king of Babylon, sent to congratulate Hezekiah on his recovery from sickness and on his delivery from the Assyrians, through which Merodach himself had been enabled to establish his independence in Babylon. Hezekiah treated the ambassadors with the utmost respect, and showed them all his treasures; but for this vanity Isaiah foretold the *Babylonian captivity*, which took place one hundred and twenty-five years after. Hezekiah then humbled himself, and the threatened punishment was postponed until after his death. 2 Kings xx. 12–19; Isa. xxxix.

513. *Peaceful State of Judah, 709–698.*—Hezekiah now reigned in peace, increased in riches, built cities, and brought water into Jerusalem through reservoirs and conduits. Meantime, ESARHADDON, who had succeeded his father Sennacherib on the throne of Assyria, recovered the allegiance of the Babylonian kingdom. 2 Kings xx. 20; 2 Chron. xxxii. 27–30.

514. *14. Manasseh, 698–643.*—Son of Hezekiah. Reigned fifty-five years. PROPHET—*Isaiah*.

---

ensuing day. This story is supposed to have arisen from the similarity of the words λαμὰς, "a mouse," and λοιμὸς, "a pestilence." Prideaux, *passim*, and Baehr's note to Herod., ii. 141.

* The eagle-headed god. Zoroaster says, "God is he that has the head of a hawk."—*Layard.*

515. *Restores Idolatry and Necromancy.*—Manasseh ascended the throne at the age of twelve years, and it seems to have been the special object of his reign to overthrow all the good which his father Hezekiah had done for Judah. He practised all the sins of Ahab and Ahaz. He rebuilt the high places, set up altars to Baal and Astarte, and worshipped the host of heaven like the Sabæans. He used enchantments, dealt with wizards and necromancers, and observed times by astrology or other methods of superstition; and when he had a son old enough he made him pass through the fire in the valley of Hinnom. Moreover, he set up altars to the host of heaven in the two courts of the temple, and introduced a graven image into the sanctuary. He also carried on a fearful persecution, and shed innocent blood very much, until he had filled Jerusalem from one end to the other. Isaiah severely remonstrated with him, and is supposed to have been martyred in consequence. 2 Kings xxi. 1–16; 2 Chron. xxxiii. 1–10.

516. *Carried into Assyrian Captivity by Esarhaddon, 677; humbles himself.*—Esarhaddon's captains now invaded Judah, and in order, probably, to prevent another disaffection, they carried Manasseh in chains to Babylon. Here the king humbled himself, and the Lord heard him and brought him back to his kingdom, and he then eradicated idolatry, restored the worship of Jehovah, and fortified Jerusalem and his fenced cities. 2 Chron. xxxiii. 11–20.

517. *15. Amon, 643–641.*—Son of Manasseh, succeeded, and restored idolatry. He was slain by his servants after reigning two years, but the conspirators were again slain by the people. 2 Kings xxi. 19–26; 2 Chron. xxxiii. 21–25.

518. *16. Josiah, 641–610.*—Son of Amon. Reigned thirty-one years. PROPHETS—*Zephaniah, Jeremiah, Habakkuk,* and *Huldah the prophetess.*

519. *Seeks God in his youth; purges Judah and Israel from Idolatry.*—Josiah ascended the throne in the eighth year of his age, and in the eighth year of his reign, when he was only sixteen years old, he began to seek after the God of his fathers. In the twelfth year of his reign he began to purge the land from idolatry. His

rule seems to have extended over both Judah and Israel, and embraced all the territory west of the Jordan, for he broke down the altars of Baal, cut down the groves, and the carved and molten images, not only in Judah and Jerusalem, but also throughout all the land of Israel. 2 Kings xxii. 1, 2; 2 Chron. xxxiv. 1-7.

520. *Cir. B. C. 630. Zephaniah prophesied.* See *Prophetical Books*—ZEPHANIAH.

521. *B. C. 629. Jeremiah began to prophesy.* See *Prophetical Books*—JEREMIAH.

522. *Cir. B. C. 626. Habakkuk prophesied.* See *Prophetical Books*—HABAKKUK.

523. *Repairs the Temple, 624.*—Josiah in the eighteenth year of his reign determined on repairing the temple at Jerusalem, and ordered the great chest to be opened in which the freewill offerings, etc. were deposited; and he delivered the money to faithful overseers, who were immediately to put the work in hand and pay the workmen. 2 Kings xxii. 3-7; 2 Chron. xxxiv. 8-13.

524. *Book of the Law found by Hilkiah, and confirmed by Huldah, 624.*—Meantime, Hilkiah the priest, and father of Jeremiah, found in the treasury-chamber an original copy of the Law, containing the fearful denunciations of Jehovah against all idolatry. The book was read to Josiah, who then sent to inquire of the Lord through Huldah the prophetess. Huldah declared that the wrath of the Lord would be executed upon the land for its idolatry, but not in the time of Josiah. The king himself then read the book publicly to the people in the temple, who thereupon entered into a covenant with Josiah to serve the Lord. 2 Kings xxii. 8-20; xxiii. 1-3; 2 Chron. xxxiv. 14-32.

525. *The Altar of Jeroboam thrown down.*—A further destruction of idolatry followed, and Josiah went to Bethel, and took "the altar which was at Bethel, and the high place which Jeroboam the son of Nebat, who had made Israel to sin, had made," and broke them down, "and burned the high place, and stamped it small to powder, and burned the grove." He also "sent and took the bones" of the deceased priests "out of the sepulchres, and burned them upon the altar, and polluted it;" thus fulfilling the prediction given to Jeroboam three hundred

and sixty years before. (See sect. 377.) 2 Kings xxiii. 4–20; 2 Chron. xxxiv. 33.

526. *Celebration of a Solemn Passover, 623.*—After this Josiah thoroughly purified the land from idolatry, witchcraft, and wizards, and restored the ark to the temple, which it is supposed Manasseh or Amon had removed; and he and the people celebrated the passover with greater strictness and solemnity than had been displayed since the days of Samuel the prophet. 2 Kings xxiii. 21–25; 2 Chron. xxxv. 1–19.

527. *Decline of the Assyrian Empire under Esarhaddon, Saosduchinus, and Chyniladanus.*—Meantime, the Assyrian power had been on the decline, and Inner Asia had been the theatre of great revolutions. ESARHADDON, the successor of Sennacherib (sect. 510), had resubdued the Babylonians, but had failed in reducing the Medes. His son SAOSDUCHINUS was the Nebuchadonosor of the book of Judith, and was succeeded by CHYNILADANUS, or Sarac, in whose reign the Chaldees revolted, took Babylonia, and, having joined the Medes, succeeded in taking Nineveh and overthrowing the Assyrian empire, about B. C. 606. (See sect. 535.)

528. *Invasion of Pharaoh-Necho; Josiah slain, 610.*—Whilst the Assyrian power was involved in wars with the Medes and Chaldees, Egypt had been consolidating its strength. When we last mentioned this country it was in a state of internal struggles between the priests and military, and Tirhakah the Ethiopian ruled in Upper Egypt (sect. 510, *note*, and sect. 508). After this a civil war arose, which ended in the division of the country into twelve independent kingdoms, called the *Dodecarthy.* About B. C. 650, Psammetichus, one of these kings, reigned at Sais, and by the adoption of Greek tactics and defensive armor, and the employment of Carian and Ionian mercenaries, he subdued all his fellow-kings and united all Egypt under a single sceptre. The policy of the Egyptian monarchy was now entirely changed; Greeks were permanently established in Egypt as merchants, and the Egyptians began to mingle in foreign affairs. NECHO, son of Psammetichus, succeeded to the throne, B. C. 617, being the twenty-fourth year of the reign of Josiah. He cut a canal from the Red Sea to

the Mediterranean and built a fleet of triremes, and at length determined to attack the Assyrian power. His march was directed to Carchemish, an important post on the Euphrates; and he accordingly followed the usual route along the sea-coast of Palestine northward. Meantime, Josiah heard of the expedition. He had probably been permitted to retain his kingdom by Assyria on condition of defending the frontier against Egypt; and accordingly he now posted his forces in the plain of Esdraelon, or Jezreel, to intercept Necho. The latter sent messengers to advise Josiah to desist from interfering, but in vain. A battle ensued, and Josiah, who went out in disguise, was slain by the archers in the valley of Megiddo. "And Jeremiah lamented for Josiah; all the singing-men and singing-women spake of Josiah in their lamentations to this day." 2 Kings xxiii. 29, 30; 2 Chron. xxxv. 20–27.

529. *17. Jehoahaz, or Shallum, 610.*—Son of Josiah, though not the eldest, and was made king by the people. PROPHET—*Jeremiah.*

530. *Reigns wickedly; deposed by Necho.*—Meantime, Necho pursued his course to the Euphrates, and after three months returned victorious, having captured Carchemish and defeated the Assyrians. He now appears to have acted as lord-paramount of Judah. He put *Jehoahaz* in bands at Riblah in Hamath in Syria, and condemned the land to pay in tribute one hundred talents of silver [£34,151] and one talent of gold [£5464]. He then went to Jerusalem and placed *Eliakim*, son of Josiah, on the throne, in the room of Jehoahaz, and changed his name to *Jehoiakim;* and afterward returned to Egypt, carrying Jehoahaz with him as a hostage. 2 Kings xxiii. 31–34; 2 Chron. xxxvi. 1-4.

531. *18. Jehoiakim, 610–599.*—Son of Josiah. Reigned eleven years. PROPHETS—*Jeremiah, Daniel, Urijah.*

532. *Reigns wickedly; Jeremiah and Urijah prophesy against him.*—The first act of Jehoiakim was to exact from the people the tribute which Necho had imposed. He reigned wickedly, and *Jeremiah* prophesied against Judah, and was threatened with death, but acquitted because he spoke in the name of the Lord, as

Micah had done in the reign of Hezekiah. *Urijah* the
prophet also prophesied against his country, and was compelled to fly to Egypt, but brought back by Jehoiakim's
orders, and slain and buried in the graves of the common
people. 2 Kings xxiii. 34–37; 2 Chron. xxxv. 5; Jer.
xxvi.

533. *Charged by Jeremiah with the Murder of
Urijah, 609.*—*Jeremiah* charged Jehoiakim with the
murder of Urijah, and with general violence and oppression, and predicted that he should be cast out of Jerusalem and buried as an ass. Jer. xxii. 16–19.

534. *Jeremiah publicly foretells the Seventy Years'
Captivity, 607.*—*Jeremiah* now contrasted the apostasy
of the Jews with the obedience of the Rechabites to their
father, *Jehonadab*, the son of *Rechab*, in drinking no wine,
living in tents, and neither possessing nor occupying any
houses, fields, or vineyards (sect. 201, *note*). (They gained
their livelihood by being scribes.) Jeremiah also caused
Baruch to write his prophecy and read it publicly in the
temple, and foretold the conquest of Egypt by Nebuchadnezzar, and THE SEVENTY YEARS' CAPTIVITY OF THE JEWS:
"And this whole land shall be a desolation, and an astonishment; and these nations shall serve the king of Babylon seventy years. And it shall come to pass when seventy years are accomplished, that I will punish the king
of Babylon, and that nation, saith the Lord." Jer. xxv.
11. 12. "After seventy years be accomplished at Babylon, I will visit you, and perform my word toward you,
in causing you to return to this place." Jer. xxix. 10.

535. *Overthrow of the Assyrian Power; Rise of
the Medo-Persian and Chaldee-Babylonian Empires.*—The Assyrian empire, which had been long on
the wane, was about this time overthrown by a powerful
combination of the new kingdoms of Media and Chaldee-Babylonia. The MEDES under Deioces had revolted from
the Assyrians about B. C. 712, after the destruction of the
army of Sennacherib (sect. 510), and, having conquered
the Persians, commenced an empire. *Cyaxares*, the third
in the Median line of kings, had defeated the Assyrians
and besieged Nineveh, but was called away by an invasion of the Scythians, a nation of Tartary which had come
down in a vast body upon Media from the country north

of the Caucasus, and held a rule in Inner Asia for twenty-eight years. Meanwhile, the CHALDEES, who anciently occupied the mountains of Armenia and had been subject to the Assyrians, revolted from the rule of the latter, and under the Assyrian general *Nabopolassar*, who is the first-mentioned king of the Chaldees, and the father of Nebuchadnezzar, they seized the kingdom of Babylon.*
Nabopolassar afterward allied with *Cyaxares*, and the two powers then took Nineveh and shared the Assyrian empire, the Medes appropriating Assyria Proper, and leaving to Nabopolassar Babylonia and its dependent provinces, including all the lower country of Mesopotamia and as much as he could conquer of Syria.

536. *Pharaoh-Necho defeated by Nebuchadnezzar.*
—During the first three years of Jehoiakim's reign Necho had been pushing his conquests eastward to the border of the Euphrates, until his progress was stopped by the newly-risen Chaldee power. Nabopolassar was fast declining in health, and had confided his army to his son NEBUCHADNEZZAR, who obtained a decisive victory over Necho at Carchemish, where the latter had formerly been so successful against Assyria. The death of Nabopolassar, however, suddenly recalled Nebuchadnezzar to Babylon; but as soon as the young prince had secured himself on his father's throne he resumed the aggressive, and within a year of his victory at Carchemish had swept off every vestige of Egyptian power in Syria, and presented his irresistible armies on the eastern side of Palestine.

537. *Nebuchadnezzar takes Jerusalem; makes Jehoiakim tributary; carries off Daniel and the Three pious Jews, 606.*—NEBUCHADNEZZAR soon appeared in Judæa at the head of his victorious armies, and no help from Egypt was now at hand. He took Jerusalem after a short siege, and plundered the temple, and bound Jehoiakim in fetters to carry him to Babylon, but liberated him on condition of his paying a large tribute and giving hostages, amongst whom were Daniel and his three companions, Shadrach, Meshach, and Abednego. 2 Kings xxiv. 1; 2 Chron. xxxvi. 6-8; Dan. i. 1-6.

---

* The city of Babylon was seated on the Euphrates, about two hundred miles to the south of Nineveh.

From this date is calculated the commencement of the seventy years' captivity, though Judah was not entirely carried away before B. C. 588.

538. *Jeremiah's Prophecies again publicly read. Jehoiakim seeks to Destroy him, 605.*—A public fast was this year proclaimed in Jerusalem, and Baruch read the roll of Jeremiah's prophecies concerning the Babylonian captivity publicly in the temple a second time. This was repeated to Jehoiakim, who then heard the roll read and burnt it, and sought to take Baruch and Jeremiah, but they lay concealed. The latter by God's direction then prepared another roll of prophecy, and in it declared that none of Jehoiakim's posterity should ascend the throne, and that his own carcass should be exposed to the heat by day and the frost by night. Jer. xxxvi.

539. *Jehoiakim revolts from Nebuchadnezzar, 603.*—For three years Jehoiakim remained faithful to his allegiance, but at length revolted. Nebuchadnezzar appears to have been unable to come in person, but at length sent up some bands of Chaldees, who with a mixed army of the neighboring Syrians, Moabites, and Ammonites ravaged Judah and carried away 3320 captives. 2 Kings xxiv. 1, 2.

540. *Jerusalem blockaded; Jehoiakim slain, 599.* —At length Jerusalem was blockaded, and Jehoiakim was taken and slain in a sally, and his body thrown out beyond the gates; and thus he was buried with the burial of an ass, according to the prophecy of Jeremiah (sect. 533). 2 Kings xxiii. 6; 2 Chron. xxxvi. 8.

541. **Daniel** *began to prophesy in this reign.* See *Prophetical Books*—DANIEL.

542. *19. Jehoiachin, or Jeconiah, or Coniah, 599.* —Son of Jehoiakim. Reigned three months. PROPHETS —*Jeremiah and Daniel.*

543. *Nebuchadnezzar besieges Jerusalem in person; carries away 10,000 captives, 599.*—Jehoiachin reigned wickedly for three months, when Nebuchadnezzar arrived in person and pressed the siege of Jerusalem with vigor. Jehoiachin, with his mother, princes, servants, and officers, at length surrendered, and Nebuchadnezzar carried them and 10,000 captives, including *Ezekiel* and

Mordecai, to Babylon, together with the treasures of the palace and temple, as predicted by Jeremiah (sect. 534). None remained but the poorer people. Nebuchadnezzar then made *Mattaniah,* uncle of Jehoiachin, king in the room of the latter, and changed his name to *Zedekiah,* and bound him with an oath to maintain fidelity. 2 Kings xxiv. 8–16; 2 Chron. xxxvi. 9, 10.

544. *Zedekiah, 599–588.*—Youngest son of Josiah and uncle of Jehoiachin. Reigned eleven years. PROPHETS—*Jeremiah, Obadiah, Daniel and Ezekiel.*

545. **False Prophets predict the speedy Return from Captivity, 598.**—Some false prophets were predicting to the Jewish captives at Babylon a speedy return to their country, when *Jeremiah* wrote a letter recommending the latter to settle quietly in the land of their captivity. *Shemaiah* the Nehelamite then wrote from Babylon to Jerusalem, urging the priests to punish Jeremiah for prophesying seventy years' captivity, and was himself punished by Jeremiah's declaring that neither he nor his posterity should return to Judæa. In B. C. 596, *Hananiah* predicted that the captivity would cease in two years, but Jeremiah prophesied that he would die within the year, which was accomplished. Jer. xxvii.; xxviii.

546. *B. C. 595.*—*Ezekiel commences his prophetical career by the river Chebar in Chaldea.* See *Prophetical Books*—EZEKIEL.

547. **Zedekiah allies with Pharaoh - Hophra (*Apries*), and rebels, 593.**—*Necho,* king of Egypt, had been succeeded by his son *Psammis,* who died after a short reign of six years. *Hophra*—called by the Greeks *Apries*—ascended the throne of his father B. C. 595. He was an enterprising and, for a long period, a successful prince. He took Gaza, and made himself master of Phœnicia and part of Palestine, and thus recovered much of that influence in Syria which the Assyrians and Babylonians had taken from Egypt. With this Hophra, Zedekiah formed a secret compact, and then in the seventh year of his reign rebelled against Nebuchadnezzar. 2 Kings xxiv. 20; 2 Chron. xxxvi. 13; Jer. xxxvii. 5.

548. **Nebuchadnezzar besieges Jerusalem; Retreat of Hophra, 590.**—From this period Nebuchadnezzar

seems to have given up the attempt to maintain Judæa as a separate state, and to have determined on incorporating it absolutely as a province with his empire. He led an army with little delay into Judæa, and besieged Jerusalem, and built forts outside it to harass the country and repel supplies. Jeremiah advised the king to save the city and temple by unreserved submission to the Chaldeans, but Zedekiah trusted in his Egyptian alliance; but, as it was a sabbatical year, he proclaimed liberty to all the Hebrew servants and slaves in Jeruralem. Hophra at the head of an Egyptian army now marched to the relief of his ally, and Nebuchadnezzar drew off his forces from Jerusalem and advanced to meet him. The Egyptian king was terrified at the strength of the Chaldean army, and retreated to Egypt, but in the mean time the Jews, believing that Nebuchadnezzar would never return, cancelled the proclamation of liberty to the Hebrew servants and indulged in demonstrations of joy at their supposed deliverance. Jeremiah, however, had previously predicted the return of Nebuchadnezzar and burning of Jerusalem, and during the absence of the Chaldeans had endeavored to escape from the city, but was seized at the gate for a deserter and imprisoned in the house of Jonathan the scribe. Jer. xxxvii. 11-15.

549. *Zedekiah secretly applies to Jeremiah; the Princes throw the Prophet into a Pit, 589.*—In the following year Nebuchadnezzar, having thus repulsed Hophra, renewed the siege, and Zedekiah applied secretly to Jeremiah concerning the fate of Jerusalem, but the prophet repeated his former predictions. The princes of Judah were now angry with Jeremiah, and removed him to the court of the prison, where he was afterward thrown into a deep pit of mire, but rescued by Ebedmelech, an Ethiopian and one of Zedekiah's eunuchs. 2 Kings xxv. 1-3; Jer. xxxviii.; xxxix. 1.

550. *Jerusalem taken, 588.*—On the seventh day of the fourth month, the city being broken up by famine and the middle gate in the hands of the enemy, Zedekiah and his men of war escaped at night, but the Chaldeans overtook him without his army in the plains of Jericho, and carried him to Nebuchadnezzar at Riblah in Hamath in Syria. Nebuchadnezzar slew his sons in his presence,

and then put out his eyes and sent him in brazen chains to Babylon, where he died in prison, having reigned eleven years. Two apparently contradictory prophecies were thus fulfilled concerning him. *Jeremiah* had declared that he should see Nebuchadnezzar, and be carried to Babylon; whilst *Ezekiel* had said that he should go to Babylon and not see it. Jer. xxxiv. 3; Ezek. xii. 13; 2 Kings xxv. 4; Jer. xxxix. 2.

551. *Nebuzaradan sacks the City.*—The walls of Jerusalem were now broken down by Nebuzaradan, Nebuchadnezzar's general, who also sacked and burnt the city and temple, and carried away nearly the whole nation captive to Babylon. 2 Chron. xxxvi. 14–21; Jer. lii. 12–23.

552. *Gedaliah appointed Governor; slain by Ishmael.*—Nebuchadnezzar then appointed *Gedaliah* to be governor over the remnant of the people who remained in Judah; and he released Jeremiah and permitted him to continue with Gedaliah at Mizpeh, as the prophet had requested. Gedaliah was afterward treacherously slain at a feast by *Ishmael*, a descendant of the royal house of Judah, who murdered many other Jews and sought to carry the remainder captive to the Ammonites. Jer. xl.; xli. 1–10.

553. *Jeremiah and Baruch go to Egypt; Remainder of the People taken to Babylon.*—Johanan, one of Gedaliah's chief officers, overtook Ishmael and recovered the captives, and fled with them to Egypt, taking Jeremiah and Baruch with him. Four years afterward Nebuzaradan carried off the few people that remained in Judah, seven hundred and forty-five in number. Meanwhile, new colonists were not introduced, as had been done by the Assyrians in Samaria; and, although nomadic tribes wandered through the country and the Idumeans settled in some southern districts, yet the land remained desolate for the appointed time. 2 Kings xxv. 22–26; Jer. xli. 11–18.

B. C. 588.—THUS WAS JUDAH CARRIED AWAY CAPTIVE OUT OF HIS OWN LAND 507 YEARS FROM THE ANOINTING OF SAUL, 468 YEARS AFTER THE ACCESSION OF DAVID, 388 YEARS FROM THE DEATH OF SOLOMON, AND 134 YEARS FROM THE CAPTIVITY OF THE TEN TRIBES.

(*History continued at p.* 244.)

554. *History of Assyria.*—The geographical limits of Assyria varied at different periods of the empire. (See *Introductory Outline of the Geography.*)

***Nimrod, cir. 2234.*—**Son of Cush, founded the kingdom of Babel, or Babylon, in the land of Shinar—*i. e.* Mesopotamia or Padan-aram—when ASSHUR or ASSUR, second son of Shem, migrated from Shinar to the country called, after him, ASSYRIA. Nimrod afterward invaded and conquered Assyria, built Nineveh, and called it after his son, NINUS. Gen. x. 10, 11.

***Chedorlaomer, cir. 1913.*—**King of Elam, with three confederate kings, took Lot prisoner, and was afterward defeated by Abram. Gen. xiv.

Interregnum of more than one thousand years.

***Cir. B. C. 862.*—**A king of Nineveh, name unknown, lived in the time of Jonah.

***1. Pul. cir. 771.*—**Invaded Israel, and obliged *Menahem* to pay one thousand silver talents.

***2. Tiglath-pileser, cir. 750.*—**Being bribed by Ahaz, B. C. 740, he carried off the Damascenes captive to Kir, or Assyria Proper, and slew Rezin. Conquered the Edomites and Philistines. Attacked Pekah, king of Israel, invaded Galilee, and carried off the Trans-Jordanic tribes of Reuben, Gad, and half Manasseh, and planted them in cities of the Medes.

***3. Shalmaneser, 730.*—**Invaded Israel and made Hoshea tributary. In B. C. 725 the latter rebelled, and Shalmaneser imprisoned him, besieged Samaria for three years, and in B. C. 721 carried the ten tribes into captivity, and placed them in the cities where Tiglath-pileser had previously stationed the Trans-Jordanic tribes.

***4. Sennacherib, 715.*—**Invaded Hezekiah, but his army was destroyed by an angel. Medes revolted B. C. 712.

***5. Esarhaddon, 710.*—**Colonized Samaria. The monarchs who succeeded him are unimportant; their power rapidly declined, and the empire was at length overthrown by the Medes and Chaldee-Babylonians. (See sect. 535.)

1 AND 2 CHRONICLES.

(*Supposed to be written by Ezra.*)

[The two books form but one in the Hebrew canon, which was called "The Book of Journals," or the "Word of Days." In the Septuagint they are called Παραλειπομενα, or "Things omitted," and were named the Books of Chronicles by Jerome.]

1 Chronicles.—Genealogical Tables from Adam to Ezra, 4004–1056.—Death of Saul, 1056.—Reign of David, 1056–1015.—Altogether, B. C. 4004 to 1015, about 2989 years.

2 Chronicles.—Reign of Solomon, 1015–975.—History of the kingdoms of Judah and Israel, 975–588.—Edict of Cyrus, 536.—Altogether, B. C. 1015 to 536, about 479 years.

The two Books of Chronicles thus extend from B. C. 4004 to 536, about 3468 years.

555. As the two Books of Chronicles relate the same history as the Books of Samuel and Kings, the summary of the facts they contain need not be repeated here; for, though they embrace many particulars which are omitted in the former books, yet we have inserted these particulars in their proper place in the history, making sufficient reference to those chapters in the Chronicles from whence they are extracted.

556. Ezra, who was probably the writer of these Chronicles, appears to have had three particular objects in their compilation—viz. 1st. To point out from the public records the state of the different families before the Captivity, that at their return they might again possess their respective inheritances. 2d. To enable the Jews to conduct the worship of God as before, by entering minutely into the duties, genealogies, families, and orders of the priests and Levites. 3d. To stir the Jews to a holy zeal for restoring the temple and its service by dwelling on those parts of the character of David, Solomon, Hezekiah, and Josiah which illustrate their pious care in these respects. One important use also of the genealogical tables is to give that succession of families through which it had been prophesied that the Messiah should come; and thus the descendants of Abraham, Isaac, Jacob, and David are marked with the greatest care.

557. The two last verses of 2 Chronicles are the same as the beginning of Ezra.

HISTORY OF THE CHALDEE-BABYLONIAN EMPIRE

DURING THE SEVENTY YEARS' CAPTIVITY,

FORMING A CONNECTION BETWEEN 2 KINGS AND 2 CHRONICLES AND THE BOOK OF EZRA. B. C. 606–536.*

[Though Jerusalem was not taken until B. C. 588, yet the seventy years' captivity is reckoned from the fourth year of Jehoiakim's reign, B. C. 606, when Nebuchadnezzar carried away Daniel the prophet and others to Babylon. The seventy years' captivity ends in B. C. 536, when Cyrus, having destroyed the Chaldee-Babylonian empire, proclaimed that all the Jews might return to Judæa and rebuild their temple; and Ezra does not commence his history until this edict of Cyrus.]

---

1. NEBUCHADNEZZAR'S reign concluded, 588–562; golden image erected at Dura; conquers Tyre, Egypt, etc.; beautifies Babylon.—His insanity.—2. EVILMERODACH, 562–560; released Jehoiachin. 3. NERIGLISSOR, 559–556; war with the Medes.—4. LABORASOARCHOD, 556.—5. BELSHAZZAR, 555–539; allied with Crœsus; Babylon taken by Cyrus after two years' siege.—CYAXARES II.—*i. e.* DARIUS THE MEDE—539–537; Daniel thrown into the lions' den; prophesies the overthrow of the Persian empire by the king of Greece. —CYRUS, 537–530.

---

558. *1. Nebuchadnezzar's Reign concluded, 588–562; Golden Image erected at Dura.*—Nebuchadnezzar, having taken Jerusalem in B. C. 588, returned to Babylon, and about B. C. 557, he erected the golden image in the plains of Dura, which he commanded all his subjects to worship. Shadrach, Meshach, and Abednego refused to obey the royal edict, and were thrown into a furnace, but

---

* The present outline has been chiefly compiled from the works of Prideaux and Jahn, who prefer Xenophon's history of Cyrus to that of Herodotus, to whom, however, reference is frequently made. The chronology of Dean Prideaux has been adopted throughout.

miraculously delivered by the direct interposition of Jehovah. Dan. iii.

559. *Conquers Tyre, Egypt, etc., 586-572.*—Nebuchadnezzar returned to Palestine and besieged Tyre for thirteen years; and as the neighboring places must have suffered severely during this period, it is probable that the prophecies of Jeremiah and Ezekiel were then accomplished against the Zidonians, Philistines, Edomites, and Moabites. Jer. xxvii.; Ezek. xxv. In B. C. 584, *Nebuzaradan*, general of Nebuchadnezzar, again invaded Palestine, probably to revenge the death of Gedaliah; and he carried away captive the residue of the Jews and Israelites, seven hundred and forty-five in number. Jer. lii. 30. (Sect. 553.) In B. C. 574, the Egyptian army revolted from Pharaoh-Hophra (called Apries by Herodotus), and made Amasis king;* and in B. C. 573, Nebuchadnezzar took Tyre, but not before the inhabitants had escaped by sea with the most valuable of their treasures; and the next year marched against Egypt, which now, on account of the intestine disturbances occasioned by the rival claims of Apries and Amasis, was still weaker than at the time when she dared not hazard a battle with the Chaldeans for the relief of Jerusalem (sect. 548). Nebuchadnezzar accordingly soon made himself master of the country, and transferred many Egyptians, as he had before Jews, Phœnicians, and Syrians, to the territory beyond the Euphrates. Megasthenes, as quoted by Josephus, says that he then laid waste a great part of Africa, penetrated to Spain, and in the greatness of his exploits excelled Hercules himself. Strabo says, "He is venerated by the Chaldeans more than Hercules by the Greeks, for he went not only to the Pillars of Hercules [Gibraltar], but marched through Spain to Thrace and Pontus;" but these accounts are manifestly fabulous. Ezek. xxvi.; xxix. 17, 18; xxx.

560. *Beautifies Babylon.*—Nebuchadnezzar now employed his wealth in ornamenting the temples at Babylon and enriching the splendor of the city. According to Berosus and others, he built the following great works, which made Babylon one of the wonders of the world:—

---

* Herod., ii. 162, 163; Joseph., *Ant.*, lib. x. c. 11.

viz. 1st. The walls; 2d. The temple of Belus; 3d. Nebuchadnezzar's palace and hanging gardens; 4th. The banks of the river; 5th. The artificial lake and artificial canals. These works were afterward attributed to the fabled Semiramis, and it has also been said that they were completed by Nitocris, the mother of Belshazzar, the last of the Chaldee monarchs.*—*Herod.*, lib. i. c. 185, 186; *Joseph., Ant.*, lib. x. c. 11.

561. *His Insanity, 569-563.*—About this time, according to the terrible prophecy of Daniel, Nebuchadnezzar was afflicted with insanity, and he "was driven from men, and did eat grass as oxen, and his body was wet with the dew of heaven, till his hair was grown like eagles' feathers, and his nails like birds' claws." Dan. iv. 33. At length, in B. C. 562, he died, in the forty-fifth year of the seventy years' captivity, after reigning forty-three years alone and two years with his father, Nabopolassar. —*Joseph., Ant.*, lib. x. c. 11.

562. *2. Evilmerodach, 562-560; released Jehoiachin.*—Son of Nebuchadnezzar. He released Jehoiachin, king of Judah, who had languished in imprisonment for thirty-seven years (sect. 543); but he proved himself an unworthy and tyrannical ruler, and was assassinated in the second year of his reign by his brother-in-law, Neriglissor. 2 Kings xxv. 27–30. *Joseph. cont. Apion*, lib. 1. The same year died *Astyages*, king of *Media*, who was succeeded by his son, Cyaxares II. (*i. e. Darius the Mede*), in the civil government, and by his grandson, *Cyrus*, in the military.—*Zenoph., Cyr.*, lib. i.

563. *3. Neriglissor, 559-556; War with the Medes.*—Neriglissor was the son-in-law of Nebuchadnezzar. He made great preparations for a war with the Medes, and invited the Lydians, Phrygians, Carians, Cappadocians, Paphlagonians, Cilicians, and all the neighboring nations to ally with him against the common enemy.

---

* " That the hanging gardens were founded by Nebuchadnezzar, and not by Semiramis, is confirmed by Diodorus, where he says that a Syrian (Assyrian) king built them to please his consort. If this consort be regarded as Herodotus's Nitocris—and according to his chronology, and his calling her the mother of the last king, Labynetus, such would appear to be the case—then becomes cleared up how Nitocris came to be mentioned as having embellished Babylon by the great works she caused to be executed."—*Heeren's Asiatic Nations.*

Meantime, *Cyrus*, in the fortieth year of his age, came to the assistance of his uncle, *Cyaxares II.*, at the head of 30,000 Persian troops, and was appointed general of the whole Median army. He defeated Neriglissor, and left him dead on the field of battle, in the fourth year of his reign.—*Zenoph., Cyr.*, lib. i.–iv.

564. *4. Laborasoarchod, 556.*—Son of Neriglissor, was unjust and cruel, and was slain after a reign of nine months.—*Joseph. cont. Apion*, lib. i.

565. *5. Belshazzar, 555–539; allied with Crœsus.*—Belshazzar was the son or grandson of Nebuchadnezzar, and is called *Nabonad* by Josephus and *Labynetus* by Herodotus. His mother appears to have been the same as the Nitocris of Herodotus—a very politic, active, and resolute woman, who completed the unfinished works of Nebuchadnezzar, and in effect governed the empire under her dissipated and thoughtless son. Belshazzar allied with Crœsus, king of Lydia, who was afterward utterly defeated by Cyrus in the eighth year of Belshazzar's reign, and Cyrus subsequently subjugated Asia Minor and all the country west of the Euphrates to the dominion of Cyaxares II. (*i. e. Darius the Mede*). Dan. v.— *Herod.*, i. 77–81, 84.

566. *Cyrus besieges Babylon, 541.*—Cyrus now commenced the siege of Babylon, but without success, and its high and strong walls, surmounted by lofty towers, its broad and deep ditches, its large magazines, and the numerous squares within the city, which were planted with corn and yielded an annual supply of provisions, seemed to secure its inhabitants for ever from all the attacks of their enemies.

567. *Takes the City, 539.*—After two years' siege Cyrus took the city by a stratagem. On the same night that the portentous writing on the wall and Daniel's fearful prophecy had prepared Belshazzar for his approaching fate, and whilst the Babylonians were engaged at a festival, he suddenly broke down the embankment between the Euphrates and the large artificial lake which had been dug to prevent the river from ever overflowing the city. The Euphrates, which ran through the centre of Babylon, was thus rendered fordable, and the army of Cyrus, being formed into two divisions, waded into the river at each end,

and finding that the inhabitants had forgotten to shut the river-gates, they easily entered the city and surrounded the palace, and Belshazzar was quickly overpowered and slain. Dan. v.—*Herod.*, i. 191; and *Xenoph., Cyrop.*, c. vi. and vii.

568. *Darius the Mede—i. e. Cyaxares II., 538-536.*—Darius, or Cyaxares II., son of Astyages, was now, at the age of sixty-two, placed by the arms of Cyrus on the throne of Babylon, which he governed according to the laws of the Medes and Persians, dividing the whole Persian and Babylonian empire into one hundred and twenty provinces. Dan. v. 31; vi. 1–3.

569. *Daniel thrown into the Lions' Den, 538.*—Daniel was thrown into the lions' den for praying to God instead of to Darius, and the same year, having reckoned that the seventy years' captivity prophesied by Jeremiah (sect. 534) was approaching to a close, he earnestly prayed that God would remember his people and restore Jerusalem. About this time also he prophesied the overthrow of the empire by the king of Greece, which was not fulfilled until B. C. 330, about two hundred years after. Dan. vi. (Sect. 626.)

570. *Cyrus, 536.*—Cyaxares II. died B. C. 537, and Cambyses being also dead in Persia, Cyrus, son of Cambyses and nephew of Darius, succeeded to the empire, which now comprised MEDIA, PERSIA, ASSYRIA, BABYLONIA, ASIA MINOR, SYRIA, PHŒNICIA, and PALESTINE. (For *Chronology of the Persian kings, with their names as given in Scripture and in Profane History*, see p. 257.)

EZRA.

(*Written by Ezra.*)

HISTORY OF THE EDICT OF CYRUS AND FIRST RETURN FROM CAPTIVITY UNDER ZERUBBABEL, AND THE GOVERNORSHIP OF EZRA. B. C. 536-456.—ABOUT EIGHTY YEARS.

[**Ezra** was written in Hebrew, except chs. iv.–vii., which are in Chaldee, either because Ezra wished to record the very words of the letters and decrees contained in those chapters, or because the Jews had become during the Babylonian captivity better acquainted with the Chaldee than the Hebrew.]

ANALYSIS.

Edict of Cyrus, 536.—First caravan of Jews under Zerubbabel and Jeshua.—Restoration of the sacrifices.—Foundation of the second temple laid, 535.—Samaritans retard the building, 534-530.—Death of Cyrus, 530.—Samaritans write to Ahasuerus (Cambyses) without effect, 529.—Artaxerxes (Smerdis Magus) prohibits the building of the temple, 522.—Darius Hystaspis king; Haggai and Zechariah incite the Jews to recommence building, 520.—Darius confirms the edict of Cyrus, 519.—Completion and dedication of the temple, 515.—State of the returned Jews.—(Death of Darius and reign of Xerxes, 485-465.)—Reign of Artaxerxes Longimanus, the Ahasuerus of Esther, 464-424.—Second caravan of the Jews under Ezra, 458.—Governorship of Ezra, 468-445.—Corrects the canon of Scripture; dies.

§ History of the high priesthood from Aaron to the return from captivity.

SUMMARY.

571. *Edict of Cyrus, 536.*—In the first year of the reign of Cyrus, the prophecies concerning his conquest of Babylon, made by Isaiah about one hundred and seventy years previous, were shown to him (probably by Daniel): "Thus saith the Lord to his anointed, to Cyrus, whose right hand I have holden, to subdue nations before him; and I will loose the loins of kings, to open before him the two-leaved gates; and the gates shall not *be shut,*"* etc. Isa. xlv. 1; Jer. xxv. 12. Cyrus also saw himself called upon by name to restore the Jewish nation to their country and temple: "Thus saith the Lord, I am the Lord that maketh all things;—that saith of Cyrus, He is my shepherd, and shall perform all my pleasure: even say-

---

* "If therefore the Babylonians had been apprised beforehand, or had known what Cyrus was about, . . . they would have closed all the little gates leading down to the river; . . . whereas the Persians came upon them by surprise."—*Herod.*, lib. i. c. 191.

ing to Jerusalem, Thou shalt be built; and to the temple, Thy foundation shall be laid." Isa. xliv. 24, 28. "Then the Lord stirred up the spirit of Cyrus," and he proclaimed throughout his empire by a herald and by a written order that all the people of the God of heaven, without exception, had liberty to return to Judæa and rebuild their temple at Jerusalem. Ezra i. 1-4.

572. *First Caravan of Jews under Zerubbabel and Jeshua, 536.*—ZERUBBABEL (Sheshbazzar), prince of Judah and grandson of King Jehoiachin, and JESHUA, grandson of Seraiah the high priest, together with ten of the principal elders, now prepared to conduct the Israelites to the land of their fathers. Accordingly, nearly 50,000 people, consisting chiefly of the tribes of Judah and Benjamin, left the countries beyond the Euphrates to return to Judæa, having been furnished with provisions for the journey and upward of 8000 horses, camels, and beasts of burden. And 5400 of the vessels of silver and gold which Nebuchadnezzar had carried away were restored by Cyrus to ZERUBBABEL, who was appointed not only leader of the caravan, but *tirshatha*, or governor of Judæa. Ezra i. 5-11; ii.

573. *Restoration of the Sacrifices.*—The journey from Babylon to Judæa must have lasted about four months, and in the seventh month the people gathered at Jerusalem, and Jeshua the high priest and the other priests set up the altar of burnt-offerings and commenced the daily sacrifices, and collected money and prepared workmen for rebuilding the temple. Ezra iii. 1-7.

574. *Foundation of the Second Temple laid, 535.*—In the second month of the second year of the return of the Jews, Zerubbabel the governor, Jeshua the high priest, and all the priests, Levites, and people assembled to lay the foundation of the temple with great solemnity; but whilst the young colonists shouted with exultation, the old priests and elders, who had seen the temple of Solomon in all its glory, could not forbear weeping even upon so joyful an occasion. Ezra iii. 8-13.

575. *Samaritans retard the Building, 534-530.*—The Cuthæans and others whom Esarhaddon had sent to colonize Samaria (sect. 507) now desired to assist the Israelites in the building of the temple and join with

them in the worship of God. This was refused by Zerubbabel and the elders, probably because the Samaritans were not of the seed of Abraham, and, moreover, mingled idolatry with the worship of Jehovah. The refusal greatly incensed the Samaritans, and thereupon they used every exertion to stop the building; and though they were unable to accomplish their object during the life of Cyrus, yet they threw so many obstacles in the way that the people were wearied out and the work went on heavily. This very naturally excited the enmity of the Jews, and thus there arose a hatred between the two nations which was continually increased by new provocations, and amongst others by the defection of Manasseh and the erection of a rival temple on Mount Gerizim, until at last all friendly intercourse entirely ceased. Ezra iv. 1-4.

576. *Write to Ahasuerus (Cambyses) without effect, 529.*—Cyrus died B. C. 530, and his son, Cambyses (called Ahasuerus by Ezra), succeeded to the throne. The Samaritans had already hired counsellors, who contrived to frustrate the purpose of the Israelites from the reign of Cyrus to that of Darius, but they now thought to stop them more effectually by sending a letter of accusation against them to Ahasuerus (Cambyses), but no reply to it seems to have been sent. Ezra iv. 5, 6.—*Herod.*, lib. ii. 1; iii. 1.

577. *Artaxerxes (Smerdis Magus) prohibits the Building of the Temple, 522.*—Cambyses, after conquering Egypt, was afflicted with insanity and killed his own brother, Smerdis, and at length died from a wound he received from the cap of the sheath of his sword falling off as he was leaping on his horse, B. C. 522, after a reign of eight years. Smerdis Magus (called Artaxerxes in Ezra iv. 7) now personated the brother whom Cambyses had slain, and seized the throne; and to him the Samaritans again wrote, accusing the Jews of building (that is, fortifying) Jerusalem—which they never thought of doing—in order to revolt from paying tribute. Artaxerxes then prohibited the Jews from proceeding with the temple, but his own fraud being discovered shortly after, he was slain by seven Persian nobles, having reigned only seven months. Ezra iv. 7-24.—*Herod.*, lib. iii. 1-38, 61-79.

578. *Darius Hystaspis king; Haggai and Zechariah incite the Jews to recommence Building, 520.*
—Darius Hystaspis obtained the throne on the death of the Magi, B. C. 521; and in the second month of his reign the prophets Haggai and Zechariah appealed so powerfully to the governor, Zerubbabel, and the high priest, Jeshua, and to the whole people, that the building of the temple was once more resumed. Upon this Tatnai, the Persian governor west of the Euphrates, came with his officers to call the Jews to account for their conduct, but on their referring to the edict of Cyrus he did not prohibit the undertaking, but wrote to Darius to investigate the affair. Ezra v.—*Herod.*, lib. iii. 88.

579. *Darius confirms the Edict of Cyrus, 519.*—Darius immediately ordered a search to be made among the royal acts, and in the archives at Acmetha (Ecbatana) the edict of Cyrus was found which directed that the temple should be built at the royal expense and of much larger dimensions. Darius sent a copy of this edict to Tatnai, with a letter commanding him to forward the building instead of obstructing it, and to defray the expenses from the royal treasury, and supply the priests with animals for sacrifice and with wheat, salt, wine, and oil; and whoever obstructed the execution of this decree was to be crucified and his house demolished. Ezra vi. 1–12.

580. *Completion and Dedication of the Temple, 515.*—The building of the temple was now carried on with renewed vigor, after having stood still for nearly fifteen years, and was at length completed in the sixth (seventh) year of the reign of Darius, twenty-one years after it had been begun and seventy-three years after the complete destruction of Jerusalem and desolation of Judah. The building was then joyfully consecrated with festive solemnities; seven hundred animals were sacrificed, and twelve he-goats offered as a sin-offering for the twelve tribes of Israel. Ezra vi. 13–22.

581. *State of the Returned Jews.*—As offerings were made for the *twelve* tribes, and as the invitation of Cyrus was proclaimed throughout the whole empire, many of the ten tribes must have returned to Palestine. The history of later periods also mentions several *Israelites* as settled in Galilee and Peræa long before the time of

Christ (1 Macc. v. 9–24); but, connecting themselves
with the tribe of Judah, they finally lost the name of
Israelites, and all Hebrews were called *Jews*, and their
country *Judœa*. But of the twenty-four courses of
priests established by David (sect. 156, *note*), only four
returned from Babylon, but the old number was still kept
up by each of the four subdividing itself into six, and
the new courses took the names of those that were
wanting. Ezra ii. 36–39; vi. 17.

582. *Death of Darius, and Reign of Xerxes, 486–
465.*—Darius died after a reign of thirty-six years, and
was succeeded by Xerxes, his son by Atossa, daughter of
Cyrus.* The principal events in the reign of Darius were
—the Babylonian revolt and retaking of the city by Zo-
pyrus, the invasion of Scythia, conquest of Thrace, Ionian
revolt and its suppression, battle of Marathon, and Egyptian revolt. The principal events in the reign of Xerxes
were—the reduction of Egypt and invasion of Greece,
which was followed by the battles of Artemisium, Thermopylæ, Salamis, Platæa, and Mycale. Xerxes was slain,
after a reign of twenty-one years, by Artabanus, captain
of his guard, who endeavored to obtain the throne, but
was circumvented by Artaxerxes Longimanus—*i. e.* "long-
handed"—the third son of Xerxes.—*Herod.*, lib. iii. c. 88–
160; iv.; ix.; *Prideaux; Jahn,* c. lviii.

583. *Reign of Artaxerxes Longimanus, the Ahas-
uerus† of Esther, 465–424.*—In the third year of his
reign he divorced his queen, Vashti; in the fifth year he
made Esther his concubine; in the seventh, he made her
his queen. (See ESTHER.)

584. *Second Caravan of Jews under Ezra, 458.*—
In the seventh year of the reign of Artaxerxes the king

---

* Jahn thinks, with Julius Scaliger, that the Artaxerxes in Ezra vii.
and the Ahasuerus in Esther was the present Xerxes I. Moreover, the
name of Amestris, wife of Xerxes, favors the supposition that she was
the same as Esther; but as it was impossible that Esther could have
committed the impious and cruel acts ascribed to Amestris, we have
followed the authority of Prideaux, who follows Josephus, and recognizes Artaxerxes and Ahasuerus in *Artaxerxes Longimanus*, the third
son and successor of Xerxes. (See also *Table of Persian Kings, with
their names according to Scripture and Profane History*, p. 257.)

† This Ahasuerus must not be confounded with the Ahasuerus of
Dan. ix. 1, who was the same as Astyages, and the father of Darius the
Mede—*i. e.* Cyaxares II. (See *Table*, p. 257.)

renewed the edict of Cyrus and Darius Hystaspis, by giving fresh permission to the Hebrews to emigrate to Judæa. Artaxerxes also appointed Ezra the priest, "a ready scribe in the law of Moses" and a lineal descendant of Aaron, to conduct the people to their native land and be governor of Judæa, with a commission to appoint judges, rectify abuses, enforce observance of the law, and make a collection for the temple amongst the Hebrews who chose to remain in exile. To this collection Artaxerxes and his counsellors not only generously contributed, but ordered the managers of the royal revenue west of the Euphrates to supply Ezra with all he should require—with silver to one hundred talents, wheat to one hundred cors, wine and oil to one hundred baths of each, and salt without limitation—that the sacrifices might be legally and regularly offered; whilst all the priests, Levites, singers, porters, and Nethinim were exempted from tribute or toll, and thus placed on an equality with the Medes and Persians. The caravan, to the number of about 6000, under the conduct of Ezra, then departed from Babylon on the first day of the first month, and reached Jerusalem on the first day of the fifth month, after keeping a solemn fast at the river Ahava, and having been just four months on the journey. They then deposited at the temple the donations they had received, including several vessels of gold and silver, and Ezra delivered his credentials to the royal officers of the district, and succeeded Zerubbabel in the governorship of the Jews. Ezra vii.; viii.

585. *Governorship of Ezra, 458-445.*—Ezra continued to be governor of the Jews until the arrival of Nehemiah. His principal political measure seems to have been the removing of strange women from amongst the Jews, which he did by assembling and exhorting the people to repent and put away the foreign wives whom many of them had married. He also read the book of the Law to the people, and having found it written therein "that the children of Israel should dwell in booths in the feast of the seventh month," the people kept the feast of tabernacles and sat under booths, which they had not done since the days of Joshua the son of Nun. Ezra ix.; x.; Neh. viii.

586. *Corrects the Canon of Scripture; Dies.*—After governing the land twelve years, Nehemiah arrived in Judæa, and Ezra resigned his office, and either returned to Babylon or retired into private life to his own country. It is believed that he then wrote the book of Ezra, assisted in compiling the books of the Chronicles, and applied himself to correcting the canon of Scripture and placing the books in their present order and condition; and some say that he changed the old Hebrew character for the Chaldee, which the Jews now use. Ezra is also said to have added in several places throughout the books of his edition of the Scriptures many passages that appeared necessary for the illustrating, connecting, or completing of them, wherein he was assisted by the same Spirit by which they had been at first written. Amongst these passages were—1st, The last chapter of Deuteronomy, which contains an account of the death and burial of Moses, who was, however, undoubtedly the author of all the rest of the Pentateuch. 2d, "And these are the kings that reigned in the land of Edom, before there reigned any king over the land of Israel" (Gen. xxxvi. 31); which could not have been said until there had been a king over Israel, and therefore could not have been written by Moses. 3d, "And the children of Israel did eat manna forty years" (Ex. xvi. 35); but Moses was dead before the manna ceased. 4th, "These are the Proverbs of Solomon, which the men of Hezekiah, king of Judah, copied out" (Prov. xxv. 1); which must have been added many years after Solomon. Ezra also changed the old names of many places that had grown obsolete for the new names which had been given them by the Israelites.

587. Ezra is said to have died in the one hundred and twentieth year of his age, and to have been buried in Jerusalem, though some say that he died in Persia. He is also called Esdras, and the rabbins, with Jerome and others, have supposed that Ezra and Malachi were the same person. (See *Prideaux, Calmet,* etc.)

History of the High Priesthood from Aaron to the Return from Captivity.

1. AARON, consecrated high priest B. C. 1491, died at Mount Hor 1452
2. ELEAZAR, third son of Aaron 1433
3. PHINEHAS 1414
4. ABIEZER or ABISHUA, ⎫
5. BUKKI, ⎬ lived under the judges.
6. UZZI, ⎭
7. ELI, of the race of Ithamar 1116
8. AHITUB I.
9. AHIAH, lived 1092
10. ABIMELECH or ABIATHAR, slain by Saul . . 1060
11. ABIATHAR, AHIMELECH, or ABIMELECH (under David) 1015
12. ZADOK I. (under Saul, David, and Solomon) . 1004
13. AHIMAAZ (under Rehoboam) 974
14. AZARIAH (under Jehoshaphat), probably Amariah of 2 Chron. xix. 11 912
15. JOHANAN, perhaps Jehoiada, under Joash, 2 Chron. xxiv. 15 (died, aged 130) 878
16. AZARIAH, perhaps Zechariah, son of Jehoiada, killed 840
17. AMARIAH, perhaps Azariah, under Uzziah . 783
18. AHITUB II., ⎫
19. ZADOK II., ⎬ under Jotham of Judah.
20. URIAH, under Ahaz, lived 739
21. SHALLUM, father of Azariah and grandfather of Hilkiah.
22. AZARIAH, in the time of Hezekiah 726
23. HILKIAH, under Hezekiah.
24. ELIAKIM, or JOAKIM, under Manasseh: he lived under Josiah to 624—called Hilkiah.
25. AZARIAH, perhaps Neriah, father of Seraiah and of Baruch.
26. SERAIAH, the last high priest before the captivity of Babylon, put to death . . . 590
27. JEHOZADAK, during the captivity . . . 590–535
28. JOSHUA, JESHUA, or JESUS, the son of Jehozadak or Josedech returned from Babylon . 536

NEHEMIAH.

(Written by Nehemiah.)

HISTORY OF THE GOVERNMENT OF NEHEMIAH, BEING A CONTINUATION TO THE HISTORY OF EZRA. B. C. 445 TO 420—ABOUT 25 YEARS.

[In the Septuagint and Vulgate this book is called the Second Book of Ezra, or Esdras.]

ANALYSIS.

Nehemiah appointed governor of Judæa, 445.—Rebuilding of the walls and towers; opposition of Sanballat and the Samaritans.—Nehemiah's first administration, 444-433.—Nehemiah's second administration, 428-420.—Close of the Old Testament history, 420.

SUMMARY.

588. *Nehemiah appointed Governor of Judæa, 445*.—In the last year of Ezra's governorship, and the twentieth year of the reign of Artaxerxes Longimanus, NEHEMIAH, son of Hechaliah, of the tribe of Judah, who was cup-bearer to Artaxerxes in his palace at Shusan (Susa) heard from Hanani and others full particulars of the desolate state of Jerusalem (which had perhaps sustained recent damage from the Samaritans, or from the war with Megabyzus, who had revolted in Syria and twice defeated the forces of Artaxerxes). This information so affected Nehemiah that the king observed his melancholy whilst being served with wine, and on learning that Nehemiah desired to go to Jerusalem and rebuild its walls, towers, and gates, he appointed him governor of Judæa, with full power to fortify Jerusalem. In compliance with a second request, Artaxerxes also gave him letters ordering the royal officers west of the Euphrates to convey him to Judæa, and to furnish the requisite timber for the fortifications from the king's forest; and Nehemiah accordingly journeyed to Jerusalem, accompanied by officers and guarded by cavalry. Neh. i.; ii. 1-9.

589. *Rebuilding of the Walls and Towers; opposition of Sanballat and the Samaritans.*—On arriving at Jerusalem, Nehemiah rode alone through the city at night, and found that the walls had been broken down and the gates burnt. He then exhorted the Jews to rebuild the walls and gates, and the work was immediately commenced; but Sanballat, Tobiah, and the Samaritans first mocked, and then threatened to attack the city and stop the progress of the building. Nehemiah, however, kept half of the workmen constantly on guard, whilst the other half labored with their swords at their sides or their weapons in their hands. When the walls were all finished except the gate, Sanballat and others craftily invited Nehemiah to meet them in the villages, and afterward charged him with intending to rebel, and used means to terrify him; which were all unsuccessful. At length, in fifty-two days, the whole was completed, and Nehemiah gave the charge of Jerusalem to his brother Hanani and to Hananiah, who were only to open the gates whilst the sun was hot, and to oblige the people to be continually on the watch. Neh. ii. 10-20; iii.; iv.; vi.; vii. 1-4.

590. *Nehemiah's First Administration, 445-433.*—Nehemiah was tirshatha, or governor, for twelve years, during which he abolished illegal usury and obliged the usurers to make restitution, revised the registry, and enjoined on the priests and Levites a strict attendance to their duties. During all this time neither he nor his brothers were, like the former governors, chargeable to the people, but he kept at his table one hundred and fifty rulers and principal Jews daily, besides giving liberally to the public works and obliging his own servants to work at the walls. At the expiration of the twelve years he returned to Artaxerxes. Neh. v.; vii. 5-73; ix.-xii.

591. *Nehemiah's Second Administration, cir. 428-420.*—Nehemiah, having obtained fresh permission from Artaxerxes to return to Jerusalem, reformed the following abuses which had crept in during his absence: 1. The gross profanation of the temple by Eliashib the priest, who, having allied with Tobiah the Ammonite, prepared a chamber for him which had been set apart for tithes

and offerings. 2. The desecration of the Sabbath in carrying burdens, treading wine-presses, and buying and selling. 3. The unjust withholding of tithes. 4. Defective offerings. 5. The intermarrying with strange women. Nehemiah is said to have assisted Ezra in revising the canon of Scripture, and is thought to have written memoirs of his government from which this book was extracted. Neh. xiii.

592. *Close of Old Testament History, cir. 420.*—Malachi prophesied about this time, and thus closes Old Testament history, for a continuation of which reference must be made to the *Apocryphal books* and *Josephus*. (See *Connection between the Old and New Testaments.*)

ESTHER.

(*Author unknown.*)

ABOUT B. C. 461-451, A PERIOD OF ABOUT TEN YEARS, COMING IN BETWEEN THE SIXTH AND SEVENTH CHAPTERS OF EZRA.

593. *Story of Esther, 461.*—In the third year of the reign of Ahasuerus (*i. e.* Artaxerxes Longimanus), the king wished Queen Vashti to exhibit herself at a feast, which she refused to do, and Ahasuerus divorced her, and a number of women were brought to him that he might choose a wife in her room. Amongst them the king's attention was particularly directed to Esther (Hebrew, *Hadassah*), the niece of Mordecai, a Jew of the tribe of Benjamin, and he made her queen in the seventh year of his reign, without knowing her nation. Soon after this Mordecai discovered that two of the king's chamberlains had conspired to slay Ahasuerus, and on telling the matter to Esther, she reported it to the king in Mordecai's name, and the conspirators were hanged. At this time Haman, a favorite of the king's took umbrage at Mordecai for not bowing to him as he passed, and persuaded Ahasuerus to issue a decree to destroy all the Jews on a certain day. Mordecai and the Jews were now in great tribulation, but contrived to send a copy of the decree to Esther, and persuade her to supplicate the king in person, though, accord-

ing to the law, whoever entered the king's presence without being called was put to death unless the royal sceptre was extended toward them. Esther and the Jews now fasted for three days, when she entered the royal presence and obtained grace, but at first she merely invited the king and Haman to her banquet. Haman was then highly elated, but being again incensed at Mordecai's not bowing to him as he passed to the banquet, he ordered a gallows fifty cubits high to be built, intending next day to ask of the king the immediate death of Mordecai. The same night King Ahasuerus could not sleep, and ordered the chronicles of his reign to be read to him, when the conspiracy of the two chamberlains was related, and the king remembered that Mordecai had gone unrewarded for his loyalty in discovering their treason. Accordingly, when Haman came the next day he desired him to clothe Mordecai in royal apparel, place him on horseback, and lead him through the city, proclaiming, "Thus shall it be done unto the man whom the king delighteth to honor." Haman obeyed the royal command, and then hasted home mourning; but whilst his wife and friends were endeavoring to comfort him with the thought that as Mordecai was a Jew he must be slain with the others of his nation, the chamberlains of the palace came to fetch him to a second banquet which Esther had prepared for him and the king. Here Esther supplicated Ahasuerus for herself and people, and pointed out Haman as their enemy, who was immediately hanged upon the gallows which he made for Mordecai, and the latter was invested with the command of Haman's house. The cruel decree was now reversed, and instead of the Jews being massacred in one day, they were themselves permitted for two days to slay all their enemies, including the household of Haman.

594. *Feast of Purim.*—In order to commemorate their deliverance the Jews henceforth celebrated the FEAST OF PURIM, or of LOTS, on the fourteenth and fifteenth days of the month Adar (February). It was called the Feast of Purim from *Pur*, "a lot," because Haman had cast lots to decide the day on which the Jews should be massacred; and the feast lasted two days, because the Jews had been permitted to destroy their enemies for two days. On this feast all the Jews attended at their syna-

gogues to hear the book of Esther read through and to curse Haman; after which the time was spent in festivity at their own houses.

Chronology of the Kings of Media and Persia, with their Names as given in Scripture and in Profane History, according to Dean Prideaux.

		B. C.	Reigned.
ARPHAXAD, Judith i. 1 . . *i. e.* DEIOCES		709	53 yrs.
(Not mentioned in Scripture) . PHRAORTES .		656	22 "
(Not mentioned in Scripture) . CYAXARES I.		634	40 "
AHASUERUS, Dan. ix. 1 . . ASTYAGES .		594	35 "
DARIUS THE MEDE, Dan. vi., ix., xi. CYAXARES .		560	23* "
CYRUS, Dan. x.; Ezra i. . . CYRUS . .		537	7 "
AHASUERUS, Ezra iv. 6 . . CAMBYSES .		530	7 "
ARTAXERXES, Ezra iv. 7–23 . SMERDIS .		522	7 mo.
DARIUS, Ezra iv. 24; vi. . . DARIUS HYSTASPIS		521	36 yrs.
(Not mentioned in Scripture) . XERXES .		485	21† "
ARTAXERXES, Ezra vii.; Neh. i. } ARTAXERXES } AHASUERUS, Esther, . . } LONGIMANUS }		464	41 "

Subsequent Kings.

	B. C.	Reigned.
XERXES II	424	45 days.
SOGDIANUS	424	6 mo.
DARIUS II., OCHUS or NOTHUS	423	18 yrs.
ARTAXERXES II., or MNEMON	405	46 "
ARTAXERXES III., or OCHUS	359	21 "
ARCES	338	2 "
DARIUS III., or CODOMANUS	336	6 "
ALEXANDER THE GREAT overthrew the Persian empire	330	

---

* This includes the two years that Darius reigned over Babylon, B. C. 538.

† Josephus and Jahn think he was the Artaxerxes of Ezra vii. and Nehemiah, and the Ahasuerus of Esther, but Prideaux has been followed in the present work, who recognizes this Artaxerxes and Ahasuerus in Artaxerxes Longimanus.

THE FIVE
POETICAL BOOKS,

OR

HOLY WRITINGS.

[ΑΓΙΟΣ, "HOLY," AND ΓΡΑΦΕ "A WRITING;" INCLUDING JOB, PSALMS, PROVERBS, ECCLESIASTES, AND SOLOMON'S SONG—CHIEFLY WRITTEN IN HEBREW METRE.—SEE INTRODUCTION.]

JOB.

(*Supposed to have been written by Job and transcribed by Moses.*)

ANALYSIS.

Chronology of the time of Job.—His country.—His condition and character.—Afflicted by Satan by divine permission.—Visited by his three friends, Eliphaz, Bildad, and Zophar.—Job and his three friends reproved by Elihu.—Jehovah appears to Job.—Job humbles himself and is restored to prosperity.—Prophetical intimations of the Messiah.

SUMMARY.

595. ***Chronology of the Time of Job.***—Job is supposed by Usher to have lived about B.C. 1520, whilst Moses was residing in Midian, but the following circumstances seem to place him much earlier: 1st. His longevity, which was considerable, as he did not die until one hundred and forty years after his afflictions, and was probably sixty or seventy years old when they commenced, for he had seven sons grown up and settled "in their houses." Job i. 4, 5. 2d. His speaking of the most ancient kind

of writing—by sculpture. xix. 24. 3d. His riches being reckoned by his cattle. xlii. 12. 4th. His acting as high priest in his family according to patriarchal usage. Gen. viii. 20. 5th. His allusions to Zabianism, or the worship of the sun and moon, which was the most ancient species of idolatry. Dr. Hales, moreover, fixes the time of Job's trial at about one hundred and eighty-four years before the birth of Abraham, and founds his opinion upon a retrograde astronomical calculation concerning the period when the principal stars referred to in Job ix. 9 and xxxviii. 31, 32, by the names of Chemah and Chesil, or Taurus and Scorpio, were the cardinal constellations of spring and autumn, as Pisces and Virgo are at present. All commentators and critics, however, are agreed that the poem of Job is the most ancient book in existence.

596. *His Country.*—Job resided in the land of Uz, which was evidently Idumæa. Lam. iv. 21. Uz was the grandson of Seir the Horite (Gen. xxxvi. 20, 28), who inhabited Idumæa prior to Abraham, and the territory was then called Seir; but his posterity being afterward expelled by the Idumæans or Edomites, the country was called Edom. Deut. ii. 12. There are two other men named Uz—the grandson of Shem and the son of Nahor, the brother of Abraham—but it is not clear whether any district was called after their names.

597. *His Condition and Character.*—Job was an Arabian emir or prince of distinguished wealth and eminent piety. His sons were in the habit of feasting in each other's houses in turns, and when their feasts were concluded Job would always send and sanctify them, and offer burnt-offerings for each one early in the morning, for he said, "It may be that my sons have sinned and cursed God in their hearts." Job i. 1–5.

598. *Afflicted by Satan by Divine Permission.*— Satan was permitted by God to afflict Job in order to try his virtue, but at first was not allowed to injure him personally. The following calamities accordingly befell Job's property and family: 1st. A company of Sabæans carried off his oxen and asses, and slew all the servants save one, who escaped to tell the tale. 2d. A fire from heaven destroyed all his sheep and all his shepherds save one. 3d. The Chaldeans carried off his camels, and killed all the

servants with them save one. 4th. Whilst his seven sons and three daughters were feasting in their eldest brother's house a violent wind blew down the house and crushed them beneath its ruins. These disasters occurred almost simultaneously, for each successive bearer of the sad tidings reached Job whilst his predecessor was yet speaking; but Job resisted the temptation to repine, and said, "The Lord gave, and the Lord hath taken away; blessed be the name of the Lord!" Satan was now suffered to afflict Job's person without taking his life, and accordingly smote him with sore boils from the sole of his foot to his crown, and his wife prompted him to curse God and die; but Job replied, "Shall we receive good at the hand of God, and not receive evil?" Job i. 6–22; ii. 1–10.

599. *Visited by his three Friends, Eliphaz, Bildad, and Zophar.*—Eliphaz the Temanite, Bildad the Shuhite, and Zophar the Naamathite now agreed to visit Job and mourn and condole with him, but when they saw his afflictions they sat down by him without speaking for seven days and nights. The grief of Job then burst forth in passionate exclamations and a vehement execration of the day of his birth, and his patience was now more exquisitely tried by the unjust suspicions, bitter reproaches, and violent altercations of his friends. The latter concluded that Job's afflictions were the expressions of the divine displeasure on account of some heinous and secret transgressions; and accordingly they reproved him for his impatience, called in question his integrity, admonished him that the chastisement of God was not to be despised, and upbraided him with arrogance and falsehood for presuming to defend himself against their accusations. Moreover they all, with a manifest though indirect allusion to Job, discoursed very copiously concerning the divine judgments, which are always openly displayed against the wicked, and of the certain destruction of hypocritical pretenders to virtue and religion. Job replied to this by enumerating his sufferings and complaining bitterly of the inhumanity of his friends and severity of God. This only irritated his visitors the more, and they severely reproached him with pride, impiety, passion, and madness. A vehement discussion then followed on the

power of the Almighty and the justice of his decrees, in which the weapons of satire and ridicule were mingled with those of reason and argument, and in which Job answered the fierce accusations of his three friends by animated and confident appeals to the tribunal of God himself. The three friends then remained silent, and Job expressed the true sentiments of his heart concerning the fate of the wicked, and allowed that their prosperity was unstable, and that they and their descendants would at last experience that God was the avenger of iniquity; but he contended that the divine counsels do not admit of human investigation, and that the chief wisdom of man consisted in the fear of God. He then beautifully descanted upon his former prosperity, and contrasted it with his present affliction and debasement; and lastly, in answer to the implications of his opponents, he related the principal transactions of his past life, asserted his integrity as displayed in all the duties of life and in the sight of God and man, and again appealed to the justice and omniscience of the Almighty in attestation of his veracity. Job ii. 11–13; iii.–xxxi.

600. *Job and his three Friends reproved by Elihu.*—Elihu the Buzite, a young man, now came forward and rebuked Job and his three friends. He declared that it was unnecessary for God to explain and develop his counsels to men, though he nevertheless admonished them by visions and revelations, and by calamities and diseases, to reprove their arrogance and reform their obduracy; and he reproved Job for pronouncing himself to be upright and for affirming that God had acted unjustly toward him. He then refuted the unjust suspicions of Job's friends, and declared that God often chastened men because they did not confide in him or humbly submit to his will; and concluded with a grand description of the omnipotence of the Creator. Job xxxii.–xxxvii.

601. *Jehovah appears to Job.*—Jehovah himself now appeared in a whirlwind and addressed Job in a sublime speech, in which he disdained to explain his divine counsels, but reproved the temerity of Job by convicting him of ignorance in being unable to comprehend the works of his creation—the nature and structure of the earth, the sea, the light, and the animal kingdom;

and then demonstrated his weakness by challenging him to emulate any single exertion of the divine energy, or even to contend with various animals of the brute creation which are particularly mentioned. Job xxxviii.–xli.

602. *Job humbles himself, and is restored to Prosperity.*—Job now humbled himself before God, and acknowledged his own ignorance and imbecility, and repented in dust and ashes. His three friends had also incurred the anger of God, and were required to sacrifice seven bullocks and seven rams for a burnt-offering, and to go to Job, who then prayed and interceded for them. Job was afterward greatly blessed by God; he had again seven sons and three daughters, and his possessions and cattle were doubled. Job xlii.

603. *Prophetical Intimation of the Messiah.*—There is an important intimation of the Messiah in this book, which may be regarded both as a prophecy and as a profession of faith on the part of Job in a promised Redeemer:

"For I know that my Redeemer liveth,
And that he shall stand at the latter day upon the earth."
Job xix. 25.

PSALMS.

AUTHORSHIP.—SUBJECTS.—CLASSIFICATION.—MEANING OF THE WORD "SELAH."

604. *Authorship.*—The book of Psalms contains one hundred and fifty lyric poems, generally supposed to have been written by MOSES, DAVID, SOLOMON, ASAPH, HEMAN, ETHAN, JEDUTHUN, and the three sons of KORAH; others have been ascribed to Adam, Melchizedek, etc., but without authority. As they have been more particularly attributed to David, and he is thought to have collected those written previously into a book, they are called "the Psalms of David," and he himself has been styled the "royal Psalmist."

605. *Subjects.*—The Psalms are said by ATHANASIUS to be an epitome of the whole Scriptures; by BASIL, to be a compendium of all theology; by LUTHER, to be a

little Bible and the summary of the Old Testament; and by MELANCHTHON, to be the most elegant writing in the whole world. According to Bishop Horne, they are an epitome of the Bible, adapted to the purposes of devotion, and treat occasionally of the creation and formation of the world; the dispensations of providence and the economy of grace; the transactions of the patriarchs; the exodus of the children of Israel; their journey through the wilderness and settlement in Canaan; their law, priesthood, and ritual; the exploits of their great men wrought through faith; their sins and captivities; their repentances and restorations; the sufferings and victories of David; the peaceful and happy reign of Solomon; the advent of the Messiah, with its effects and consequences, his incarnation, birth, life, passion, death, resurrection, ascension, kingdom, and priesthood; the effusion of the Spirit; the conversion of the Jews; the establishment, increase, and perpetuity of the Christian Church; the end of the world; the general judgment; the condemnation of the wicked; and the final triumph of the righteous with their Lord and King.

606. *Classification.*—The Psalms are generally divided into five books. BOOK I. begins with Ps. i.; BOOK II., with Ps. xlii.; BOOK III., with Ps. lxxiii.; BOOK IV., with Ps. xc.; and BOOK V., with Ps. cvii. The first four books terminate with "AMEN," and the last with "HALLELUJAH."

607. *Selah.*—This word occurs seventy times in the Psalms and three times in Habakkuk. It has been supposed by some to signify a rest or change in the song or modulation; by others, to be equivalent to our word "slow;" and by others, to mean a repeat, or "Amen," or "the end."

PROVERBS.

(Written chiefly by Solomon.)

608. *Authorship and Scope.*—The book of Proverbs was written chiefly by Solomon, and probably included a selection from the 3000 proverbs which he composed.

1 Kings iv. 32. Its object is to instruct men in the deepest mysteries of true wisdom and understanding, the height and perfection of which is THE SINCERE FEAR OF THE LORD. The book is thus filled with the choicest sententious aphorisms, infinitely surpassing all the ethical sayings of the ancient sages, and comprising in themselves distinct doctrines, duties, and rules of piety toward God, of equity and benevolence in dealings with the world, and of sobriety and temperance in the government of self. It likewise includes precepts for the right education of children, and for the relative situation of subjects, magistrates, and sovereigns.

ECCLESIASTES.

(Εκκλεσιαστης, "*a preacher.*"—*Written by Solomon.*)

609. *Authorship and Scope.*—The beautiful descriptions which this book contains of the phenomena in the natural world and the economy of the human frame prove it to have been the work of a philosopher; accordingly, it is generally supposed to have been written by SOLOMON in his old age, when he had repented of his sin and folly, and, having drained the cup of pleasure to its dregs, had become fully convinced of the vanity of everything except piety toward God.

610. The scope of this book is to demonstrate the vanity of all earthly objects, and to draw off men from pursuing them as an *apparent* good, and direct them to the highest and only *permanent* good in this life—namely, to the fear of God and communion with him. The object of the Preacher's inquiry is, therefore, What is the SOVEREIGN GOOD of man? and after discussing various erroneous opinions, he finally determines that it consists in TRUE WISDOM; and his whole argument then consists in the praise and recommendation of WISDOM as the supreme good to creatures responsible for their actions. In this WISDOM is not included a single particle of that which is worldly and carnal, so frequently pursued by men ad-

dicted to vice, the minions of avarice, and the slaves of their passions; but that which is from above, that which is holy, spiritual, undefiled, and which, in the writings of Solomon, is but another word for RELIGION.

SONG OF SOLOMON.

(*Written by Solomon.*)

611. Subject and Meaning.—This nuptial song or lyrical drama is supposed to have been included in the 1005 songs of Solomon mentioned in 1 Kings iv. 32. It is of a pastoral character, and has been divided into seven parts, according to the seven days of the marriage-feast amongst the Jews; but some critics have regarded it as a series of poems or idyls, each distinct and independent of the other.

612. The subject of this beautiful composition is supposed to have been the marriage of Solomon with Pharaoh's daughter, though Horne and others think that the bride must have been of Hebrew origin, as she declares herself to be a native of Sharon, which was a canton of Palestine. Cant. ii. 1. But all ages seem to have determined that this marriage afforded the veil of a sublime and mystical allegory, delineating the bridal union between Jehovah and his pure and uncorrupted Church. God had selected a peculiar people, of the posterity of Abraham, from among the nations, and ratified his choice by a solemn compact which was founded upon reciprocal conditions—on the one part, love, protection, and support; on the other, faith, obedience, and pure and devout worship. This solemn union between God and his Church has been celebrated by almost all the sacred writers under a similar image; the word adultery has denoted idolatrous worship, and our Lord himself has adopted the title of Bridegroom (Matt. ix. 15; xxv. 1); and the Lamb's spouse—*i. e.* THE CHURCH—is represented as a bride adorned for her husband. Rev. xxi. 2, 9.

THE
SIXTEEN PROPHETICAL BOOKS.

[There are sixteen Prophetical authors and seventeen Prophetical Books, but the latter are only calculated at sixteen, as the Lamentations of Jeremiah are considered as a supplement to his Prophecies.

The prophetical Authors are divided into two classes—viz. I. THE FOUR GREATER PROPHETS, *Isaiah, Jeremiah, Ezekiel, and Daniel.* II. THE TWELVE MINOR PROPHETS, *Hosea, Joel, Amos, Obadiah, Jonah, Micah, Nahum, Habakkuk, Zephaniah, Haggai, Zechariah, and Malachi.*]

CHRONOLOGICAL TABLE

OF THE PROBABLE PERIODS IN WHICH THE PROPHETS FLOURISHED.

[The Greater Prophets are in bold letters.]

I. *Before the Captivity.*

PROPHETS.	B. C.	JUDAH.	ISRAEL.
1 JONAH	856–784.		Jehu and Jehoahaz, or Joash and Jeroboam II.
2. AMOS	810–785.	Uzziah.	Jeroboam II.
3. HOSEA	810–725.	Uzziah, Jotham, Ahaz, and Hezekiah.	Jeroboam II.
4. Isaiah	**758–698.**	Uzziah, Jotham, Ahaz, Hezekiah, and Manasseh.	Jeroboam II., Zechariah, Shallum, Menahem, Pekahiah, Pekah, and Hoshea.
5. JOEL	810–660, or later.	Uzziah or Manasseh.	Ditto.
6. MICAH	758–699.	Jotham, Ahaz, and Hezekiah.	Pekah and Hoshea.
7. NAHUM	720–698.	Hezekiah.	
8. ZEPHANIAH	640–609.	Josiah.	
9. Jeremiah	**628–586.**	Josiah, Jehoahaz, Jehoiakim, Jehoiachin, and Zedekiah.	

II. *During the Captivity.*

PROPHETS.	B. C.	JUDAH.
10. HABAKKUK	612–598.	Jehoiakim.
11. Daniel . .	606–534.	During the whole of the Captivity.
12. OBADIAH .	588–583.	Between the taking of Jerusalem by Nebuchadnezzar and his destruction of the Edomites.
13. Ezekiel .	595–536.	During part of the Captivity.

III. *After the Captivity.*

14. HAGGAI .	520–418, or longer.	Under Zerubbabel, after the return from captivity.
15. ZECHARIAH	520–548, or longer.	Ditto.
16. MALACHI	436–420.	Nehemiah.

THE
FOUR GREATER PROPHETS.

I. Isaiah—his life and period, cir. 758–698.—Scope of his prophecies.—Principal subjects.—Prophecies of the Messiah.

II. Jeremiah—his life and period, cir. 628–586.—Subjects of his prophecies.—*Book of Lamentations.*

III. Ezekiel—his life and prophecies, 595–536.

IV. Daniel—his early life, cir. 626–606.—Interprets Nebuchadnezzar's first dream: the image of four empires, cir. 603.—Nebuchadnezzar sets up a golden image, cir. 580.—His second dream: the tree, 570; his madness, cir. 569–563.—Daniel's vision of four beasts, 555.—Vision of the ram and he-goat, 553.—Belshazzar's feast and death, 538.—Daniel in the lion's den, 538.—Foretells the exact time of the coming and death of the Messiah, 538.—His other prophecies.

I. ISAIAH.

613. *Life and Period of Isaiah, cir. 758-698.*— Isaiah was the son of Amoz, and flourished during the reigns of Uzziah, Jotham, Ahaz, Hezekiah, and is said to have been martyred by being sawn asunder in the first year of Manasseh's reign. According to the lowest computation, and reckoning from the last year of Uzziah's reign to the first of Manasseh's, he must have prophesied during B. C. 758–698, about sixty years. At the beginning of this period both the kingdoms of Judah and Israel

were in a most flourishing condition; Judah had conquered the Philistines, made the Ammonites tributary, and subdued some Arabian tribes in Arabia Deserta, whilst Israel had recovered the Trans-Jordanic territory from Benhadad and conquered Damascus and Hamath. But Isaiah lived to see idolatry established in Judah and Israel carried into Assyrian captivity.

614. *Scope of his Prophecies.*—The scope of Isaiah's predictions is threefold:

1. *To detect, reprove, aggravate, and condemn the sins of the Jews especially*, and also the iniquities of the ten tribes of Israel and the abominations of the Gentiles.

2. *To invite both Jews and Gentiles* to repentance and reformation by numerous promises of God's pardon and mercy.

3. *To prophesy the coming of the Messiah*, which he does so much more clearly and copiously than any other prophet that he has been emphatically styled the "EVANGELICAL PROPHET."

615. *Principal Subjects.*—The chief subjects of Isaiah's prophecies are:

1. The captivities and restoration of Judah and Israel. xxxix. 6, 7.

2. The ruin and desolation of Babylon, Tyre, Damascus, Egypt, etc., and the destruction of Syria and Israel for confederating against Judah; Syria being designated by its chief city, Damascus, and Israel by its chief city, Ephraim. vii. 1, 2; xlvii. 7, 15. This was afterward accomplished by Tiglath-pileser, king of Assyria. viii. 4, and sect. 493.

3. The conquests and conduct of Cyrus, who is mentioned by name, and his relieving the Jews, nearly two hundred years before his birth. xliv. 28; xlvi. 1–5.

4. The prophecies concerning the Messiah—viz.:

1. His divine character. vi.; vii. 14; ix. 6; xxxv. 4; xl. 5, 9, 10; xlii. 6–8; lxi. 1.

2. His miracles. xxxv. 5, 6.

3. His peculiar virtues and qualities. ix. 2, 3; xl. 11; xliii. 1–3.

4. His rejection. vi. 9–12; viii. 14, 15; liii. 3.

5. His sufferings for our sins. l. 6; liii. 4–11.

6. His death and burial. liii. 8, 9.

7. His victory over death. xxv. 8; liii. 10–12.
8. His final glory. xlix. 7, 22, 23; lii. 13–15; liii. 4, 5.
9. The establishment, increase, and perfection of his kingdom. ii. 2–4; ix. 2, 7; xi. 4–10; xvi. 5; xxix. 18–24; xxxii. 1; xl. 4, 5; xlii. 4; xlvi. 13; xlix. 9–13; li. 3–6; lii. 6–10; lv. 1–3; lix. 16–21; lx.; lxi. 1–5; lxv. 25.*

616. *Prophecies of the Messiah.* — The principal prophecies of Isaiah in reference to the Messiah are the following:

---

* The grandest specimen of Isaiah's poetry is presented in the fourteenth chapter of his book, which is one of the sublimest odes occurring in the Bible and contains the noblest personifications.

The prophet first predicts the liberation of the Jews from their Babylonian captivity and their restoration to Judæa (ver. 1–3), and then introduces a chorus of Jews, who express their surprise and astonishment at the downfall of Babylon and overthrow of her king. The nations whom the king of Babylon had oppressed are represented under the image of fir trees and cedars of Libanus, who, whilst the whole earth shouts for joy, taunt the fallen tyrant and boast their security now he is no more. ver. 4–8. Hades, or the regions of the dead, is now personified. ver. 9. Hades excites his inhabitants—the shades of princes and the departed spirits of monarchs—who rise from their couches as from their thrones, and, meeting the king of Babylon at the entrance of their cavern, they insult and deride him on his impotence and dissolution. ver. 10, 11. The Jews now resume the speech (ver. 12); they address the king of Babylon as the morning-star fallen from heaven, and contrast his extravagant vaunts with his present low and abject condition. ver. 13–15. A new scene immediately follows, which diversifies the subject and gives it a new turn and additional force. Certain persons are introduced who light upon the corpse of the king of Babylon, lying, naked and covered with wounds, upon the bare ground and among the common slain, just after the taking of the city, upon which they severely taunt the tyrant, and bitterly reproach him with his destructive ambition and cruel usage. ver. 16–20. To complete the whole, God is introduced, declaring the fate of Babylon, the utter extirpation of the royal family, and the total desolation of the city, the deliverance of his people, and the desolation of their enemies; confirming the irreversible decree by the awful sanction of his oath. ver. 21–27.

"How forcible," says Bishop Lowth, "is this imagery! how diversified! how sublime! how elevated the diction, the figures, the sentiments! The Jewish nation, the cedars of Lebanon, the ghosts of departed kings, the Babylonish monarch, the travellers who find his corpse, and, last of all, JEHOVAH himself, are the characters which support this beautiful lyrical drama. . . . There is nothing wanting in this ode to defeat its claim to the character of perfect beauty and sublimity, nor do I know a single instance in the whole compass of Greek and Roman poetry which in every excellence of composition can be said to equal or even to approach it."—*Lowth, Jahn, and Horne.*

1. *His Forerunner.*

"The voice of him that crieth in the wilderness,
Prepare ye the way of the Lord,
Make straight in the desert a highway for our God." ch. xl. 3.

2. *His Birth.*

"Behold, a virgin shall conceive, and bear a son,
And shall call his name Immanuel." ch. vii. 14.

3. *His Family.*

"And in that day there shall be a root of Jesse,
Which shall stand for an ensign of the people;
To it shall the Gentiles seek:
And his rest shall be glorious." ch. xi. 10.

4. *His Name and Kingdom.*

"For unto us a child is born,
Unto us a son is given:
And the government shall be upon his shoulder:
And his name shall be called
Wonderful, Counsellor, The mighty God,
The everlasting Father, The Prince of Peace.
Of the increase of his government and peace there shall be no end,
Upon the throne of David, and upon his kingdom;
To order it, and to establish it
With judgment and with justice, from henceforth even for ever."
ch. ix. 6, 7.

5. *Rejection by the Jews.*

"And he shall be for a sanctuary;
But for a stone of stumbling and for a rock of offence
To both the houses of Israel,
For a gin and for a snare to the inhabitants of Jerusalem." ch. viii. 14.

6. *Accepted by the Gentiles.*

"I will also give thee for a light to the Gentiles,
That thou mayest be my salvation unto the ends of the earth."
ch. xlix. 6.

7. *His Miracles.*

"Then the eyes of the blind shall be opened,
And the ears of the deaf shall be unstopped.
Then shall the lame man leap as an hart,
And the tongue of the dumb sing." ch. xxxv. 5, 6.

II. JEREMIAH.

617. *Life and Period of Jeremiah, cir. 628-586.*
—Jeremiah, son of Hilkiah, was of sacerdotal race and a native of Anathoth, a city set apart for the priests in the tribe of Benjamin. He began to prophesy when very young, and continued for about forty-two years, reckoning from the thirteenth year of Josiah's reign. During the reign of JOSIAH he reproved the Jews for their wickedness and hypocrisy; and in the latter part of the reign, when they seem to have forgotten the solemn covenant they had made with God in Josiah's youth, he sharply rebuked them for their disobedience, and predicted the Babylonian captivity as the punishment for their universal and incorrigible depravity (sect. 534). During the following reigns the roll of his prophecies was publicly read by Baruch, but one copy was burnt by Jehoiakim, and Jeremiah narrowly escaped death. In Zedekiah's reign the prophet was consulted by the king and imprisoned by the nobles; but he was afterward released by Nebuchadnezzar at the taking of the city, and remained in Judæa whilst Gedaliah was governor. After the murder of Gedaliah by Ishmael, Jeremiah followed the remnant of the Jews to Egypt, where it is said he was stoned by his countrymen for his faithful remonstrances against their idolatrous practices. Others, however, say that he returned and died in Judæa; and others, that he died at Babylon.

618. *Subjects of his Prophecies.*—The principal subjects of Jeremiah's prophecies are—1. The fates of Jehoiakim and Zedekiah. xxii.; xxxiv. 2. The divine judgments against Judah. ii.-xx., etc. 3. The Babylonian captivity, the precise time of its duration, and the return of the Jews. xxiii.; xxv. 4. The destruction of Babylon and downfall of Persia, Egypt, Philistia, Tyre, Moab, Ammon, Edom, Damascus, etc. xlvi.; xlix. 5. The miraculous conception of the Messiah, the virtue of his atonement, his covenant, and his laws. xxxi.; xxxii.

619. *Book of Lamentations.*—Besides his prophecies, Jeremiah composed the "Book of Lamentations," which consists of five distinct elegies of twenty-two periods each, according to the twenty-two letters of the Hebrew alphabet. The following calamities are deplored: viz. the impositions of the false prophets who had seduced the people by their lying declarations, the destruction of the holy city and temple, the overthrow of the state, and the extermination of the people.

III. EZEKIEL.

620. *Life and Prophecies of Ezekiel, 595-536.*—Ezekiel, son of Buzi, and, like Jeremiah, of the sacerdotal race, was carried away captive with Jehoiachin, B. C. 599, and prophesied twenty years, commencing in the fifth year of his captivity and the thirtieth from the renewal of the covenant with God in the reign of Josiah. Whilst Ezekiel was among the captives on the river Chebar—which flows into the Euphrates about two hundred miles north of Babylon—the Lord appeared to him in a vision on a throne borne by four cherubim supported by four wheels, and commanded him to shut himself up in his house. Whilst thus confined he represented the siege of Jerusalem on a tile or slate, and lay on his left side three hundred and ninety days, and on his right side forty days, to prefigure the number of years (three hundred and ninety) during which God endured the idolatry of the TEN TRIBES, and the years (forty) during which he bore with the sins of JUDAH from the solemn renewal of the covenant with Jehovah to the destruction of Jerusalem. During this period his food was to be polluted and limited in quantity, to represent the severity of the famine during the actual siege. iii.-v. After this Ezekiel was carried in spirit to Jerusalem, where he beheld the idolatry of the people (viii.); and the principal subjects of his prophecies are—the calamities of Judæa, the conquest and downfall of the Moabites, Ammonites, Edomites, Philistines, and of Tyre, Sidon, and Egypt (xxv.-xxviii.), the deliverance of the Jews under Cyrus, and their final return from their dispersion (xxxix.), together with clear intimations of the coming of the Messiah. xxxiv.

IV. DANIEL.

621. *Early Life of Daniel, cir. 626-606.*—The prophet Daniel belonged to the tribe of Judah, and was

of royal descent. In B. C. 606, being the fourth year of Jehoiakim's reign, Nebuchadnezzar took Jerusalem (sect. 537), and carried off hostages, amongst whom were Daniel, who was then about twenty years old, with Hananiah, Mishael, and Azariah. The hostages, being brought to Babylon, were educated in the palace, and Daniel was called Belteshazzar, and the three others Shadrach, Meshach, and Abednego. These four afterward lived on pulse and water, and not on the king's wine and meat, as it was proved, after ten days' trial, that their countenances were not injured by the poorness of their diet. They then became rapidly renowned for their wisdom and rise in the king's favor. Dan. i.

622. *Interprets Nebuchadnezzar's First Dream —the Image of Four Empires, cir. 603.*—In the third year of Nebuchadnezzar's reign, about B. C. 603* or 601, the king had a troublous dream, but forgot its details, and ordered his magicians to both tell it and interpret it, with promises of rewards if they succeeded, but of death and destruction if they failed. The magicians excused themselves in vain, and were condemned, when Daniel, having with his three companions prayed to God, was favored by the Almighty with a revelation of the secret, and being taken into the king's presence he told and interpreted the dream, which was as follows: Nebuchadnezzar had seen a bright and terrible image, with head of fine gold, breast and arms of silver, belly and thighs of brass, legs of iron, and feet partly of iron and partly of clay; when a stone cut out without hands dashed it to pieces, and it became like chaff scattered in the wind, but the stone became a great mountain and filled the whole earth.

Daniel then told Nebuchadnezzar that he (the Babylonian kingdom) was the head of gold; that a second kingdom, of silver, (Medo-Persian, under Cyrus) should rise up after him; that a third, of brass (the Macedonian, under Alexander), should rule over the earth; that a fourth, of iron (the Roman commonwealth and first part of the empire), should break and subdue like iron; and that a

---

* Prideaux says B. C. 601, which is apparently the most correct date, as Nebuchadnezzar began to reign alone about B. C. 604.

fifth, of iron and potter's clay (the Roman empire divided), should be partly strong and partly broken. Daniel then interpreted the stone cut out without hands to signify the kingdom which God should set up (the kingdom of Christ), which should never be destroyed, but should overthrow the nations and fill the whole earth. Nebuchadnezzar then rewarded Daniel and made him ruler over the province of Babylon. Dan. ii.

623. *Nebuchadnezzar sets up a Golden Image, cir. 580.*—Nebuchadnezzar set up a golden image, sixty cubits high, in the plain of Dura in the province of Babylon, and commanded all his subjects to worship it on penalty of being thrown into a furnace. Shadrach, Meshach, and Abednego refused compliance; the furnace was heated seven times its usual heat, and the three Jews were thrown in; but a form "like the Son of God" delivered them, whilst they who threw them in were consumed. Nebuchadnezzar then blessed God, and issued a decree threatening death to any one who should malign the three Jews, whom he then promoted in the province of Babylon. Dan. iii.

624. *Nebuchadnezzar's Second Dream—the Tree, cir. 570: his Madness, cir. 569–563.*—Nebuchadnezzar about B. C. 570 dreamed that he saw a tall and spreading tree, when a watcher and holy one came down from heaven and cried, Hew it down, but leave his stumps in the earth with a band of iron and brass, and let his portion be with the beasts, and his heart be changed from man's to a beast's for seven times (years). Daniel interpreted this to signify that Nebuchadnezzar should lose his understanding, and be driven from men and dwell with beasts for seven years.

The next year, B. C. 569, Nebuchadnezzar was vaunting his power in his palace at Babylon, when the dream was fulfilled (B. C. 569–563); but at the end of seven years he lifted up his eyes, his understanding returned, and he praised, extolled, and honored the God of heaven. Dan. iv.

625. *Daniel's Vision of Four Beasts, 555.*—Nebuchadnezzar died, and his son EVILMERODACH, his son-in-law NERIGLISSOR, and LABORASOARCHOD, son of Neriglissor, reigned in succession after him. (See sect. 562.) At length (B. C. 555) Belshazzar, grandson of Nebuchadnez-

zar, ascended the throne, and in the first year of his reign Daniel had a vision of four beasts: 1st. A LION with eagle's wings (Babylon); and its wings were plucked and it stood like a man (was checked by the armies of Cyrus, Darius, or Cyaxares). 2d. A BEAR (Persia), with three ribs in its mouth (Babylon, Lydia, and Egypt). 3d. A LEOPARD, with four fowl's wings and four heads (Alexander the Great and his four successors). 4th. A TERRIBLE BEAST, with iron teeth and brazen nails (Roman empire) and ten horns (ten kingdoms, variously enumerated); and a little horn rose amongst them with eyes and mouth speaking great things (Antichrist, the Papacy), which plucked up three of the first horns. Daniel then beheld the thrones cast down, and the ANCIENT OF DAYS sitting, the judgment set, and the books opened; and one like the Son of man came with the clouds of heaven, and power was given him over all nations, an everlasting dominion, and a kingdom which could not be destroyed.

One that stood by then told Daniel that the four beasts were four kingdoms, and that the little horn would war upon the saints until the ANCIENT OF DAYS came, when the MOST HIGH would have everlasting dominion and the saints possess the kingdom. Dan. vii.—*Lowth and Horne.*

626. *Vision of the Ram and He-goat, 553.*—In the third year of Belshazzar's reign Daniel saw a vision of a ram with two horns (Medo-Persian empire), which was crushed by a he-goat with one horn (Macedo-Grecians under Alexander); the he-goat increased in power, and his one horn was fractured, and succeeded by four horns (Greece, Thrace, Syria, and Egypt). A little horn arose amongst the four horns (the Romans, who reduced Jerusalem to that desolation which was to last for 2300 prophetic days—*i. e.* years, ver. 14). Dan. viii.—*Lowth and Horne.*

627. *Belshazzar's Feast and Death, 538.*—Belshazzar made a feast to 1000 of his lords, and profaned the sacred vessels which Nebuchadnezzar had brought from Jerusalem, when a hand wrote upon the wall, and none of the astrologers could decipher the writing. Daniel was then introduced by the grandmother of Belshazzar and wife of Nebuchadnezzar. He declared the words to be MENE, MENE, TEKEL, UPHARSIN:

MENE—God hath numbered thy kingdom and finished it.

TEKEL—Thou art weighed in the balances and found wanting.

PERES—Thy kingdom is divided and given to the Medes and Persians.*

Daniel was then rewarded, and proclaimed the third ruler in the kingdom; but the same night Babylon was taken by Cyrus and Belshazzar slain. (See sect. 567.) Dan. v.

628. *Daniel in the Lions' Den, 538.*—Darius the Mede having ascended the throne at the age of sixty-two (sect. 568), appointed one hundred and twenty princes over the whole kingdom under three presidents, of whom Daniel was the first. The presidents and princes were jealous of Daniel, but could bring no charge against him; and therefore, knowing his piety to God, they persuaded Darius to issue a decree that for thirty days no one should pray to God or man, but to King Darius only, on pain of being thrown into the den of lions. Daniel disobeyed the decree by continuing his usual practice of praying to God three times a day, and was immediately apprehended. Darius tried to save him, but was unable, as the laws of the Medes and Persians were unchangeable, and the prophet was thrown into the den. Next morning the king went to the den, after passing a sleepless night, and found Daniel unhurt, who was then released, and his accusers and their wives and children thrown in, when the lions immediately devoured them. Dan. vi.

629. *Daniel foretells the Exact Time of the Coming and Death of the Messiah, 538.*—Daniel, having learnt from the prophecies of Jeremiah that the seventy years' captivity was drawing to a close, commenced fasting and prayer for the restoration of Jerusalem.

Whilst thus engaged the angel Gabriel appeared to him, and revealed to him the exact time of the coming and death of the Messiah and duration of the temple:—

---

* The verb *paras*, whence *Peres* is derived, as an appellative signifies to "divide" or "break;" it is likewise the proper name of the Persians, who were to be sharers in the division of the Babylonian empire. *Upharsin* is a particle of the verb *paras;* it literally signifies, "And they divide it."—*Lowth.*

"From the going forth of the commandment to restore and to build Jerusalem unto the Messiah the Prince shall be seven weeks, and threescore and two weeks: the street shall be built again, and the wall, even in troublous times. And after threescore and two weeks shall the Messiah be cut off, but not for himself; and the people of the prince that shall come shall destroy the city and the sanctuary." Dan. ix. 25, 26.

This prophecy was thus fulfilled:

The commencement of the building of the temple is fixed in the seventh year of the reign of Artaxerxes Longimanus, B. C. 458, when the order was issued to Ezra. (See sect. 584.)

	Prophetic weeks.	Years.
The building of the temple lasted from B. C. 458 to 409, or	7	49
The period from the completion of the temple to the public manifestation of the Messiah at the beginning of John the Baptist's preaching, extending from B. C. 409 to A. D. 25, or	62	434
From the manifestation of the Messiah to his passion (A. D. 25 to 32) were	1	7
From the building of the temple to the passion of our Lord, B. C. 458 to A. D. 32	70	490

(Our Lord is supposed to have been born four years before the vulgar era of Anno Domini.)

630. *Daniel's other Prophecies, cir. 534.*—Daniel having thus prophesied the rise and successive downfall of the Assyrian, Grecian, Persian, and Roman empires; the rise and fall of Antichrist, and duration of his power; the exact time of the coming and death of the Messiah, and his victories over his enemies, and second destruction of Jerusalem,—he was favored in his old age by a fourth and last prophetic vision of events which extended through successive ages, and only ended with the general resurrection. In the third year of the reign of Cyrus, whilst Daniel was fasting and making supplication, an angel comforted him, and unfolded to him—1st. The destruction

of the Persian empire by Greece, which was accomplished by Alexander; 2d. The partition of Alexander's dominions into four kingdoms (Greece, Thrace, Syria, and Egypt, erected by Cassander, Lysimachus, Seleucus, and Ptolemy); 3d. The wars between the kingdoms of Egypt, which lay to the south of Judæa, and of Syria on the north, together with the conquest of Macedon by the Romans; 4th. The tyranny of the papal Antichrist, which was to spring up under the Roman empire; and 5th. The invasion of the Saracens from the south and the Turks from the north in the *time of the end*, or latter days of the Roman monarchy. This amazing and comprehensive prophecy concludes with foretelling the general resurrection, and with announcing the time when all these great events were to have their final consummation, when the Jews were to be restored, Antichrist destroyed, the fulness of the Gentiles brought in, and the millennium, or reign of saints, was to begin; but the exact period, until Providence shall open more of the seals, cannot be fully ascertained. Dan. x.-xii.*

THE TWELVE MINOR PROPHETS.

(Called MINOR from the brevity of their works, not from the inferiority of their writings.)

631. *1. Hosea, cir. 810-725.*—Hosea, son of Beeri, prophesied during the reigns of Uzziah, Jotham, Ahaz, and in the third year of Hezekiah, kings of Judah, and during the reign of Jeroboam II., king of Israel. His subjects are—the guilt and disobedience of the Jewish nation, the heavy judgments that awaited them, their

---

* The book of Daniel was written partly in Hebrew and partly in Chaldee. The History of Susanna, and Bel and the Dragon, are ascribed to him, but their authenticity is more than doubtful. These three books, however, with Ezekiel's prophecies, are the only writings extant of those prophesied in Babylon during the Captivity; but part of the prophecies of Jeremiah, Habakkuk, and Obadiah were written in Judæa about the same time.

final conversion and re-establishment in the Land of Promise, and their restoration to God's favor and to a condition of the greatest national prosperity, under the immediate protection of the Messiah, in the latter ages of the world. Hosea also predicts the ingrafting of the Gentiles into the Church of God, and alludes to the calling of our Lord from Egypt, the resurrection on the third day, the overthrow of the Antichristian army in Palestine by the immediate interposition of Jehovah, and the Saviour's final victory over death and hell.

The most singular circumstances in Hosea's prophetical career were—his being desired by God to marry, first, a harlot, and afterward an adulteress, as a type of the then and after state of the Jews.

632. *2. Joel, cir. 810-660, or later.*—It is difficult to determine the chronology of Joel, son of Pethuel. His prophecies are exceedingly poetic. By a cloud of locusts he represents an enemy's army which desolated Judæa, and this, together with caterpillars and drought, brought on a terrible famine. God, being moved by the calamities and prayers of his people, then scattered the locusts, and the wind blew them into the sea. Subsequently, Joel foretells the day of the Lord and his vengeance. He speaks of the TEACHER OF RIGHTEOUSNESS to come from God, and of the Holy Spirit to descend upon all flesh. He says that Jerusalem will eternally be inhabited, that salvation will come from thence, and that whosoever shall call on the name of the Lord shall be saved. Acts ii. 6.

633. *3. Amos, cir. 810-785.*—Amos was a herdsman and gatherer of sycamore-fruit at Tekoah in Judah, about four leagues south of Jerusalem, and prophesied about the times of Uzziah of Judah and Jeroboam II. of Israel. He prophesied against Damascus, the Philistines, Tyrians, Edomites, Ammonites, Moabites, Judah, and Israel, and foretold the invasions of Pul, Shalmaneser, Tiglath-pileser, Sennacherib, and Nebuchadnezzar, and captivity of the ten tribes.

634. *4. Obadiah, cir. 588-583.*—His time is uncertain. His prophecies are in one chapter, in which he denounces judgments on the Edomites for their enmity to the Jews, and foretells the restoration of the latter and their victories and flourishing state.

635. **5. *Jonah*, *cir. 856–784*.**—Son of Amittai, and a native of Gath-hepher in Galilee. He prophesied about the time of Jeroboam II. of Israel, during whose reign he predicted the recovery of the *coasts of Israel*, which had been seized by the Syrians. 2 Kings xiv. 25, 26. (See sect. 471.)

Jonah was sent by God to cry against Nineveh, but, being fearful, he embarked at Joppa to fly to Tarshish. During the voyage a storm arose, and the mariners, having thrown their wares overboard, cast lots to ascertain who was the cause of the evil, when the lot fell upon Jonah, and they threw him overboard and the storm ceased. A great fish swallowed up Jonah, who remained in its belly three days and three nights, but upon praying to God he was vomited upon dry ground. God then a second time sent Jonah to Nineveh, which was three days' journey, or about sixty miles, round, and Jonah, having made one day's journey into it, cried, "In forty days shall Nineveh be overthrown." The Ninevites then repented, and their destruction was postponed, which displeased Jonah (as it affected his veracity as a prophet); upon which God caused a gourd to grow up in one night to shelter him from the sun's rays, but to wither the next night, as a reproof to the prophet, who desired to spare the gourd, but murmured that God should have spared Nineveh and its 120,000 inhabitants.

Jonah's preservation for three days and three nights in the belly of the fish is considered to be typical of our Saviour's being held in the jaws of death for a similar period. "An evil and adulterous generation seeketh after a sign; and there shall no sign be given to it, but the sign of the prophet Jonas: for as Jonas was three days and three nights in the whale's belly; so shall the Son of man be three days and three nights in the heart of the earth. The men of Nineveh shall rise in judgment with this generation, and shall condemn it: because they repented at the preaching of Jonas; and, behold, a greater than Jonas is here." Matt. xii. 39–41; xvi. 4; Luke xi. 29–32.

636. **6. *Micah*, *cir. 758–699*.**—Born at Morasthi in Southern Judæa, and prophesied during the reigns of Jotham, Ahaz, and Hezekiah, kings of Judah. He fore-

told the invasions and triumphs of Shalmaneser and Sennacherib in Israel and Judah; the captivities, dispersion, and deliverance of Israel; the cessation of prophecy; the destruction of Assyria and Babylon; the representatives of the Christian Church; the birth of the everlasting Ruler at Bethlehem Ephratah; the establishment and exaltation of Christ's kingdom over all nations; the influence of the gospel; and the destruction of Jerusalem. —*Dr. Gray.*

" But thou, Bethlehem Ephratah,
Though thou be little among the thousands of Judah,
Yet out of thee shall He come forth unto me that is to be ruler in Israel;
Whose goings forth have been from of old, from everlasting."
Mic. v. 2.

637. *7. Nahum, cir. 720-698.*—Nahum is supposed to have been a native of Elkosh or Elkosha, a village in Galilee, and of the tribe of Simeon. His prophecy is one entire poem, which, opening with a sublime description of the justice and power of God, tempered with long-suffering, foretells the destruction of Sennacherib's forces and the subversion of the Assyrian empire, together with the deliverance of Hezekiah and death of Sennacherib. The destruction of Nineveh is then predicted, and described with singular minuteness.

638. *8. Habakkuk, cir. 612-598.*—His tribe and birthplace are unknown. His prophecies are in two parts. The first is a kind of dialogue between God and the prophet, in which the Babylonian captivity is threatened, the Messiah promised, and the destruction of Babylon foretold. The second part is a psalm or prayer, in which Habakkuk recounts the wonderful works of the Almighty, and implores him to hasten the deliverance of his people.

639. *9. Zephaniah, cir. 640-609.*—Son of Cushi, and prophesied during the reign of Josiah. He denounced Judah for her idolatry; preached repentance as the only means to avert the divine vengeance; prophesied against the Philistines, Moabites, Ammonites, Ethiopia, and Nineveh; and predicted the Babylonian captivity and future restoration and prosperity of the Church.

640. **10. Haggai, cir. 520-518, or longer.**—His birthplace and tribe are unknown, but the times of his predictions are distinctly marked by himself—viz. B. C. 520, when the Jews, discouraged by the impediments thrown in their way by the Samaritans, had ceased to prosecute the rebuilding of the temple. Haggai was then raised up to exhort the Jews to complete the building. Ezra v. 1, and sect. 578. He predicted that the glory of the *second* temple should exceed that of the *first*, which was fulfilled when Christ *entered it;* and he foretold the setting up of the Messiah's kingdom under the name of Zerubbabel.

641. **11. Zechariah, cir. 520-518, or longer.**—Son of Berechiah and grandson of Iddo, but his tribe and birthplace are unknown. Like Haggai, he returned from the Captivity with Zerubbabel. His prophecies are in two parts. In the first he enjoins the restoration of the temple, and intersperses predictions relative to the advent of the Messiah. In the second he foretells more distant circumstances—the destruction of Jerusalem by the Romans; the future condition of the Jews; their compunction at having pierced the Messiah; their admission by baptism to the privileges of the gospel covenant; and the final re-establishment of Christ's kingdom.

After Isaiah, the prophet Zechariah referred most particularly to the coming of our Saviour. He intimated—1st, The entrance of our Lord into Jerusalem riding on an ass. Zech. ix. 10; Matt. xxi. 2-9. 2d, The selling of our Lord and the fate of the money. Zech. xi. 12, 13; Matt. xxvi. 15; xxvii. 3-10. 3d, The piercing of our Lord's side. Zech. xii. 10; John xix. 34-37.

642. **12. Malachi, cir. 434-420.**—Malachi was the last of the prophets, and completed the canon of the Old Testament; his exact time and birthplace are unknown. He was commissioned to reprove the priests and people for the irreligious practices into which they had fallen during and after the governorship of Nehemiah, their disrespect to God in their sacrifices, and their unlawful intermarriages with idolatresses. He prophesied the rejection of the Jews, the calling of the Gentiles, the coming of Christ, and the ministry of his forerunner, John the Baptist: "Behold, I will send my messenger, and he shall

prepare the way before me: *and the Lord, whom ye seek, shall suddenly come to his temple, even the messenger of the covenant whom ye delight in:* behold, he shall come, saith the Lord of hosts. . . . Behold, I will send you Elijah the prophet before the coming of the great and dreadful day of the Lord." Mal. iii.; iv.; Matt. xi. 14; xvii. 11; Mark ix. 11; Luke i. 17.

PRINCIPAL PROPHECIES, INTIMATIONS, AND TYPES OF THE MESSIAH IN THE OLD TESTAMENT.

643. ***By God to the Serpent.***—" He (the seed of the woman) shall bruise thy head, and thou shalt bruise his heel." Gen. iii. 15. (See Gal. iv. 4 and 1 John iii. 18.)

644. ***By God to Abraham.***—" In thee shall all the families of the earth be blessed." Gen. xii. 3; xviii. 18; xxii. 18. To Isaac, Gen. xxvi. 4; and to Jacob, Gen. xxviii. 14. (See Gal. iii. 9, 16; Matt. i. 1.)

645. ***By Jacob to Judah.***—" The sceptre shall not depart from Judah, nor a lawgiver from between his feet, until Shiloh come; and unto him shall the gathering of the people be." Gen. xlix. 10. Fulfilled by the high priests continuing to exercise their authority until A. D. 70.

646. ***By Balaam.***—" I shall see him, but not now:
I shall behold him, but not nigh:
There shall come a Star out of Jacob,
And a Sceptre shall rise out of Israel."
Num. xxiv. 17; Rev. xxii. 16.

647. ***By Moses to the Israelites.***—" The Lord thy God will raise up unto thee a Prophet from the midst of thee, of thy brethren, like unto me." Deut. xviii. 15. (See Acts vii. 37.)

648. ***By Job.***—" For I know that my Redeemer liveth, and that he shall stand at the latter day upon the earth." Job xix. 25. (See 1 Thess. iv. 16, 17; 1 Cor. xv. 24–26; 1 Tim. iii. 16.)

649. ***By God to David.***—" I will set up thy seed after thee, which shall proceed out of thy bowels, and I will establish his kingdom. He shall build an house for my

name, and I will establish the throne of his kingdom for ever." 2 Sam. vii. 12, 13. (See Matt. i. 1.)

650. *By David.*—

"For thou wilt not leave my soul in hell;
 Neither wilt thou suffer thy Holy One to see corruption."
Ps. xvi. 10. (See Acts ii. 31; xiii. 33–37; 1 Cor. xv. 44.)

"The Lord said unto my Lord,
 Sit thou at my right hand, until I make thy enemies thy footstool." Ps. cx. 1. (See Matt. xxii. 42–44;
Acts ii. 33; Heb. v. 6; vii. 2, 3, 17.)

"Sacrifice and offering thou didst not desire;
Mine ears hast thou opened;
Burnt-offering and sin-offering hast thou not required.
Then said I, Lo, I come:
In the volume of the book it is written of me,
I delight to do thy will, O my God;
Yea, thy law is within my heart."
Ps. xl. 6–8. (See Heb. x. 5.)

"Yea, my own familiar friend, in whom I trusted,
 Which did eat of my bread, hath lifted up his heel against me." Ps. xli. 9. (See Matt. xxvi. 47.)

"The stone which the builders refused is become the headstone of the corner.
 Blessed be he that cometh in the name of the Lord."
Ps. cxviii. 22, 26. (See Matt. xx. 9, 42; Eph. ii. 20; 1 Pet. ii. 7.)

651. *By Isaiah.*—

"The voice of him that crieth in the wilderness,
 Prepare ye the way of the Lord,
 Make straight in the desert a highway for our God."
Isa. xl. 3. (See Matt. iii. 1–3; Luke iii. 4.)

"Behold, a virgin shall conceive, and bear a son,
 And shall call his name Immanuel."
Isa. vii. 14. (See Matt. i. 20, 23.)

"And in that day there shall be a root of Jesse,
 Which shall stand for an ensign of the people;
 To it shall the Gentiles seek:
 And his rest shall be glorious."
Isa. xi. 10. (See Rom. ix. 33; 1 Pet. ii. 8; John i. 32; iii. 34; Col. ii. 3.)

" For unto us a child is born,
Unto us a son is given:
And the government shall be upon his shoulder:
And his name shall be called
Wonderful, Counsellor, The mighty God,
The everlasting Father, The Prince of Peace.
Of the increase of his government and peace there shall
be no end.
Upon the throne of David, and upon his kingdom,
To order it, and to establish it,
With judgment and with justice from henceforth even
for ever."
   Isa. ix. 6, 7. (See John iii. 16; Matt. xxviii. 18.)

" The Spirit of the Lord God is upon me;
Because the Lord hath anointed me
To preach good tidings unto the meek;
He hath sent me to bind up the broken-hearted,
To proclaim liberty to the captives,
And the opening of the prison to them that are bound;
To proclaim the acceptable year of the Lord,
And the day of vengeance of our God."
   Isa. lxi. 1, 2. (See Luke iv. 18, 19, 21.)

" The people that walked in darkness have seen a great
light:
They that dwell in the land of the shadow of death,
Upon them hath the light shined."
   Isa. ix. 2. (See Matt. iv. 14–16.)

" Then the eyes of the blind shall be opened,
And the ears of the deaf shall be unstopped.
Then shall the lame man leap as an hart,
And the tongue of the dumb sing."
   Isa. xxxv. 5, 6. (See Matt. xi. 5.)

" I will also give thee for a light to the Gentiles,
That thou mayest be my salvation unto the end of the
earth." Isa. xlix. 6. (See Luke ii. 32.)

" He is despised and rejected of men;
A man of sorrows, and acquainted with grief.
He was wounded for our transgressions,
He was bruised for our iniquities:

The chastisement of our peace was upon him;
And with his stripes we are healed.
All we like sheep have gone astray;
We have turned every one to his own way;
And the Lord hath laid on him the iniquity of us all."
   Isa. liii. 3, 5, 6. (See Matt. xxvi.; xxvii.)

652. *By Jeremiah.*—
"Behold the days come, saith the Lord,
That I will raise unto David a righteous Branch,
And a King shall reign and prosper,
And shall execute judgment and justice in the earth. . . .
And this is his name whereby he shall be called,
THE LORD OUR RIGHTEOUSNESS."
                  Jer. xxiii. 5, 6. (See Luke i. 32, 33.)

653. *By Ezekiel.*—
"And I will set up one Shepherd over them, and he shall feed them,
Even my servant David." Ezek. xxxiv. 23; xxxvii. 24. (See John i. 49; x. 1, 16; xix. 19, 21.)

654. *By Daniel.*—"I saw in the night visions, and, behold, one like the Son of man came with the clouds of heaven, and came to the Ancient of Days, and they brought him near before him. And his dominion is an everlasting dominion, which shall not pass away, and his kingdom that which shall not be destroyed." Dan. vii. 13, 14. (See Matt. xxiv. 30; xxvi. 64; xxviii. 18.)

"Seventy weeks are determined upon thy people, and upon thy holy city, to finish the transgression, and to make an end of sins, and to make reconciliation for iniquity, and to bring in everlasting righteousness, and to seal up the vision and prophecy, and to anoint the most Holy." Dan. ix. 24. (See Heb. ix. 26; John i. 41. See also sect. 629.)

655. *By Hosea.*—
"When Israel was a child, then I loved him,
And called my Son out of Egypt."
                  Hos. xi. 1. (See Matt. ii. 19, 20.)

656. *By Micah.*—
"But thou, Bethlehem Ephratah,
Though thou be little among the thousands of Judah,

Yet out of thee shall He come forth unto me that is to be ruler in Israel;

Whose goings forth have been from of old, from everlasting." Mic. v. 2. (See Acts ii. 1, 6; Luke ii. 4, 5.)

657. *By Zechariah.*—

" Behold the man whose name is THE BRANCH;

And he shall grow up out of his place,

And he shall build the temple of the Lord."

Zech. vi. 12. (See Luke i. 78, 79.)

" Rejoice greatly, O daughter of Zion;

Shout, O daughter of Jerusalem;

Behold, thy King cometh unto thee:

He is just, and having salvation;

Lowly, and riding upon an ass,

And upon a colt the foal of an ass."

Zech. ix. 9. (See Matt. xxi. 5; John xii. 15.)

"So they weighed for my price thirty pieces of silver.

And the Lord said unto me,

Cast it unto the potter:

A goodly price that I was prized at of them."

Zech. xi. 12, 13. (See Matt. xxvi. 15.)

" And they shall look upon me whom they have pierced,

And they shall mourn for him, as one mourneth for his only son."

Zech. xii. 10. (See John xix. 34, 36; Acts ii. 23.)

658. *By Malachi.*—

" Behold, I will send my messenger,

And he shall prepare the way before me:

And the Lord, whom ye seek, shall suddenly come to his temple,

Even the messenger of the covenant."

Mal. iii. 1. (See Matt. iii. 1, 3; xi. 10.)

659. *The Persons typical of the Messiah* in the Old Testament are—Adam, Noah, Abraham, Isaac, Melchizedek, Jacob, Joseph, Moses, Aaron, Joshua, David, Solomon, Zerubbabel, etc.

660. *The Things typical of the Messiah* are—Noah's ark, manna, the rock in Horeb, the brazen serpent, the passover, the Pentecost, the feast of atonement, the high priest, the paschal lamb, circumcision, the ark of the covenant, the golden candlestick, the mercy-seat, the temple, etc.

CONNECTION
BETWEEN THE
OLD AND NEW TESTAMENTS,
INCLUDING
THE HISTORY OF THE JEWS FROM THE ADMINISTRATION OF NEHEMIAH TO THE BIRTH OF JESUS CHRIST.

ANALYSIS.

I. *Jewish History from Nehemiah to the Revolt under the Maccabees*, B. C. 420-166.

Persia, B. C. 420-330.—Chasm in the Jewish history from Nehemiah to Alexander the Great.—Joshua slain in the temple by Jonathan the high priest, 366.—Samaritans build the temple at Gerizim; Manasses, high priest.—Decline of the Persian empire.

Alexander the Great and his Successors, 330-300.—Alexander's first conquests; visits Jerusalem, 332.—Conquers Egypt and overthrows Persia, 332-330.—His death, 323; disputes among his generals.—Four kingdoms established by permanent treaty.

Egypt—the Ptolemies, 300-202.—Government under the Ptolemies.—Death of Simon the Just, 292: completion of the canon of Scripture.—Septuagint completed.—Ptolemy Philopator enters the Holy of Holies; persecutes the Jews at Alexandria, 217.

Syria—the Seleucidæ, 202-166.—Conquest of Palestine by Antiochus the Great, 202.—Jewish temple saved from plunder by a miracle, 176.—Jesus, or Jason, introduces Greek idolatry amongst the Jews, 175.—Menelaus supplants Jason in the high priesthood, 172.—Antiochus Epiphanes profanes the temple and plunders Jerusalem.—Dreadful persecution of the Jews.—Revolt under Mattathias, 168.

II. *History of the Maccabees, or Asamonean Princes*, B. C. 166-37.

Judas Maccabæus, 166.—Character of the war.—Judas restores the temple; feast of dedication instituted, 166.—Neighboring nations league against the Jews; death of Antiochus Epiphanes, 164.—Victories of Judas over the neighboring nations; Jews in Galilee transplanted to Judæa.—Victory over Lysias; first peace with Syria.—Judas carries on a border war, and attempts to reduce Acra.—Lysias and Antiochus Eupator invade Judæa; take Bethsura, and besiege Jerusalem.—Second peace between Judas and Syria, 163.—Alcimus, high priest, deposed; Demetrius Soter sends an army against Judæa.—Judas forms an alliance with Rome; slain in battle, 161.

Jonathan Maccabæus, 161.—Persecution revives; Jonathan chosen leader of the people.—Death of Alcimus; fresh wars between Bacchides and Jonathan, which are concluded by a peace.—Alexander Balas, the impostor, obtains Syria; Jonathan made high priest, 153.—Demetrius Nicator obtains the throne of Syria; confirms Jonathan in the high priesthood.—Jonathan assists Antiochus against Demetrius.—Allies with Rome and Lacedæmon; fortifies Judæa.—Falls by the treachery of Tryphon.

Simon Maccabæus, 143.—His independence confirmed by Demetrius Nicator.—Completes the fortification of Judæa and reduces and levels Acra.—Public memorial of his acts; his powers recognized by Rome.—Treacherous invasion of Antiochus Sidetes.—Murder of Simon.

John Hyrcanus, 136.—Besieges Ptolemy.—Invasion of Antiochus Sidetes; peace at length concluded with Syria.—Accompanies Antiochus against Parthia.—Regains his independence and raises the Asamonean power to its greatest height.—Joins the Sadducees; Pharisees and Sadducees become political factions.—Dies.

Aristobulus I., 106.—Cruelty to his family; seizes the high priesthood and assumes the diadem.—Conquers the Itureans; kills his brother Antigonus.

Alexander Jannæus, 105.—Petty wars with his neighbors.—Civil dissensions fomented by the Pharisees.—Conquers Moab and Gilead, but loses his army in Gaulonitis.—Rebellion of the Pharisees for six years; his army destroyed.—Regains his kingdom; his cruelty to the rebels.—His dying advice to his queen.

Queen Alexandra, 78.—Domination of the Pharisees: Hyrcanus high priest.—Aristobulus joins the opposite party.

Hyrcanus II., 69.—Struggles between Hyrcanus and Aristobulus.

Aristobulus II., 69.—Antipater, father of Herod, espouses the cause of Hyrcanus.—Intrigues with Aretas, who defeats Aristobulus.—Roman interference; Pompey arbitrates between Hyrcanus and Aristobulus.—Pompey takes Jerusalem and restores Hyrcanus to the throne.

Hyrcanus II. restored, 63.—Roman supremacy; Antipater at the head of affairs.—Alexander, son of Aristobulus II., invades Judæa; defeated by Antipater and the Romans.—Gabinius changes the government to an aristocracy; constitution of the Sanhedrims.—Defeat and death of Aristobulus II. and his son Alexander.—Rise of the Herodians; Herod defies the Sanhedrim.—Julius Cæsar assassinated, 44; Antipater poisoned by Malichus.—Hyrcanus joins the faction of Malichus, but is reconciled by

Herod's espousing Mariamne.—Faction of Malichus headed by Antigonus, son of Aristobulus II., 42-41.—Parthians place Antigonus on the throne.—Herod escapes to Rome, 40.

Antigonus, 40.—Herod obtains the kingdom from the Triumvirate.—Reduces Antigonus; *end of the Maccabœan Dynasty*, 37.

III. *History of the Herodians to the commencement of New Testament History.*

Herod the Great, 37-3.—Massacres his opponents and propitiates Antony.—Appoints Ananel high priest.—Aristobulus, brother of Mariamne, obtains the office, but is drowned.—Herod summoned by Antony.—First secret instructions respecting Mariamne.—Fall of Antony at Actium; Herod conciliates Augustus, and is confirmed on the throne.—Second secret instructions respecting Mariamne; her execution.—Herod introduces heathen customs and public games.—Conspiracy of Ten.—Increases the fortifications, erects public works, and rebuilds the temple.—Famine in Judæa; Herod's generosity.—Intrigues of Salome and Antipater; trial and execution of Alexander and Aristobulus, sons of Mariamne.—Conspiracy and trial of Antipater.—Golden eagle pulled down at Jerusalem.—Herod's sickness and cruelty.—Shuts up the principal Jews in the hippodrome; execution of Antipater.—Death of Herod; his will.—Character of Herod.—*Conclusion.*

SUMMARY.

I. *Jewish History from Nehemiah to the Revolt under the Maccabees*, B. C. 420-166.

Persia.
B. C. 420-330.

1. *Chasm in Jewish History from Nehemiah to Alexander the Great, 420-330.* —From the administration of Nehemiah to the conquests of Alexander there is a chasm in the Jewish records which Josephus has neglected to fill up. The Jews still continued subject to Persia, and paid a yearly tribute, whilst the high priest conducted the internal government of Judæa under the Persian satrap of Syria.

2. *Joshua slain in the Temple by Jonathan the High Priest, 366.*—The murder of Joshua and building of the Samaritan temple are, however, recorded as occurring within this period. About B. C. 366, Bagoses was satrap, and Jonathan or Johanan was high priest. Joshua, brother of Jonathan, became a favorite with Ba-

goses, who appears to have invested him with the high priesthood to the exclusion of Jonathan. Joshua accordingly went to Jerusalem; a quarrel ensued in the temple between the two brothers, and Joshua was slain by the hand of Jonathan. When the news reached Bagoses, he marched to Jerusalem and avenged the death of his favorite on the whole nation by imposing a tribute of fifty drachmas (about £1 12s.) upon every lamb offered for sacrifice; and this continued to be exacted for seven years.

3. ***Samaritans build the Temple at Gerizim; Manasses High Priest.***—Jaddua, son of Jonathan, afterward succeeded to the high priesthood. His brother Manasses married the daughter of Sanballat,* governor of Samaria, but the elders at Jerusalem condemned the marriage. Manasses would have repudiated his wife, but Sanballat persuaded him to accept the high priesthood of Samaria. He also promised that, in case of his own death, Manasses should succeed him in the governorship, and having obtained the permission of Darius, he about this time built the Samaritan temple on Mount Gerizim, corresponding to that at Jerusalem.†

4. ***Decline of the Persian Empire.***—Meantime, the occurrence of frequent rebellions in the provinces dependent on the Persian power, the increase of luxury amongst the people, and the power exercised by the royal seraglio, all caused and indicated the gradual decline of the empire, which was at length overturned by the new power of Macedonia.

5. ***Alexander's First Conquests; visits Jerusalem, 332.***—Alexander the Great succeeded his father Philip in B. C. 336. Having crossed the Hellespont, he defeated a Persian army at GRANICUS. Darius advanced against him in person, but was completely routed at ISSUS, and forced to fly. Alexander then subdued Phœnicia, and spent seven months in besieging Tyre, during which JADDUA, the high priest and successor of Jonathan, had refused to break his oath of

---

* Dean Prideaux supposes that this Sanballat was the same Sanballat the Horonite who opposed Nehemiah (sect. 589). This, however, cannot be reconciled with the chronology, and it is probable that two different governors of Samaria may have borne the same name.

† For the origin of the Samaritans see sect. 507.

fealty to Darius by supplying him with provisions. Accordingly, Alexander marched to Jerusalem to punish him for his refusal. The terrified high priest was directed in a celestial vision to array himself and the other priests in their sacerdotal dress, and to meet the conqueror attended by the citizens clothed in white garments. The sacred procession so affected ALEXANDER that he adored the name of God written on the high priest's tiara (sect. 163), and saluted JADDUA; and, entering Jerusalem, he offered sacrifices to Jehovah as the priests directed, and was shown the prophecy of Daniel that Greece should overcome Persia (sect. 630). He subsequently remitted the payment of tribute in the sabbatical year. The Samaritans envied these privileges conferred on their neighbors, and endeavored, but without success, to obtain the same for themselves.

6. *Conquers Egypt and overthrows Persia, 332–330.*—ALEXANDER next marched to Egypt, which gladly submitted, B. C. 332; and the next year (B. C. 331) he founded Alexandria, and proceeded into the desert to sacrifice in the temple of Jupiter Ammon. The same spring he set out toward Syria to meet DARIUS, who had collected another army. On his way he punished the Samaritans for burning the house of Andromachus, whom he had appointed to be their governor, and then marched through Phœnicia and Syria, crossed the Euphrates and Tigris, defeated Darius and his 1,000,000 troops with immense slaughter on the plains of Gaugamela, and pursued the fugitives to ARBELA, which place has given its name to the battle, though it was nearly fifty miles distant from the spot where it was fought. DARIUS fled to Ecbatana in Media, whilst Babylon, Susa, and Persepolis surrendered to his conqueror; but the next year (B. C. 330) ALEXANDER again marched against him, but Darius fell by the treachery of Bessus, satrap of Bactria, though the burning of Persepolis had previously made known to Asia that the empire of Persia was destroyed and that the East must henceforth acknowledge a new lord and master.

Successors of Alexander. B. C. 323–300.

7. *Death of Alexander, 323; Disputes amongst his Generals.*—It is not within our province to pursue further the narration of Alexander's conquests. He died at BABYLON, B. C. 323;

but after his death violent disputes broke out amongst his generals, who divided the empire amongst themselves. For the present, however, they only bore the titles of governors of provinces under Alexander Ægeus, the posthumous son of Alexander the Great by Roxana, whom they had declared king jointly with Aridæus, an illegitimate son of King Philip.

8. *Ptolemy Lagus takes Jerusalem.*—Wars soon broke out between these generals, in the course of which Ptolemy Lagus conquered Judæa. Josephus says that he came to Jerusalem to sacrifice in the temple, and that he took the city without a blow by entering it on the Sabbath. He carried off several Samaritans and many thousand Jews to Egypt, but treated them kindly. For some years Syria and Egypt were perpetually at war with each other, and as Palestine lay between those countries, it was often not only the prize of the contest, but the arena upon which the combatants fought for the victory.

9. *Four Kingdoms established by a Permanent Treaty, 300.*—The great horn of the he-goat, as prophesied by Daniel, was broken by the death of Alexander, and the generals of the latter, who had carried on almost a continual war since the death of their sovereign, were in the space of a few years reduced to four in number— viz. Cassander, Lysimachus, Ptolemy Lagus, and Seleucus. The four horns of the he-goat and four heads of the leopard were therefore now to be represented by the four kingdoms established by a permanent treaty, by which the four generals were to be kings of the following provinces:

1. CASSANDER was to have Macedonia and Greece.

2. LYSIMACHUS, Thrace, Bithynia, and some of the adjoining provinces.

3. PTOLEMY LAGUS, Libya, Egypt, Arabia Petræa, *Palestine*, and Cœle-Syria.*

4. SELEUCUS, all that remained, comprehending many

---

* **Cœle-Syria**, or *Hollow Syria*, was the name given after the Macedonian conquest to the great and fertile valley between the two ranges of Lebanon—Libanus and Anti-Libanus—in the south of Syria, bordering upon Phœnicia on the west and Palestine on the south. In the wars between the Ptolemies and Seleucidæ the name was applied to the whole of Southern Syria, including Damascus; and it was this latter territory that now became subject to the kings of Egypt.

provinces in Asia Minor, Syria, Mesopotamia, Babylonia, and the East as far as India.

10. *Government under the Ptolemies, 300–202.* — According to the foregoing treaty, Palestine was included in the dominions of the Ptolemies, under whom it continued for nearly a century. During this period the revenues were farmed to the high priests, who appear to have continued to govern the Jews with the same powers they had enjoyed under the Persian satraps of Syria.

Egypt. Ptolemy I., Lagus. B. C. 300-283.

11. *Death of Simon the Just, 292; Completion of the Canon of Scripture.* — SIMON THE JUST, who was the grandson of *Jaddua*, had succeeded to the high priesthood B. C. 300, and is said by the Jews to have been the last of the *Great Synagogue*, which consisted of one hundred and twenty persons. These had returned with Ezra from the captivity in Babylon, and had been engaged in restoring the observance of the Law, and in collecting all the sacred books into one body and composing the canon of Scripture.* This "Great Synagogue" was followed by a "New Synagogue," which expounded and commented upon the completed canon. Simon the Just was succeeded in the high priesthood by his brother Eleazar, but the founder and first president of the New Synagogue † was *Antigonus Socho*,‡ or Sochæus, the first of the Mishnical teachers who studied the traditions.

12. *Septuagint completed.* — The Jews now appear to have lived in uninterrupted tranquillity. They began to spread over the known world, and studied Greek literature, and compiled the *Septuagint* at Alexandria, which was so called because, according to tradition, it was supposed to have been made

Ptolemy II., Philadelphus. B. C. 283.

---

* Many stories are related of Simon the Just in the Jerusalem Talmud and elsewhere, which it would be unnecessary to repeat here.

† The *Synagogue* has been sometimes confused with the council of the *Sanhedrim*, but this latter assembly did not exist before the time of the Maccabees.

‡ The Jews ascribe the origin of the *Sadducees* to the method of instruction pursued by *Socho*, for the latter having taught that man ought to serve God disinterestedly, and not from fear of punishment or hope of reward, his two pupils, *Sadoc* and *Baithus*, inferred that there was no future state of rewards or punishments.

in seventy-two days by seventy elders, or learned Jews, who had been sent by Eleazar the high priest to Alexandria at the request of Ptolemy Philadelphus, king of Egypt.

13. ***Ptolemy Philopator enters the Holy of Holies; persecutes the Jews at Alexandria, 217.***—No event of importance now occurred in Jewish history until the war broke out between *Ptolemy Philopator* and *Antiochus the Great*, during which Palestine suffered greatly from the contending armies. At length Philopator defeated Antiochus in the battle of Raphia, after which the Jews sent to renew their homage to Ptolemy, who then visited their temple and offered sacrifices, and even ventured to enter the Holy of Holies contrary to the expostulations of the priests; but he is said to have been seized with supernatural terror and to have rushed hastily out. On returning to Egypt, however, he visited his anger against the Jews at Jerusalem upon those of Alexandria, and published a decree forbidding any to enter his presence who refused to worship his gods. He is subsequently said to have shut up large numbers in the hippodrome or circus, for the purpose of destroying them with his elephants; but when the animals were made drunk with wine and brought forth, they fell upon the spectators instead of attacking the Jews.

Ptolemy III., *Euergetes.* B. C. 247. Ptolemy IV., *Philopator.* B. C. 222. Ptolemy V., *Epiphanes.* B. C. 205.

14. ***Conquest of Palestine by Antiochus the Great, 202.***—Ptolemy V., or *Epiphanes*, had succeeded his father, Ptolemy Philopator, B. C. 205, to the kingdom of Egypt, at the early age of five years. Antiochus the Great, who had ascended the throne of Syria, which included Asia Minor, Syria, Mesopotamia, Babylonia, etc., was now in the zenith of his glory, and had carried his conquests to the borders of India. In B. C. 203 he allied with Philip of Macedon to share the territories of the youthful Ptolemy, and then seized Palestine, Phœnicia, and Cœle-Syria. A war ensued in which the Jews suffered more from the Egyptian than the Syrian armies, and being otherwise alienated from the Ptolemies, they tendered their submission to Antiochus, supplied his army with provisions, and assisted him in expelling the Egyptian garrison from the castle

Syria. Antiochus the Great. B. C. 233-187.

of Zion. Antiochus liberally rewarded the Jews for their attachment; he gave an annual pension toward the sacrifices, and decreed that no foreigner should enter the limits of their temple.

Seleucus Philopator. B. C. 187.
15. *Jewish Temple saved from Plunder by a Miracle, 176.*—Antiochus the Great was succeeded on the throne of Syria by Seleucus Philopator. During the reign of the latter, Simon, a Benjamite, and governor of the temple, quarrelled with Onias the high priest, and in revenge reported to Apollonius, the governor of Cœle-Syria under Seleucus, the great wealth hoarded in the temple at Jerusalem. Heliodorus, the king's treasurer, was accordingly sent to bring away the riches, but on approaching the treasury it is said (2 Macc.) that a vision of a man on horseback struck him to the ground, and it was with great difficulty he recovered.

Antiochus Epiphanes. B. C. 176.
16. *Jesus, or Jason, introduces Greek Idolatry amongst the Jews, 175.*—Antiochus, surnamed Epiphanes, ascended the throne of Syria on the death of his brother Seleucus, and by seeking to combine the popular manners of a Roman with the ostentatious luxury of a Syrian he became to his subjects an object of hatred and contempt. As soon as he was settled in his kingdom, Jason, the brother of Onias the high priest, being ambitious of obtaining the pontifical office for himself, bribed Antiochus with the large sum of three hundred and sixty talents [£86,400] to invest him with the high priesthood and to summon Onias to Antioch. Jason warmly espoused the principles of Antiochus, and labored to introduce Greek institutions and worship into Judæa. He established a Greek gymnasium and idolatrous games at Jerusalem, encouraged apostasy from the law of Moses, and did his utmost to induce the people to adopt heathen customs.

17. *Menelaus supplants Jason in the High Priesthood, 172.*—After three years Jason sent his younger brother Menelaus* to carry tribute to Antioch, when

---

* Jason had changed his name, which was at first *Jesus*, in order to show his devotion to Greek superstitions. Menelaus had in the same manner changed his name, which was originally the same as that of his eldest brother Onias, whom Jason had supplanted.

the latter, by an increased bribe to Antiochus, obtained the high priesthood for himself, and Jason in his turn was deposed from the office. Menelaus was subsequently unable to raise the promised money, and was at last obliged to sell the golden vessels belonging to the temple. Onias, the real high priest, who was imprisoned at Antioch, heard of the sacrilege, and severely rebuked Menelaus; upon which the latter persuaded Andronicus, the governor of Antioch, to put Onias to death.

18. *Antiochus Epiphanes profanes the Temple, and plunders Jerusalem.*—About this period a war broke out between Syria and Egypt, and Antiochus invaded the latter country as far as Alexandria. Meantime, it was reported that Antiochus was dead, and Jason, thinking this a favorable moment to regain the priesthood, marched against Jerusalem with 1000 Ammonites and took the city, whilst Menelaus secured himself in the castle of Zion. When the news reached Antiochus, he thought that the whole Jewish nation was in a state of revolt. He immediately marched to Jerusalem, retook the city, and in the course of three days slew 40,000 of the inhabitants and sold as many more as slaves. Jason fled to the country of the Ammonites, and subseqently died in exile in Lacedæmonia, whilst Menelaus was again invested with the high priesthood. But the fury of Antiochus could not be satiated by slaughter. Guided by the impious apostate Menelaus,* he entered the inmost courts of the temple, and even the Holy of Holies, and sacrificed a sow upon the altar. He then carried off the table of shew-bread, the golden candlestick, the altar of incense, and all the offerings which had been made in the temple, and after plundering the city in the same way he returned to Antioch loaded with treasure.

19. *Dreadful Persecution of the Jews.*—Antiochus was subsequently repulsed in Egypt by the Romans, and whilst returning to Syria he again vented his anger upon

---

* The after career of Menelaus is uncertain, but he is said to have been put to death in the reign of Antiochus Eupator by being thrown into a high tower filled with ashes at Beræa, the modern Aleppo. 2 Macc. xiii. 4–8.

the Jews, whose religion he appears to have held in especial abhorrence, and on whose account he now issued a decree commanding his whole empire to worship Greek gods. In his way through Palestine from Egypt he detached 22,000 men from his army, and sent them under Apollonius to destroy Jerusalem. This general entered the place peaceably, but on the following Sabbath he committed the most horrible massacre upon the people, plundered the whole city, and then set it on fire. Athenæus, an old man, was commissioned to instruct the Jews in the Greek religion and compel them to celebrate its rites. Circumcision, the keeping of the Sabbath, and every observance of the Jewish law were punished by death; copies of the sacred books were destroyed, groves planted, and idolatrous altars built in every city; and the citizens were compelled to sacrifice to the Olympian Jupiter and other gods, and to eat swine's flesh on the king's birthday and keep the feast of Bacchus. Many Jews submitted from fear, and others from attachment to Greek customs, yet others resisted all the threats and tortures of this unparalleled persecution.

20. *Revolt of the Jews under Mattathias, 168.*— At length Mattathias, a priest, publicly set Antiochus at defiance. He refused to sacrifice at the idolatrous altar, and struck down a Jew who approached it as a rebel to Jehovah, and then, with the assistance of his sons and others, he slew the royal officers, broke down the altar, and fled to the wilderness of Judæa.* Here his party rapidly increased, and he soon emerged from his concealment, demolished the idolatrous altars throughout the country, circumcised the children, and slew the apostates; but died in the midst of his expedition, B. C. 166, and appointed his third son, Judas, surnamed Maccabæus, or the Hammerer, to be military leader, and his second son, Simon Thassi, to be counsellor to his brother.

---

* It is related that about this time a body of 1000 Jews, being pursued by the army of Antiochus on the Sabbath day, patiently submitted to being cut to pieces rather than violate the sacred rest. Upon this Mattathias and his friends made it lawful to resist the attack of an enemy on the Sabbath.

II. *History of the Maccabees, or Asamonean Princes*, B. C. 166–37.

21. ***Character of the War.***—The primary object of the Jewish insurrection was not political independence, but religious freedom; and during the leaderships of Judas and his brother Jonathan the nation continued to pay tribute to the kings of Syria; but in B. C. 143, Demetrius Nicator, the reigning monarch, acknowledged Simon as high priest and prince of the Jews, and relinquished all claims for tribute, customs, or taxes.*

<small>Judas Maccabæus. B. C. 166–161.</small>

22. ***Judas restores the Temple: Feast of Dedication instituted, 166.***—Judas soon followed in the steps of his father Mattathias. In the first two years of his reign he defeated the generals of Antiochus four times, and having thus deterred the king from an immediate renewal of the contest, he led his victorious army to Jerusalem for the purpose of cleansing and dedicating the sanctuary. This must have been a task of considerable difficulty, as the temple was commanded by the fortress on Mount Acra, called in the Hebrew *Millo* (see note to sect. 326), which was still garrisoned by the forces of the heathen. Judas, however, built up a new altar, furnished the temple with fresh vessels, set up the candlestick, table of shew-bread, and altar of incense, and hung up the veils before the Holy of Holies. Having thus repaired and purified the temple just three and a half years after it had been polluted by Antiochus, sacrifices were recommenced, and a festival celebrated for eight days, which was afterward commemorated by the annual FEAST OF DEDICATION. (See sect. 193.) Thus was fulfilled the prophecy of Daniel (xii. 7), that three years and a half—or, in the language of prophecy, "a time, times, and half a time"—should be the period of its desolation. But Mount Mo-

---

* In the establishment of the Asamonean power under Judas, Jonathan, and Simon we see the reward of valor exerted in defence of religion and law, and the happy effects of family concord; whilst from the dissensions which prevailed amongst their descendants, and paved the way for the aggrandizement of the Herods, princes may learn the useful lesson that family feuds are more to be dreaded than the rebellion of subjects; the one may for a time deprive the prince of power, the other wrest the sceptre from the family for ever.—*Hales.*

riah, on which the temple was built, was rather lower than Acra, and the people were much annoyed on their way to the temple by the heathen garrison. Judas therefore protected the Lord's house with walls and towers, and posted a detachment of troops to guard it. In subsequent reigns Acra was lowered and the valley between the two hills was filled up, so that the buildings of the temple overhung the fortifications on Acra.

23. *The Neighboring Nations league against the Jews; Death of Antiochus Epiphanes, 164.*—After this Judas fortified Bethsura, a town between Hebron and Jerusalem, as a barrier against the Idumæans or Edomites. Meantime, the neighboring nations formed a league for utterly extirpating the Jewish nation, which was, however, defeated by the death of Antiochus and energy of Judas. Antiochus was proceeding to Babylon when he heard of the defeat of his generals, rededication of the temple, and destruction of the idolatrous altars. He immediately returned to Judæa, vowing vengeance against the whole Jewish nation; but on his way was seized with a fatal disease, and died in the most dreadful agonies of body and soul.

24. *Victories of Judas over the Neighboring Nations; Jews in Galilee transplanted to Judæa.*— Judas now heard of the confederacy formed against him and prepared to take the field. He first fell upon the Edomites on his southern borders, defeated them in battle, besieged and took their fortresses, and put their garrisons to the sword. He then entered the country east of the Jordan, and defeated Timotheus, the Syrian governor, who marched against him. The Phœnicians on the northwest and the inhabitants of Gilead on the east immediately commenced an active war. Judas now separated his army into three divisions: with the first he marched to the relief of the Jews resident in Gilead; the second he despatched under his brother Simon to defend Galilee; whilst the third remained at home for the protection of Judæa and Jerusalem. A marked success attended this judicious proceeding. Judas with his division quickly overran Gilead, took the towns, and returned laden with spoil. Simon defeated the enemy in Galilee, but finding the Jews there too few to defend themselves, he wisely induced them to

remove to Judæa, where they would strengthen the population, which had been weakened by the persecutions of Antiochus Epiphanes. The generals of the division who remained at home, wishing to share the glory of the two brothers, led their forces against Jamnia, a seaport on the Mediterranean, but were defeated by Gorgias, the governor of that district, with the loss of 2000 men, which misfortune, however, did not detract from the rising fame of the Maccabees.

25. *Victory over Lysias; First Peace with Syria.*—Antiochus Eupator had now succeeded his father Antiochus Epiphanes, on the throne of Syria; and Lysias, the guardian and kinsman of Eupator, determined to avenge the insult which the Maccabees had inflicted on the Syrian empire. Accordingly, Lysias invaded Judæa with an army of 80,000 men, including a large body of cavalry and eighty elephants, and commenced the siege of Bethsura (sect. 23). Judas marched to the attack, and succeeded not only in relieving the garrison, but in dispersing the invading forces. Lysias then made a peace with Judas, which was ratified by Antiochus; and on this occasion the Jewish nation was benefited by the friendly interference of the Roman ambassadors at the Syrian court.

26. *Judas carries on a Border War, and attempts to reduce Acra.*—When Lysias had retired to Antioch, Judas again invaded Gilead and overthrew Timotheus, and then marched against Gorgias and the Idumæans, and by a hardly-earned victory avenged the death of those who had fallen in the expedition against Jamnia (sect. 24). He afterward tried to reduce the fort of Acra, from which the Syrian garrison was perpetually sallying out and disturbing the peace of the city and service of the temple. Some apostate Jews, however, escaped from the fort to Antioch, and informed the Syrian king of the threatened danger.

27. *Lysias and Antiochus Eupator invade Judæa; take Bethsura and besiege Jerusalem.*—Antiochus Eupator and his guardian Lysias were now afraid lest the city of Jerusalem should be entirely lost, and accordingly they invaded Judæa with a vast army of 120,000 men, thirty-two elephants, three hundred chariots, and again

commenced the siege of Bethsura. Judas immediately raised the siege of Acra, and marched to the relief of the fortress; but after some slight successes, in which his brother Eleazar fell, he found himself unable to cope with the overwhelming forces of the enemy, and retreated to Jerusalem. The garrison at Bethsura was at length compelled to surrender, and the Syrian army then marched to besiege Jerusalem.

28. *Second Peace between Judas and Syria, 163.*—The city was almost reduced, when the news reached Lysias that Philip, the rival guardian of Antiochus Eupator, had raised an army and seized Antioch, and taken upon himself the government of the empire. Accordingly, he found it necessary to conclude a peace with the Jews, by which Judas was appointed governor of Judæa under the king of Syria.

29. *Alcimus, High Priest, deposed; Demetrius Soter sends an Army against Judæa.*—Menelaus, the high priest, was now dead (sect. 17, *note*), and Antiochus appointed Alcimus, or Jacimus, to be his successor, to the exclusion of Onias, son of that Onias who had been murdered at Antioch (sect. 17). Onias fled to Egypt, and obtained permission from Ptolemy Philometor to build a temple at Heliopolis. Thus, three temples existed—viz. the Samaritan at Gerizim, that of the Jews at Jerusalem, and that of Onias. Alcimus, however, from his profligacy and idolatry, was not long permitted by the people to exercise his office; and by his subsequent intrigues he persuaded Demetrius Soter, who had now succeeded Antiochus Eupator to the throne of Syria, to send a large invading force against Judæa under Nicanor, which was, however, signally defeated by Judas and his followers, and in the second action Nicanor was slain.

30. *Judas forms an Alliance with Rome; slain in Battle, 161.*—Judas now saw that no dependence could be placed upon the kings of Syria, and accordingly sent ambassadors to Rome to endeavor to form an alliance. The Romans decided to receive the Jews amongst their friends and allies, and wrote a letter to Demetrius requiring him to desist from harassing that nation, but before the letter could be delivered Judas was dead. On the death of Nicanor, Demetrius had sent Bacchides with Al-

cimus a second time into Judæa at the head of a large army, to which Judas could only oppose a force of 3000 men, all of whom, with the exception of eight hundred, fled at the approach of the enemy. But the intrepid leader scorned to fly, and with this handful of men he boldly engaged the whole army of Bacchides. By the impetuosity of his charge he routed the right wing of the enemy, but the left wing remained entire, and Judas, being overpowered by numbers, fell on the field of battle; and all Israel mourned many days, saying, "How is the valiant man fallen that delivered Israel?"

31. *Persecution revives; Jonathan chosen Leader of the People, 161.*—After the death of Judas Maccabæus, Alcimus and his apostate party returned to power, and openly persecuted the followers of Judas; and all the Maccabæans that could be found were brought before the general Bacchides and cruelly tortured and put to death. Under these circumstances the people chose Jonathan, brother of Judas, for their leader, and committed themselves to his guidance. At first Jonathan and his brother Simon retired to a strong position on the banks of the Jordan, from whence they avenged the death of their brother John, who had been slain by some Arabs of the tribe of Jambria. Their position was, however, soon known to Bacchides, who accordingly assaulted their camp on the Sabbath day. But Jonathan exhorted his troops to remember the decision of Mattathias (sect. 20, *note*), and his forces courageously resisted the attack and slew 1000 of the enemy, and on finding their numbers unequal to a further contest, they sprang into the Jordan and escaped by swimming to the other side. Bacchides then fortified Judæa, especially Acra, and took the children of the inhabitants as hostages for the fidelity of their parents.

Jonathan Maccabæus. B. C. 161–143.

32. *Death of Alcimus; Fresh Wars between Bacchides and Jonathan, which are concluded by a Peace.*—Alcimus, the high priest, was at length struck with palsy and died; after which Bacchides returned to Antioch, and the Jews for two years dwelt in peace under the government of Jonathan. At the expiration of this time Bacchides was informed by the opposition that all the Maccabæan party might be seized in a single night,

and he accordingly came to Judæa to execute the plan. But Jonathan discovered the plot, and put fifty of the conspirators to death; but, being unable to cope with Bacchides, he retired and fortified a place in the wilderness, and successfully withstood a siege. Bacchides, enraged at the defeat, slew the advisers who had brought him back to Judæa, concluded a peace with Jonathan, exchanged prisoners, and swore never more to molest the land; and Jonathan settled in peace at Michmash, about nine miles north of Jerusalem, where he administered the laws with impartiality and pursued his schemes of reformation.

33. *Alexander Balas, the Impostor, obtains Syria; Jonathan made High Priest, 153.*—In this year the famous impostor, Alexander Balas, pretended to be a son of Antiochus Epiphanes, and claimed the empire of Syria; and being supported by the Romans, he sailed to Ptolemais in Phœnicia, seized the city, and proclaimed himself king of Syria. The disputes between this pretender and Demetrius Soter, the reigning monarch, proved of infinite advantage to Jonathan, as each party vied with the other in offers to secure his co-operation. Demetrius appointed him the king's general in Judæa, and offered him numerous immunities and privileges; but Alexander Balas granted him the high priesthood, and sent him a purple robe and crown of gold; and Jonathan preferred an alliance with the latter to accepting the proposals of the insincere Demetrius.

34. *Demetrius Nicator obtains the Throne; confirms Jonathan in the High Priesthood.*—The Syrians soon grew disaffected toward Alexander Balas, and Demetrius Nicator, son of Demetrius Soter, whom Alexander Balas had deposed, now asserted his claim to the empire, and, being assisted by Egypt, he defeated Alexander and obtained the throne. Jonathan was still in quiet possession of Judæa, and, being determined to expel the garrison from Acra, he commenced a regular siege. Demetrius, hearing this, summoned Jonathan to Ptolemais, but the latter gave orders to press the siege during his absence, and then carried such valuable presents as he thought would influence the king and his licentious court. Demetrius, in return, confirmed Jonathan in

the high priesthood, ratified the offers of immunity from tribute, etc. which his father had made, and promised to withdraw the garrison from Acra if Jonathan would assist him in putting down a revolt at Antioch, which was then in a state of tumult. Jonathan despatched 3000 men to the aid of the king, who was, however, no sooner relieved than he forgot his promises and refused to exempt the Jews from tribute.

35. *Jonathan assists Antiochus against Demetrius.*—This ingratitude of Demetrius was quickly punished. A new claimant now appeared for the kingdom of Syria. Tryphon, who had been governor of Antioch under Alexander Balas, brought forward Antiochus, son of his old master, and defeated Demetrius and placed the young prince on the throne. He then sent an embassy to Jonathan, soliciting assistance and promising to fulfil the engagements which Demetrius had broken. Jonathan readily accepted the proposal, defeated Demetrius, who invaded Galilee, and reduced Joppa, Gaza, and Bethsura.

36. *Allies with Rome and Lacedæmon; fortifies Judæa.*—On returning to Judæa, Jonathan renewed the treaty which Judas had made with the Romans, and formed an alliance with the Lacedæmonians. He also held a council at Jerusalem to take into consideration the fortification of Judæa; and at this assembly it was agreed that the walls of Jerusalem should be heightened and a line of circumvallation should be drawn round the fort of Acra under the superintendence of Jonathan, whilst Simon should have the oversight of the fortifications throughout the country.

37. *Falls by the Treachery of Tryphon.*—Meantime, it appeared that Tryphon had elevated Antiochus, the son of Alexander Balas, to the throne, for the sole purpose of murdering him and usurping the crown himself, but whilst Jonathan remained to oppose the plot he despaired of success. Accordingly, he marched his army against Judæa, but being met by Jonathan with 40,000 men, he put on the mask of friendship, and pretended that he had only come to consult about their common interests and to put the city of Ptolemais in Phœnicia into his hands. Jonathan was thus persuaded to dismiss

his army and proceed with Tryphon to Ptolemais with only 1000 troops, but on entering the city he was taken prisoner and his men were slain. Tryphon then invaded Judæa, carrying Jonathan as a captive; and being met by Simon at the head of a large army, he declared that he only detained Jonathan for a debt of one hundred talents [about £24,000], and that if the debt was paid, and his two sons given up as hostages, he should be released. Simon complied, but Tryphon failed to fulfil his promise, and, being encouraged by messages from the garrison at Acra, he attempted to invade Judæa. Simon, however, baffled his efforts, and Tryphon at last retired to the district east of the Jordan surrounding Mount Gilead, called Galaaditis, and put Jonathan to death at Bascama.

Simon Maccabæus. B. C. 143-136.

38. *His Independence confirmed by Demetrius.*—Simon, brother of Jonathan and Judas, succeeded to the high priesthood and government on the death of the former. Meantime, Tryphon murdered Antiochus and proclaimed himself king of Syria, and Demetrius Nicator, who now wanted the assistance of the Jews in deposing the tyrant, confirmed the authority of Simon as high priest and prince, and relinquished all claims for tribute, customs, and taxes. From this grant the Jews calculate the deliverance of their country from a foreign power, and they dated all their instruments and contracts by the years of Simon and his successors.

39. *Completes the Fortification of Judæa, and reduces and levels Acra.*—Simon's first measure was to complete the fortifications which were erecting throughout Judæa and to reduce some of the enemy's fortresses which still held out. The garrison at Acra now began to feel the effects of the circumvallation, and, their provisions being exhausted, they at last surrendered, and were permitted to leave unmolested. From the beginning of the revolt this garrison had occasioned infinite annoyance and trouble to Jerusalem. Simon therefore not only destroyed the fort, but employed three years in reducing the hill on which it stood to a level with Mount Moriah. He also fortified the latter, and built his palace within the wall, probably on the site where the castle

Antonia was afterward erected, and he made his son, John Hyrcanus, generalissimo of all his forces.

40. *Public Memorial of his Acts; his Powers recognized by Rome.*—The state was now in a flourishing condition, and the people made a public acknowledgment of their allegiance to the Maccabees. The valiant deeds of Simon and his predecessors were engraved on tables of brass, and these were set up in a conspicuous part of the temple. About the same time Simon sent an embassy to the Romans, bearing a golden shield weighing 1000 minæ, and worth at least £50,000, as a present to the senate, who thereupon renewed the league and recognized his powers as high priest and prince of Judæa.

41. *Treacherous Invasion of Antiochus Sidetes.*—Meantime, Demetrius Nicator had retired from before Tryphon to Babylon, and was subsequently taken prisoner by the Parthians, whilst his younger brother, Antiochus Sidetes, married Cleopatra, wife of Demetrius, and attempted to dispossess Tryphon. Antiochus was desirous of obtaining the assistance of Simon, and accordingly confirmed him in his authority and granted him the privilege of coining money as an independent prince. When, however, he had deposed Tryphon and ascended the throne of Syria, he laid claim to the citadels of Jerusalem, Joppa, and Gazara (probably Gadara), demanded five hundred talents for tribute and damages, and invaded Judæa. But John Hyrcanus and his brother Judas, the two sons of Simon, defeated the general of Antiochus and obliged him to retreat from the country.

42. *Murder of Simon.*—Antiochus Sidetes at length obtained the death of Simon. Ptolemy, one of his officers and governor of Jericho, had married the daughter of Simon, and having concerted measures with Antiochus for usurping the government of Judæa, he invited Simon and his sons Judas and Matthias to his castle near Jericho, and then treacherously murdered them. Messengers were also sent to despatch John Hyrcanus, but he fortunately escaped to Jerusalem and secured the city before Ptolemy could seize it.

43. *Besieges Ptolemy.*—Hyrcanus was now chosen by the people to succeed his

John Hyrcanus. B. C. 136-106.

father, Simon, in the high priesthood and principality. He first marched against Ptolemy, and besieged him in a castle near Jericho; but the latter still held the mother and surviving brethren of Hyrcanus in his clutches, and, bringing them to the walls, threatened to throw them down headlong if the siege was continued. Hyrcanus accordingly gradually relaxed, and then raised, the siege; though, according to Josephus, his mother loudly exhorted her son from the walls to disregard her sufferings and pursue his revenge. Ptolemy then slew the mother and brethren of Hyrcanus, and fled to Philadelphia in Asia Minor.

44. *Invasion of Antiochus Sidetes; Peace at length concluded with Syria.*—The following year Antiochus Sidetes invaded Judæa and besieged Hyrcanus in Jerusalem, and as it was a sabbatical year there was soon such a scarcity of provisions that the besieged were reduced to the greatest distress. On the approach of the feast of tabernacles Hyrcanus requested a truce for the purpose of keeping it, which Antiochus most graciously granted, and even sent animals for the sacrifice. This conduct led to proposals for a peace, which was at length concluded, Hyrcanus engaging to dismantle Jerusalem and pay tribute for the towns possessed by the Jews out of Judæa. Antiochus also required the fort of Acra to be rebuilt, but Hyrcanus chose rather to pay five hundred talents [£120,000]; and hostages being delivered for the fulfilment of these terms, the siege was raised.

45. *Accompanies Antiochus against Parthia; regains his Independence, and raises the Asamonean Power.*—Four years after this Antiochus invaded Parthia to recover his brother Demetrius, and was accompanied by Hyrcanus, who greatly distinguished himself in the war. Here Antiochus was slain, and Demetrius Nicator, being at length enabled to return to Syria, regained the kingdom. Hyrcanus seized the opportunity of these disturbances to deliver himself from Syria and completely establish the independence of Judæa, and neither himself nor his successors were ever afterward tributary to the Syrian kings. He seized several of the bordering cities in Syria, Phœnicia, and Arabia; subdued the Idumæans, and obliged them to embrace the Jewish religion;

subjugated Samaria, and destroyed the temple of Sanballat on Mount Gerizim; and obtained from the Romans an acknowledgment that the treaty which he had been forced to make with Antiochus Sidetes was null and void, being a violation of the freedom guaranteed by the senate to the Jewish nation. Hyrcanus was thus master of all Judæa, Galilee, and Samaria, and having raised the glory of the Asamonean princes to its greatest height, he passed the remainder of his reign respected by the neighboring states and free from foreign war.

46. *Hyrcanus joins the Sadducees; Pharisees and Sadducees become Political Factions.* —During the foregoing period two parties had arisen among the Jews—the Pharisees and the Sadducees. (See sects. 94–100.)

The Pharisees rigidly adhered to the very letter of the old law, and explained the Scriptures themselves by the light of tradition. The Sadducees, by an epicurean philosophy and a latitudinarian system of morals, had fallen into the opposite extreme, and affixed a mere human interpretation to Scripture, and even questioned the doctrine of the immortality of the soul. The Pharisees, being the more orthodox sect, were supported by the many; the Sadducees, from the laxity of their principles, were favored by the wealthy few. Hyrcanus was originally a Pharisee, but, according to Josephus, one of that party once told him that he ought to resign the high priesthood and content himself with the civil government, because, as his mother had been a captive, it was uncertain whether he was a descendant of Aaron or of a stranger. Hyrcanus was incensed at this insult, and probably perceiving symptoms of disaffection amongst the whole Pharisaic party, and a desire to separate the offices of high priest and king, which he united in his own person, he left their sect and went over to the Sadducees. The Pharisees and Sadducees, from being mere religious sects, now became political factions. Domestic broils arose, which estranged the affections of a large party of Jews from Hyrcanus and his family; and the factious opposition of the Pharisees, first to their own princes and afterward to the Romans, ultimately led to the declension of the Asamonean power, and finally to the downfall of the Jewish nation.

310 CONNECTION BETWEEN THE B. C. 106-78.

Aristobulus I.
B. C. 106.

47. *Cruelty to his Family; seizes the High Priesthood and assumes the Diadem.* —The events of the succeeding reign are a series of domestic tragedies, which may be ascribed with probability to the intrigues of party and the turbulent ambition of the Pharisees. Hyrcanus had left the civil government to his wife, but his eldest son, Aristobulus, seized the government and put his mother in prison, where she perished of hunger. Having thus obtained the high priesthood and principality, he put the royal diadem on his head and assumed the title of king, being the first Jewish prince who had done so since the Babylonian captivity.

48. *Conquers the Itureans; kills his brother, Antigonus.* —Aristobulus then admitted his brother Antigonus to a share in the kingdom, but imprisoned his then remaining brethren. He subdued Iturea east of the Jordan, and offered the inhabitants the alternative of circumcision or expatriation, upon which they preferred the former. On his return from this expedition he was seized with sickness, during which his queen, Salome, and her party excited his jealousy against Antigonus, his favorite brother. Accordingly, he summoned Antigonus to his presence unarmed, and gave orders to a guard of soldiers to kill him if he came in armor. But the messenger appointed to bear the summons was seduced by the enemies of Antigonus to direct the prince to go to the royal castle in his armor, as the king desired to see it. Antigonus was accordingly slain, but the reproaches of conscience, aggravated by the recollection of the cruel murder of his mother, increased the disorders of Aristobulus, and he died the same year in the bitterest agony of mind and body.

Alexander Jannæus.
B. C. 105-78.

49. *Petty Wars with his Neighbors.* — Immediately after the death of Aristobulus I., his widow, Alexandra or Salome, released his three younger brothers from the prison in which they had been confined, and Alexander Jannæus, the eldest of them, was invested with the high priesthood and ascended the throne of Judæa. One of his first acts was to put his next brother to death for entertaining treasonable designs, and the remainder of his reign was a series of petty wars with his neighbors, varied by civil war and dissensions at home. He besieged Ptolemais in Phœnicia, but the citizens applied for aid to Ptolemy Lathyrus, who had been compelled by his mother, Cleopatra, to exchange the kingdom of Egypt for that of Cyprus. Ptolemy Lathyrus obliged Alexander to raise the siege, and invaded Galilee and Judæa; and Jannæus would probably have been entirely ruined had not Cleopatra sent an army from Egypt to his assistance. Alexander subsequently took Gadara, a fortified city east of the Jordan, but after a few other petty successes, in which he met with great resistance, he returned to Jerusalem without being in the least enriched by his conquests.

50. *Civil Dissensions fomented by the Pharisees.*—The heroic line of the Maccabæan princes had ended with John Hyrcanus, and we now enter upon a period in which the fury of faction had converted the Pharisees into the most dangerous enemies of the state, and ultimately led to civil war. At the feast of tabernacles, whilst Alexander Jannæus was officiating as high priest at the altar, he was pelted with citrons by the populace and insulted by the most opprobrious language, implying that he was descended from a slave and unworthy of being high priest or king. The royal guards then fell upon the people and slaughtered 6000 persons, and Alexander, to prevent a recurrence of the like insult, railed in the court of the priests from the approach of the crowd, and took upward of 6000 mercenaries into his pay.

51. *Conquers Moab and Gilead, but loses his Army in Gaulonitis.*—Alexander now endeavored to divert the attention of the Jews from their intestine divisions by engaging in war. Accordingly, he succeeded in making the lands of Moab and Gilead tributary, but three years afterward lost nearly all his army in an expedition against Gaulonitis, a district in the northern division of Batanæa, east of the Jordan.

52. *Rebellion of the Pharisees for Six years; the Army of Alexander destroyed.*—When Alexander returned to Jerusalem after this disaster the discontent of the Pharisees was shared by the whole nation, and the Jews openly rebelled against his government. For six

years, in spite of frequent defeats, they maintained a bloody civil war, and when at length he sought an accommodation they desired him to cut his throat, as these were the only terms upon which they could be at peace with him. They sent to Demetrius Eucerus, king of Syria, for succors, who accordingly, with a powerful army of Jews and Syrians, overthrew Alexander and cut to pieces his mercenaries to a man, whilst most of the Jews of his party perished, and Alexander himself was forced to fly to the mountains.

53. *Alexander regains the Kingdom; his Cruelty.*—Six thousand of the rebels now pitied the misfortunes of their king and espoused his cause; and Demetrius, fearing a still greater defection, returned to Damascus. Jannæus was again successful, and at length obtained a decisive victory, in which the greater part of the rebels were slain. The remainder took refuge in the fortress of Bethsura, which he besieged and took the following year, and carried the prisoners to Jerusalem. But these successes were sullied by his barbarous cruelty. He crucified eight hundred of the captives in one day, and massacred their wives and children before their eyes, whilst he gave a feast to his wives and concubines in view of the horrid scenes, that they might glut their eyes with the spectacle.

54. *His Dying Advice to his Queen.*—The remainder of the rebels now fled the country, and Alexander spent three years in recovering the fortresses which had revolted during the civil war, and also extended his conquests beyond the Jordan. He then returned victorious to Jerusalem, and gave himself up to luxury and drunkenness, which brought on a quartan ague that subsequently proved fatal, and he died whilst besieging Ragaba, east of the Jordan. In his last moments he advised Alexandra his queen to conceal his death until the capture of the fortress, and then, on returning to Jerusalem, to convene the Pharisees, and first, to offer to govern the kingdom according to their counsels; and secondly, to resign his dead body to their discretion, whether to treat it with ignominy or with respect. She followed this advice, and the funeral obsequies of her husband were celebrated with more splendor than those of any of his

predecessors, whilst she herself was quietly established in the government.

55. ***Domination of the Pharisees; Hyrcanus High Priest.***—Alexandra was now settled on the throne, and appointed her eldest son, Hyrcanus, to be high priest, but she gave up the reins of government to the Pharisees, and thus, as Josephus observes, Alexandra had the kingdom and the Pharisees the power. The exiles of their party were now recalled, and revenge was executed upon those who had persuaded Alexander Jannæus to crucify the eight hundred rebels.

<small>Queen Alexandra. B. C. 78-69.</small>

56. ***Aristobulus joins the Opposite Party.***—Hyrcanus, the high priest, was of a weak disposition, and did not oppose their proceedings; but his younger brother, Aristobulus, incensed at the persecutions of his father's former adherents, put himself at the head of the party opposed to the Pharisees, and openly remonstrated with the queen, Alexandra, against their proceedings. The queen then put some fortresses into the hands of Aristobulus and his friends, where they might find refuge from the tyranny of the Pharisees; but Aristobulus was subsequently sent on a foreign expedition, and took that opportunity of securing the affections of the army. Alexandra died at the age of seventy-three, after a reign of nine years.

57. ***Struggles between Hyrcanus and Aristobulus.***—The reign of Hyrcanus II. did not exceed three months, for his younger brother Aristobulus had already obtained the affections of the army, and the people, being weary of the tyranny of the Pharisees, were ready for a change of government. A battle ensued between the forces raised by the Pharisees in favor of Hyrcanus and the partisans of Aristobulus, after which Hyrcanus resigned the kingdom and high priesthood, and was contented to lead a retired life under the protection of his brother.

<small>Hyrcanus II. B. C. 69.</small>

58. ***Antipater, Father of Herod, espouses the Cause of Hyrcanus.***—Aristobulus II. now ascended the throne, but soon found a more subtle enemy than his imbecile brother. ANTIPATER, the father of *Herod the Great*, an Idumæan

<small>Aristobulus II. B. C. 69-63.</small>

by birth, but Jew by religion, had been brought up in the court of Alexander Jannæus, and contracted a firm friendship with Hyrcanus, the heir-apparent to the crown. The deposition of the latter frustrated his hopes, but he insinuated to Hyrcanus that his life was in danger from Aristobulus, and at length prevailed on him to fly to Aretas, king of Arabia Petræa.

59. *Antipater intrigues with Aretas, who defeats Aristobulus.*—Antipater had previously engaged Aretas to furnish an army for the assistance of Hyrcanus, and accordingly the Arabian king led 50,000 men into Judæa, and, being joined by the Jewish partisans of Hyrcanus, he defeated Aristobulus and forced him to retire to the temple, where he besieged him.

60. *Roman Interference; Pompey arbitrates between Hyrcanus and Aristobulus.*—Meantime, Pompey was carrying on his conquests in Asia, and had sent a division of his army under Scaurus into Syria. The two brothers sent offers to Scaurus for his assistance, who accepted those of Aristobulus, and ordered Aretas to retire, under pain of an invasion. After this Pompey reduced Cœle-Syria, and was met at Damascus by ambassadors both from the Jewish nation and the two brothers to request that he would decide the quarrel. He accordingly subsequently listened to the statement of the ambassadors from Judæa, and permitted the brothers to plead their cause before him. The representatives of the Jewish people declared their wish to be subject to priests only, and not to kings. Hyrcanus pleaded the injustice of his younger brother in depriving him of the crown, whilst Aristobulus urged the imbecility of Hyrcanus and his evident unfitness for government. Pompey, however, would not openly declare his sentiments, though he saw that the weakness of Hyrcanus presented the fewest obstacles to the extension of the Roman conquests; and Aristobulus, perceiving clearly that the decision would not be in his favor, withdrew to make preparations of defence.

61. *Pompey takes Jerusalem, and restores Hyrcanus II. to the throne.*—After this Pompey reduced Aretas and took Petra, the capital of Arabia Petræa, and then marched against Aristobulus, whom he found in the

frontier fortress of Alexandrium. Pompey summoned the Jewish prince to his presence. who accordingly came down and had several interviews with him, but was at length required to sign an order for the surrender of all the fortresses to the Romans before he quitted the camp. Aristobulus now saw that negotiations were useless, and was no sooner dismissed than he fled to Jerusalem and prepared for a siege. On the approach of Pompey he submitted, and came out and offered a sum of money to prevent a war. Pompey accepted the proposal, and sent Gabinius to receive the money, but the latter found the gates shut and returned to the camp, and Aristobulus was put in chains. Pompey then marched in person to Jerusalem; the gates were opened by the party of Hyrcanus, whilst that of Aristobulus withdrew into the temple, and for three months sustained a siege. Pompey at length found that, whilst the Jews would resist an attack on the Sabbath day, they would not hinder the besieging works. On that day, therefore, he advanced the battering-rams and filled up the ditches, and at last took the place by assault and slew 12,000 of the Jews, including many priests, whose blood was mingled with the blood of their sacrifices. He then entered the temple and viewed the sanctuary and "Holy of Holies," but left the sacred vessels untouched, though it may be observed that he, who had hitherto experienced the greatest successes, never prospered in any of his undertakings after this profanation. He appointed Hyrcanus to be high priest and prince of the country, but on condition that he should submit to the Romans and pay tribute, and that he should not assume the diadem nor extend his territories beyond their ancient boundaries. Pompey then took Aristobulus and his two sons, Alexander and Antigonus, prisoners to Rome, to grace his triumph; but they subsequently escaped at different periods, and caused great disturbances.

62. *Roman Supremacy; Antipater at the Head of Affairs.*—The restoration of Hyrcanus II. to the throne was purely nominal, for Antipater was the actual governor of Judæa. But for the future the Jewish state was entirely dependent on Rome, and this yoke was confirmed by the subsequent

Hyrcanus II. (restored). B.C. 63–40.

policy of Antipater and his sons, who followed the general maxim of entire devotion to the Roman power, in order to succeed in wholly removing the reigning family of the Maccabees.

63. *Alexander, Son of Aristobulus, invades Judæa; defeated by Antipater and the Romans.*—Alexander, the eldest son of Aristobulus, had escaped from Pompey whilst being carried prisoner to Rome, and now reappeared in Judæa at the head of 10,000 infantry and 1500 horse, took several fortresses, and ravaged the country. Hyrcanus was obliged to apply to Gabinius, the Roman proconsul of Syria, for assistance, who thereupon sent some troops into Judæa under the celebrated Mark Antony, whilst he prepared to follow with a larger army. Mark Antony united his forces with those of Antipater and Hyrcanus, defeated Alexander, and compelled him to retire to the fortress of Alexandrium. Gabinius now arrived, and by the intervention of the mother of Alexander he made peace with the latter, on condition of his surrendering Alexandrium and the other fortresses which he had taken.

64. *Gabinius changes the Government to an Aristocracy; Constitution of the Sanhedrims.*—Gabinius now went to Jerusalem, and confirmed Hyrcanus in the high priesthood, but changed the government from a monarchy to an aristocracy, probably at the request of the Jews themselves, who had formerly desired such a change from Pompey (sect. 60). Hitherto, justice had been administered throughout Judæa by two Sanhedrims or tribunals. The *Lesser Sanhedrim* consisted either of twenty-three or of seven judges,* and existed in every city; the *Greater Sanhedrim*,† of which the high priest was presi-

---

* **The Lesser Sanhedrim.**—The Talmud says that this smaller court consisted of twenty-three members, but Josephus, who must have been intimately acquainted with all the judicial institutions of his nation, does not mention this smaller council, but says that the court next below the Sanhedrim was composed of seven members. Several attempts have been made to reconcile the two accounts, but without success, and it seems now generally agreed that the account of Josephus is to be preferred.

† **The Greater Sanhedrim,** which appears to have been established during the reigns of the first Maccabees, included amongst its members, 1st, *chief priests*—that is, ex-high priests—and the heads of the twenty-four classes of priests; 2d, *elders*, or princes of the tribes, and heads

dent, was composed of seventy or seventy-two persons, and sat only at Jerusalem, and tried all the appeal cases brought up from the Lesser Sanhedrims. By this constitution Jerusalem was the chief place of authority, and the principal ecclesiastical and judicial powers were necessarily vested in the high priest, apart from the royal dignity which the Maccabæan princes had previously enjoyed. Gabinius now established five independent but Great Sanhedrims—at Jerusalem, Jericho, Gadara, Amathus, and Sepphoris—and thus transferred all the civil powers of Hyrcanus to the nobles, and deprived the nation of a common centre of union. This form of government continued until B. C. 44, when Julius Cæsar restored Hyrcanus to his former power.

65. *Defeat and Death of Aristobulus and his Son Alexander.*—Aristobulus at length escaped from Rome, and raised an army, but was defeated by Gabinius and taken prisoner; and his son Alexander, who repeated the attempt whilst Gabinius was invading Egypt, met with similar ill-success on the return of the Roman general. Gabinius was subsequently superseded in the government of Syria by Crassus, who plundered the temple of 10,000 talents. In the civil wars between Pompey and Cæsar, Aristobulus and Alexander espoused the cause of the latter; but Aristobulus, who was released by Cæsar, and sent with two legions to promote his interests in Judæa, was poisoned on his way by the adherents of Pompey, and his son Alexander, who had raised forces in Judæa in expectation of the arrival of his father, was carried to Antioch and beheaded after a formal trial.

66. *Antipater assists the Romans; appointed Procurator of Judæa by Julius Cæsar.*—Meantime, Antipater was using every means to ingratiate himself with the Romans, and was rapidly rising in power and distinction. In B. C. 56 he had greatly assisted Gabinius and Mark Antony in the invasion of Egypt, and after the death of Pompey, in B. C. 48, he warmly espoused the cause of Julius Cæsar, and brought to his aid in the

---

of the family associations (sect. 134); and 3d, *scribes*, or learned men. All the *elders* and *scribes*, however, did not hold a seat, but became members either by election or by a nomination from the ruling executive authority.

Egyptian campaign the forces concentrated in Judæa, Idumæa, and part of Arabia. In return, Cæsar refused to listen to the claims of Antigonus, the only surviving son of Aristobulus, abolished the aristocratical constitution of Gabinius, restored the supreme authority to Hyrcanus, and made Antipater procurator of Judæa under the latter; and he subsequently confirmed Hyrcanus in the high priesthood and ethnarchy, and remitted the tribute to be paid to the Romans during the sabbatical year.

67. *Rise of the Herodians; Herod defies the Sanhedrim.*—Antipater had now four sons grown up—Phasael, whom he made governor of Jerusalem; HEROD, whom he appointed governor of Galilee; Joseph; and Pheroras; together with a daughter named Salome. The prosperity of Antipater and his family now rendered them odious to the Jews of the aristocratic party. Herod, by his heroism and enterprise against the banditti of his district, had gained both the admiration of the people and the esteem of Sextus Cæsar, a relative of Julius Cæsar, who had been invested with the government of Syria. But the popularity of Herod aroused the jealousy of the aristocracy. He had put the leader of the robbers to death on his own authority and without any formal trial, and his enemies persuaded Hyrcanus to summon him to Jerusalem to answer for his conduct before the Sanhedrim. Herod came clothed in purple, attended by his guards, and bearing a menacing letter from Sextus Cæsar commanding the Sanhedrim to acquit him. The assembly was overawed, but Samias stepped boldly forward, arraigned him for his crime and presumption, and predicted that the day would come when Herod would refuse them the pardon which they were now but too ready to extend to him. (See sect. 74.) The Sanhedrim now seemed inclined to act, but Hyrcanus adjourned the sitting, and thus gave Herod the opportunity to fly to Damascus; but it was with great difficulty that the youthful general was afterward dissuaded by his father and brother from marching an army to Jerusalem to avenge the insult.

68. *Julius Cæsar assassinated, 44; Antipater poisoned by Malichus.*—The assassination of Julius Cæsar, which took place shortly after, threw the Roman

empire into the greatest confusion. Cassius, one of the conspirators, seized Syria, and taxed the territory of Hyrcanus at seven hundred talents, one half of which Antipater commissioned his sons Phasael and Herod to raise, and entrusted the collection of the other half to Malichus, a nobleman who was attached to the interests of Hyrcanus. Malichus failed in procuring the proper supply, and would have been put to death, had not Antipater paid one hundred talents out of the treasury of Hyrcanus. But shortly after, Malichus, who thus owed his life to Antipater, formed a party against his preserver, and poisoned him at a banquet, and seized Jerusalem; but he met with a just punishment, for through the interference of Phasael and Herod he was afterward put to death by the Roman garrison at Tyre.

69. *Hyrcanus joins the Faction of Malichus, but is reconciled by Herod's espousing Mariamne.*—But the defeat of Brutus and Cassius at Philippi deprived the sons of Antipater of their strongest support, and the party formed by Malichus continued their opposition after the death of their leader. This faction at length gained over Hyrcanus by arousing his jealousy, but the sons of Antipater upbraided him with his desertion, and the differences between them were speedily removed by Herod's espousing Mariamne, the beautiful granddaughter of Hyrcanus, and thus connecting himself with the Maccabæan line.

70. *Faction of Malichus headed by Antigonus, 42, 41.*—On the defection of Hyrcanus the adverse party placed Antigonus, the only surviving son of Aristobulus, at their head, and even persuaded the Roman governor of Damascus to enforce the claims of the latter to the throne of Judæa. But Antigonus was totally defeated by Herod, and compelled for a period to relinquish his purpose. The next year the discontented party sent a deputation to Mark Antony to complain that Phasael and Herod were undermining the authority of Hyrcanus. Meantime, however, Herod had reminded Antony of the services which his father Antipater had formerly rendered in the Egyptian expedition (sect. 66), and had conciliated the Triumviri by valuable presents, and thus induced the latter to disregard the complaints of

a faction and to make him and his brother Phasael tetrarchs of Palestine.

71. *Parthians place Antigonus on the Throne; Herod escapes to Rome, 40.*—Antony now proceeded to Egypt, where he wasted his time in luxurious ease and dalliance with Cleopatra, leaving the affairs of Syria and Asia Minor to fall into the utmost confusion. The people of Syria, exhausted by successive exactions, refused to pay further tribute. The Parthians, under their king's son, Pacorus, marched to aid the revolt, and after mastering Syria, Pacorus was induced, by the offer of 1000 talents and five hundred female slaves, to assist in placing Antigonus on the throne. An undecisive struggle ensued between the forces of the Parthians and those of the two brothers, after which Phasael and Hyrcanus were induced, contrary to the advice of Herod, to visit the Parthian governor of Syria and submit the dispute to his arbitration. The Parthian governor, however, treacherously put them both in chains; Phasael committed suicide, Hyrcanus was barbarously mutilated to incapacitate him from exercising the high priesthood, whilst Herod escaped from Jerusalem and hastened to Rome.

Antigonus.
B. C. 40-37.
72. *Herod obtains the Kingdom from the Triumvirate.*—At Rome, Herod had intended to request the Triumvirate—Octavius Cæsar, Antony, and Lepidus—to confer the throne of Judæa on Aristobulus, brother of Mariamne, but he found Antony so willing to advance his interests that a decree was obtained from the senate appointing himself king of the Jews.

73. *Reduces Antigonus; End of the Maccabæan Dynasty, 37.*—Herod now returned to Jerusalem, raised an army, and carried on the war against Antigonus. The Romans, who had already driven the Parthians beyond the Euphrates, now assisted him in obtaining the throne, and after three years he had besieged and taken Jerusalem and gained possession of Judæa. During the siege, which lasted six months, Herod endeavored to conciliate the people by consummating his marriage with Mariamne, and thus contracting an affinity with the Maccabæan family, but Antigonus was sent in chains to

Antioch, where he was executed by Antony as a common malefactor. Thus ignominiously ended the dynasty of the Maccabees, one hundred and twenty-nine years from the commencement of the authority of Judas Maccabæus, and one hundred and twenty-six years from the acknowledgment of his power by Antiochus Eupator.

III. *History of the Jews under the Herodians to the Commencement of New Testament History.*

74. ***Massacres his Opponents and Propitiates Antony.***—Immediately after Herod had taken Jerusalem and ascended the throne it was necessary that he should confirm his authority in Judæa and discharge his obligations to Mark Antony. In effecting the former his conduct was marked by cruelty and revenge. All the Sanhedrim were massacred except Pollio and Samias, who had counselled the surrender of the city, and all the adherents of Antigonus who could be discovered were summarily put to death. Meantime, the Romans, exasperated at the length of the siege, had filled Jerusalem with bloodshed and rapine. Herod declared that they would make his kingdom a desert, and paid them a large sum of money to desist. Nevertheless, he found means, by forcing contributions from the wealthy and confiscating the property of the slain, to send sufficient plunder to Antony as would in part discharge his obligation.

<small>Herod the Great. B. C. 37–4.</small>

75. ***Appoints Ananel High Priest.***—The office of high priest was now vacant by the execution of Antigonus and mutilation of Hyrcanus, who returned to Judæa, but was put to death a few years afterward on a suspicion of treason. According to hereditary succession, it belonged of right to Aristobulus, brother of Mariamne, for whom Herod had at first intended to ask the kingdom; but the king was afraid lest the influence attached to the office should prove dangerous to himself, and, not being able to undertake it in his own person, he gave it to an obscure Babylonian priest named Ananel.

76. ***Aristobulus obtains the Office, but is Drowned.***—The pride of Alexandra, the mother of Mariamne and Aristobulus, was now aroused at this insult. She appealed

to Cleopatra, who immediately began to interest Antony in the matter, and Herod found it necessary to depose Ananel and elevate Aristobulus to the high priesthood. But the latter soon excited the fatal jealousy of the monarch. Aristobulus was tall and eminently handsome, and exhibited in his countenance the noble qualities and lineaments of the Maccabæan race; and at the feast of tabernacles, whilst officiating at the altar in the splendid robes of his office, the assembled multitude burst into loud acclamations of joy and goodwill. After the festival Herod was entertained by Alexandra near Jericho, and at his instigation Aristobulus bathed in the midst of his attendants and acquaintance, and in a pretended sport was drowned after repeated immersion.

77. *Herod summoned by Antony.*—Herod affected to shed tears at the accident, but Alexandra was convinced of his participation in the murder, and again applied to Cleopatra. The latter had now joined Antony at Laodicea in Syria, and through her influence Antony was persuaded to summon Herod to Laodicea to answer for his conduct. Herod was obliged to obey, but by a profusion of gifts so propitiated Antony that on his arrival he was immediately acquitted.

78. *First Secret Instructions respecting Mariamne.*—Before Herod left Jerusalem he privately instructed his uncle Joseph (husband of his sister Salome) to put Mariamne to death in case he should be condemned, as he feared, lest Antony should make her his partner. Joseph foolishly divulged the secret to Mariamne as a proof of her husband's love. Meantime, Salome, who was the firebrand of the family, had become indignant at the proud treatment she received from Mariamne, and on the return of Herod insinuated to the latter that Mariamne had carried on an illicit intercourse with Joseph. Mariamne soon persuaded Herod of the unfounded nature of the charge, but subsequently betrayed her knowledge of the secret instructions he had given to Joseph. This he considered to be a proof of her guilt, and, though he restrained himself from putting her to death, yet he immediately ordered the execution of Joseph.

79. *Fall of Antony at Actium; Herod conciliates*

Augustus, and is confirmed on the Throne.—In B. C. 31, Antony met with a decisive overthrow at Actium. Herod immediately sent a special message exhorting him to slay Cleopatra, seize her treasures and kingdom, and thus raise another army with which to contend for empire. Antony, however, seemed bent on his own ruin, and Herod obtained an audience with Augustus at Rhodes. In this interview he boldly acknowledged all he had done, and all he would have done, for Antony, and even stated the last counsels he had given to that infatuated man; and having thus enabled Augustus to judge of his fidelity to others, he plainly offered him the same friendship and engaged to be equally faithful. This manly frankness, seconded by liberal presents, obtained the favor of Augustus and secured the kingdom to Herod, whose dominions included the whole of the territories possessed by the late Maccabees, and were divided into five districts— namely, *West of the Jordan*—1. Judæa; 2. Samaria; 3. Galilee. *East*—4. Peræa.* *South*—5. Idumæa. And when Augustus visited Herod some years afterward he was received with the most royal liberality and magnificence.

80. *Second Secret Instructions respecting Mariamne; her Execution.*—Before Herod left Jerusalem this second time he committed Mariamne and her mother Alexandra to the care of his friend Soemus, with similar directions to those he had previously given to Joseph— viz. that if Augustus compassed his death, Mariamne and Alexandra should not be permitted to survive him. But Soemus was induced by the entreaties of the women, by their kind presents, and by his own belief that Herod

---

* **Division of Peræa.**—Peræa, which signifies the country on the opposite side, was a general name for any district belonging to or closely connected with a country from the main part of which it was separated by a sea or river. The name *Peræa* was therefore applied in its more extended sense to the whole territory stretching from the river Arnon to Mount Hermon, between the Jordan and the desert, and was subdivided into eight districts or cantons—viz. 1. Peræa, in the more limited sense, which only extended from the Arnon to the Jabbok; 2. Gilead, or Galaaditis; 3. Decapolis, or Ten Cities, of which little is known for certain; 4. Gaulonitis; 5. Batanea, the ancient Bashan; 6. Ituræa or Auranitis; 7. Trachonitis; 8. Abilene, in the extreme north, among the mountains of Anti-Libanus between Baalbec and Damascus.

would never return in safety, to reveal the orders for their destruction. Accordingly, when Herod came back to Jerusalem after his interview with Augustus he was received by Mariamne with coldness and dislike. For a whole year the king fluctuated between love and resentment, but at length Mariamne brought matters to a crisis by pointedly refusing to return his love, and by upbraiding him with the murder of her grandfather and brother. Salome, actuated by a fiendish desire of revenge, seized this opportunity for suborning the cup-bearer of Herod to assert that Mariamne had bribed him to administer a potion to her husband. The king immediately put his wife's confidential eunuch to the torture, thinking he must be aware of the cause of her altered conduct; but the eunuch disclosed nothing relating to the potion, but admitted that her estrangement arose from her knowledge of the orders with which Soemus had been entrusted. Herod was now persuaded that nothing but an illicit intercourse with Mariamne could have wrung the secret from so faithful an officer as Soemus. Accordingly, he ordered the latter to be instantly executed, and then summoned his more immediate friends to try his wife for administering the potion. Mariamne was found guilty and condemned to death, but Herod commuted the sentence to imprisonment. His bloodthirsty sister Salome, however, persuaded him that her death was necessary as a security against a popular tumult, and she was led away to execution. Mariamne met her death with a firmness which became her race, though her own mother Alexandra, from the fear of sharing in her punishment, assailed her on the way with the most violent and indecent reproaches. The vehement love of Herod for this beautiful princess outlived his jealousy, and his remorse could not be removed by the pleasures of the table or the chase. He retired from society, and was at length seized with fever and delirium. Alexandra, thinking it impossible for him to recover, laid a plot for seizing the government, but it was discovered to Herod by the officers whom she endeavored to corrupt, and he instantly ordered her to be put to death.

81. ***Herod introduces Heathen Customs and Public Games.***—When Herod had recovered his health he sedulously endeavored to remove the prejudices of the

Jews and Romanize Judæa. He instituted horse- and chariot-races and public games in honor of Augustus, and built a theatre and amphitheatre in Jerusalem in which celebrated musicians contended for victory, animals were exhibited, and gladiators fought with wild beasts and with each other.

82. *Conspiracy of Ten.*—By these proceedings, and especially by the adornment of the public places with the trophies of the conquests of Augustus, Herod had acted in direct opposition to the Jewish prejudices, and appeared as the enemy of their country and their God. Ten of the most zealous malcontents formed a conspiracy to assassinate him in the theatre. The plot was discovered, the conspirators were arrested with daggers concealed about their persons, and were immediately put to death with the most cruel tortures.

83. *Increases the Fortifications, erects Public Works, and rebuilds the Temple.*—Herod now determined to increase his fortifications as a security for himself and a provision against rebellions, and to display his power and gratify his magnificence by the erection of costly and splendid public works. In Jerusalem he already possessed two fortresses, the palace and castle of Antonia, which had been named after Antony. He now rebuilt the city of Samaria, and bestowed on it the name of Sebaste in honor of Augustus, and erected a temple in it which he dedicated to Cæsar. He converted the Tower of Strato into a grand city and seaport, and built an artificial harbor with moles and breakwater and surrounded with a wall and towers, and to this new city he gave the name of Cæsarea. He also erected at the source of the Jordan, called *Panium*, a temple of white marble, which he dedicated to Augustus. And at length he was led to form the bold design of pulling down the old temple at Jerusalem, which had sustained great damage during the civil wars, and of rebuilding it entirely on a more magnificent scale. (An account of this stupendous work may be found at sect. 360, *note.*)

84. *Famine in Judæa; Herod's Generosity.*—In the thirteenth year of the reign a dreadful famine visited Judæa and Samaria, during which Herod made such sacrifices to relieve his people, and exhibited such noble

generosity, that had not his crimes branded his memory with the indelible mark of tyranny he would have ranked amongst the kings who had been benefactors to their subjects. He stripped his palaces of every ornament of silver and gold, and, loading a vessel with the spoils, sent it to Egypt to purchase corn, and for a long time fed the whole mass of the population at his own cost. By his kind interference also Agrippa relieved the Jewish colonies of Asia from the exactions they suffered, and obtained a restitution of the privileges which had been previously confirmed to them by the Romans.

85. *Intrigues of Salome and Antipater; Trial and Execution of Alexander and Aristobulus, the Sons of Mariamne.*—Herod ruled from his confirmation on his throne by Augustus until his death, a period of nearly thirty years, undisturbed by a single war, for the occasional hostilities with the robbers of Trachonitis and the Arab chiefs that supported them scarcely deserve the name of warfare. But his prosperity as a sovereign is strangely contrasted with the long series of domestic tragedies that mark the latter years of his life. The details of this complicated tissue of crimes and intrigues will be found in the pages of Josephus, but the following is a summary of the events: Herod, though not wanting in natural affection for his children, was still more jealous of the maintenance of his authority as monarch, and when the latter was threatened his ungovernable passions quickly overcame the dictates of Nature and justice. By Mariamne he had two sons, Alexander and Aristobulus, whom he sent to be educated for three years at Rome under the immedate inspection of Augustus, and at the expiration of that time he himself brought them back to Judæa. The return of the young men diffused general satisfaction, but aroused the fears of Salome and of all those who had participated in the condemnation of their mother Mariamne. The latter party accordingly spread reports that the young men disliked their father, and only regarded him as the murderer of their mother; and at length Herod was informed by his sister Salome and brother Pheroras of the pretended revengeful temper of the sons of Mariamne. Herod was exceedingly afflicted at the intelligence. He had a son, Antipater, by his first

wife, Doris, born before he ascended the throne, and he now sent for Antipater to court, and hoped by taking him into favor to repress the rebellious spirit of Alexander and Aristobulus. Antipater followed the policy which his aunt and uncle had commenced, and did his utmost to irritate Herod against the sons of Mariamne. Being subsequently sent to Rome, he wrote frequent letters from thence to exasperate the king and awaken his fears, and at length Herod carried the two brothers to Rome to accuse them before Cæsar. Augustus heard the charge, but the eloquence of Alexander moved the compassion of the emperor, and by the advice of the latter a reconciliation was effected. Herod and his three sons then returned home together, but Salome and Antipater were soon enabled to persuade the king that Alexander and Aristobulus were plotting against him, and he sought and obtained permission to accuse them before a Roman council at Berytus. The Roman governors of Syria, the members of Herod's family, and one hundred and fifty of the chief persons of Syria now assembled together, and Herod appeared before them and accused his two sons with all the vehemence of a bitter enemy. The two young men, however, could only be proved guilty of uttering some reproachful speeches, and not of any malice or conspiracy against their father. Part of the assembly confirmed to Herod the power of life and death over his sons, but did not consider that their crimes deserved a capital punishment; but the majority decreed that the princes deserved to die; and, though Herod did not immediately act upon this decision, yet learning shortly afterward of the interest taken by the people in the fate of the criminals, he became satisfied of their guilt and ordered them to be executed.

86. *Conspiracy and Trial of Antipater.* — Antipater was now afraid lest Herod should discover his participation in the destruction of the sons of Mariamne, and accordingly plotted with Pheroras, the brother of Herod, to despatch the king by poison. Antipater then removed to Rome, that he might not be suspected of taking a part in the murder, but meantime Pheroras fell sick and died, and Herod, being informed that the latter had been poisoned by his wife, set on foot the most strict investigation, and at length discovered the plot against

himself. Antipater returned without suspecting any danger, but on reaching Sebaste was seized and brought before the council. His guilt was distinctly proved, and he was condemned and thrown into prison, and an embassy was despatched to Cæsar to request his final decision in the matter.

87. *Golden Eagle pulled down at Jerusalem.*—Whilst the embassy was at Rome, Herod was attacked by a violent and painful disease. Judas and Matthias, who were the chief among the teachers of the law, believed that he could never recover, and induced the people to throw down the golden eagle which Herod had erected over the temple contrary to the laws and customs of the Jewish nation. The conspirators were seized, and though Herod was so ill that he could not sit up, yet he assembled his council, who recommended the punishment of the ringleaders, and Herod ordered them to be burned.

88. *Herod's Sickness and Cruelty.*—Herod's disease soon increased in violence. The lower parts of his body ulcerated, and he was frequently thrown into strong convulsions. He tried the warm baths of Callirrhoe, but without deriving any benefit, and his torments, instead of moving him to repentance, incited him to fresh cruelties.

89. *Shuts up the Principal Jews in the Hippodrome; Execution of Antipater.*—Maddened by his agony, Herod shut up the principal Jews in the hippodrome at Jericho, and gave orders that they should be put to death immediately after his own decease, that mourners might not be wanting at his funeral.* At length the embassy returned from Rome, bringing Cæsar's permission either for the exile or execution of Antipater. Though revived for a moment by the news, Herod was soon again distracted by his torments, and endeavored to commit suicide. An alarm spread through the palace and reached the ears of Antipater, who then tried to bribe his jailer to permit his escape, but the man communicated the proposal to Herod, and Antipater was immediately put to death.

---

* It must also have been about this time that Herod gave orders for the murder of the infants, as recorded in St. Matthew's Gospel, ii. 16–18.

90. *Death of Herod; his Will.*—On the fifth day after the execution, Herod died, having reigned thirty-four years from the death of Antigonus and thirty-seven years from the time of receiving the kingdom from the Roman Triumvirate. By his will he gave the kingdom of Judæa to *Archelaus;* the tetrarchy of Galilee and Peræa, in its more limited sense (sect. 79, *note*), to *Antipas;* Ituræa, Gaulonitis, Trachonitis, and Batanea to *Philip;* and a large sum of money, with the cities of Jamnia, Azotus, and Phasaelis, to his sister Salome; besides handsome estates and money to each of his relations and legacies to the emperor Augustus and his wife Julia. This will was read aloud to the soldiers amidst loud acclamations, and Archelaus was proclaimed king, whilst the Jewish chiefs were released from their previous confinement in the hippodrome.

91. *Character of Herod.*—The character of Herod has been well summed up by Josephus. He was universally cruel and of an ungovernable anger, but, though he trampled justice under foot, he was always a favorite of fortune. From a private station he rose to the throne, escaped a thousand dangers, and prolonged his life to the full boundary of old age. In his own family he appeared most miserable, but in himself most prosperous, for there was not one of his enemies whom he did not overcome.

92. We have thus brought the Old Testament History, a period of probation and preparation, to its natural close. In the last year or two of the reign of Herod the Forerunner appeared and Christ was born. The fulfilment of the Law and the Prophets in the person of the Messiah, and the history of the Jewish nation from the death of Herod to the destruction of Jerusalem, are included in the New Testament period, to which the author has devoted a separate volume.

JEWISH SECTS.

93. Classification.—Several religious sects appear to have sprung up amongst the Jews during the government of the Asamonean princes, of which the principal were the PHARISEES, SADDUCEES, and ESSENES. To these may be added the SCRIBES, HERODIANS, SAMARITANS, GALILÆANS, and SICARII.

94. I. The Pharisees, originated about B. C. 135.—From *pharash*, "separated" or "set apart." These were the most numerous and distinguished sect amongst the Jews, and were instituted in the reign of John Hyrcanus (p. 310), B. C. 135, though they are supposed to have first appeared soon after the institution of the Sadducees, B. C. 250.

95. Tenets.—The Pharisees held the following tenets: 1. The existence of angels and spirits; 2. The resurrection of the dead; 3. Pre-existence and transmigration of souls; and, 4. The eternal happiness of the Jews in the terrestrial kingdom of the Messiah, which they derived from the merits of Abraham, their practice of circumcision, their offering of sacrifices, and their knowledge of God.

96. Practices.—I. THE PHARISEES WERE MOST STRICT IN THEIR MANNERS. They offered up long prayers in public places, sanctimoniously repaired the sepulchres of the prophets, considered themselves defiled by the company of sinners, and compassed sea and land to make Jewish proselytes of the Gentiles.

II. THE PHARISEES INTERPRETED CERTAIN OF THE MOSAIC LAWS MOST LITERALLY. They considered the laws of retaliation and divorce, which Moses had *tolerated*, to be morally right; that an oath was not binding unless the name of God was specified in it; and that it was unlawful to pluck ears of corn or heal the sick on the Sabbath.

III. THE PHARISEES REVERENTLY OBSERVED THE TRADITIONS OR DECREES OF THE ELDERS. They punctiliously paid tithes in temple-offerings, even of the most trifling thing; wore broad phylacteries and large fringes to their garments; fasted twice a week with great austerity; purified cups, vessels, and couches after meals; and washed their hands up to the wrists both before and after meat.

97. *II. Sadducees, originated about B. C. 250.*—Derived their name from Sadok, pupil of Antigonus Sochæus, president of the Sanhedrim, B. C. 250 (sect. 11). Sochæus taught that man ought to serve God disinterestedly, and not from fear of punishment or hope of reward. Sadok, his pupil, inferred from this that there was no future state of rewards or punishments. The Sadducees, or followers of Sadok, were inconsiderable in point of numbers, but of the first distinction and eminence.

98. *Tenets.*—The Sadducees believed—1. That there was no resurrection, neither angel nor spirit; 2. That there was no fate or overruling Providence; 3. That no faith was to be placed in the traditions, but that the letter of Scripture was to be adhered to only, and the five books of Moses to be preferred.

99. *III. Essenes, originated about B. C. 110.*—These are not mentioned in the New Testament, though they are supposed to be alluded to in Matt. xix. 12; Col. ii. 18, 23. They were divided into two classes—viz. 1. *The Practical Essenes*, who lived in society, and even married, though with much circumspection; 2. *The Contemplative Essenes*, also called Therapeutæ, or Physicians, because they cured the diseases of the soul. These devoted themselves to a life of celibacy and meditation.

100. *Tenets.*—Both classes of Essenes were exceedingly abstemious, exemplary in their moral deportment, averse to profane swearing, and rigid in the observance of the Sabbath. They believed—1. That the soul was immortal, though there was no resurrection of the body; 2. That there was a state of future rewards and punishments; and, 3. That everything was ordered by an eternal fatality or chain of causes.

101. *Scribes and Lawyers.*—These generally belonged to the sect of Pharisees, and took their names from their employment, which at first was *transcribing* the Law, but they subsequently became public teachers

of it, and were consulted in all difficult points of doctrine or duty. Lawyers and Scribes appear to be synonymous terms, but Macknight conjectures the Scribes to have been the public expounders of the Law, whilst the Lawyers studied it in private.

102. **Herodians, Samaritans, Galilæans, and Sicarii.**—Several other sects are alluded to in Scripture, of whom may be mentioned the following: I. THE HERODIANS, who were a political faction rather than a religious sect, and derived their name from Herod the Great, to whose family they were strongly attached. They were distinguished by their concurring in Herod's plan of subjecting himself and the country to the Romans, and in his heathen practices. II. THE SAMARITANS, of whom full mention is made in sect. 507. III. GALILÆANS and ZEALOTS, who were followers of that Judas the Galilæan who persuaded the people to refuse to pay tribute to Rome, because it was due to God alone. Acts v. 37. IV. THE SICARII, or Assassins. Acts xxi. 38.

THE

FOURTEEN APOCRYPHAL BOOKS.

103. **1 Esdras, or Ezra.**—This is only extant in Greek. It contains an account of the celebration of the passover in the reign of Josiah; the story of the three competitors for the favor of Darius; and the history of the return of the Jews from their Babylonian captivity, the building of the temple, and re-establishment of divine worship. It is full of improbabilities and contradictions, defies the Scripture narrative and all chronological order, but contains nothing exceptionable in doctrine or precept.

104. **2 Esdras.**—This is only extant in Latin, and its author is unknown. It contains a series of pretended revelations and predictions concerning the restoration of Jerusalem, character of the Messiah, etc., and abounds with absurd rabbinical tales and fables.

THE FOURTEEN APOCRYPHAL BOOKS. 333

105. *Tobit.*—Professes to relate the history of Tobit and his family, who were carried into captivity to Nineveh by Shalmaneser (sect. 505); it contains, however, so many rabbinical fables and allusions to Babylonian demonology that it has been looked upon as an amusing fiction inculcating pious and moral lessons.

106. *Judith.*—Originally written in Chaldee and translated into Latin. It professes to relate the defeat of the Assyrians through the instrumentality of Judith, who beheaded their general Holofernes, but in consequence of its numerous geographical, historical, and chronological difficulties it has been considered rather as a drama or parable.

107. *Rest of the Chapters of the Book of Esther.*—These are seven in number, and were written by some Hellenistic Jew. Both Jerome and Grotius consider them to be pure fiction.

108. *Wisdom of Solomon.*—Commonly ascribed to Solomon, though the style is not like him, and it was never extant in Hebrew. It contains—first, an encomium on Wisdom, and then a series of reflections on the early history of the Jews and their subsequent proneness to idolatry.

109. *Ecclesiasticus, or Wisdom of Jesus the Son of Sirach.*—This book has been ascribed to Solomon, but the style and other internal evidence disprove the supposition. It was written in Hebrew—or rather in Syro-Chaldee—by Jesus son of Sirach, who appears to have travelled in pursuit of knowledge, and, being thoroughly versed in the Scriptures, had blended many things from the prophets with the sentences ascribed to Solomon and the result of his own observation. This was subsequently translated into Greek for the use of the Alexandrian Jews by his grandson, who seems to have been also named Jesus, and to have been the son of another Sirach. The book has been held in general and deserved esteem by the Western Church, and was introduced into the public service by the venerable Reformers and compilers of the English Liturgy.

110. *Book of Baruch.*—The author and original language of this book are uncertain, and it is only extant in Greek and Syriac. The principal subject of the book is

an epistle pretended to be sent by Jehoiakim and the captive Jews in Babylon to their brethren in Judah and Jerusalem.

111. *Song of the Three Children.*—This does not appear to have been ever extant in Hebrew, and though it has always been admired for the piety of its sentiments, yet it was never admitted to be canonical until recognized by the Council of Trent.

112. *History of Susanna.*—This is evidently the work of some Hellenistic Jew, and is considered by some modern critics to be both spurious and fabulous.

113. *Bel and the Dragon.*—This is not extant either in Hebrew or Chaldee, and was always rejected by the Jewish Church, and, indeed, obtained little credit until admitted to be canonical by the Council of Trent. The author designed to make idolatry ridiculous, but he transported to Babylon the worship of animals, which was never practised there.

114. *Prayer of Manasses.*—Said to have been composed by that monarch during his captivity, but, though not unworthy of the occasion, it has been rejected as spurious even by the Church of Rome.

115. *1 and 2 Maccabees.*—These books are so called because they relate the patriotic and gallant exploits of Judas Maccabæus and his brethren, and are both admitted to be canonical by the Romish Church.

116. BOOK I. relates the history of the Jews from the beginning of the reign of Antiochus Epiphanes to the death of Simon, and it was probably written in the reign of John Hyrcanus, either by himself or under his superintendence. It is a most valuable historical monument.

117. BOOK II. is very inferior to Book I., and is a compilation from various histories by an unknown author, and must therefore be read with caution. It contains the history of about fifteen years—viz. from the sending of Heliodorus by Seleucus to plunder the temple to the defeat of Nicanor by Judas Maccabæus.

EXAMINATION QUESTIONS,

INCLUDING THE

CAMBRIDGE EXAMINATION-PAPERS IN OLD TESTAMENT HISTORY
FOR VARIOUS YEARS, IN CHRONOLOGICAL ORDER.

[The figures at the end of each Question refer to the sections, or pages where marked p., where the Answer may be found.]

Give the derivation of the word Pentateuch (p. 35).

Give the derivation of Genesis (p. 35).

How many years does the history of this book occupy? (p. 35.)

What are the principal events recorded in Genesis? (p. 35.)

State in order the work of each of the six days occupied by God in the creation. Sect. 1.

What were the words of God immediately before creating man? 2.

Explain these words, and say how far they lead us to imagine a plurality of Persons to have been engaged in the creation of the world. 2.

What blessing did God pronounce on man after his creation? 3.

By what rivers was the garden of Eden watered? 4.

Of what were the ordinances of the Sabbath and of marriage typical? 4, *note*.

Relate the circumstances connected with the fall of our first parents. 5.

What curse did God pronounce on the serpent? 5.

Can you trace here the promise of a Redeemer? 6.

Describe the events connected with the murder of Abel. 7.

Give the names of the heads of families mentioned as the posterity of Cain. 8.

To whom is the invention of musical instruments ascribed? 8.

State the posterity of Adam through Seth. 9.

Who was the father of Enoch? 9.

What was his end? 9.

What is said of Enoch in the Old and New Testament? 9.

For what is Methuselah noted? 9.

What circumstances led to the building of the ark? 10.

Of whom was Noah the son? 9.

From which of Adam's sons was he descended? 9.

Who was the father of the Canaanites? 15.

Give the date of the Deluge. 11.

How long did Noah live after it? 12.

What allusion is made to Noah in St. Peter's Epistles? 10.

What curse was pronounced by Noah on Ham, and what blessing on Shem and Japheth respectively? and on what occasion? 12.

What is the meaning of the promise given to Japheth, "he shall dwell in the tents of Shem"? 14.

From which of the three were the Jews descended? 16.

What other parts of the globe were peopled by his posterity? 14–16.

What portions of the world were peopled by the descendants of Japheth, and what by those of Ham? 14–16.

What blessing or promise did God make to Noah after the Flood, and by what token was the promise confirmed? 11.

Of what is Noah's ark a type or figure? 79.

"Whoso sheddeth man's blood, by man shall his blood be shed." On what occasion were these words first pronounced? 11.

When was man forbidden to eat flesh? and under what restriction? 11.

Where was the tower of Babel built? 17.

What does the name signify? 17.

What were the objects for which the tower of Babel was built? 17.

Wherein did the sin of those engaged in building it consist? 17.

How was that sin visited? 17.

Relate the circumstances which led to the confusion of tongues at Babel. 17.

What city was afterward built upon or near the site of Babel? 17.

What promises did God make to Abraham? and on what occasions were they renewed? 20, 21, 26, 28, 29.

Name the generations from Noah to Abram. 18.

Give the probable date of the birth of Abram. 19.

How many children had Haran? and who were they? 19.

What was the religion of Abraham's father, and probably his own? 20.

Was Abraham always called "father of the faithful"? 42.

What rite did God ordain at this time? 29.

What was the distinguishing feature of Abraham's character? 42.

Illustrate it by incidents of his life. 20, 36.

What command did Abram receive from God at Ur? 20.

What peculiar appellations did the patriarch Abraham receive? 28.

What were the three distinct acts of great faith for which he became so eminently distinguished? 42.

To which of these in particular is reference made when it is said that "his faith was imputed to him for righteousness"? 42.

What was the native place of Abraham? 20, *note*.

State where Abraham was living before his call, the relationship between him and Lot, and the date of his call. 20.

When was his name changed from "Abram" to "Abraham," and what is the signification of the latter? 29.

Why is he called the "father of the faithful"? 28.

Who was Melchizedek? 24.

EXAMINATION QUESTIONS.

How is he described in the Epistle to the Hebrews? 25.

Where, and on what occasion, did Abraham meet with him? 24.

State what is recorded to have taken place during the interview. 24.

Which is the first mention of tithes? 24.

Give an account of the subsequent movements of Abraham. 32.

By what different races was Canaan at this time peopled? 23.

For how long a time did God say that his seed should be afflicted? 26.

At what time must this affliction have commenced, according to chronology? 26.

Show how the promises made to him were fulfilled. 28.

Who was the child of promise? 28.

How may Isaac be called a type of Christ? 36, *note.*

What is the meaning of a type? 78.

State the different particulars which we gather from Scripture of the history of Lot. 20, 22, 24, 31.

What is the earliest account given of making wine? 12.

The earliest mention of money? 32.

State the circumstances attending the birth of Ishmael. 27.

"And he will be a wild man; his hand will be against every man, and every man's hand against him." Of whom was this said? 27.

How has the prediction been fulfilled? 34.

What circumstances are connected with the destruction of Sodom? 31.

Why was Ishmael cast forth from Abraham's family? 34.

What remarkable deliverance did he experience immediately after his ejection? 34.

What nation descended from him? 34.

When did Sarah die? and where was she buried? 37.

Relate the circumstances attendant on the marriage of Isaac. 38.

Who was Abraham's second wife? and what nation was descended from one of his sons by her? 39.

What is the meaning of the word "Jacob"? 40.

In what year did Abraham die? and where was he buried? 41.

Relate the deception practised by Jacob upon his father Isaac. 46.

What were the consequences to which it led, and under what circumstances did the brothers, Esau and Jacob, meet after their separation? 47, 53, 55.

Give a brief sketch of the life of Isaac. (See Index, *Isaac,* 33, 36, 38, 40, 46.)

Who was his mother? 30, 33.

In what way was Jacob deceived by his sons? 61.

Give an account of the life of Esau. Who were his posterity? 40, 43, 45, 46, 48.

Relate the circumstances of Jacob's vision at Bethel. 47.

What was his vow? 47.

What did God afterward say to Jacob at Bethel? 57.

Explain the meaning of the term "Israel." 54.

Where and how did Jacob obtain that name? 54.

What was the occasion of his fear and distress at the time? 53.

How was his prayer answered? 55.

Give a brief account of the history of Jacob. (See Index, *Jacob.*)

Give the names of the family of Jacob by his two wives. 50.

What prediction did he utter on his deathbed respecting Levi? and how was it fulfilled? 72.

What were his prophecies with reference to his other children? 72.

Show briefly how these prophecies were fulfilled. 73.

At what age did he die? and where was he buried? 74.

What were the circumstances under which Joseph was sold into Egypt? and by what steps did he attain to the office which he ultimately held? 61, 64, 65.

Relate the dreams of Pharaoh which led to Joseph's release from prison. 65.

How did Joseph interpret these dreams? and what was his consequent promotion? 65, 66.

Relate the principal events in the life of Joseph. (See Index, *Joseph.*)

How is Joseph a type of Christ? 77.

What first led to the establishment of the Israelites in Egypt? 69.

What proportion of the produce of land in Egypt in the time of Joseph was the king entitled to? 65.

By whom was the law fixing the proportion first established? 65.

Sum up the typical intimations and prophecies of a Saviour to be found in the book of Genesis. 79.

What is the meaning of the word "Exodus"? p. 68.

State the circumstances attendant on the birth of Moses and his preservation. 81, 82.

What is the meaning of his name? 82.

Relate the circumstances of his flight into Midian and of his call by God at Horeb. 83, 84.

By what name did God make himself known to him? 84.

Where did he meet with Aaron? 85.

How did Pharaoh entertain their demand? 86.

What length of time were the Israelites in Egypt? 100.

Give a brief account of their condition during the closing years of their residence there. 81.

By what signs was he ordered to convince the Israelites that he was sent by God. 85.

Name the plagues of Egypt. 88-96, 98.

What institution commemorated the last of them? 99.

What were the circumstances of the institution of the feast of the passover? 97.

Was it known by any other name? 99.

What answers to it under the Christian dispensation? 196.

What persons were excluded from the observance of it? 97.

Give a brief account of the ceremonies to be observed in the celebration of it. 97.

EXAMINATION QUESTIONS.

Of what was the paschal lamb a type? 152.

In what year did the Israelites leave Egypt? 100.

How were they led, and where did they encamp? 100.

How was the passage of the Red Sea effected? 101.

What was the fate of their enemies? 101.

Trace their wanderings to Sin. 102.

By what means were the children of Israel fed during their travels in the barren wilderness? 102.

And what peculiarity attended the supply of their food? 103.

What is the meaning of the word "manna"? 103.

What circumstances occurred in their journey to Rephidim? 104.

With what enemy was Joshua here engaged? and what was the result of the battle? 105.

By whom was Moses visited? and what measures did he adopt in consequence of the advice given him? 106.

Where did the Israelites encamp in the third month of the Exodus? 107.

Enumerate the different miracles which were wrought on behalf of the children of Israel from the time of their departure from Egypt until they came into the wilderness of Sinai, and show what some of those miracles typified. 101, 102, 104, 152.

State the circumstances attending the promulgation of the moral, civil, and ceremonial law. 108, 109.

During the absence of Moses what crime did the Israelites commit? 110.

What were the consequences of their idolatry? 110.

What circumstances attended Moses' second abode on Mount Sinai? 111.

What building was afterward raised? and who were consecrated priests? 111.

In what commandments and precepts were the Jews warned against false prophets, divination, etc.? 112.

When is the Sabbath first mentioned in the history of the children of Israel? 114.

Is it then spoken of as a new appointment for the first time made, or as an institution already existing? 114.

When was it first instituted? 1.

How does the reason assigned in the fourth commandment for its observation show its universal obligation? 114.

What was the object of the cities of refuge? 116.

How many of them were there? 116.

Under what limitations were they available? 116.

What law of sale existed among the Jews? 126.

What were the laws of usury? of pledges? of heirship? 127, 128.

Mention some of the miscellaneous precepts regarding covetousness. 130.

What was the law respecting slavery? 132.

What was the condition of the slaves? 132.

From what funds was the tabernacle built? 139.
Give a description of its external form. 139.
What was the Holy of Holies? 140.
Who was privileged to enter into it? and when? 153.
What were the contents of the ark of the covenant? 144.
What was the ark of the covenant? 144.
Where was it placed? 144.
What was its fate at different periods? and where was it ultimately deposited? 144, *note*.
Where was the altar of incense placed? 141.
What other furniture had the Most Holy Place besides the ark? 145, 146.
What was the Shechinah? 147.
Describe the court of the tabernacle. 148.
What was its furniture? 149, 150.
When was the tabernacle completed? 151.
What typical intimations do you find of the Messiah in Exodus? 152.
What is the meaning of the word "Leviticus"? p. 95.
To what family amongst the Israelites was the priesthood appropriated? 154.
Into how many classes were the priests divided? and by whom? 156, *note*.
Who and what were the Nazarites? 201.
Describe the sacerdotal orders. 153.
What provision was made for the tribe of Levi? 164.
What were the office and the robes of the high priest? 157.
What was his typical character? 158.
What were the duties and the livelihood of the Levites? 164.
Who were the Nethinim? 165.
How were the Jewish offerings classified? 167.
What species of animals might be sacrificed? and how were the victims selected? 168.
What were the burnt-offerings? 169.
What were the peace-offerings? 170.
What were the sin-offerings? 171.
What was the sin-offering for the priest? 172.
What other distinctions of persons were there with reference to this offering? 173–175.
What was the trespass-offering? 176.
What was the typical character of the Levitical sacrifices? 177.
How many kinds of oblations were there? 178–180.
What were the ordinary oblations? 178.
What were the free oblations? 179.
What were the prescribed oblations? 180.
What was the law regarding first-fruits and firstlings? 181, 182.
What were the regulations with regard to tithes? 183.
What were the meat- and drink-offerings? 184, 185.
How many kinds of national sacrifices were there? 186.

EXAMINATION QUESTIONS.

Give a classification of the annual festivals instituted by Moses. 187.

What were the three principal feasts? and what was the design of the institution of each of them? 188–190.

What was their typical meaning? 196.

What was the reason of the feast of Pentecost? and when did it take place? 189.

By what other names was it designated? 189.

With what event in subsequent times do we find it connected? 189.

To what festival does it correspond in the Church of England? 189.

How many times in the year were the males of the children of Israel bound to appear before the Lord? and on what occasions? 187.

What was the sabbatical year? 194.

Give a short account of the sabbatical year and of the year of jubilee. 194, 195.

What was the latter a type of? 196.

What was the scape-goat? 192.

Describe the ceremonies connected with it. 192.

On what day did they take place? 192.

What other circumstances were peculiar to this day? 192.

What was its typical meaning? 196.

Sum up the typical intimations generally of the Messiah to be found in these festivals. 196.

Classify the vows prevalent among the Jews. 199.

How many kinds of Nazarites were there? 201.

To which class did John the Baptist belong? 201.

What was the Cherem? 202.

How many kinds of purification were there? 203.

What were the laws with reference to leprosy? 207.

What typical intimations besides those already referred to do we find in Leviticus? 169, *note.*

Why is the book of Numbers so styled? p. 120.

How long did the children of Israel tarry at Mount Sinai? 215.

What detained them there? 215.

What sign was given for their departure? 216.

What was the direction of their course from thence as far as Kadesh? 217, 218, 220, 221.

When did they begin to wander in the wilderness? and what was the cause of their wandering? 222.

Where did Kadesh-barnea lie? 221.

What miracle was performed there for the children of Israel? 225.

Where had a similar miracle been wrought for them before? 104.

What sin did Moses commit in connection with the miracle of Kadesh? 225.

And how was he visited for it? 225.

What were the names of the two faithful spies? 222.

How did Caleb and Joshua first distinguish themselves? 222.

Where were the bones of Joseph finally deposited? 267.

Give the history of the rebellion of Korah, Dathan, and Abiram. 223.

What was the result of it? 223.

Explain the allusion of St. Jude. 223.

What is meant by "Aaron's rod that budded"? Give an account of the rebellion which preceded this miracle. 224.

Who died at Kadesh? 225.

Why were the Israelites compelled to take a circuitous route on leaving Kadesh? 226.

When did Aaron die? and who succeeded him in the priesthood? 226.

In what contest were the Israelites now engaged? and with what success? 227.

What course did they take from Hor? 228.

For what crime were they punished during their journey? and what was the mode of punishment? 228.

How were they relieved? 228.

Of what was the lifting up of the serpent typical? 238.

What afterward became of it? 228.

What reception did the Israelites meet with from Sihon and Og? 229.

What was the result? 229.

What portion of the country now fell into the hands of the Israelites? 229.

Give a brief account of Balaam's interview with the king of Moab. 230.

What advice did he give Balak when not allowed to curse Israel? 230.

What was his end? 232.

Quote his prophecy of the Star of Jacob. 230.

Reconcile his being the son of Bosor. 232, *note*.

By what rivers were the Israelites now separated from Canaan? 233.

On the review of the whole of the Israelites, who only were found belonging to the old generation? 233.

Compare this with the former census. 234.

Which of the tribes of Israel received their inheritance on the east side of Jordan? 235.

On what conditions were they allowed to do so? 235.

To what unknown book is allusion made in Numbers? and what different opinions are entertained with regard to it? 237.

What typical and prophetical intimations of the Messiah can you find in Numbers? 238.

What is the meaning of the word "Deuteronomy"? p. 130.

Relate the events connected with the death of Moses. 239.

How long were the Israelites in the wilderness? and from what point did Moses see the Promised Land? 239.

At what age did he die? 239.

EXAMINATION QUESTIONS.

Of whom was he the son? 240.

What relation was he to Aaron? 85.

What part of the Pentateuch was probably not written by him? 242.

Give a brief review of his life and character. 240.

What prophecies with reference to the Messiah do you find in Deuteronomy? 241.

Where in the New Testament do you find one of these prophecies especially applied? 241.

What number of years does the book of Joshua occupy? p. 136.

What circumstances are here related relative to the previous life of Joshua? 252.

Give a summary of the contents of the book of Joshua. p. 136.

Give an account in detail of the conquest of Palestine by Joshua. 253, 254, 256–261.

Who concealed the spies sent by Joshua? where were they hidden? and by what token was the house to be known when the city was taken? 253.

Through what river, and opposite to what city, did the Israelites enter Canaan? 254.

Describe the passage of the Israelites over Jordan. 254.

By what means was Jericho taken? 255.

What was the name of Jerusalem before its occupation by the Israelites? 326.

Where was Gilgal? 254.

Give an account of the twelve stones set up there. 254.

By what device did the Gibeonites save themselves from destruction? 258.

What conditions were imposed upon them by Joshua? 258.

By whom were their rights afterward invaded? 259.

How far did the Promised Land extend to the north and to the south? *Introd.* 23.

To what limits in these directions did the Jews under the Judges gain possession of it? *Introd.* 23.

What remnants of the old inhabitants were left to dwell within those limits? 261.

How did these remnants afterward affect the children of Israel? 271.

How does Joshua confirm his own account of the miracles at Gibeon? 259, *note.*

Where was the tabernacle constructed? 215.

Where was it first set up in the Land of Promise? 144, *note.*

What was the supposed age of Joshua at his death? What other celebrated men died about the same time? and where were they each buried? 267.

What is known of the "book of Jasher"? 269.

By whom is the book of Judges supposed to be written? p. 145.

What period of time is included in it? p. 145.

In what way have its chronological difficulties been explained? p. 145.

What was the number of the judges? 15.

Mention some of the most remarkable of them. 15.

When was the office abolished? 303.

What steps were taken to follow up the conquest of Canaan after the death of Joshua? 270.

What circumstances occasioned a relapse of the Israelites into idolatry? 270, 271.

What idols did they now worship? 271.

State the circumstances attending the idolatry of Micah. 272.

What tragedy now took place in the country of Benjamin? 273.

Who were the Philistines? 277, *note*.

What did Shamgar do? 277.

Give a short account of Deborah and Barak. 277.

"Blessed above women shall Jael the wife of Heber the Kenite be!" On what occasion was this blessing pronounced on Jael? 277.

Who was Gideon? 280.

By what token was Gideon assured of God's assistance against the Midianites? 280.

What means did he employ in selecting his army, and what was the result of his attack upon the Midianites? 281.

By what other name was Gideon known, and on what occasion was that name conferred on him? 280.

What occurred to Oreb, Zeeb, Zebah, and Zalmunna? 281.

Where do we find the earliest example of an apologue? 283.

State the occasion on which it was used. 283.

What was the end of Abimelech? 285.

What was Jephthah's vow? 291.

What peculiarity of pronunciation is recorded as belonging to the Ephraimites? 291.

Give an account of the life, exploits, and death of Samson. 296, 297.

Give an account of the birth and education of Samuel. 298.

Relate the circumstances of his call to the prophetic office. 300.

Who was his mother? 298.

Give a short account of Eli. 298.

How did two of the sons of Eli die? 301.

Of what were they to be the sign? 299.

What were their names? 299.

Under what circumstances was the ark of God captured by the Philistines? 301.

How long did they retain it? 302.

What was done with it afterward? 302.

What judgments attended its presence when carried among the enemies of the children of Israel? 302.

How long did the sons of Samuel judge the land? 303.

What causes led to the establishment of monarchy among the Jews? 303.

Whom did Samuel anoint as the first king? and what signs did he give him? 303.

EXAMINATION QUESTIONS.

Give a brief abstract of the book of Ruth. 304.
What is the character of this book? 304.
By whom was it written? p. 162.
Of what tribe was Boaz? 305.
Who was Obed? 305.
Who were the mothers of Dinah, Solomon, Samuel, and Obed? 50, 333, 298, 305.
How far do the books of Samuel bring the narrative down? p. 162.
By what other name are they known? p. 162.
What was the first event which signalized the reign of Saul? 306.
How and when did Jonathan distinguish himself? 307.
By what means was the kingdom afterward divided? 364.
Give an account of Saul. 303, 306, 307, 320–322.
What was the cause of Saul's desertion and rejection by the God of Israel? 308.
How did he die? 321.
How was David anointed king? 309.
What was the origin of the ill-will which Saul bore David? 311.
What course did Saul's persecution eventually compel David to take? 312.
What act of forbearance did David show him? 317.
Upon what occasions did David counterfeit madness? 314.
And upon what occasions did he spare the life of Saul? 317, 319.
By whose hand did Saul die? and in what battle had he been engaged? 321.
What sin of Saul drew forth the words, "It repenteth me that I have set up Saul to be king"? 308.
What was Saul's end? 321.
Of what tribe was his successor? How does the book of Ruth bear upon the history of his family? 304.
What was David's origin? 305.
By what mighty deeds did he distinguish himself in his youth? 310, 319.
By whom was he anointed king? 309.
What justified such an act so many years before the death of Saul? 308.
Where did David at first reign? 323.
What place did he afterward take and make his residence? 326.
What part did Abner take in the political revolutions of his time? 324.
Why was not David allowed to build the temple at Jerusalem? 328.
Give an account of Absalom, his wicked conduct toward his father, and his punishment. 335, 337, 342.
How did David receive the tidings of his death? 342.
Give a full account of Absalom. 335–337, 339, 342.
Give a short account of Ahithophel. 337, 340.

What are we told of Shimei? of Ziba? of Barzillai? 343.

Give an account of the dissensions which took place between Israel and Judah in the reign of David. 344.

Who was Joab? and what was his conduct in this war? 354.

What act of presumption did David commit? and what punishment ensued? 348.

What advantage did Adonijah take of his father's advanced age? 349.

Whom did David appoint as his successor? 349.

Where was David buried? 350.

What was the character of David? 351.

Under whom did the kingdom of Israel attain its greatest extent? and what were then its limits? 352.

Give an account of the vision which Solomon had soon after his accession to the throne. 356.

How was his wisdom displayed immediately afterward? 356.

What relation did he form with Egypt? 356.

Whence did he import linen and war-chariots? 357.

With what contemporary king did Solomon form a friendly alliance? 357.

What was the spot on which the temple was erected? 359.

Where had the ark been kept before its erection? 144, *note*.

Supposing 975 B. C. to be the date of Solomon's death, give the following dates: of Saul being anointed king by Samuel; of David being anointed king of all Israel at Hebron. 369, 323.

To what tribes did the following persons respectively belong: Moses, David, Daniel, Ezra, Saul, Korah, Zerubbabel, and Boaz? 82, 304, 621, 584, 303, 223, 360, *note*, 305.

What was the fate of Abiathar? of Adonijah? of Joab? 353.

What relation was Joab to David? and what was his character? 354.

What was the end of Shimei? 355.

In what year of his reign did Solomon commence the building of the temple? 358.

How many persons were employed on the structure? 358.

Give an exact description of the temple. 359.

In what manner was the temple dedicated? 360.

How many temples were there at Jerusalem? and who built them? 359 and 360, *note*.

In what respects did the first and second temples differ? 360.

How was the prophecy fulfilled that the second temple should excel the first? 360, *note*.

Illustrate the great glory of Solomon. 361.

What circumstances disturbed the latter part of his reign? 362.

What account have we of Jeroboam the son of Nebat previous to his establishing himself on the throne of Israel? 362.

Who was Rehoboam? 364.

In what way was the revolt of the ten tribes of Israel foretold in the time of Solomon? 362.

What occasion was given by Rehoboam for their revolt? 364.

EXAMINATION QUESTIONS.

Did he ever make an attempt to bring them again into subjection? 372.

State clearly the changes which took place in the governing power among the Jews between the time of Samuel and that of Solomon. (See *Introduction*.)

Describe briefly the events which took place connected with the succession to the throne on Solomon's death. 364.

Relate the circumstances of the separation and the revolt of the ten tribes of Israel from Judah. 364.

Under whom did the tribes revolt? 364.

Mention the chief events in the life of Jeroboam. 371, 373, 374, 377.

What is the title by which the memory of his conduct is perpetuated? 371.

What means were employed by Jeroboam to prevent the ten tribes from returning to the house of David? 374.

Why was it said of Jeroboam the son of Nebat that he "made Israel to sin"? 374.

Why were the two calves of gold set up? 374.

How did God manifest his displeasure to Jeroboam at Bethel? 377.

What did the man of God prophesy at Bethel? 377.

What king of Judah is connected with the transaction? 377.

State the principal events in the life of Elijah. 401, 403, 406, 410.

What were the circumstances of his death? 428.

In whose reigns did he live? 399, 420, 426.

Elijah said to Ahab, "Thus saith the Lord, In the place where dogs licked the blood of Naboth shall dogs lick thy blood, even thine." How was this prophecy fulfilled? 417.

By what means did Ahab obtain the vineyard of Naboth? 414.

What judgment was denounced against him and his wife by Elijah? and how was that judgment fulfilled? 414, 417, 445.

Who was Jezebel? 401.

How was Ahab killed? 415.

How was Ahab worse than Jeroboam? 417.

For what special objects were Elijah and Elisha raised up? 428, 463, *notes*.

By whom, and with what remarkable observances, was Jericho rebuilt? 418.

Who was Jehoshaphat? and how long and in what manner did he reign? 398.

Who succeeded Elijah in the prophetic office? 428.

Mention some of the most remarkable events in the life of Elisha. 463, *note*.

What kings reigned over Judah and Israel in his time? 463, *note*.

Who raised to life the Shunammite's son? 437.

What prophet fed miraculously a large number of people with a few loaves of bread? 463, *note*.

By whom was Elisha called? and what was to be the sign that the spirit of the former prophet was upon him? 428.

Give an account of the cure of Naaman's leprosy, and of the circumstances immediately connected with it. 430.

What miracle was wrought at Elisha's sepulchre? 463, *note.*

What was the character of Jehoram? 427.

What prophecies were delivered against him? and by whom? 435.

Show their fulfilment. 436.

State the circumstances attending the siege of Samaria by Benhadad. 433.

What was the character of Ahaziah and his fate? 439, 442.

Under what circumstances did Joash come to the throne of Judah? 447.

How was Jehu appointed king over Israel? 441.

Whom did he succeed? 441.

What measures did he take to destroy the worshippers of Baal? 450.

What was his general character? 453, 455.

Jezebel says to Jehu, "Had Zimri peace, who slew his master?" Who was Zimri's master? 445.

What was Zimri's end? 395.

Why did Jezebel remind Jehu of Zimri's fate? 441.

Why was she condemned by Elijah? 414.

Give a sketch of the history of Syria as mentioned in Scripture. 471.

What mention is there in the Old Testament of contrivances for measuring time? 499.

Give an account of Hezekiah, the sufferings to which he was subjected, and the miracles which God performed for him. 502, 511.

How is the excellency of King Hezekiah described? 502.

What reformation did he make? 502.

What did he do to the brazen serpent? 502.

How was his piety manifested when threatened by the king of Assyria? 510.

Who was Merodach-baladan? What circumstance in the life of Hezekiah is connected with him? 512.

What miraculous interposition took place for deliverance? 510.

What prophet lived in his time? 512.

How old was Josiah when he began to reign? 519.

How was his piety manifested when the book of the Law found in the house of the Lord was for the first time read to him? 524.

How did Josiah meet with his death? 528.

What great reformation did he effect through his kingdom? 525.

How is the solemn passover which was then kept described? 526.

How was his death for years after lamented? 528.

Give some account of the acts and deeds of the king. 519, 523, 525.

Of what prophecy was he the object? 525.

Who were the Assyrian and Babylonian kings mentioned in Scripture previous to Nebuchadnezzar? 535.

Whence originated the Samaritans? 507.

EXAMINATION QUESTIONS. 349

Who was Zedekiah? 544.

What is known of him? 547–550.

What two remarkable prophecies were fulfilled concerning him? 550.

How did the king of Judah treat Jeremiah during the siege of Jerusalem? 549.

What became of the king of Judah and Jeremiah after the city was taken? 550, 552.

Describe the circumstances that immediately led to the seventy years' captivity. 535, *et seq.*

What were the respective durations of the kingdoms of Israel and Judah after their separation, and by whom were the inhabitants respectively carried into captivity? 368, 369.

What were the different forms of government to which the Israelites were subject at different periods before the captivity? (See *Introduction*.)

State the occasions of the different changes. (See *ibid.*)

State the names of the last king of Israel and his conqueror, with date, and of the last three kings of Judah, mentioning briefly the circumstances of the final subjugation of the latter kingdom. pp. 166–169.

What period of history is embraced in the Chronicles? p. 239.

What period of time do they comprehend? p. 239.

By whom are they supposed to have been written? and what particular objects had the author in view? p. 239.

What is the most important use of the genealogical tables contained therein? p. 239.

What were the operations of Nebuchadnezzar in Palestine after the capture of Jerusalem? and what prophecies were then probably fulfilled? 559.

Give the principal events in the subsequent life of Nebuchadnezzar. 558–561.

In what year of his reign and of the Captivity did he die? and by whom was he succeeded? 561.

By whom, and on what occasion, was the Babylonish captivity first foretold? 534.

Give the date of the fall of the Babylonian empire and the name of the last king. 565.

To what monarch did it then become subject? 568.

Which of Cyrus' successors are mentioned in the Old Testament? 576.

Under whose conduct did the Jews return home from Babylon after their captivity? 572, 584.

Who was Ezra? and what was his office? 584.

What are the principal contents of his book? p. 245.

What were his labors respecting the canon of Scripture? 586.

By what kings of Persia were the three decrees in favor of the Jews, recorded in the book of Ezra, issued? 571, 579, 584.

From which of the three were the seventy weeks of Daniel to be reckoned? 584.

Who were the chief persons concerned in the restoration of the Jews and in the rebuilding of the temple? 574, 578.

Under what circumstances was the building of the second temple commenced? 575.

What interruptions did it experience? and from what prophets did the Jews receive encouragement in the work? 575, 578.

Who was Nehemiah? 588.

When did he flourish? 588.

And what did he do for the Jews? 589.

What office did Nehemiah hold under Artaxerxes? 588.

In what way did he exert himself for the rebuilding of Jerusalem? 589.

Who were the principal persons that opposed him? 589.

Give the names of the high priests from Aaron to the return from captivity. p. 252.

What gave rise to the feuds between the Jews and the Samaritans? 575.

Where did the Samaritans worship? 575.

What are the chief contents of the book of Nehemiah? p. 253.

Who was Sanballat? and on what occasion is his name mentioned? 589.

To what year B. C. does direct history in our canon of the Old Testament extend? 592.

Give a summary of the contents of the book of Esther. 593.

Over what period does it extend? 593.

By what name is Ahasuerus (mentioned in the book of Esther) known in profane history? 593.

Relate the circumstances of the plot formed by Haman against the Jews, and show how it was frustrated. 593.

What is the signification of the word "Purim"? 594.

How did the Jews observe this festival? 594.

INDEX.

The references are made to the Sections; those to the Connection between the Old and New Testaments, and to the Introduction, are distinctly marked.

A.

	Sect.
Aaron meets Moses in the wilderness	85
with Moses goes to Pharaoh	86
lays up some manna in a pot	103
with Hur holds up Moses' hands	105
the people delegated to them	109
persuaded by the people to make a golden calf	110
a type of Christ	152
his family appointed priests	154
consecrated	166
his sedition with Miriam at Hazeroth	220
his rod blossoms	224
his sin at Meribah	225
his death on Mount Hor	226
Abdon, a judge in North Israel	294
Abednego, given as an hostage to Nebuchadnezzar	537
(Hebrew, Azariah), educated at Babylon	621
cast into the fiery furnace	623
Abel, son of Adam, a keeper of sheep; his sacrifice; killed by Cain	7
Abel of Beth-maachah; Sheba slain there	345
Abel-mizraim ("the mourning of the Egyptians")	74
Abiathar, son of Ahimelech	315
the priest, bears the ark after David; ordered to carry it back	338
revolts with Adonijah	349
banished to Anathoth	353
Abib	97 and *note*
Abigail, wife of Nabal, marries David	318
Abihu, son of Aaron, with Nadab, attends Moses in the mount	109
their sin	169
Abijah, or Abijam, son of Rehoboam	378
defeats Jeroboam	379

	Sect.
Abijah, son of Jeroboam	380
Abimelech, king of Gerar, deceived by Abraham	32
his covenant with Abraham	35
deceived by Isaac	44
Abimelech, son of Gideon by a concubine	283
killed by a mill-stone	285
Abinadab, ark remained in house of	302
son of Jesse	309
Abiram ("deceit"), rebellion of	223
son of Hiel	256, 418
Abishag, a Shunammite virgin	349
Adonijah requests to marry her	353
Abishai, son of Zeruiah, conquers Ammonites	331
wishes to slay Shimei	338
marches against Absalom	341
against Sheba	345
succors David, and slays Ishbi-benob	347
Abner, son of Ner, Saul's uncle, commander of Ishbosheth's army, slain by Joab	324
Abram, son of Terah, age of; marries Sarai	19
early life and call of	20
enters Canaan; land promised to his seed; goes to Egypt; deceives Pharaoh	21
returns; separates from Lot; and goes to Mamre	22
rescues Lot, and pays tithes to Melchizedek	24
a son promised to him, and the Egyptian bondage foretold	26
Ishmael born	27
God's promises renewed	28
circumcision instituted; name changed to Abraham	29
visited by three angels; intercedes for Sodom	30
deceives Abimelech at Gerar	32
Isaac born	33

INDEX.

	Sect.
Abraham sends away Hagar and Ishmael	34
enters into covenant with Abimelech	35
commanded to offer Isaac	36
Sarah dies; buys the cave of Machpelah	37
marries Isaac to Rebekah	38
marries Keturah	39
sends away her sons with gifts,	*note*
dies; buried by Isaac and Ishmael	41
the father of the faithful	42
Absalom, son of David, receives Tamar into his house	334
assassinates Amnon and flees to Geshur	335
returns; Joab effects a reconciliation for him with David	336
revolts	337
insults David's concubines	339
rejects Ahithophel's counsel	340
defeated and slain by Joab	342
Achan: his sin; stoned to death with his family and burned in the valley of Achor ("trouble")	257
Achish, king of the Philistines; David flees to him	314
gives Ziklag to David	319
dismisses David	323
Achsah, daughter of Caleb, Othniel's wife	264
Acra, or Millo, a hill of Jerusalem, 326, *note*, and *Con.*	22
Adah, wife of Lamech, mother of Jabel and Jubal	8
or Bashemath, wife of Esau	45
Adam, creation of	1
God blesses him	3
placed in Eden; beasts named and woman made	4
fall and sentence of God on him; clothed with skins and expelled Paradise	5
his sons	7
his posterity through Cain	8
his age, and posterity through Seth	9
Psalms ascribed to him	604
Adar, a month	594
Adonibezek, king of Bezek, defeat of	270
Adonijah, son of David by Haggith; his revolt	349
slain by Benaiah	353
Adonizedek, king of Jerusalem, defeated by Joshua	259
Adoram stoned in revolt of ten tribes	364
Adriel, Merab given to him	346
Adullam, cave of; David concealed there	314
Adultery, law respecting	118
Africa peopled by descendants of Ham	15

	Sect.
Agag, king of Amalek, slain by Samuel	308
Ahab, king of Israel, son of Omri; duration of reign	399
marries Jezebel; his idolatry	401
accuses Elijah with troubling Israel	406
his affinity with Jehoshaphat	409
Benhadad threatens him; his victory	411
his second victory over Benhadad	412
his alliance with Benhadad	413
covets Naboth's vineyard	414
Jehoshaphat unites with him against the Syrians	415
his death	417
events in his reign	418
Ahara, a river	584
Ahasuerus, or Cambyses; Samaritans write to him	576
divorces Vashti and marries Esther	593
Ahaz, son of Jotham, king of Judah	487
his idolatry	488
Isaiah prophesies to him	491
defeated by Pekah and Rezin	492
applies to Tiglath-pileser	493
worships the gods of Damascus	494
his sun-dial	499
Ahaziah, king of Israel, son of Ahab; duration of reign	420
idolatry	421
his sickness; sends to Baalzebub	424
sends three companies of fifty each to arrest Elijah; his death	425
Ahaziah, king of Judah; son of Jehoram by Athaliah	439
joins Jehoram, king of Israel	440
slain by Jehu	442
Ahiah, a son of Eli	301
Ahijah, the Shilonite prophet, promises to Jeroboam ten tribes	362
Abijah sends to consult him	380
Ahimaaz, son of Zadok the priest	338
Ahiman, son of Anak	264
Ahimelech, a high priest, gives shew-bread to David	314
slain by Doeg	315
Ahinoam of Jezreel; David marries her	318
Ahithophel the Gilonite, David's counsellor, revolts	337
his counsel	338
followed	339
rejected	340
commits suicide	342
Ahitub, a son of Eli	301
Aholiab, an inspired architect	139
Aholibamah, or Judith, a wife of Esau	45

INDEX. 353

Ai; distance from Jericho; taken by Joshua............ 257
Alcimus, or Jacimus, high priest, deposed............*Con.* 29
Alexander the Great; his first conquests; visits Jerusalem; adores the name of God............*Con.* 5
  conquers Egypt and overthrows Persia............*Con.* 6
  his death............*Con.* 7
Alexander Balas, the impostor, obtains Syria............*Con.* 33
Ægeus, a posthumous son of Alexander the Great......*Con.* 7
Jannæus, high priest, brother of Aristobulus I.............*Con.* 49
  insulted by the populace....*Con.* 50
  rebellion of Pharisees........*Con.* 52
Alexander Jannæus; regains the kingdom; his cruelty......*Con.* 53
  his dying advice to his queen..............*Con.* 54
Alexander, son of Aristobulus II., invades Judæa............*Con.* 63
  carried to Antioch and beheaded............*Con.* 65
Alexandra, queen of Alexander Jannæus............... *Con.* 54
  ascends the throne............*Con.* 55
  mother of Mariamne.........*Con.* 80
Altar of incense......................... 141
  of burnt-offerings.................. 149
Amalekites, account of................. 247
  defeated by Joshua.............. 105
  defeat the Israelites................. 222
  defeated by Saul..................... 308
  David 319 and *note,* 323
Amasa, commander of the host of Absalom......................... 342
  commander-in-chief to David. 344
  slain by Joab......................... 345
Amasis, king of Egypt, rival of Apries................................ 559
Amaziah, king of Judah, son of Joash; duration of reign.... 460
  slays his father's murderers... 462
  defeats the Edomites............... 464
  worships the Edomite gods.... 466
  challenges Joash, king of Israel, and defeated................ 467
  slain at Lachish...................... 468
Amittai, father of Jonah............... 635
Ammiel, father of Machir............ 341
Ammonites, history of..............*Int.* 21
  descended from Ben-ammi..... 31
  oppress the Israelites eighteen years................................. 288
  defeated by Jephthah............. 291
  by Saul..................... 305
  by David.................. 331
  subject to Solomon.................. 352
  defeated by Jehoshaphat........ 422
Amnon, son of David by Ahinoam, abuses Tamar........... 334
  slain by Absalom.................... 335

Amon, king of Judah, son of Manasseh........................... 517
Amorites, the, their position in Canaan............................ 23
  defeated by the Israelites....... 229
  by Joshua................. 261
Amos prophesies.......................... 476
  his time, etc............................ 633
Amram, father of Moses............... 82
Amraphel, king of Shinar............ 24
Anak, three sons of...................... 264
Anakims defeated by Joshua....... 259
Ananel, high priest..................*Con.* 75
Anath, father of Shamgar............ 277
Anathema, or Cherem.................. 202
Anathoth, Abiathar banished to.. 353
Andromachus, governor of the Samaritans...........................*Con.* 6
Andronicus, governor of Antioch...................................*Con.* 17
Aner, an Amorite, joins Abraham. 24
Animals created............................ 1
  named by Adam...................... 4
Antigonus, brother of Aristobulus I........................*Con.* 48
  son of Aristobulus, defeated by Herod..........................*Con.* 70
  Parthians place him on the throne............................*Con.* 71
  sent in chains to Antioch and executed.........................*Con.* 73
Antigonus Socho, founder of the New Synagogue............*Con.* 11
  his doctrine......................*Con.* 97
Antiochus the Great, defeated by Philopator......................*Con.* 13
  his conquest of Palestine...*Con.* 14
Antiochus Epiphanes, brother of Seleucus, establishes idolatrous games at Jerusalem...............................*Con.* 16
  bribed by Menelaus............*Con.* 17
  profanes the temple, etc.....*Con.* 18
  persecutes the Jews............*Con.* 19
Antipas, son of Herod the Great.*Con.* 90
Antipater, father of Herod the Great...............................*Con.* 58
  intrigues with Aretas........*Con.* 59
  his policy...........................*Con.* 62
  defeats Alexander..............*Con.* 63
  appointed procurator of Judæa..................................*Con.* 66
  poisoned by Malichus.........*Con.* 67
Antipater, a son of Herod the Great.................................*Con.* 85
  put to death by order of Herod....................................*Con.* 89
Antonia, a palace and castle of Jerusalem.........................*Con.* 83
Antony, Mark, assists Antipater.....................................*Con.* 63
  his conduct in Egypt..........*Con.* 71
  executes Antigonus............*Con.* 73
  his overthrow at Actium...*Con.* 79
Aphek; Benhadad II. defeated there................................... 412

INDEX.

Apocryphal books, account of...*Int.* 59
  history of..................*Con.* 103-107
Apollonius, a general of Antiochus...................................*Con.* 18
Apologues; Jotham's earliest recorded...................................... 284
  Joash's.. 467
Apries, or Pharaoh-Hophra, allies with Zedekiah..................... 547
  retreat of................................ 548
Arabia, geography and history of................................*Int.* 17-22
Arabians tributary to Jehoshaphat.............................. 408
Arad, king of a Canaanite nation................................. 227
Aram, geography of.........*Int.* 9 and 39
Araunah the Jebusite.................. 348
Araxes, a river of Eden................. 4
Arbela..................................*Con.* 6
Archelaus, son of Herod the Great.
  Con. 90
Aretas, king of Arabia Petræa..*Con.* 58
  assists Hyrcanus............*Con.* 59
Aridæus, an illegitimate son of Philip........................*Con.* 7
Arioch, king of Ellasar, defeated by Abram............................ 24
Aristobulus I. seizes the government............................*Con.* 47
  conquers the Itureans; kills Antigonus..........................*Con.* 48
Aristobulus II., brother of Hyrcanus.................................*Con.* 56
  battle with Hyrcanus........*Con.* 57
  ascends the throne............*Con.* 58
  defeated by Antipater........*Con.* 59
  Pompey arbitrates between the brothers..................*Con.* 60
  taken prisoner to Rome.....*Con.* 61
  escapes; is defeated and poisoned..............................*Con.* 65
Aristobulus, a son of Herod the Great, executed...............*Con.* 85
Ark, the, built; a type of salvation by Christ..................... 10
  of the tabernacle, contents....p. 91
  subsequent history of...... 144, *note*
  taken by the Philistines......... 301
  disasters attending, and its restoration............................ 302
  removal to Jerusalem by David................................. 328
Armenia, geography of..............*Int.* 40
Arnon, a river; march from Hor to.. 228
Aroer.. 291
Arphaxad, son of Shem; his descendants................................ 16
  his age................................... 18
Arphaxad, king of the Medes......p. 257
Arses, king of the Medes..............*ib.*
Arson, law against...................... 124
Artabanus slays Xerxes, captain of the guard..................... 582
Artaxerxes (Smerdis Magus) prohibits the building of the temple.................................... 577
Artaxerxes Longimanus, or Ahasuerus................................... 583
  appoints Ezra conductor of the people............................ 584
  appoints Nehemiah governor. 588
  divorces Vashti; marries Esther.................................... 593
Artemisium, battle of.................. 582
Arza, steward of Baasha.............. 393
Asa, king of Judah, son of Abijah; duration of reign............... 381
  suppresses idolatry................ 384
  defeats Zerah......................... 387
  bribes Benhadad I.................. 390
  his death................................. 391
Asahel, son of Zeruiah, slain by Abner..................................... 324
Asaph, a writer of the Psalms...... 604
Asenath, wife of Joseph.............. 66
Ashdod, a government of the Philistines.......................... 277, *note*
  taken by Sennacherib........... 509
Asher, son of Zilpah, born.......... 50
  Jacob's prophecy respecting him....................................... 72
  the territory of his tribe........ 263
Ashtaroth, worshipped by the Israelites................................ 271
  by Ahab, 401 and *note*
Asia Minor, geography of...........*Int.* 8
  peopled by the descendants of Japheth................................. 14
Asia, Northern, peopled by the descendants of Japheth............ 14
  Central, peopled by the descendants of Shem................ 16
Askelon, a government of the Philistines....................... 277, *note*
Assemblies, legislative; the comitia.. 134
  method and place of convening...................................... 135
  powers of............................... 136
Asshur, son of Shem; his descendants... 16
Assyria, geography and history of...*Int.* 46
  summary of history.............. 554
  also tables, at..............pp. 165-169
Assyrians, descended from Shem.. 16
Astarte, worshipped by Ahab, 401 and *note*
Astyages, king of Media, death of.. 562
Atad, threshing-floor of.............. 74
Athaliah, queen of Judah, daughter of Ahab, marries Jehoram....................................... 400
  usurps the throne................... 443
  slain....................................... 447
Atonement, day of...................... 192
Atossa, mother of Xerxes............ 582
Azariah, a prophet...................... 381
  encourages Asa...................... 387

INDEX. 355

Azariah, probably same as Amariah 587
Azariah, king of Judah. See UZZIAH.
Hebrew name of Abednego... 621

B.

Baal, introduction of, among the Israelites............................. 271
   Gideon throws down the altar of................................... 280
   worshipped by Ahab; account of................. 401 and *note*
   prophets slaughtered by Elijah...................................... 406
   worshippers slaughtered by Jehu...................................... 450
Baal-zebub ("lord of flies"), god of Ekron, sent to by Ahaziah.. 424
Baanah, captain and murderer of Ishbosheth, slain by David. 325
Baasha, king of Israel; duration of reign............................ 385
   his idolatry............................. 386
   allies with Benhadad I............ 388
   fortifies Ramah....................... 389
   assassinated by Zimri............ 393
Babel built and kingdom founded. 17
Babylon besieged by Cyrus......566, 567
Babylonia, geography and history of........................*Int.* 41–43
   rise of empire......................... 535
Bacchides sent by Demetrius Soter into Judæa.................*Con.* 30
Bagoses, a satrap of Syria.........*Con.* 2
Bahurim, Shimei curses David at. 338
Balaam; Balak sends to him........ 230
   his counsel............................. 231
   slain..................................... 232
Balak, king of Moab..................... 230
Barachah, supposed the valley of Jehoshaphat....................... 422
Barak defeats Sisera...................... 278
Baruch reads Jeremiah's prophecy in the temple................. 534–538
   book of............................*Con.* 110
Barzillai, the Gileadite, succors David................................... 341
   congratulates David................ 343
Bashan 229
Bashemath, or Adah, wife of Esau. 45
Bathsheba, wife of Uriah; David's adultery with................. 332
   death of her child; Solomon born.................................. 333
   tells David of Adonijah's revolt.................................... 349
   her request for Adonijah....... 353
Beeri, father of Hosea.................... 631
Beeroth, a city of the Gibeonites.. 258
Beersheba ("well of oath"), wilderness of............................ 34
   digging of the well of.............. 35
   Elijah flies thither.................. 410
Bel and the Dragon.................*Con.* 113

Belshazzar, allies with Crœsus.*Con.* 565
   slain................................*Con.* 567
   his feast and death............*Con.* 627
Belteshazzar, name given to Daniel.................................*Con.* 621
Benaiah, proclaims Solomon king. 349
   slays Adonijah and Joab........ 353
   slays Shimei......................... 355
Benammi, father of the Ammonites, born............................. 31
Benhadad I. bribed by Asa; attacks Baasha....................... 390
   II.; 1st campaign; siege of Samaria................................ 411
   2d campaign; defeated at Aphek................................... 412
   alliance with Ahab................. 413
   defeats Ahab at Ramoth-gilead 415
   his death foretold by Elijah... 438
   III., son of Hazael.................. 458
   (For an account of these three Syrian kings see also 493, *note*.)
Benjamin, son of Rachel, born..... 58
   his father refuses to send him to Egypt................................ 68
   is sent, and the cup found in his sack................................ 69
   Jacob's prophecy respecting him....................................... 72
   territory of his tribe.............. 263
   the tribe utterly routed......... 273
   forcibly obtain wives............. 274
Benoni ("son of my sorrow")..... 58
Berechiah, father of Zechariah.... 641
Berith, an idol, worship of, by Israelites................................. 285
Bessus, satrap of Bactria...........*Con.* 6
Bethel ("house of God"), so called by Jacob.............................. 47
   golden calf set up there......... 374
   man of God comes to............. 377
   Josiah breaks down the altar at.. 525
Beth-maachah.............................. 345
Beth-rehob, a Syrian state........... 331
Bethshan, or Scythopolis............ 321
Bethshemites slain for looking into the ark......................... 302
Bethsura, a town between Hebron and Jerusalem. ....*Con.* 23
Bethuel, son of Nahor, father of Rebekah.............................. 38
Bezaleel, son of Uri, an inspired architect............................... 139
Bezek, 10,000 men of, slain........... 270
Bezer, a city of refuge................. 236
Bible, the...............................*Int.* 53
Bildad the Shuhite, Job's friend... 599
Bilhah, handmaid of Rachel........ 49
   her sons................................. 50
   Reuben commits incest with her... 59
   misconduct of her sons........... 61
Blasphemy, law against............... 113

INDEX.

Boaz marries Ruth..................... 305
Bread, unleavened, feast of..99 and 188
Breastplate of judgment, the........ 162
Brutus, defeat of, at Philippi........ 69
Buzi, father of Ezekiel................. 620

C.

Cæsar, Julius, restores Hyrcanus, *Con.* 64
   releases Aristobulus...........*Con.* 65
   appoints Antipater procurator................................*Con.* 66
   assassination of...................*Con.* 68
   Sextus, governor of Syria...*Con.* 67
   Octavius............................... 72
   secures the kingdom to Herod. 79
Cæsarea, built by Herod the Great, *Con.* 83
Cain, murders Abel..................... 7
   his posterity.......................... 8
Cainan, son of Enos, descendant of Seth................................ 9
Caleb, sent to spy out Canaan; his conduct........................ 222
   drives out the three sons of Anak................................. 264
Calf, the golden................ 110 and *note*
Calves, the golden, set up by Jeroboam 374
Cambyses. *See* AHASUERUS.
Canaan, son of Ham.................. 12-15
   land of, prior to conquest by Israelites............................ 243
   boundaries......................... 244
   description of the country...... 245
   early inhabitants..............246-250
   divided among the twelve tribes... 263
Candlestick, the golden............... 143
Captain of a thousand........... 311, *note*
Carchemish, an important post on the Euphrates....................... 528
   captured by Necho................. 530
Carmel, Mount; the contest between Elijah and the priests of Baal............................... 406
Cassander, a general of Alexander................................*Con.* 9
Cassius, seizes Syria.................*Con.* 68
   defeated at Philippi............*Con.* 69
Census of the Israelites............... 234
Ceremonial law, how divided. (See *note*, p. 90)
Chaldee, Babylonian empire, rise of................................... 555
   history of............................. 558
Chebar, a river....... 620
Chedorlaomer, king of Elam, defeated by Abram............. 24, 554
Chemosh, worshipped by Solomon. 362
Chephirah, a city of the Gibeonites................................. 258
Cherem, or Anathema................ 202
Cherethites, follow David..338 and *note*
   march of, under Abishai........ 345

Cherith, Elijah fed by ravens at the brook................... 428, *note*
Cherubim, the............................ 146
Child-birth, purification after....... 206
Chimham, son of Barzillai............ 343
Chronicles, Books of................555-557
Cimbri, the, or Cimmerians, descended from Gomer, son of Japheth............ 14
Circumcision, instituted............... 29
   re-established....................... 255
Cleopatra; Antony falls in love with her......................*Con.* 71
Cœle-Syria..........................*Con.* 9, *note*
Comitia, the. *See* ASSEMBLIES, LEGISLATIVE.
Commerce of Solomon.................. 357
Constitution, the Jewish..133 and *note*
Covetousness, law against............ 130
Cozbi, a Midianitish woman, slain by Phinehas....................... 231
Crassus, governor of Syria.......*Con.* 65
Creation, the............................ 1, 2
Crœsus, king of Lydia, defeated by Cyrus............ 565
Cush, son of Ham...................... 15
Cushites, descendants of Cush...... 15
Cuthæans, or Samaritans............. 507
Cyaxares II., placed by Cyrus on the throne of Babylon......... 568
   death of............................... 570
   III. in Median line, allies with Nabopolassar and takes Nineveh. See page 168...... 535
Cyrus, succeeds Astyages in the military government.......... 562
   assists his uncle Cyaxares II.. 563
   besieges Babylon.................... 566
   takes Babylon....................... 567
   succeeds to the empire........... 570

D.

Dagon, a god of the Philistines.... 297
   falls down before the ark....... 302
Damascus, seized by Rezon.......... 362
   kingdom of.................... 493, *note*
Dan, son of Bilhah, born............. 50
   Jacob's prophecy concerning him................................. 72
   the territory of his tribe........ 263
   the tribe carry off Micah's gods, and take Laish........... 272
   golden calf set up at............... 374
Daniel, carried to Babylon............ 537
   called Belteshazzar................ 621
   interprets the king's dreams, 622, 624
   his vision of the four beasts... 625
   of the ram and he-goat..................... 626
   deciphers the writing............ 627
   thrown into the lions' den...... 628
   his prophecies..................629, 630
   his history..........621-630 and *note*
Darius the Mede. *See* CYAXARES II.

INDEX. 357

Darius Hystaspis, obtains the throne................................ Sect. 578
confirms the edict of Cyrus... 579
his death, and principal events of his reign........................ 582
Dathan, ("laws"), rebellion of...... 223
David, son of Jesse, anointed king. 309
slays Goliath............................ 310
thrice escapes death; marries Michal........................ 311
flies to Ramah......................... 312
his covenant with Jonathan... 313
his wanderings..................314–319
forbearance at Engedi and Ziph........................... 317, 319
marries Abigail and Ahinoam. 318
defeats Amalekites and proclaimed king....... 3_3, 325
takes Jerusalem...................... 326
defeats Philistines, etc. 327, 329, 331
adultery with Bathsheba....... 332
reconciled to Absalom........... 336
leaves Jerusalem..................... 338
his concubines insulted......... 339
grief for Absalom................... 342
returns to Jerusalem.............. 343
attacked by Ishbi-benob......... 347
numbers the people............... 348
his death and character.....350, 351
Psalms of............................... 604
Dead bodies, purification after touching............................. 205
Dead Sea, formation of............... 31
Debir, king of Eglon, defeated by Joshua.............................. 259
Deborah, nurse of Rebekah, dies.. 57
the prophetess, defeats Sisera. 278
Dedication, feast of.................... 193
institution of....................Con. 22
Delilah betrays Samson............... 297
Deluge, the................................. 11
Demetrius Euceres, Pharisees send to him......................... Con. 52
Nicator, acknowledges Simon as high priest............... Con. 21
obtains the throne............ Con. 34
his ingratitude punished....Con. 35
Soter, sends an army against Judæa........................ Con. 29
Deuteronomy; analysis of its contents............................ p. 130
prophecies in......................... 241
authenticity of the last chapter........................ 242
Dinah, daughter of Leah, born.... 50
carried off by Shechem........ 56
Divination, law against............... 112
Divorce, law of........................... 120
Dodecarthy, the.......................... 528
Doeg, the Edomite, marches against Nob.................... 315
Doris, the first wife of Herod the Great................. Con. 85
Dothan, Joseph finds his brethren there................................ 61
besieged by Benhadad............ 431

Dura; Nebuchadnezzar's image erected there...............558, 623

E.

Ebal, a mountain of Palestine...... 245
Ebed, father of Gaal..................... 285
Ebedmelech rescues Jeremiah...... 549
Ebenezer, Israelites defeated there. 301
so called by Samuel................ 302
Eber, son of Salah, descendant of Shem............................. 18
Ecbatana; Darius flees thither...Con. 6
Ecclesiastes, authorship of........... 609
scope of............................... 610
Ecclesiasticus, or Wisdom of Jesus son of Sirach.............Con. 109
Edar, a tower................................ 59
Eden, garden of, situation...4 and note
Edom, or Esau (" red ")............... 43
land of, Israelites refused a passage through.............. 226
wilderness of........................ 429
Edomites, history of................Int. 22
defeated by Saul.................... 308
rendered tributary by David.. 329
subject to Solomon................. 352
defeated by Amaziah............ 464
Edrei, Og defeated at.................. 229
Eglon, king of Moab..................... 259
slain by Ehud....................... 276
Egypt, geography and history of, Int. 2–6
peopled by descendants of Mizraim, son of Ham............... 7
Abram, goes thither.............. 21
Joseph carried thither........... 61
Ehud, a judge, delivers Israel from Moabites............................ 276
Ekron, a government of the Philistines.......................277, note
Elah, son of Baasha, king of Israel. 392
Elam, son of Shem....................... 16
Elath.. 357
Eleazar, made high priest........... 226
dies.................................... 267
brother of Simon the Just....Con. 11
brother of Judas Maccabæus..Con. 27
Eli, high priest........................... 298
his criminal leniency toward his sons........................... 299
prophecy of Samuel against him................................. 300
his death............................ 301
Eliab, eldest son of Jesse............. 308
Eliadah, father of Rezon............. 362
Eliakim, or Jehoiakim, king of Judah, son of Josiah........... 530
Eliezer, Abraham's servant.......... 38
son of Moses......................... 106
a prophet............................. 398
Elihu the Buzite reproves Job and his three friends................ 600
Elijah, summary of his life....428, note
Elim, Israelites wander to........... 102
Elimelech, husband of Naomi...... 305

358 INDEX.

	Sect.
Eliphaz the Temanite, Job's friend	599
Elisha, summary of his life....463, *note*	
Elkanah, father of Samuel	298
Elkosh, or Elkosha, a village in Galilee	637
Ellasar	24
Elon, a judge	293
Endor, witch of, Saul consults her	320
Engedi, David's forbearance there	317
English translation of Bible......*Int*.	63
Enoch, son of Cain	8
son of Jared, descendant of Seth	9
Enos, son of Seth	9
Ephod, the	160
Ephraim, son of Joseph, born	67
blessed by Jacob	72
territory of his tribe	263
Ephraim, wood of, Absalom defeated there	342, *note*
Ephrath, Benjamin born and Rachel buried there	58
Er, son of Judah and the daughter of Shuah	62
Esarhaddon, colonizes Samaria	507
reigns	510, 554
Esau, born	40
sells his birthright	43
marries Judith and Bashemath.	45
loses his father's blessing	46
marries Mahalath	48
meets Jacob on his return from Haran	55
Esdras, books of	*Con.* 103, 104
Eshcol, an Amorite, joins Abram..	24
Essenes, a sect of the Jews	*Con.* 93
Esther, her history	593
the book of	593, 594
apocryphal chapters of	*Con.* 107
Etam, a rock	296
Etham, a writer of the Psalms	604
Ethbaal, king of the Zidonians, father of Jezebel	401 and *note*
Ethiopia, geography of	510 and *note*
Ethiopians, the, descended from Ham	15
Euphrates, a river of Eden	4
Eve, created; given to Adam and named by him	4
tempted; tempts Adam, and the curse upon her; clothed in skins and expelled Paradise	5
her sons	7, 8, 9
Evilmerodach, releases Jehoiachin.	562
succeeds Nebuchadnezzar	625
Exodus, contents of the book	p. 68
Expiation, feast of	192
Ezekiel, carried to Babylon by Nebuchadnezzar	543
his life and prophecies	620
Ezion-geber, a port on the Red Sea.	357
Jehoshaphat builds a navy there	419
Ezra, probably wrote the Books of Chronicles	556

	Sect.
Ezra, conducts a caravan of Jews to Judæa	584
his governorship	585
corrects the canon of Scripture.	586
dies; supposed same as Malachi	587
the book of, Analysis	p. 245

F.

Fall, the	5
Firmament created	1
First-fruits and firstlings	181, 182
Fishes created	1
Fornication, law against	121
Furniture of the Holy Place	141–143
Most Holy	144–147
court	149, 150

G.

Gaal, son of Ebed, defeated by Abimelech	285
Gabinius, sent by Pompey to Jerusalem	*Con.* 61
changes the government	*Con.* 64
Gad, son of Zilpah, born	50
Jacob's prophecy respecting him	72
the territory of his tribe	263
a prophet, directs David	314
sent to David	348
Gadi, father of Menahem	484
Galileans, the sect of	*Con.* 102
Gath, a government of the Philistines	277, *note*
taken by David	329
Gath-hepher, in Galilee	635
Gaza, a government of the Philistines	277, *note*
Samson's exploit there	297
taken by Hophra, or Apries	547
Gedaliah, appointed governor over Judah; slain	552
Gehazi, Elisha's servant; Naaman's leprosy transferred to him,	430, 463, *note*
Genesis, Analysis of	p. 35
Gerar, Abraham removes thither..	32
Isaac goes there	44
Gerizim, temple built on Mount,	507, and *Con.* 3
Gershom, son of Moses, born	83
circumcised	85
brought to him by Jethro	106
Gershonites, a family of the Levites	164
For their charge and situation see p. 91.	
Geshur, Absalom flies to the king of	335
Geshurites, a nomad race on southern border of Palestine	261
David makes excursions against them	319 and *note*
Gezerites, a nomad race on southern border of Palestine;	

	Sect.
David makes excursions against them	319 and note
Gibbethon, Nadab slain there	383
Gibeah, a murder in the streets of; taken by the eleven tribes,	273 and note
Gibeon, a city of the Gibeonites	258
Gibeonites, the first of the Nethinim	165
deceive Joshua	258
atonement for Saul's slaughter of the	346
Gideon, judgeship of	279
called, and throws down altar of Baal	210
defeats the Midianites	281
refuses to be king; dies	282
Gilboa, a mountain of Palestine	245
defeat and suicide of Saul there	321
Gilead, a mountain of Palestine,	245 and note
Gilgal, twelve stones pitched there.	254
a national assembly at	306
Girgashites, their position in Canaan	23
war with	261
Gittites, follow David	338 and note
Godhead, plurality of persons in	2
Golan, a city of refuge	236
Goliath, slain by David	310
Gomer, son of Japheth, father of the Cimbri	14
Gomorrah, Abraham intercedes for it	30
destruction of	31
Gonorrhœa, purification from	206
Gorgias	Con. 24
Goshen, land of, assigned to Israelites	70 and note
Greeks, the, descended from Japheth	14

H.

Habakkuk, his prophecies	522, 638
Hadad, a prince of Edom	362
Hadadezer. king of Zobah; David's victory over	329, 331
his servant Rezon seizes Damascus	362, 493, note
Hadassah. Hebrew name of Esther.	593
Hagar, becomes Abram's concubine; bears Ishmael	27
exiled	34
Haggai, incites the Jews to recommence building	578
his predictions	640
Ham, son of Noah, cursed	12
his posterity	15
Haman, a favorite of Ahasuerus, hanged	593
Hamoth, a Syrian state	329, 530
Hamor, father of Shechem	56
Hanani, the prophet, remonstrates with Asa	381, 390

	Sect.
Hanani, brother of Nehemiah.	589
Hananiah, a false prophet	545
brother of Nehemiah	5 9
Hebrew name of Shadrach	621
Hannah, mother of Samuel	298
Hanun, son of Nahash; conduct to David	331
Haran, son of Terah, father of Lot	19, 20
a place in Mesopotamia	20
Hareth, forest of	314
Harosheth	278
Haroth-jair—i. e. villages of Jair.	287
Havilah, situation of	308 and note
Hazael, king of Syria; Elijah ordered to anoint him	410, 428, note
accession of, foretold by Elisha,	438, 463, note
seizes the territory east of Jordan	453, 456
stifles Benhadad I.; summary of history of	492, note
Hazeroth, Aaron and Miriam sin there	220
Hazor	260, 278
Heber, the husband of Jael	278
Hebron, a city of refuge	236
the king of, defeated by Joshua.	259
Hebron, the sons of Anak driven out from	264
David proclaimed there	323
Heirships, law respecting	128
Helam, Hadadezer defeated at	331
Heliodorus, treasurer of Seleucus Philopator	Con. 15
Heliopolis, temple built there by Onias	Con. 29
Heman, a writer of the Psalms	604
Hermon, Mount	229, 245
Herod the Great, temple of	360, note
appointed governor of Galilee,	Con. 67
espouses Mariamne	Con. 69
made tetrarch by Antony	Con. 70
escapes to Rome	Con. 71
obtains the kingdom from the Triumvirate	Con. 72
reduces Antigonus	Con. 73
massacres the Sanhedrim	Con. 74
appoints Ananel high priest,	Con. 75
deposes him, elevates and murders Aristobulus	Con. 76
propitiates Antony	Con. 77
first secret instructions respecting Mariamne	Con. 78
conciliates Augustus; is confirmed on the throne	Con. 79
second secret instructions respecting Mariamne	Con. 80
introduces heathen customs	Con. 81
rebuilds the temple	Con. 83
his generosity	Con. 84
executes Mariamne's sons	Con. 85
his sickness and cruelty	Con. 88
executes Antipater	Con. 89

INDEX.

	Sect.
Herod, his death and character,	Con. 90, 91
Herodians, rise of the	Con. 67
sect of	Con. 102
Hezekiah, king of Judah, breaks brazen serpent	228, 502
son of Ahaz, duration of reign.	501
restores the worship of Jehovah	504
rebels against Shalmaneser	506
submits to Sennacherib	508
his sickness; fifteen years added to his life	511
his vanity	512
peaceful state of Judah	513
Hezion. See REZON.	
Hiddekel, the, a river of Eden	4
Hiel, the Bethelite, rebuilds Jericho	256, 418
High priest, the, his office	157
his typical character	158
his robes, etc	159-163
history of them to return from the Captivity	p. 252
Hilkiah, father of Jeremiah, finds a copy of the Law	524
Hinnom, valley of	515
Hippodrome, the, at Jericho; Jews shut up in it	Con. 89
Hirah, a Canaanite	62
Hiram, king of Tyre, assists David.	326
an ally of Solomon	357
Historical books, account of	Int. 56
History of Susanna	Con. 112
Hittites, the, their position in Canaan	23
conquered by Joshua	261
Hivites, conquered by Joshua	261
Hobab, brother-in-law of Moses	216
Hobah, north of Damascus	24
Hoham, king of Hebron, slain by Joshua	259
Holofernes, beheaded by Judith,	Con. 106
Hophni, son of Eli, misconduct of.	299
death of	301
Hophra (see PHARAOH)	547
Hor, Mount, Aaron dies there	226
Horeb, Mount, Moses called at	84
Elijah goes there	410
Hormah ("utter destruction"), Canaanites defeated at	227
Hosea, his prophecies and time,	469-631
Hoshea, king of Israel, son of Elah, slays Pekah	495
duration of reign	497
allows Hezekiah to invite the people to the passover	498
made tributary to Shalmaneser	500
rebels, and is imprisoned	503
Huldah, the prophetess	524
Hur, holds up Moses' hands	105
with Aaron, has the charge of the people	109

	Sect.
Hushai, the Archite, joins Absalom	338
defeats Ahithophel's counsel	340
Hyrcanus, John, escapes to Jerusalem	Con. 42
succeeds Simon as high priest,	Con. 43
besieged by Antiochus Sidetes,	Con. 44
regains his independence; raises Asamonean power	Con. 45
joins the Sadducees	Con. 46
Hyrcanus II., son of Alexandra, high priest	Con. 55
resigns the kingdom and high priesthood	Con. 57
Pompey arbitrates between him and Aristobulus	Con. 60
restored by Pompey	Con. 61
confirmed by Gabinius in high priesthood	Con. 64
joins Malichus	Con. 69
barbarously mutilated	Con. 71

I.

	Sect.
Ibzan, a judge	292
Iddo, grandfather of Zechariah	641
Idolatry, law against	112
Injuries, corporal, law of	117
Isaac, born	33
Abraham commanded to offer him	36
a type of Christ	36, note
marries Rebekah	38
Jacob and Esau born	40
goes to Gerar and deceives Abimelech	44
blesses Jacob	46
Jacob comes to reside with him; his death	60
Isaiah, begins to prophesy	480
his predictions to Ahaz	491
his life and period	613
scope of his prophecies	614
chief subjects of his prophecies	615
his prophecies of the Messiah.	616
Iscah (see SARAI)	19
Ishbi-benob, a gigantic Philistine, slain by Abishai	347
Ishbosheth, son of Saul, reigns over eleven tribes	323
quarrels with Abner	324
murdered by his two captains.	325
Ishmael, son of Hagar, born; prophecy respecting him	27
exiled; becomes a great archer; his children, and death	34
Ishmaelites, Joseph sold to them	61
Israel. See JACOB.	
history of the divided monarchy of	365
Issachar, son of Leah, born	50

INDEX.

	Sect.
Issachar, Jacob's prophecy respecting him	72
the territory of his tribe	263
Issus, Darius routed at	Con. 5
Ithamar, youngest son of Aaron	231
Ittai, the Gittite, follows David	338
sent to battle by David	341
Ituræa, subdued by Aristobulus,	Con. 48

J.

	Sect.
Jabal, son of Adah and Lamech	8
Jabbok, a river	245
Jabesh-gilead, four hundred virgins of, sent to the Benjamites	274
besieged by Nahash	306
Jabesh-gileadites bury the bodies of Saul and his sons	321
Jabin, king of Hazor, defeated by Joshua	260
defeated by Barak	278
Jacob, born; why so named	40
obtains Esau's birthright	43
his father's blessing	46
goes to Laban; his dream	47
marries Leah and Rachel	49
his family	50
his new covenant with Laban	51
leaves, and is pursued by Laban; reconciled	52
his vision at Mahanaim; message to Esau	53
wrestles with a man at Peniel; name changed to Israel	54
meeting with Esau	55
dwells at Succoth	56
buries the idols and goes to Bethel; God's promise renewed	57
leaves Bethel	58
joins his father at Mamre	60
deceived by his children	61
sends his sons to Egypt for corn	68
sends Benjamin	69
goes to Egypt	70
his dying acts and prophecies	72
their fulfilment	73
his death and burial	74
Jaddua, son of Jonathan, high priest	Con. 3
Jaddua, saluted by Alexander	Con. 5
Jael, slays Sisera	278
Jahaziel, a prophet	398
Jair, a judge	287
Jamnia, a seaport on the Mediterranean	Con. 24
Japheth, son of Noah	12
his posterity	14
Japhia, king of Lachish, slain by Joshua	259
Jarmuth, Piram, king of, slain by Joshua	259
Jared, father of Enoch	9
Jasher, book of	260, *note*, and 269

	Sect.
Jason, introduces Greek idolatry among the Jews	Con. 16
supplanted by Menelaus in high priesthood	Con. 17
Javan, descendant of Japheth, father of the Greeks	14
Jebusites, position in Canaan	23
subdued by Joshua	261
Jerusalem taken from them by David	326
Jeconiah. See JEHOIACHIN.	
Jeduthun, a writer of the Psalms	604
Jehoahaz, king of Israel, son of Jehu; duration of reign	457
his idolatry; oppressed by Hazael, etc.	458
Jehoahaz, king of Judah, son of Josiah	529
deposed by Necho	530
Jehoash, king of Judah, son of Ahaziah; duration of reign	448
restores the worship of Jehovah	449
repairs the temple	452
worships Baal; commands Zechariah to be stoned	454
bribes Hazael	456
slain by his servants	459
Jehoash, king of Israel, son of Jehoahaz; duration of reign	461
his idolatry; Elisha's promise,	463 and *note*
defeats Syrians three times	465
defeats Amaziah	467
Jehoiachin, king of Judah, son of Jehoiakim; duration of reign	542
carried away captive by Nebuchadnezzar	543
Jehoiada, the high priest	446
regent	449
his death	454
Jehoiakim, son of Josiah; duration of reign	531
Jeremiah and Urijah prophesy against him	532
charged by Jeremiah with murder of Urijah	533
made tributary by Nebuchadnezzar	537
seeks to destroy Jeremiah	538
revolts	539
slain	540
Jehonadab, the son of Rechab, meets Jehu	445
obedience of Rechabites to	534
Jehoram, king of Israel, son of Ahab; duration of reign	426
his idolatry	427
allies with Jehoshaphat	429
seeks to slay Elisha	433
slain by Jehu	441
Jehoram, king of Judah, son of Jehoshaphat; duration of reign	434
his idolatry	435

INDEX.

	Sect.
Jehoram, king of Judah, his death.	436
Jehoshaphat, king of Judah, son of Asa; duration of reign..	398
worships Jehovah	400
organizes the national education	402
fortifies Judah; levies an army	404
appoints judges	407
flourishing state of his kingdom	408
his affinity with Ahab	409
nearly killed at Ramoth	415
rebuked by Jehu	416
tries to revive the commerce of Solomon, etc	419
defeats Moabites and Ammonites	422
allies with Jehoram	4 9
Jehosheba, wife of Jehoiada, saves Joash	446
Jehovah-jireh ("the Lord will provide"), so called by Abraham	36
Jehovah-nissi ("the Lord my banner"), an altar built by Moses	105
Jehu, son of Hanani, a prophet	389
Jehu, son of Nimshi, anointed king of Israel; slays Ahaziah and Jehoram	441, 442
king of Israel; duration of reign	444
slays Jezebel	445
destroys Baal's worshippers	450
his idolatry	455
Jephthah, judgeship of	288
captain of a band of men in Tob	289
sends to the king of Ammon.	290
defeats Ammonites; his vow	291
Jeremiah, prophesies	521–531
prophesies against Jehoiakim.	532
charges him with the murder of Urijah	533
foretells seventy years' captivity	534
prophecies publicly read	538
writes to the captives of Babylon	545
cast into a pit	549
his prophecy against Zedekiah	550
his life and period	617
Jericho, spies sent thither	253
taken by Joshua	256
rebuilt by Hiel	418
Jeroboam, son of Nebat, promised the government of ten tribes by Ahijah; flies to Egypt	362
returns from Egypt	364
king of Israel; duration of reign	371
fortifies Shechem	373
his idolatry	374

	Sect.
Jeroboam, man of God sent to; his hand withered	377
Ahijah's prophecy against him	380
Jeroboam II., son of Joash; duration of reign	469
Jonah's promise	471
recovers all Hazael had taken away; his idolatry	473
Jerubbaal ("let Baal plead"), name given to Gideon	280
Jerusalem, taken by David	326
description of	326, note
capital of Judah; called Salem and Jebus..	p. 201
taken by Joash, king of Israel	467
Nebuchadnezzar	550
sacked by Nebuzaradan	551
Alexander visits	Con. 5
taken by Antiochus Epiphanes	Con. 18
Pompey	Con. 61
Herod the Great.	Con. 73
Jeshua, grandson of Seraiah	572
high priest	574
Jesse, son of Obed	305
father of David	309
Jesus. See JASON.	
Jethro, priest of Midian; his daughters meet with Moses.	83
his advice to Moses	106
Jewish constitution, account of,	133 and note
See ASSEMBLIES, LEGISLATIVE.	
connection of the tribes with each other	137
the tribunal of seventy instituted by Moses	138
Jezebel, daughter of Ethbaal, marries Ahab	401
persecutes the prophets	405
threatens Elijah	410
advises Ahab to seize Naboth's vineyard	414
slain by Jehu	445
Joab, son of Zeruiah, slays Abner.	324
made chief captain	326
conquers Ammonites and Syrians	331
reduces Rabbah	333
mediates between Absalom and David	336
marches against Absalom	341
slays Absalom	342
superseded in command by Amasa	344
slays Amasa	345
remonstrates with David on his numbering the people.	348
slain by Benaiah	353
his character	354
Joash, father of Gideon	280
See JEHOASH.	
Job, chronology of the time of	595
his country	596

INDEX.

	Sect.
Job, his condition and character	597
afflicted by Satan	598
visited by his three friends	599
reproved by Elihu	600
Jehovah appears to him	601
is restored to prosperity	602
prophetical intimation of Messiah in book of	603
Jochebed, mother of Moses	82
Joel, son of Samuel	302
Joel, prophesies	470, 632
Johanan, a chief officer of Gedaliah	552
John Hyrcanus. *See* HYRCANUS.	
Jonah, prophesies	451
his history; sent against Nineveh	635
Jonathan, son of Saul: his heroic conduct	307
his friendship with David	312
his death	321
Jonathan, son of Abiathar	338
the high priest	Con. 2
(*See* MACCABÆUS)	Con. 31
Joram, son of Toi, king of Hamath, visits David	329
See JEHORAM.	
Jordan, the, crossed by the Israelites	254
Joseph, son of Rachel, born	50
sold by his brethren	61
sold to Potiphar and cast into prison	63
interprets the dreams of the butler and the baker	64
interprets the dreams of Pharaoh	65
made chief ruler of Egypt; marries Asenath	66
his sons	66
his brethren visit him	68
a second time; sends for his father and family	69
his policy during the famine,	71, note
Jacob's prophecy respecting him	72
buries Jacob	74
again forgives his brethren	75
death and burial	76
a type of Christ	77
burial of his bones in Canaan.	267
Joseph, a son of Antipater	Con. 67
executed by Herod the Great,	Con. 78
Joshua, previous life of; his name changed	252 and note
defeats the Amalekites	105
attends Moses in the mount	109
one of the twelve spies; his conduct	222
appointed Moses' successor.	235, 239
sends spies to Jericho	253
crosses the Jordan	254
an angel appears to him	255

	Sect.
Joshua, takes Jericho	256
takes Ai; punishes Achan	257
allies with the Gibeonites	258
defeats Adonizedek and four kings	259
defeats Northern kings	260
divides Canaan among the tribes	263
district assigned to him	264
his last days and death	266, 267
Joshua, book of, Analysis of its contents	p. 136
Joshua, a Bethshemite	302
Joshua, slain in the temple by his brother Jonathan	Con. 2
Josiah, king of Judah, son of Amon; duration of reign	518
worships Jehovah	519
repairs the temple	523
throws down the altar of Jeroboam	525
celebrates the passover	526
slain	528
Jotham, Gideon's son	283
his parable of the trees	284
Jotham, king of Judah, son of Uzziah; duration of reign	481
reigns righteously	483
Jubal, son of Lamech and Adah, descendant of Cain	8
Jubilee, the	195
Judah, son of Leah, born	50
proposes to sell Joseph	61
marries the daughter of Shuah; his sons, and incest with Tamar	62
his address to Joseph	69
Jacob's prophecy respecting him	72
the territory of his tribe	263
defeats Adonibezek	270
prefatory history of the kingdom	365
Judas Maccabæus. *See* MACCABÆUS.	
Judges, book of, obscurity of chronology, and Analysis of its contents	p. 145
Judgeships, the	275–296
Judith, book of	Con. 106

K.

Kadesh-barnea, spies sent thence.	221
Israelites return thither	225
Kadmonites, a people of Canaan	23
Kedesh, a city of refuge	236
Keilah, David rescues it from the Philistines	316
Kenites, a people of Canaan	23
Kenizzites, a people of Canaan	23
Keturah marries Abraham; her sons	39
Kibroth-hattaavah ("the graves of lust"), Israelites murmur there for flesh	218

INDEX.

Kings, Analytical Table of..........p. 166
Kir-haraseth, capital of Moabites, besieged by Jehoram and Jehoshaphat.................... 429
Kish, father of Saul...................... 303
Kishon, a river of Palestine......... 245
    Baal's prophets slaughtered at...................................... 406
Kohathites, a family of the Levites................................... 164
    their charge and situation....p. 91
Korah, rebellion of........................ 223
    Psalms ascribed to the sons of. 604

L.

Laban, brother of Rebekah.......... 47
    welcomes Jacob; deceives him. 49
    new covenant with Jacob...... 51
    pursues Jacob; is reconciled to him................................... 52
Laborasoarchod, son of Neriglissor. 564
    son-in-law of Nebuchadnezzar. 625
Labynetus, name given to Belshazzar by Herodotus.......... 565
Lachish, reduced by Joshua......... 259
    Amaziah slain there............... 468
Laish, taken by Danites; called Dan..................................... 272
Lamech, son of Methusael, descendant of Cain................ 8
    son of Methuselah, father of Noah.................................. 9
Lamentations, book of.................. 619
Land, dry, created......................... 1
Landmarks, law respecting........... 124
Language, original, of the Old Testament.............................Int. 60
    but one after the death of Noah................................... 17
Lapidoth, husband of Deborah.... 278
Laver, the.................................... 150
Law, the moral, given.................. 108
    the ceremonial....................... 109
Lawyers.............................. Con. 101
Leah, daughter of Laban, marries Jacob.................................. 49
    her children........................... 50
Lehi, Samson taken there............. 296
Leprosy, how Moses acted respecting................................... 207
    different kinds........................ 208
    first, in man........................... 209
    laws, for distinguishing......... 210
    purification from.................... 211
    second, in houses.................... 212
    third, in clothes..................... 213
Levi, son of Leah, born................ 50
    his cruelty to the Shechemites..................................... 56
    Jacob's prophecy respecting him..................................... 72
    the tribe, slay 3000 of the idolaters................................ 110
    devoted to temple-service..153–164
Levites, the................................ 164

Leviticus, Analysis of its contents....................................p. 96
    typical intimations in............ 214
Libnah, reduced by Joshua.......... 259
    besieged by Sennacherib........ 509
Light, creation of......................... 1
Lot, son of Haran........................ 19
    leaves Ur with Abram........... 20
    dwells at Sodom.................... 22
    rescued by Abram.................. 24
    escapes from Sodom; fate of his wife; incest with his daughters............................. 31
Lud, descendant of Shem, father of Lydians.......................... 16
Lydians, the, descended from Shem.................................. 16
Lysias invades Judæa; defeated by Judas Maccabæus............... 25
Lysimachus, a general of Alexander............................Con. 9

M.

Maacah, a king in North Palestine................................... 331
Maachah, grandmother of Asa, deposed by him..................... 384
Maachathites, war with............... 261
Maccabæus (Hammerer), Judas, third son of Mattathias...Con. 20
    restores the temple; institutes feast of dedication..........Con. 22
    his victories................... Con. 24, 25
    his wars........................Con. 24–27
    peace with Syria...........Con. 25, 28
    defeats force of Demetrius Soter............................. Con. 29
    allies with Rome; slain......Con. 30
    Jonathan, brother of Judas, chosen leader by the people.................................Con. 31
    war with Bacchides...........Con. 32
    made high priest................Con. 33
    assists Antiochus................Con. 35
    allies with Rome and Lacedæmon; fortifies Judæa......Con. 36
    falls by the treachery of Tryphon..............................Con. 37
    Simon, second son of Mattathias...........................Con. 20
    succeeds Jonathan..............Con. 38
    completes fortifications; reduces Acra.......................Con. 39
    public memorial of his acts; his powers recognized by Rome..............................Con. 40
    his murder.........................Con. 41
Maccabees, rule of......................Con. 20
    books of....................Con. 115–117
Machir, son of Ammiel, succors David.................................. 341
Machpelah, cave of, purchased; the burial-place of Sarah, of Rebekah, and of Leah........ 37
    of Abraham........................... 41

INDEX. 365

	Sect.
Machpelah, burial-place of Jacob.	74
of Joseph	267
Madai, father of Medes, descendant of Japheth	14
Magog, father of Scythians, descendant of Japheth	14
Mahalaleel, son of Cainan, descendant of Seth	9
Mahalath, daughter of Ishmael... marries Esau	34, 48
Mahanaim ("God's host"), Jacob met by angels there	53
Makkedah, cave of, five kings take refuge in	259
Malachi, prophesies,	592
his prophecies	642
Malichus, poisons Antipater; death of	Con. 68
faction of	Con. 69, 70
Mamre, Abram dwells there,	22 and *note*
an Amorite, assists Abram	24
Man created and blessed	1–3
Manasseh, son of Joseph; born	67
blessed by Jacob	72
territory of his tribe	263 and *note*
Manasseh, king of Judah, son of Hezekiah; duration of reign.	514
his idolatry	515
Manasseh, carried into captivity by Esarhaddon	516
Prayer of	Con. 114
Manasses, high priest of Samaria,	Con. 3
Manna, sent.	102
properties of; Aaron lays up an omer	103
a type of Christ	152
ceases	255
Manoah, a Danite, father of Samson	296
Manslaughter, law against	116
Maon, wilderness of; David goes there	316
Marah ("bitter"), Moses heals the water of	102
Marathon, battle of	582
Mariamne, granddaughter of Hyrcanus, espoused to Herod	68
her marriage	73
first secret instructions respecting her	78
second secret instructions respecting her, and death	80
her sons executed	85
Marriage, instituted	4 and *note*
unlawful marriages	119
Massah ("temptation"), (*see* MERIBAH)	104
Mattan, a priest of Baal, slain by Jehoiada	449
Mattaniah, king of Judah (*see* ZEDEKIAH)	543
Mattathias, a priest; revolt of Jews under; father of Judas Maccabæus	Con. 20

	Sect.
Matri, Saul's family	303
Matrimonial laws	119–122
Medes, descended from Japheth	14
Media, History and Geography of,	*Int.* 48, 49
Megabyzus	588
Megiddo, Ahaziah slain at	442
Josiah slain in valley of	528
Mehujael, son of Irad, descendant of Cain	8
Melchizedek, king of Salem; meets Abram	24
his character and office	25
psalms ascribed to him	604
Menahem, king of Israel, assassinates Shallum.	482
his idolatry; duration of reign.	484
bribes Pul	486
Mene	627
Menelaus, supplants Jason in high priesthood	Con. 17 and *note*
guides Antiochus into the temple	Con. 18 and *note*
Menses, purification from	206
Men-stealing, law against	125
Mephibosheth, son of Jonathan; adopted by David	330
falsely reported to David by Ziba	338
testifies his loyalty to David...	343
Merab, Saul's eldest daughter	310
promised to David	311
Merarites, a family of the Levites.	164
(For their charge and situation see p. 91.)	
Mercy-seat, the	145
Meribah ("strife"), Moses and Aaron sin there	104, 225
Merodach-baladan, king of Babylon, sends to Hezekiah	512
Merom, the waters of	245, 260
Meschech, father of Muscovites, descendant of Japheth	14
Meshach, given as a hostage to Nebuchadnezzar	537
(Hebrew Mishael), educated at Babylon	621
cast into the fiery furnace	623
Mesopotamia. History and Geography of	*Int.* 39
Messiah, prophecies and typical intimations of	643 *et seq.*
Methusael, son of Mehujael, descendant of Cain	8
Methuselah, son of Enoch, oldest of all men	9
Micah, a native of Mount Ephraim; idolatry of	272
Micah, the prophet, prophesies	485
his prophecy	636
Micaiah, prophesies	399
sent for by Ahab	415
Michal, Saul's daughter, marries David	311
assists David's flight	312
given to Phalti	318

INDEX.

Michal, restored to David............ Sect. 324
   reproves him........................ 328
Michmash 307
Midian, Moses flees thither.......... 83
   son of Abraham and Keturah, progenitor of Midianites....... 39
Midianites, the, descended from Midian............................. 39
   defeated by the Israelites...... 232
   harass the Israelites............. 279
   defeated by Gideon............... 281
Milcah, daughter of Haran, marries Nahor......................... 19
   grandmother of Rebekah...... 38
Minnith 291
Miriam, sister of Moses................ 101
   sedition; smitten with leprosy................................. 220
   her death.............................. 225
Miscellaneous precepts................. 131
Mishael, Hebr. name of Meshach... 621
Mitre, the................................... 163
Mizpeh, Samuel assembles Israel at..................................... 302
Mizraim, father of the Egyptians, descendant of Ham............ 15
Moab, his birth........................... 31
Moabites, history of...............*Int.* 20
   descended from Moab 31
   10,000 slain by Ehud............. 276
   defeated by Saul.................. 308
     by David................... 319
   subject to Solomon................ 352
   defeated by Jehoshaphat........ 422
Molech, worshipped by Solomon... 362
     by Ahaz........ 488
Moon, created............................. 1
Morasthi, Micah born there......... 636
Mordecai, carried to Babylon by Nebuchadnezzar................. 543
   honored............................... 593
Moreh, Abram goes there.. 21 and *note*
Moriah, Mount, Abraham tempted to offer Isaac there........ 36
   Jerusalem built on it...... 326, *note*
   temple built on it.................. 359
Moses ("saved from water"), born. 82
   writer of Pentateuch...........*Int.* 55
   flight to Midian; marries Zipporah................................. 83
   called at Horeb..................... 84
   returns to Egypt; circumcises his son.............................. 85
   stands before Pharaoh........... 86
   leads Israelites out of Egypt.. 98
   divides the Red Sea.............. 101
   heals water at Marah............ 102
   commands Joshua to attack the Amalekites................... 105
   visited by Jethro................... 106
   ascends Mount Sinai............. 109
   reprimands Aaron for idolatry.................................... 110
   reascends Mount Sinai.......... 111
   consecrates Aaron and his sons.................................. 166

Moses, institutes festivals............. Sect. 187
   numbers the twelve tribes..... 216
   appoints seventy elders to assist in governing................ 219
   sends out the twelve spies...... 221
   his sin at Meribah................. 225
   puts the sacerdotal garments on Eleazar.......................... 226
   sets up the brazen serpent..... 228
   reviews the people in plains of Moab............................. 233
   appoints Joshua his successor............................ 235, 239
   appoints the cities of refuge... 236
   his last acts and death.......... 239
   review of his life and character.................................... 240
Mountains of Canaan................... 245
Murder, law against..................... 116
Muscovites, descended from Japheth................................ 14
Mycale, battle of......................... 582

N.

Naamah, daughter of Lamech and Zillah................................. 8
Naaman, his leprosy cured by Elisha.................................. 430
Nabal, husband of Abigail, death of...................................... 318
Nabonad, name given to Belshazzar by Josephus.................. 565
Nabopolassar, an Assyrian general, king of Chaldees, and father of Nebuchadnezzar... 535
Naboth, his vineyard coveted by Ahab; his death.................. 414
Nadab, son of Aaron, with Abihu attends Moses in the mount. 109
Nadab and Abihu, their sin......... 169
Nadab, king of Israel, son of Jeroboam; duration of reign.. 382
   his idolatry; slain by Baasha................................... 383
Nahash, king of the Ammonites, defeated by Saul................. 306
   death of............................... 331
Nahor, his descent and age.......... 18
   marries Milcah..................... 19
   grandfather of Rebekah........ 38
Nahum, the prophet..................... 637
Naioth, Samuel takes David thither........................ 312 and *note*
Naomi, mother-in-law of Ruth..... 305
Naphtali, son of Bilhah, born...... 50
   Jacob's prophecy respecting him.................................... 72
   territory of his tribe.............. 263
Nathan, a prophet, forbids David to build a temple................ 328
   reproves him for his sin......... 332
   proclaims Solomon king........ 349
Nazaritism................................. 201
Nebat, father of Jeroboam........... 371
Nebo, Mount....................... 245, *note*

INDEX. 367

Nebuchadnezzar, son of Nabopolassar... 535
- defeats Pharaoh-Necho... 536
- takes Jerusalem, etc... 537
- besieges Jerusalem, carries captive Ezekiel and Mordecai... 543
- slays the sons and puts out the eyes of Zedekiah... 550
- erects a golden image... 558
- conquers Tyre, etc... 559
- beautifies Babylon... 560
- his insanity... 561
- his restoration and death.. 624, 561

Nebuchadonosor... 527
Nebuzaradan sacks Jerusalem... 251
Necho. *See* PHARAOH.
Nehemiah, book of, Analysis of..p. 253
- appointed governor of Judæa. 588
- rebuilds the walls, etc. of Jerusalem... 589
- his first administration... 590
- second... 591
Neriglissor, son-in-law of Nebuchadnezzar... 563
Nethaneel, a son of Jesse... 309
Nethinim, the... 165
- origin of... 258
New moon, festival of...... 313 and *note*
Nimrod, son of Cush... 17
- founds the kingdom of Babel. 554
Nimshi, father of Jehu... 444
Nineveh, or Nimroud... 486, *note*
- Sennacherib flies to... 510
- taken by Cyaxares and Nabopolassar... 535
- Jonah sent by God to... 635
Nisroch, Sennacherib slain in the temple of... 510 and *note*
Nitocris, mother of Belshazzar... 560
- completes unfinished works of Nebuchadnezzar... 565
Noah, son of Lamech, born... 9
- builds the ark... 10
- leaves the ark and sacrifices to Jehovah... 11
- prophecies concerning his sons... 12
- his posterity... 13–16
Nob, Saul massacres the priests at. 315
Numbers, book of, Analysis of...p. 120
- typical intimations in... 238

O.

Obadiah, governor of Ahab's house, feeds the prophets... 405
- meets Elijah... 406
Obadiah, the prophet... 634
Obed, son of Ruth, father of Jesse. 305
Obed the prophet... 490
Obed-edom, David leaves the ark in his house... 328
Oblations... 167
- first, ordinary... 178
- second, free... 179

Oblations, third, prescribed... 180
- *See* DRINK-OFFERINGS... 185
Oded, the prophet, remonstrates with Pekah... 492
Offerings, first, burnt-... 169
- second, peace-... 170
- third, sin-... 171–175
- fourth, trespass-... 176
- drink-... 185
Og, king of Bashan, defeated by Israelites... 229 and *note*
Old Testament, world of... *Int.* 1
- Critical History of... p. 25
Olives, Mount of, Solomon erects high places on... 362
Omri, king of Israel, besieges Zimri... 395
- his party prevails over that of Tibni... 396
- builds Samaria; death of... 397
On, or Heliopolis... 66, *note*
Onan, son of Judah and the Canaanite... 62
Ophir... 357, 419
Ophrah, in Manasseh... 280
Oreb, prince of the Midianites; slain by Ephraimites... 281
Orpah, daughter-in-law of Naomi. 305
Othniel, takes Debir; marries Achsah... 264
- judgeship; delivers the people. 275
Ozem, a son of Jesse... 309

P.

Palestine, Geography of, and History at different periods...*Int.* 23
- description of... 245
- early inhabitants of... 246
- the highway between Egypt and the Asiatic empires... 251
Palmyra, or Tadmor, built by Solomon... 357
Paran, wilderness of... 216
- David goes there... 318
Parents, law against disobedience to... 115
Passover, instituted... 97
- described... 188
- a type of the Messiah... 196
- kept by Joshua... 255
- by Hezekiah... 504
Pekah, king of Israel, assassinates Pekahiah... 489
- son of Remaliah; duration of reign... 490
- allies with Rezin invades Judah... 491
- second invasion... 492
- slain by Hoshea... 495
Pekahiah, king of Israel, son of Menahem; duration of reign ; his death... 489
Peleg, son of Eber... 18
Pelethites, follow David... 338
- march against Amasa... 345

INDEX.

Peniel ("face of God"), name given by Jacob.......... 54
Peninnah, wife of Elkanah.......... 298
Pentateuch.......... *Int.* 55
Pentecost, feast of.......... 189
   a type of the Messiah.......... 196
Peres.......... 627 and *note*
Perizzites, the, their position in Canaan.......... 23
   subdued by Joshua.......... 261
Persia, Geography and History of.......... *Int.* 50
Pethor, in Mesopotamia.......... 230
Pethuel, father of Joel.......... 632
Petra, taken by Pompey.......... 61
Phalti, son of Laish, Michal given to.......... 318
Pharaoh, different dynasties of... *Int.* 4
   deceived by Abram.......... 21
   his dreams interpreted by Joseph.......... 64
   commands male infants of Hebrews to be destroyed... 81
   his death.......... 83
   to whom Moses is sent.......... 83
   pursues the Hebrews.......... 101
Pharaoh-Hophra. *See* APRIES.
Pharaoh-Necho, invasion of.......... 528
Pharez, son of Judah and Tamar. 62
Pharisees, the, become a political faction.......... *Con.* 46
   a sect of the Jews.......... *Con.* 94
   their tenets.......... *Con.* 95
   practices.......... *Con.* 96
Phasael, son of Antipater, made governor of Jerusalem... *Con.* 67
   made a tetrarch of Palestine.......... *Con.* 70
   commits suicide.......... *Con.* 71
Pheroras, son of Antipater...... *Con.* 67
   plots against Herod; his death, *Con.* 86
Philip.......... *Con.* 28
   a son of Herod the Great... *Con.* 90
Philistia, Geography and History of.......... *Int.* 36, 37
Philistines, their origin...... { *Int.* 37 / 278, *note* }
   attack the southern Jewish tribes; repulsed by Shamgar.......... 277
   forty years' oppression of...... 295
   defeated by Samson.......... 296
   defeat Israelites at Ebenezer. 301
   defeated by Saul.......... 307
      by David.......... 310
   defeat Saul.......... 321
   defeated by David.......... 327-329
   David's last expedition against them.......... 347
   subject to Solomon.......... 332
   tributary to Jehoshaphat...... 408
   smitten by Hezekiah.......... 506
Phinehas, son of Eleazar, slays Zimri and Cozbi.......... 231
Phinehas, son of Eli, misconduct of 299

Phinehas, son of Eli, death of...... 301
Phœnicia, Geography and History of.......... *Int.* 11, 12
Phœnicians, descended from Ham. 15
   account of.......... 248
Phut, father of Libyans, son of Ham.......... 15
Pihahiroth, Israelites encamp at.. 100
   Moses divides the Red Sea at.......... 101
Piram, king of Jarmuth, slain by Joshua.......... 259
Pisgah, Moses views Land of Promise from.......... 239
Pison, a river of Eden.......... 4
Pithom, a treasure-city, built by Israelites.......... 81
Plagues, the ten.......... 87-98
   individual design and character of.......... 98, *note*
Platæa, battle of.......... 582
Pledges, law respecting.......... 127
Poetical books, account of......... *Int.* 57
Pollio, a member of the Sanhedrim, *Con.* 74
Pompey, reduces Cœle-Syria.... *Con.* 60
   takes Jerusalem.......... *Con.* 61
   death of.......... *Con.* 66
Potiphar, captain of Pharaoh's guard, Joseph sold to.......... 63
Potipherah, priest of On, father-in-law of Joseph.......... 66
Prayer of Manasses.......... 114
Priests, the.......... 153
   classification of.......... 153
   their duties and requirements; family of Aaron appointed.. 154
   dress.......... 155
   sources of their livelihood..... 156
   divided into twenty-four courses by David.......... 156, *note*
   four courses return from Babylon.......... 581
Prophets, their chronological order.......... p. 266
Prophetical books, account of... *Int.* 58
Proverbs, the book of, authorship and scope.......... 608
Psalms, the book of, authorship... 604
   subjects.......... 605
   classification.......... 606
   occurrence of word Selah in... 607
Psammetichus, father of Pharaoh-Necho.......... 528
Psammis, son of Pharaoh-Necho.. 547
Ptolemies, government under... *Con.* 10
Ptolemy I., Lagus, takes Jerusalem.......... *Con.* 8
   his provinces.......... *Con.* 9
   II., Philadelphus; Eleazar sends 70 elders to.......... *Con.* 12
   III., Euergetes.......... *Con.* 13
   IV., Philopator, enters the Holy of Holies.......... *Con.* 13
   V., Epiphanes.......... *Con.* 14
Puah, a Hebrew midwife.......... 81

INDEX. 369

Pul, king of Assyria, invades Israel............486, 554
Purifications, first, as a religious ceremonial............ 205
   second, from personal uncleanness............ 206
   third, from leprosy....... 207–213
Purim, feast of............ 193
   origin of............ 594

R.

Raamses, a treasure-city, built by Israelites............ 81
Rabbah, Joab sent by David to besiege............ 331
   taken by David............ 333
Rabshakeh, sent by Sennacherib to Hezekiah............ 509
Rachel, daughter of Laban, marries Jacob............ 49
   her children............ 50
   steals Laban's images............ 52
   death and burial of............ 58
Raddai, a son of Jesse............ 300
Ragaba............Con. 54
Raguel. See JETHRO.
Rahab, hides the spies; their promise to her............ 253
   with her family, saved............ 256
Ramah, David goes there............ 312
   fortified............ 389, 390
Rameses, Israelites leave............ 100
Ramoth-gilead, a city of refuge... 236
   Ahab defeated there............ 415
Rebekah, daughter of Bethuel, marries Isaac............ 38
   assists the deception of Jacob. 46
   Esau's threat reported to her.. 47
   buried at Machphelah............ 37
Rechab, a captain and murderer of Ishbosheth; slain by David............ 325
   father of Jehonadab............ 445
Rechabites, the.........201 and note, 534
Red Sea, passage of............ 101
Refuge, cities of, law respecting... 116
   appointed by Moses............ 236
Rehoboam, king of Judah, son of Solomon and Naamah; ten tribes revolt from him............ 364
   duration of reign............ 370
   assembles an army to recover Israel............ 372
   rebuked by Shemaiah............ 375
Rephaims, the, their position in Canaan............ 23
Rephidim, journey of Israelites to. 104
Reu, son of Peleg............ 18
Reuben, eldest son of Leah, born. 50
   his incest with Bilhah............ 59
   opposes the killing of Joseph. 61
   offers his sons a security for Benjamin's life............ 68
   Jacob's prophecy respecting him............ 72

Reuben, the territory of his tribe, 235, 263
Reuel. See JETHRO.
Rezin, allies with Pekah; invades Judah............ 491
   second invasion of............ 492
   slain by Ahaz............493 and note
Rezon, son of Eliadah; founds Damascus............ 362
Rezon, or Hezion............493, note
Riblah, Jehoahaz put in bands there............ 530
Rimmon, rock, Benjamites abide there............ 274
Rivers of Canaan............ 245
Rizpah, concubine of Saul............ 324
   her sons given to Gibeonites.. 346
Ruth, book of............304, 305
   story of............ 305

S.

Sabæans............ 515
Sabbath instituted............4, note
Sabbatical year, the............ 194
Sacrifices............ 167–177
   See OFFERINGS and OBLATIONS.
   classified............ 167
   selection of victims............ 168
   their typical character............ 177
   national............ 186
Sadducees, become a political faction............Con. 46
   their origin............Con. 97
   tenets............Con. 98
Sais............ 528
Salah, son of Arphaxad............ 18
Salamis, battle of............ 582
Sale, law of............ 126
Salome, queen of Aristobulus I. (see ALEXANDRA)............Con. 48
Salt, valley of, 18,000 Edomites slain in............ 329
   Edomites conquered in, by Amaziah............ 464
Samaria, built by Omri............ 396
   besieged by Benhadad II....... 433
   taken by Shalmaneser............ 505
   colonization of............ 507
Samaritans, who so called............ 507
   hinder building of temple..575, 589
   sect of............Con. 102
Samias, a member of the Sanhedrim............Con. 67
   counsels surrender of the city, Con. 74
Samson, judgeship of............ 295
   born; life and exploits of...... 296
   capture and death............ 297
Samuel, son of Elkanah and Hannah............ 298
   prophecy of............ 300
   calls on the people to put away idolatry............ 302
   his sons; anoints Saul king... 303
   rebukes Saul for disobedience. 307

INDEX.

	Sect.
Samuel, slays Agag	308
anoints David king	309
death of	318
appears after death to Saul	320
books of, Analysis of	p. 164
Sanballat, hinders building of the temple	589
governor of Samaria	Con. 3
Sanhedrim, its supposed origin,	138, 219
defied by Herod	Con. 67
massacred by Herod	Con. 74
Saosduchinus	527
Sarai, daughter of Haran, marries Abram	19
deals hardly with Hagar	27
a son promised to her	28
her name changed to Sarah	29
laughs at the promise	30
death of	37
Saul, son of Kish, anointed king	303
defeats Ammonites	306
his disobedience; defeats Philistines	307
reproved by Samuel	308
endeavors to kill David	311
sends messengers after David	312
massacres the priests of Nob	315
the skirt of his robe cut off by David	317
his spear and cruse of water carried away by David	319
consults witch of Endor	320
defeat and suicide of	321
character of	322
Scape-goat, the	192
Scaurus, a general of Pompey	Con. 60
Scribes, the	Con. 101
Scythopolis	321
Sects, Jewish	Con. 93
Segub, son of Hiel	256, 418
Seir	596
Selah	607
Seleucus, a general of Alexander; his provinces	Con. 9
Seleucus Philopator, succeeds to the throne of Syria	Con. 15
Seminis emissio, purification from	206
Semiramis	560
Sennacherib, succeeds to the throne; Hezekiah submits to	508
takes Ashdod; invades Judah	509
destruction of his army	510, 554
Septuagint	Int. 61
completed	12
Seraiah, a high priest	572
Serpent, the, tempts Eve	5
the brazen, set up by Moses	229
destroyed by Hezekiah	502
Serpents, the fiery	228
Serug, father of Nahor	18
Servitudes, the	275–298
Seth, son of Adam	9
Sethon	508, note

	Sect.
Seventy, the tribunal of, instituted by Moses	138
appointed	219
Shadrach, given as a hostage to Nebuchadnezzar	537
Shadrach (Hebrew Hananiah), educated at Babylon	621
cast into the fiery furnace	623
Shallum, assassinates Zechariah	479
duration of reign	482
a name of Jehoahaz	529
Shalmaneser, makes Hoshea tributary	500
besieges Samaria	505, 554
Shamgar, judgeship of	277
Shammah, son of Jesse	309
Sharon, a canton of Palestine	612
Sheba, revolt of	344
death of	345
Sheba, queen of, visits Solomon	361
Shechem, Jacob resides at; son of Hamor	56
a city of refuge	236
laws set up at, on Mount Ebal	239
capital of Israel	369
	See 283, note
Shechemites, circumcised, and slaughter of	56
Shechinah, the	147
Shelah, son of Judah and the Canaanite	62
Shelomith, the son of, blasphemes and is stoned	113
Shem, son of Noah	12
his posterity	16
Shen	302
Shemaiah, the prophet	370
forbids Rehoboam to fight against Israel	372
Shemaiah, a false prophet; his punishment	545
Shepherds, an abomination to the Egyptians	69
Sheshai, son of Anak	264
Sheshbazzar. (See ZERUBBABEL)	572
Shew-bred, the table	142
David obtains some from Ahimelech	314
Shibboleth, Ephraimites made to pronounce	291
Shiloh, the tabernacle set up there	262
daughters of, carried off by Benjamites	274
Shimei, curses David	338
David forgives him	343
slain by Benaiah	355
Shinar	24
Shiphrah, a Hebrew midwife	81
Shishak, king of Egypt, invades Judah	375
Shittim, Israelites led to, by Joshua	253
Shobach, commander-in-chief of Hadadezer	331
Shobi, son of Nahash, succors David	341

INDEX. 371

	Sect.
Shuah, a Canaanite	62
Shunammite, the, her son restored by Elisha	437
Shur, wilderness of; Hagar goes thither	27
Israelites enter	102
Sicarii, the, sect of	Con. 102
Sichem, Abram passes through,	21 and note
Siddim, vale of	24
Sidonians, the, war with	261
Sihon, king of the Amorites, defeated by Israelites	229
wrests territory from Ammonites	290
Siloam, pool of	340
Simeon, son of Leah, born	50
his cruelty to Shechemites	56
kept as a pledge by Joseph	68
Jacob's prophecy respecting him	72
territory of his tribe	263
tribe of, defeats Adonibezek	270
Simon the Just, high priest, death of	Con. 10
See MACCABÆUS.	
Sin, wilderness of, Israelites enter	102
Sinai. (See HOREB)	84
the Jews encamp before it	107
Sisera, general of Jabin, slain by Jael	278
Slavery, law respecting	132
Slaves, fugitive, law respecting	125
Smerdis Magus. See ARTAXERXES.	
Sodom, Lot dwells there	22
Abraham intercedes for it	30
destruction of	31
Soemus, a friend of Herod the Great	Con. 80
Solomon, son of Bathsheba, born	330
proclaimed king	349
extent of his kingdom	352
ascends the throne; executes Adonijah and Joab	354
puts Shimei to death	355
marries Pharaoh's daughter	356
commerce of	357
builds the temple	358
his idolatry	362
his death and character	363
a writer of the Psalms	604
the Proverbs	608
Ecclesiastes	609
Song of	611
Wisdom of	Con. 108
Song of the Three Children	Con. 111
Sorek, valley of	297
Spies, twelve, sent into Canaan	221
two, sent to Jericho	253
Stars, created	1
Stealing, law against	123
Succoth ("booths")	100, note
Sun, created	1
Susanna, History of	Con. 112
Syria, Geography and History of,	Int. 9, 10

	Sect.
Syria, History of	493, note
(See pp. 166-169, note.)	
Syrians defeated by David	331

T.

	Sect.
Taberah ("a burning") march of Israelites to	217
Tabernacle, the, external description	139
court of	148
completion of	151
set up in Shiloh	262
Tabernacles, feast of	190
a type of the Messiah	196
kept by Ezra	585
Tabor, mountain of Canaan	245
Tabrimon, father of Benhadad I.,	493, note
Tadmor, or Palmyra, built by Solomon	357
Tamar, wife of Ur, Judah's incest with	62
daughter of David; abused by Amnon	334
Tatnai, a Persian governor	578
Tekel	627
Tekoah, Jehoshaphat obtains a victory there	422
Temple, the, built by Solomon	358
description of	359
dedication of	360
the second	360, note
Herod's	360, note
Ten tribes, revolt of	364
Terah, father of Abram, his descent	19
leaves Ur; his death	20
Tarshish	357, 419
Thebez, Abimelech slain in besieging	285
Thermopylæ, battle of	582
Thracians, descended from Japheth	14
Thummim	162
Tibarenians, descended from Japheth	14
Tibni, faction of; death of	396
Tidal, king of nations	24
Tiglath-pileser, Ahaz applies to; slays Rezin	493, 554
Timnath	62, 296
Timnath-serah given to Joshua	264
Tiras, father of the Thracians, descendant of Japheth	14
Tirhakah, king of Ethiopia	510
Tirzah, burnt by Zimri	395
Tithes	183
Tob, land of	289
Tobiah hinders building of the temple	589
Tobit, book of	Con. 105
Toi, father of Joram, king of Hamath	329
Tola, a judge	286

INDEX.

	Sect.
Trespass, law of	124
Tribes, connection with each other	137
Trumpets, feast of	191
Tryphon, treachery of	Con. 37
Tubal-Cain, son of Lamech and Zillah	8
Type, a scriptural meaning of	78
Tyre, kings of	Int. 12

U.

Uncleanness, purification from.... 206
Upharsin................................ 627, *note*
Ur, Abram born there................. 20
Uriah, husband of Bathsheba, his death................................ 332
Urijah, a prophet, slain by Jehoiakim............................. 532
Urim 162
Uz, land of.............................. 596
Uzzah, slain for touching the ark.. 328
Uzziah, or Azariah, king of Judah; duration of reign...... 470
   influence of Zechariah over him................................ 472
   smitten with leprosy.............. 475

V.

Vashti, queen of Ahasuerus, divorced............................... 593
Vow, Jephthah's................. 291, *note*
Vows, nature of....................... 197
   classification...................... 199
   I. of dedication................... 200
   II. of self-interdiction and Nazaritism........................ 201
Vulgate, the........................ Int. 62

W.

Wars of the Lord, book of........... 237
Wisdom of Solomon............... Con. 108
Witness, false, law respecting..... 129
World, the, of Old Testament...... 1

X.

Xerxes, succeeds Darius.............. 582
   See Table........................ p. 257

Y.

Yarmuk, a river of Palestine....... 245

Z.

Zabad, expedition of the sons of, 81, *note*
Zabianism, Job alludes to........... 595
Zadok, the priest, bears the ark after David; ordered to carry it back........................ 338
   ordered by David to proclaim Solomon king................... 349

	Sect.
Zalmunnah, a king of the Midianites, slain by Gideon	281
Zarrah, son of Judah and Tamar..	62
Zared, a river	228
Zarephath, a Phœnician city	403
Zealots, the	Con. 102
Zebah, a king of the Midianites, slain by Gideon	281
Zebul, governor of Shechem	285
Zebulon, son of Leah, born	50
Jacob's prophecy respecting him	72
the territory of his tribe	263
Zechariah, son of Jehoiada, stoned by Joash	454
Zechariah, king of Israel, son of Jeroboam II.; duration of reign; assassinated by Shallum	479
Zechariah the prophet, son of Berechiah	641
Zedekiah, king of Judah, son of Josiah; duration of reign...	544
allies with Pharaoh-Hophra...	547
applies to Jeremiah	549
his eyes put out by Nebuchadnezzar; carried to Babylon; death, and contradictory prophecies concerning him	550
Zeeb, prince of the Midianites, slain by Ephraimites	281
Zelophehad, daughters of	128
Zemaraim, a mountain on the borders of Ephraim	379
Zephaniah, the prophet	518
his prophecies	639
Zerah, the Ethiopian, defeated by Asa	387
Zerubbabel, grandson of Jehoiachin, appointed tirshatha of Judæa	572
refuses assistance from Samaritans in the building the temple	575
Zeruiah, sister of David	326, *note*
mother of Joab	354
Ziba, David places Mephibosheth under his care	330
falsely accuses Mephibosheth to David	334
Mephibosheth complains of his treachery	343
Ziklag, given to David by Achish.	319
Zillah, a wife of Lamech	8
Zilpah, Leah's handmaid	49
her sons	50
Zimri, slain by Phinehas	231
Zimri, king of Israel, assassinates Elah	393
duration of reign	394
besieged by Omri; his death..	395
Zion, taken by David	326
Ziph, wilderness of, David goes there	316
his forbearance at	319

	Sect.		Sect.
Zipporah, daughter of Jethro, marries Moses	83	Zobah, invaded by David	329
circumcises her son	85	Zophar the Naamathite, Job's friend	599
brought to Moses by Jethro	106	Zopyrus, retakes the city of Babylon	582
Zobah, kings of, defeated by Saul.	308, *note*		

THE END.

TESTIMONIALS.

"THIS is not a commonplace book. It is the result of labor and learning. It is fitted to render much help to the student in his endeavor to become acquainted with the contents of the Bible analytically and chronologically, and by means of a judicious classification of them. . . . It presents an excellent summary of matters adapted to facilitate an intelligent study of the sacred volume."—*British Quarterly Review*.

"This *Analysis* cannot fail to be useful to a large class of students. Numerous tables, summaries of events, analyses of law systems, and other important matters, are appended."
—*Athenæum*.

"Of the first edition of this work we had the pleasure of speaking in terms of hearty praise; and if then it claimed acceptance as an intelligently-conceived and well-executed hand-book to the study of the Old Testament, it now deserves more specific and emphatic commendation, so thoroughly has the author perfected what at first he achieved so happily. Amongst the chief additions are the following: An account of Canaan prior to its conquest by the Israelites; synchronistical tables of the history of Israel and Judah; a review of the history of these divided monarchies, prefacing a thorough rearrangement of this portion of the general history, by which greater clearness is attained than we ever found in any similar work; and a new connection of the Old and New Testaments, including the history of the Jews from the governorship of Nehemiah to the birth of our Lord, which is marked by many great improvements and is admirable for lucidity and completeness. Another feature of the work worthy of special mention is the excellent analysis of the laws of Moses.

"We know of no manual for the student of the Old Testament so perfect in method, so comprehensive in its contents, so thorough in its information, and so reliable in its treatment of the most intricate portions of Jewish history, as is this volume. Clear intelligence, historical learning, and great carefulness of labor are stamped on every page. To students preparing for theological examinations, to teachers under training in normal schools, and to ministers conducting Bible-classes of young men, we can give it our best word, assured that they will find it of high value."—*Nonconformist.*

"The volume before us is well described by its title. It is very simple in its plan, but, simple as the plan seems, its execution must have been a work of time and labor, and the author has lost sight of nothing that might conduce to the object in view. The summary and analysis of the text, which is of itself a work of no small difficulty, is cleverly done, especially in the Mosaic laws and ordinances; and the author generally endeavors to explain or illustrate any obscure points in Jewish history—'particularly,' as he frankly remarks, 'those portions which are most frequently the subjects of college examinations.'"—*Dr. Kitto's Journal of Sacred Literature.*

www.ingramcontent.com/pod-product-compliance
Lightning Source LLC
Chambersburg PA
CBHW072132220426
43664CB00013B/2215